AFRICAN PERSPECTIVES ON TRADE AND THE WTO

Twenty-first century Africa is in a process of economic transformation, but challenges remain in areas such as structural reform, governance, commodity pricing and geopolitics. This book looks into key questions facing the continent, such as how Africa can achieve deeper integration into the rules-based multilateral trading system and the global economy. It provides a range of perspectives on the future of the multilateral trading system and Africa's participation in global trade. It also underlines the supportive roles that can be played by multilateral and regional institutions during such a rapid and uncertain transition.

This volume is based on contributions to the Fourth China Round Table on WTO Accessions and the Multilateral Trading System, which took place just before the WTO's Tenth Ministerial Conference in Nairobi in December 2015.

PATRICK LOW is a visiting professor at the University of Hong Kong and a fellow at the Asian Global Institute. He was formerly Chief Economist at the World Trade Organization and previously worked at the GATT Secretariat.

AMBASSADOR CHIEDU OSAKWE is Trade Advisor to the Honorable Minister and Chief Negotiator for the Federal Ministry of Industry, Trade and Investment, Nigeria, while he is on special leave from the WTO. In the WTO, he has worked as director of various divisions for many years, including most recently as Director of the Accessions Division.

MAIKA OSHIKAWA is Officer in Charge of the Accessions Division of the WTO, having served in various divisions within the WTO Secretariat, including most recently as Head of the Asia and Pacific Desk in the Institute for Training and Technical Cooperation.

AFRICAN PERSPECTIVES ON TRADE AND THE WTO

Domestic Reforms, Structural Transformation and Global Economic Integration

Edited by

PATRICK LOW
University of Hong Kong

CHIEDU OSAKWE
World Trade Organization

MAIKA OSHIKAWA
World Trade Organization

CAMBRIDGE
UNIVERSITY PRESS

CAMBRIDGE
UNIVERSITY PRESS

University Printing House, Cambridge CB2 8BS, United Kingdom

Cambridge University Press is part of the University of Cambridge.

It furthers the University's mission by disseminating knowledge in the pursuit of education, learning, and research at the highest international levels of excellence.

www.cambridge.org
Information on this title: www.cambridge.org/9781107174474
10.1017/9781316795873

First published 2016

Printed in the United Kingdom by Clays, St Ives plc

A catalogue record for this publication is available from the British Library.

Library of Congress Cataloging in Publication Data
Names: World Trade Organization. China Round Table (4th : 2015 : Nairobi, Kenya), author. | Low, Patrick, 1949– editor. | Osakwe, Chiedu I. (Chiedu Igwebuike), editor. | Oshikawa, Maika, editor. | World Trade Organization. Ministerial Conference (10rh : 2015 : Nairobi, Kenya)
Title: African perspectives on trade and the WTO : domestic reforms, structural transformation, and global economic integration / edited by Patrick Low, Chiedu Osakwe, Maika Oshikawa.
Description: New York : Cambridge University Press, 2016. | "This volume, the work of over twenty authors, grew out of the Fourth China Round Table and the WTO's Tenth Ministerial Conference, two seminal events held back-to-back in Nairobi, Kenya, in December 2015" – Introduction. | Includes bibliographical references and index.
Identifiers: LCCN 2016038551 | ISBN 9781107174474 (alk. paper)
Subjects: LCSH: Africa – Foreign economic relations – Congresses. | Africa – Commerce – 21st century – Congresses. | Free trade – Africa – Congresses. | International trade – Congresses. | World Trade Organization – Africa – Congresses. | Globalization – Economic aspects – Africa – Congresses. | Economic development – Africa – Congresses.
Classification: LCC HF1611 .W67 2015 | DDC 337.6–dc23
LC record available at https://lccn.loc.gov/2016038551

ISBN 978-1-107-17447-4 Hardback
ISBN 978-1-316-62652-8 Paperback

CONTENTS

Colour plates are to be found between pp. 242 and 243.

FIGURES

PLATES

Message

H.E. Mr Uhuru Kenyatta, President, Republic of Kenya
(© Office of the President, Nairobi, Kenya)

Joint foreword

Mr Roberto Azevêdo, Director-General, World Trade Organization
(© WTO)
H.E. Mrs Amina Mohamed, Cabinet Secretary for Foreign Affairs and
International Trade, Republic of Kenya (© Ministry of Foreign Affairs,
Nairobi, Kenya)
H.E. Mr Gao Hucheng, Minister of Commerce, People's Republic of China
(© Department of Foreign Affairs and Trade website – www.dfat.gov.au)

Inside photo plates

Forecourt of the Kenyatta International Convention Centre, Nairobi,
Kenya, venue for the Tenth WTO Ministerial Conference from 15 to
18 December 2015.
(© WTO/Admedia Communication)
WTO Director-General Roberto Azevêdo and H. E. Mr Shouwen Wang,
Vice Minister of Commerce of the People's Republic of China, open
the Fourth China Round Table, which took place on 13–14 December
2015. The Government of China pledged at the Round Table to contribute a further USD 500,000 (CHF 494,636) to the China Programme
for 2016.
(© WTO/Admedia Communication)

H.E. Mr Wang Shouwen, Vice Minister of Commerce of the People's
Republic of China, delivering one of the opening addresses during the
Fourth China Round Table on 14 December 2015.
(© WTO/Admedia Communication)

H.E. Mr Uhuru Kenyatta, President of Kenya, gives a keynote speech at
the Opening Ceremony of the High Level Session of the Fourth China
Round Table on 14 December 2015.
(© WTO/Admedia Communication)

Mr Roberto Azevêdo, WTO Director-General, at the Opening Ceremony
of the High Level Session of the Nairobi Fourth China Round Table on
14 December 2015.
(© WTO/Admedia Communication)

H.E. Mrs Amina Mohamed, Cabinet Secretary for Foreign Affairs and
International Trade of Kenya, speaking at the High Level Session of the
Fourth China Round Table on 14 December 2015.
(© WTO/Admedia Communication)

Mr Chiedu Osakwe, Director of the Accessions Division of the WTO,
speaking at the High Level Session of the Fourth China Round Table
on 14 December 2015.
(© WTO/Admedia Communication)

H.E. Ms Fatima Haram Acyl, Commissioner for Trade and Industry,
African Union Commission, speaks at the Nairobi Fourth China
Round Table on 14 December 2015.
(© WTO/Admedia Communication)

H.E. Mr Okechukwu E. Enelamah, Minister of Industry, Trade and
Investment of Nigeria, speaks at the Nairobi Fourth China Round
Table on 14 December 2015.
(© WTO/Admedia Communication)

H.E. Mr Rob Davies, Minister of Trade and Industry of South Africa,
speaking at the High Level Session of the Fourth China Round Table
on 14 December 2015.
(© WTO/Admedia Communication)

H.E. Mr Joshua Setipa, Minister of Trade and Industry of Lesotho,
speaking at the High Level Session of the Fourth China Round Table
on 14 December 2015.
(© WTO/Admedia Communication)

Ms Arancha González, Executive Director of the International Trade
Centre, speaking at the High Level Session of the Fourth China Round
Table on 14 December 2015.
(© WTO/Admedia Communication)

Mr Joakim Reiter, Deputy Secretary-General at the United Nations
    Conference on Trade and Development, speaking at the High Level
    Session of the Fourth China Round Table on 14 December 2015.
(© WTO/Admedia Communication)
Ms Anabel González, Senior Director of the Global Practice on Trade and
    Competitiveness of the World Bank Group, during the High Level
    Session of the Fourth China Round Table on 14 December 2015.
(© WTO/Admedia Communication)
H.E. Mrs Ellen Johnson Sirleaf, President of Liberia, meeting with H.E.
    Mr Uhuru Kenyatta, President of Kenya, during the Tenth WTO
    Ministerial Conference in Nairobi, Kenya, on 15 December 2015.
(© WTO/Admedia Communication)
H.E. Mr Uhuru Kenyatta, President of Kenya, and WTO Director-
    General Roberto Azevêdo, accompanied by other participants in the
    High Level Session of the Fourth China Round Table on 14 December
    2015.
(© WTO/Admedia Communication)

CONTRIBUTORS

Editors

PATRICK LOW is a Visiting Professor at the University of Hong Kong and a Fellow at the Asian Global Institute.

AMBASSADOR CHIEDU OSAKWE is Trade Advisor to the Honorable Minister and Chief Negotiator for the Federal Ministry of Industry, Trade and Investment, Nigeria, and an Adjunct Professor at the International University in Geneva.

MAIKA OSHIKAWA is Officer in Charge of the Accessions Division of the WTO.

Contributors

FATIMA HARAM ACYL is the Commissioner for Trade and Industry at the African Union Commission.

UKAMAKA ANAEDU is a research assistant in the Accessions Division of the WTO.

ROBERTO AZEVÊDO is the Director-General of the WTO.

CHRISTINA BUSCH works in the Trade and Competitiveness Global Practice of the World Bank Group.

VICKY CHEMUTAI is an Economic Affairs Officer in the Accessions Division of the WTO.

ROB DAVIES is the Minister of Trade and Industry of South Africa.

MOULAY HAFID ELALAMY is the Minister of Industry, Trade and New Technologies of Morocco.

OKECHUKWU E. ENELAMAH is the Minister of Industry, Trade and Investment of Nigeria.

MICHAEL FINGER worked as an international economist in the Research Division of the GATT/WTO.

ANABEL GONZÁLEZ is Senior Director of the Global Practice on Trade and Competitiveness of the World Bank Group.

ARANCHA GONZÁLEZ is Executive Director of the International Trade Centre.

BERNARD M. HOEKMAN is the Director of the Research strand 'Global Economics: Multilateral Cooperation and Policy Spillovers' at the European University Institute.

MARCUS BARTLEY JOHNS is a Trade Specialist in the World Bank Group Geneva Office.

STEPHEN N. KARINGI is the Director of the Regional Integration, Infrastructure and Trade Division of the United Nations Economic Commission for Africa.

UHURU KENYATTA is the President of Kenya.

ALEXEI P. KIREYEV is a Senior Economist at the International Monetary Fund.

GERARD MCLINDEN is Senior Trade Facilitation Specialist in the Global Practice on Trade and Competitiveness of the World Bank Group.

SIMON MEVEL is an Economic Affairs Officer at the United Nations Economic Commission for Africa.

AMINA MOHAMED is Cabinet Secretary for Foreign Affairs and International Trade of Kenya.

OTTAVIA PESCE is an Economist at the United Nations Economic Commission for Africa.

JOAKIM REITER is Deputy Secretary-General at the United Nations Conference on Trade and Development.

JOSHUA SETIPA is the Minister of Trade and Industry of Lesotho.

YUAN YUAN is Director of the Division of Trade Policy Review and Notification, Department of WTO Affairs of the Ministry of Commerce of China.

MESSAGE

UHURU KENYATTA
President of Kenya

H.E. Mr Uhuru Kenyatta, President, Republic of Kenya

This volume celebrates two important events that took place in Nairobi in December 2015. The World Trade Organization held its Tenth Ministerial Conference in Kenya, and we took advantage of that occasion to host the Fourth China Round Table back-to-back with the Conference. The people and Government of Kenya are honoured to have been accorded the opportunity to provide the location for these meetings.

The choice of an African venue conveys a message I cherish as much as the events themselves and their substantive outcomes. The WTO was established in Marrakesh some two decades ago with a sense of novelty and optimism that marked a deepening of multilateral, non-discriminatory trade cooperation across the globe.

Twenty years on from the entry into force of the WTO in 1995, the WTO came back to Africa, holding its first ministerial conference on the continent. This time Africa was hosting not a birth, but an institution that has made a valuable contribution over the years to open trade, policy predictability, the rule of law and enhanced economic welfare. Yet the WTO that came to Nairobi also confronts serious challenges, having struggled with an unfinished negotiating agenda since the turn of the century.

The Nairobi meeting confronted these challenges with determination, tenacity and political will that yielded as positive an outcome as anyone could have hoped for. In addition to specific gains in such areas as agriculture, better trade opportunities for least-developed countries, and a new deal on trade in information technology products, the Nairobi Package has potentially broken a logjam that has frustrated progress in the Doha Round. It has also created an opportunity to address other issues that many believe are ripe for multilateral negotiation. E-commerce could be one such issue of interest for Africa, considering the growing role of the digital economy across the continent. Even more, in Nairobi, decisions were taken to enlarge the WTO with the membership of Afghanistan and Liberia, hence advancing ever closer to the strategic objective of universality of membership.

The WTO success complements a good year for multilateral cooperation. In July 2015, in Addis Ababa, Ethiopia, we had a successful Third International Conference for Financing for Development, arising from the Monterrey Consensus. This was followed by the adoption of the 2030 Agenda for Sustainable Development Goals in September 2015, in New York, by world leaders. Subsequently, at a meeting of the United Nations Framework Convention on Climate Change, in Paris, France, we reached an historic agreement to combat climate change.

In Nairobi, we also spent a couple of days before the WTO Conference thinking about trade as a motor for growth and development especially for the least-developed countries (LDCs). Of the forty-eight economies bearing this designation, thirty-four are in Africa.

The China Round Table was instituted by China in 2011 as part of a mechanism to assist LDCs to participate more effectively in the WTO and support those seeking accession to the WTO in negotiating their membership. The Fourth meeting of the Round Table provided a valuable opportunity to discuss the challenges facing LDCs and identify the role of trade and the multilateral trading system in underwriting their economic progress. A number of valuable reflections delivered and discussed at the Round Table can be found in this volume.

Returning to the WTO Ministerial Conference, this was not only an occasion to advance the work of the institution, but also a chance to reflect on the place of Africa in the global community of nations. No more than a decade or two ago, Africa was often referred to by the Western press and other commentators as a bleak continent of basket-case economies. That negative image has been laid to rest.

For the last two decades, Africa's growth rate has exceeded that of the global economy. Africa's share of world production has expanded by 30 per cent and that of trade by more than one-third. Africa's share of foreign direct investment has doubled. In 2014, six of the ten fastest growing economies were African.

All this speaks of a continent on the move. Yet we must not delude ourselves. Our continent faces manifold challenges. Our growth performance is too narrowly based on primary commodities. Trade opportunities within the continent have only started to be tapped. We face an urgent task in tackling poverty, enhancing inclusiveness and fitting the continent into a rapidly evolving global digital economy. We have huge investment needs in terms both of physical infrastructure and human capital. We need to improve our governance.

We know well that trade can be a vital support to the continent's growth and development, as well as a buttress against social and political instability. We also know that the WTO can make a critical contribution to our success. This is why the Nairobi outcome is so welcome. But Nairobi is only a beginning, a harbinger of opportunity – a platform.

Much remains to be done. The progress on export subsidies in agriculture was a very welcome development. But trade rules in agriculture must be made fairer still. Trade-distorting domestic support is damaging African agriculture and industry. If we are to industrialize, tariff escalation and peak tariffs need to be eliminated. African economies producing competitively should not be frustrated by defensive trade remedies. Standards should not be the next frontier of protectionism.

The Trade Facilitation Agreement (TFA) struck at the Ninth Ministerial Conference in Bali in 2013 was a welcome development. Now we need more governments to ratify the TFA, as Kenya did in the run-up to the Nairobi Conference. The TFA will permit goods and services to flow more freely amongst countries with all the benefits that brings in terms of jobs, growth and development.

What does Africa itself need to do in order to take maximum advantage of opportunities offered by intensified engagement in the world economy? I believe we face four major tasks.

First, we must build on recent growth successes in Africa to undertake a profound structural transformation. This is a multifaceted undertaking, with industrial development, diversification, and high-quality job creation at the core of our efforts.

Second, we must address poverty and enhance opportunities for the millions of individuals and families presently on the periphery of African development.

Third, as individual states and as a continent, we must integrate better into the global economy in order to benefit more from international trade and investment. The first step is to develop the enormous untapped opportunities for intensified intra-African integration. This will provide a natural springboard for deeper engagement in the global economy.

Fourth, we must improve the quality of governance across the continent.

WTO Director-General Roberto Azevêdo and Kenya's Cabinet Secretary for Foreign Affairs and International Trade Amina Mohamed demonstrated exemplary leadership in working with ministers.

In closing, I have no hesitation in recommending this volume for what it tells us about how international trade and the WTO mesh with Africa's development priorities and aspirations.

JOINT FOREWORD

Mr Roberto Azevêdo   H.E. Mrs Amina Mohamed   H.E. Mr Gao Hucheng

The Tenth WTO Ministerial Conference in Nairobi in December 2015 achieved successful outcomes of historic proportions. This success built on the foundations laid at the Ninth Ministerial Conference in Bali in December 2013. A WTO that regularly delivers will be a more robust institution that responds to the growth and development requirements of its members. Now, collectively, we must forge ahead to consolidate our successes, build on them and advance the organization to respond to the trade and economic challenges that members face.

Bali culminated in the landmark Trade Facilitation Agreement (TFA), which will lower trade costs and support trade expansion, and resulted in decisions on agriculture, food security and development. The welfare effects for individual economies, when fully implemented and with appropriate companion policies, are very significant indeed.

The contributions from Nairobi were also extremely significant. In agriculture, the Ministerial Conference ended decades of struggle over the issue of export subsidies on agricultural products. These have been banned once and for all. This is an historic achievement that further levels the agricultural playing field at a stroke. This was overdue and was an indispensable step for development in the right direction. Moreover, it means that the WTO is delivering on a key target of the UN's Sustainable Development Goals, which were set just three months before.

Other achievements in agriculture dealt with food aid and addressed aspects of food security, including public stockholding and a special safeguard mechanism. A long-standing issue regarding the negative effects of cotton subsidies on poorer cotton producers was also addressed, through the elimination of export subsidies and the provision of duty-free, quota-free market access in major markets. In addition, a package for least-developed countries (LDCs) included revised rules of origin requirements for those suppliers under preferential trade agreements. Further work was done on securing preferential access for services traded by LDCs.

The Ministerial Conference also concluded negotiations aimed at removing tariffs on a range of information technology products, amounting to the removal of tariffs on 10 per cent of global merchandise trade, building on an early agreement reached in 1996.

During the Nairobi Ministerial Conference, the terms of WTO entry for Afghanistan and Liberia were approved and the WTO welcomed the accessions of Yemen, Seychelles and Kazakhstan, all of which had become WTO members since the Bali Ministerial Conference. The WTO now covers 98 per cent of world trade and is well on its way to attaining universal membership.

Nairobi opened a window on the future of the WTO. It opened up the possibility of adopting new and creative ways of carrying issues forward. Moreover, it confirmed the collective understanding that trade plays a vital role in sustaining economies, promoting jobs, facilitating growth and fostering development.

The WTO's Tenth Ministerial Conference was made more substantive and symbolically significant because it was held in Africa, home to more than one quarter of the entire WTO membership. Africa is a continent on the move, with tremendous promise and a prominent future in global affairs. But because there are many emerging economies in Africa, the continent faces multi-dimensional challenges on its road to development. Millions need to be lifted out of poverty. Much must be done to diversify sources of income and trade and to enhance value-added across a broad range of activities involving both goods and services. Huge infrastructure deficits must be met. By working more closely together, governments can achieve more than when they work alone. Full participation in the multilateral trading system will be an essential ingredient for moving forward.

Of course the Nairobi Ministerial Conference did not solve all the WTO's difficulties or address all its challenges. It highlighted differences that exist among WTO members regarding the Doha Round. However, in Nairobi, members underlined their commitment to delivering on the remaining Doha Round issues, and they recognized that some members are keen to discuss other issues as well. Conversations are now underway about how we can take all of this work forward – and there is a clear desire among the membership to deliver more, and to do it more quickly.

2015 was a successful year for multilateralism, marked by the Third International Conference on Financing for Development, the adoption of the Sustainable Development Goals by the United Nations and the finalization of the Paris Agreement on climate change (COP21) just before the WTO's Ministerial Conference in Nairobi. Nairobi formed part of the success of multilateralism in 2015 – and it was particularly satisfying to do so on the occasion of the WTO's 20th anniversary.

Ultimately, decision-makers are well aware that all economies need trade and that trade needs a framework of global rules. The WTO provides the core underpinning for trade relations. Its role shall remain critical for stability, certainty and order in trade relations. The GATT/ WTO has made significant contributions to growth and development over the decades. It has written and enforced rules, contributed to greater trade openness, increased market access opportunities, and resolved hundreds of disputes over the years. We have no doubt that the organiza- tion will go from strength to strength in the years to come.

The contributions in this collection reflect on all of these elements. It will be a lasting record of the Nairobi Ministerial Conference and the Fourth China Round Table, which was held in Nairobi, back-to- back with the Ministerial Conference. The China Round Table is a joint activity of the WTO Secretariat, the Government of China and the WTO member that hosts the Round Table – in this case, Kenya. The Round Table is one of the four pillars of 'China's LDCs and Accessions Programme' – usually known as 'The China Programme'. This initiative was established in 2011 by a Memorandum of Understanding between the WTO Secretariat and the Government of China. The Round Table promotes a process to deliver technical assistance and capacity-building to LDCs, share experiences based on accession-related domestic reforms and support a policy dialogue to deepen the integration of LDCs and other developing economies into the rules-based multilateral trading system. We jointly opened the Fourth China Round Table and are very pleased that this volume reflects the valuable contribution that this initiative made to a very memorable week in Nairobi.

The book contains important discussions and analyses of a range of issues facing the WTO – specifically its African members – and the numerous challenges facing all members as they struggle to make things better for their populations. We congratulate the editors and all the contributors and recommend this book not only as a valuable record of the WTO's success in Nairobi but also as a timely and important contribution to the literature on sound policy-making at the international level.

Mr Roberto Azevêdo
WTO Director-General

H.E. Mrs Amina Mohamed
Cabinet Secretary for Foreign Affairs and International Trade of the Republic of Kenya

H.E. Mr Gao Hucheng
Minister of Commerce of the People's Republic of China

ACKNOWLEDGEMENTS

This book project was prepared for the Nairobi Fourth China Round Table, which was held in the context of the Tenth Ministerial Conference, the first gathering of WTO ministers to be held on the African continent during the WTO's 20th anniversary. These two events offered unique opportunities for African trade policy decision-makers and their partners to reflect and exchange views on the continent's participation in the rules-based multilateral trading system in the twenty-first century. As editors of this book, we express our profound appreciation to all the authors whose contributions feature in this volume. We are immensely grateful for the time, energy and intellect they have invested in this project. The range of perspectives represented in these chapters will help to improve understanding of engagement with Africa and contribute to the maximization of the continent's potential as the next growth frontier. Many colleagues were indispensable in the preparation of this book. We received inspiration, strong support and thoughtful reflections, at every stage, from WTO Deputy Director-General David Shark and Graça Andresen-Guimaraes, Senior Advisor in the Office of WTO Director-General Roberto Azevêdo. For their editorial work in preparing the manuscript and refining it through many stages, we are very grateful indeed to Souda Tandara-Stenier, Anthony Martin and Helen Swain. We received research assistance from Vicky Chemutai. We are also grateful to the Government of China, which provided financial support for the Nairobi Fourth China Round Table at which most of the chapters contained in this volume were first presented. Last but not least, we are grateful to Finola O'Sullivan at Cambridge University Press, whose support was indispensable for this book to move ahead in a short period of time.

ABBREVIATIONS

ACP	African Caribbean and Pacific Group of States
AEC	African Economic Community
AGOA	African Growth and Opportunity Act
ASEAN	Association of Southeast Asian Nations
ASYCUDA	Automated SYstem for CUstoms DAta
AU	African Union
AUC	African Union Commission
AVE	*ad valorem* equivalents
BADR	Base Automatisée des Douanes en Réseau
BCEAO	Central Bank of West African States
CBN	Central Bank of Nigeria
CEMAC	Central African Economic and Monetary Community
CEN-SAD	Community of Sahel–Saharan States
CET	common external tariff
CFTA	Continental Free Trade Area
CIMA	Inter-African Insurance Conference
COBAC	Bank of Central African States
COMESA	Common Market for Eastern and Southern Africa
CU	customs union
CVA	WTO Customs Valuation Agreement
DCFTA	Deep and Comprehensive Free Trade Agreement
DDA	Doha Development Agenda
DID	difference-in-difference
DSB	WTO Dispute Settlement Body
DSM	WTO Dispute Settlement Mechanism
DSU	WTO Dispute Settlement Understanding
EAC	East African Community
ECA	UN Economic Commission for Africa
ECCAS	Economic Community of Central African States
ECO	Economic Cooperation Organization
ECOWAS	Economic Community of West African States

EDI	electronic data interchange
EGA	Environmental Goods Agreement
EPAs	economic partnership agreements
EPZ	export processing zone
ESA	Eastern and Southern Africa
EUROMED	Euro-Mediterranean Partnership
FDI	foreign direct investment
FIEs	foreign-invested enterprises
f.o.b.	free-on-board
FOCAC	Forum on China-Africa Cooperation
FTA	free trade agreement
GAFTA	Greater Arab Free Trade Area
GATS	General Agreement on Trade in Services
GATT	General Agreement on Tariffs and Trade
GNI	gross domestic income
GPT	general preferential tariff
GSP	Generalized System of Preferences
GVCs	global value chains
HACCP	Hazard Analysis Critical Control Point
HICs	high-income countries
HPAEs	High Performing East Asian Economies
IDB	Integrated Data Base
IGAD	Intergovernmental Authority on Development
IMF	International Monetary Fund
IPR	intellectual property rights
IT	information technology
ITA	WTO Information Technology Agreement
ITC	International Trade Centre
LDCs	least-developed countries
LICs	low-income countries
LMCs	lower-middle-income countries
LPI	World Bank's Logistics Performance Index
MFN	most-favoured nation
MOFCOM	China's Ministry of Commerce
MOU	Memorandum of Understanding
MRTAs	mega-regional trade agreements
MTS	multilateral trading system
NAMA	non-agricultural market access
NIRP	Nigeria Industrial Revolution Plan
NTMs	non-tariff measures

ODCs	other duties and charges
OECD	Organisation for Economic Co-operation and Development
PIDA	African Development Bank Group's Programme for Infrastructure Development in Africa
PSI	preshipment inspection
PTAs	preferential trade arrangements
QRs	quantitative restrictions
RCEP	Regional Comprehensive Economic Partnership
RECs	Regional Economic Communities
REER	real effective exchange rate
RoO	rules of origin
RTA	regional trade agreement
RVC	regional value chain
SACU	Southern African Customs Union
SADC	Southern African Development Community
SADCC	Southern African Development Coordinating Conference
SAPs	IMF's structural adjustment programmes
SCM	WTO Agreement on Subsidies and Countervailing Measures
SCT	supply chain trade
S&D	special and differential treatment
SDGs	United Nations Sustainable Development Goals
SDR	special drawing rights
SEZ	special economic zone
SIDS	small-island developing state
SITA	Supporting Indian Trade and Investment for Africa
SME	small and medium-sized enterprise
SPS	sanitary and phytosanitary measures
SSA	Sub-Saharan Africa
STEs	state trading enterprises
STRI	World Bank's Services Trade Restrictiveness Index
TA	technical assistance
TBT	technical barriers to trade
TDCA	Trade, Development and Cooperation Agreement
TFA	WTO Trade Facilitation Agreement
TFTA	Tripartite Free Trade Area Agreement
TISA	Trade in Services Agreement
TISI	trade and investment support institution

TiVA	OECD-WTO Trade in Value Added database
TLs	tariff lines
TPP	Trans-Pacific Partnership
TPR	WTO Trade Policy Review
TPRM	WTO Trade Policy Review Mechanism
TRIMs	trade-related investment measures
TRIPS	WTO Agreement on Trade-Related Aspects of Intellectual Property Rights
TRQ	tariff rate quota
TTIPA	Trans-Atlantic Trade and Investment Partnership
UEMOA	West African Economic and Monetary Union
UMA	Arab Maghreb Union
UMCs	upper-middle-income countries
UN	United Nations
UNCTAD	UN Conference on Trade and Development
UNDAP	UN Development Assistance Plan
UNWTO	UN World Tourism Organization
VAT	value-added tax
VCS	value chains
WAEMU	West African Economic and Monetary Union
WCO	World Customs Organization
WFOEs	wholly-foreign owned enterprises
WTO	World Trade Organization

DISCLAIMER

The opinions, arguments and conclusions contained in this publication are the sole responsibility of the individual authors. This includes contributions prepared by individual staff of the Secretariat of the World Trade Organization. None of the chapters purports to reflect the opinions or views of WTO members or the Secretariat, directly or indirectly. Any citation of the chapters should ascribe authorship to the individuals who have written the contributions. This book should not be viewed as advancing any form of legal interpretation or any policy position, and no views or analysis in this publication should be attributed to the WTO, its Secretariat or its members.

1

Introduction and Overview

PATRICK LOW, CHIEDU OSAKWE AND MAIKA OSHIKAWA

Introduction

This volume, the work of more than twenty authors, grew out of the Fourth China Round Table and the WTO's Tenth Ministerial Conference, two seminal events held back-to-back in Nairobi, Kenya, in December 2015. The work presented here provides comprehensive, substantive insights of the African trade policy and development context in which these two meetings took place.

The Fourth China Round Table is an annual event, coordinated by the WTO with the Government of China on the basis of a 2011 Memorandum of Understanding (MOU) and hosted by a WTO member. The policy round table process assists least-developed countries (LDCs) in improving the effectiveness of their participation in the multilateral trading system by facilitating a deeper understanding of trade rules and trends and an exchange of views on global best practices, accompanied by the provision of advice and support for those still in the process of acceding to the WTO. This was the first time the Round Table was held in Africa. The Fourth Round Table, hosted by the Government of Kenya, operated in synergy with the Tenth Ministerial Conference in Nairobi.

Holding the meeting in Africa was something of a homecoming, since more than 70 per cent, or thirty-four out of the forty-eight UN-designated LDCs originate from the continent. The two days over which the Round Table took place, immediately prior to the Ministerial Conference, provided a valuable opportunity for LDC government officials, representatives of international agencies and other invitees to exchange views and listen to policy presentations, some of which are reproduced in this volume.

The WTO's Tenth Ministerial Conference was also infused with an extra sense of occasion, as it was the first WTO ministerial gathering to take place in Africa. The venue was highly auspicious when it came to generating results, and these have been spelled out in some detail by WTO Director-General Roberto Azevêdo, Kenya's Cabinet Secretary for Foreign Affairs and International Trade, Amina Mohamed, and China's Minister of Commerce Gao Hucheng, in their joint foreword to this volume.

Another positive aspect of the chosen venue for the WTO's Tenth Ministerial Conference was that it brought Africa and African developmental challenges and imperatives into sharp focus. Africa has the potential to become a global economic powerhouse, but it still faces formidable development challenges. It is generally acknowledged that engagement in the global economy, through trade and foreign investment, is an indispensable accompaniment of progress. The nature of that engagement and the domestic environment from which it is issued are crucial to prospects for progress through development, growth and quality job creation.

It is important that the WTO focus on Africa due to the economic, social and political realities facing the continent, particularly given Africa's importance to the WTO. No less than one quarter of the WTO's membership is African, and seven of the nineteen current candidates for WTO accession are from the continent. What happens in Africa will increasingly leave an imprint on multilateral trade relations.

The contributions to this volume fit into two broad categories. Part I contains short chapters, most of which are based on contributions made by African policy-makers and their partners in the discussion at the Fourth China Round Table. The eight chapters in that part raise a range of issues vital to Africa's development, largely with a focus on international economic engagement. The chapter by Fatima Haram Acyl (Chapter 2) emphasizes the importance of the right kind of engagement with the multilateral trading system to support development and poverty eradication, and the challenges of fulfilling the UN Sustainable Development Goals spelled out in Agenda 2030. Okechukwu Enelamah (Chapter 3) explains the transformational policies that Nigeria is pursuing to raise incomes and promote development, including through economic diversification (particularly on the trade front), industrial and infrastructural investment, institutional reform and improved governance.

Rob Davies (Chapter 4) also highlights the imperative for structural transformation. He emphasizes industrialization, African economic integration, an appropriate degree of protection from competing imports and the need for a WTO that supports African industrial development. Joshua Setipa (Chapter 5) notes the dependence of Lesotho on the textiles and clothing sector and on agriculture. Lesotho's government has been pursuing a strategic approach to lower costs, facilitate trade and provide sectoral incentives aimed at diversifying the production base of the economy. Moulay Hafid Elalamy (Chapter 6) discusses how Morocco leveraged itself out of the economic doldrums that afflicted the country in the 1980s through a comprehensive economic reform programme that included joining the GATT in 1987 and tying in domestic reforms at the international level.

Like a number of the other contributions to the Fourth China Round Table discussions, that of Arancha González (Chapter 7) emphasizes the opportunities offered by participation in global value chains. A particular focus is on the importance of small and medium-sized enterprises and how the challenges they face can be met by openness, 'smart' reforms and connectivity. Joakim Reiter (Chapter 8) examines the importance of foreign direct investment (FDI) within a sound policy framework across a range of sectors including services, supported by fuller participation in the WTO, and notes that many African states will not attain the UN Sustainable Development Goals unless the FDI gap is addressed. Anabel González (Chapter 9) focuses on the potential contribution to development and poverty reduction of greater African economic integration in a less costly and more competitive operating environment.

Part II and Part III of this volume consist of a collection of commissioned papers for the Fourth China Round Table. Those in Part II cover various aspects of African trade development and the role of policy in shaping the continent's performance and prospects. Part III focuses on specific aspects of development policy and experiences that are not necessarily particular to Africa but are nevertheless of considerable relevance in that context.

The first chapter in Part II, by Michael Finger (Chapter 10), examines Africa's trade performance over the last two decades, which in aggregate has been relatively dynamic in comparison to that of many other regions. It notes Africa's commodity dependence, particularly on the trade front, but also detects indications of growing diversification. The chapter looks at the experience of six African economies that have done particularly well and considers the ingredients of their success.

In Chapter 11, Maika Oshikawa, Ukamaka Anaedu and Vicky Chemutai trace African policy developments through the medium of successive WTO Trade Policy Reviews. Against a process of trade policy reform in many African economies, they conclude that scope exists for making better use of trade policy to sustain and deepen the transformation process. In this context, the authors contend that better use could be made of the WTO system to support reform and improve governance. Thus, the WTO accession template could be useful in driving progress.

Stephen Karingi, Ottavia Pesce and Simon Mevel (Chapter 12) examine Africa's regional integration experiences. These efforts have been supported by the Common African Position on the Post-2015 Development Agenda and the African Union's Agenda 2063. It is acknowledged by governments that trade is crucial in ensuring the full benefits of Africa's transformation process. The drive for regional integration through trade is reflected in the Tripartite Free Trade Agreement and the drive towards a Continental Free Trade Area (CFTA). Sequencing and the scope of international trade agreements are important elements in developmental outcomes.

Bernard Hoekman (Chapter 13) considers how Africa's agriculture and natural resource base can be leveraged to diversify and develop industry and services through increasingly higher value-added participation in international vertical production arrangements. In this context, intra-regional trade remains well below potential, although the indications are that growing attention to trade facilitation and the CFTA should help to lower trade costs, improve logistics and infrastructure and grow competiveness through enhanced productivity.

Marcus Bartley Johns, Christina Busch and Gerard McLinden (Chapter 14) concentrate on the role of trade facilitation in the continent's development, noting that trade-related costs are higher in Africa than any other region. This obstructs intra-African integration as well as participation in global markets. Progress in this domain is essential to Africa's diversification efforts aimed at fostering higher value-added activities in agribusiness, manufacturing and services. Reducing trade-related costs is also an important component of poverty reduction.

In the first chapter of Part III of the volume (Chapter 15), Chiedu Osakwe takes a detailed look at industrial policy and its potential contribution to Africa's development and structural transformation. He argues that industrial policy is resurgent and that, in developing economies, it is driven by a variety of factors, including the post-2008–09 crisis and reduced global growth, a perceptible process of de-industrialization, balance-of-payments pressures that will become more acute with tumbling commodity prices, and demographic trends across the continent. Industrial policies aimed at improving competitiveness and at diversifying and modernizing economies in the increasingly digitized global economy must be smart, focusing on enhanced capacities and technological adaptation, thus avoiding the pitfalls of inward-looking and ultimately stultifying import substitution. Such policies can be accommodated within the WTO framework, notwithstanding concerns about the trading system squeezing out policy space.

Alexei Kireyev (Chapter 16) undertakes a statistical analysis of the impact of reforms associated with WTO accession on competitiveness. The findings are quite different among recently acceded economies in various parts of the world, and the overall impact attributable is relatively small. The author nevertheless argues that policy reform based on the WTO accession template would yield significant dividends in terms of credible reform packages that could be locked in internationally. Such efforts could be supported by an examination of the experiences of other economies that have managed complex reform agendas in the context of WTO accession.

The final chapter in Part III (Chapter 17), by Yuan Yuan, provides a detailed account of China's reform process that led to a thirty-year growth miracle. She explains how this was brought about by adding capital and labour, relying on foreign investment and export markets, and emphasizing cost efficiency. This phase of China's development is being balanced by greater emphasis on domestic consumption and developing the services economy. Economic growth will be slower but is likely to remain high in comparison to many other economies, and trade will remain important. Some of China's development experiences could provide useful illustrations of the ingredients of success in building up Africa's manufacturing base and diversifying the economy.

Salient Features of Africa's Trade Performance, Opportunities and Challenges

The summary above of the contributions to this volume provides only a hint of their richness and their comprehensive treatment of the issues at hand. What follows is a more systematic account of the main themes emerging from the volume. A recapitulation of this nature is no substitute for the profuse detail and subtle argumentation of the chapters themselves, but we thought it would be useful to provide a reasonably complete summary of the issues that have captured the attention of the authors.

History has repeatedly demonstrated that no economy can prosper without trade. Trade is both a reflection and cause of the health of the domestic economy. As Michael Finger points out in his chapter, growth has on average been vigorous in recent years. In the twenty-first century, supported by trade, Africa's economy has grown at an average of 5 per cent per year, outpacing global GDP growth by a significant margin.

Ten of the world's sixteen fastest-growing economies are in Africa. In the last twenty years, Africa's share of global production has risen by 30 per cent and its share of trade by more than one-third. The continent's share of world foreign direct investment has doubled. These expansion rates are built from a very low base. But they are indicative of an Africa on the move.

In terms of the destination of exports, Africa's trade is skewed against the continent. Only about 18 per cent of Africa's trade is with itself. The lack of intra-African trade represents a significant loss of opportunity. Virtually all of the chapters in Parts I and II of the volume refer to the challenges of fostering deeper economic links across the continent. It would be very difficult to find a commentator who does not consider the sparseness of intra-African economic links a foregone development opportunity awaiting remedy. The continent's core trade destinations are China, the European Union and the United States, which among themselves take a very large share of the total. Just as product diversification of exports is desirable, so too is greater geographical dispersion.

Africa's trade performance has been driven to a large degree by oil and other commodity exports. The commodity price boom fed trade growth. Recent price developments will reverse some of those gains.

Commodity dependency in trade points to a structural challenge facing many African economies. They need to diversify into manufacturing and services, thus building greater economic resilience at home, more and better jobs and trading opportunities abroad. Manufacturing and services provide vital conduits for adding more value domestically and regionally. Foreign direct investment is often an important ingredient in this context, as emphasized by Joakim Reiter in his contribution. The drive for transformational change goes to the very structure of economies. Effective change calls for clarity of purpose, consistency and a sound decision-making apparatus. Efforts must focus on deepening development, generating growth, creating employment and eradicating poverty.

Pro-poor policies are sometimes treated as an add-on, but many argue that addressing poverty must form a customized, integral part of any viable reform package. The importance of addressing poverty is considered in the contributions by Fatima Haram Acyl in relation to the UN's

Sustainable Development Goals, and more generally by Anabel González and by Gerard McLinden and Marcus Bartley Johns in their chapters. Practically every contribution to the volume has specific observations on the structural transformation imperative.

There is a credible basis for economic convergence for a number of African economies with diversification and modernization of their economies and consistent implementation of sound policies.

Some, but by no means all, African economies have already embarked on the path of diversification, building manufacturing capabilities and fostering services activities. It has been estimated that only one-third of Africa's GDP growth record is attributable to economic activity in the natural resource sector.

Clearly, a diversified domestic platform is emerging in a number of economies. Okechukwu Enelemah, Joshua Setipa and Moulad Hafid Elalamy, for example, all identify specific policy frameworks at the national level that are geared to economic transformation in Nigeria, Lesotho and Morocco, respectively. Many of the other chapters also discuss the issue. The broad-based acknowledgement of the need for far-reaching economic transformation is encouraging and is a trend that will persist. If domestic industrial and service industry growth is competitive or has the potential to become so, the diversification will spread to exports. If such activities are uncompetitive, they will eventually be a drain on the entire economy.

Significant trade and diversification opportunities have emerged in recent years with the development of vertically integrated production structures that span multiple borders. Global value chains (GVCs) allow economies to specialize in specific production lines without having to produce entire products. Rob Davies, Arancha González, Joakim Reiter, Anabel González, Stephen Karingi and his co-authors, and Bernard Hoekman are some of the contributors who allude, in greater or lesser detail, to the pivotal developmental role that participation in GVCs can make in the right policy environment.

These opportunities for component trade through participation in GVCs in both goods and services offer new scope for adding value domestically and regionally. This is especially relevant in primary commodity production in Africa, where rather than exporting primary products largely in their raw form, further value can be added prior to exportation.

Another genre of GVCs does not determine where to locate on the basis of the presence of underground resource deposits or farming land, but simply on the basis of a favourable operating environment. The challenge in the case of both resource-based and footloose GVCs is for local producers to become involved in a continuing process of upgrading and ultimately the establishment of home-grown, internationally oriented lead firms.

The Policy Challenges

Policy is obviously at the core of this volume and is discussed in one guise or another by all authors. Strictly speaking, no such thing as policy neutrality exists. Even where an economy decides not to intervene in the market, it is effectively taking a policy decision. If there is no escaping policy, it makes it doubly important to ensure that policies are sound and conducive to progress.

Too often, policy can become a millstone around the neck of growth and development. This can be for three main reasons. One is to do with policy design. Either through neglect or poorly formulated policies, costs in the economy are needlessly increased. A second problem may be poor implementation because of a lack of adequate resources, or adequately trained resources, which leads to inefficiencies and added costs.

A third problem is corruption, which not only adds costs to production in a variety of ways, but diverts significant resources from development and, more seriously, fractures the moral integrity and the legitimacy of elected leaders to govern. It is within the powers of governments to address all these shortcomings and make their own policy-based contributions to productivity and growth.

In broad terms, policy reform may assume a number of different forms. Some policies are enabling or facilitating, in the sense that they remove what might be considered inadvertent costs of doing business. Trade facilitation, customs reform, streamlined regulation and investment in human and physical infrastructure are among the instruments of enablement.

A second kind of policy reform involves removing or adjusting policies deliberately put in place in pursuit of specific economic, political or social objectives. These policies may have become outdated in terms of their original purpose or they may reflect errors of judgement, such as an excessive reliance on import-substituting industrialization, which was a feature of early industrialization efforts in some economies.

A third reform genre involves the introduction of new policies. New policies may respond to changed circumstances or may reflect past neglect. Like anywhere else, policy change in Africa is bound to involve a combination of these three kinds of change.

The idea that prosperity born of growth and economic progress is assured with as little policy intervention as possible is more ideological than scientific. But it is also clear there can be too much intervention, whether as a result of ideology or wrong-headedness leading to flawed policies. The precise policy mix that will do the best job is not always easy to identify, as is amply demonstrated by Maika Oshikawa and her co-authors in their chapter, which reviews more than one hundred WTO Trade Policy Reviews on African economies. Interesting pointers on policy options for economic transformation are offered by Yuan Yuan in her analysis of China's experiences over the last three decades or so.

The reasons for intervention may stem from the external consequences of transactions that are unpriced or incorrectly priced in the market. These so-called externalities and other kinds of market failure may have good or bad consequences, but they both warrant intervention.

This discussion is related to so-called industrial policy, which has sparked fierce debates, often with a certain ideological overlay. There is nothing wrong in principle with governments deploying policy levers to change resource allocation decisions in an economy. As Chiedu Osakwe's chapter discusses, virtually all governments have deployed industrial policy under various guises, sometimes (but not always) to good effect.

The challenge is, indeed, to do it well. This means that the objectives must be clear and the policies must be well designed for efficiency and monitored. Adequate government capabilities are a prerequisite for the successful conduct of industrial policies, as is adequate information and analysis for understanding cause and effect.

In Africa's case, as elsewhere, plenty of scope exists for improving and streamlining the regulatory framework for doing business. In other cases too, there will be justification for lessening the impact of certain interventions. It is argued in some quarters, for example, that import tariffs tend to be too high in some sectors.

Awareness has grown rapidly in recent years that trade and investment relationships among African economies are poorly developed, and big opportunities lurk behind the interaction. Moves are afoot to eradicate some of the barriers to exchange across the continent, be they of a fiscal or regulatory nature. These are the ideas driving regional integration initiatives, as discussed at some length by Stephen Karingi and his colleagues. These initiatives will need to be supported by enhanced continent-wide infrastructure in order to facilitate and lower the costs of transport and communications in particular. Bernard Hoekman mentions the importance of addressing these challenges, and Marcus Bartley Johns and his co-authors focus particularly on the trade facilitation aspects.

The Role of the WTO

Just as many African economies have tended to maintain relatively high tariffs on many products, they have been reluctant to commit to maximum tariff levels through WTO 'bindings'. Where there are bindings, these are often set at levels considerably higher than the relevant applied tariffs. Several reasons can be adduced as to why this may be so, but it does deny the economies concerned an opportunity to use internationally negotiated commitments as a means of locking in policy. Maika Oshikawa and her co-authors have something to say about the advantages of international policy lock-in in their contribution, as does Alexei Kireyev.

Apart from any gains economies might enjoy as a result of tying down their policy commitments through international obligations, they can also rely on the WTO system of rules for protection against discrimination and other non-conforming policy behaviour. These possibilities help to level the playing field and ensure a greater degree of certainty regarding the external policy environment.

Many African economies did not accede to the GATT – the WTO's predecessor – through negotiations. Rather they were 'successor' members of the organization following their political independence from colonial powers.

Those economies in Africa and elsewhere that accede to the WTO through negotiations are frequently required to undertake far-reaching reforms. They benefit from such reforms in various ways, including the enhancement of the capacity to compete. Alexei Kireyev analyses the relationship between WTO accession and enhanced competitiveness in some detail. He also argues that African economies that have not been through this process might consider adopting long-term reform programmes similar to a WTO accession package. The chapters by Fatima Haram Acyl and Rob Davis emphasize that WTO support for economic transformation in Africa must be sufficiently accommodative of different policy approaches. In his contribution on industrial policy, Chiedu

Osakwe argues that the WTO does not prevent governments from pursuing well-designed and effective industrial policies.

We urge readers to take the time to study the chapters that follow. They are an eclectic set of contributions, nuanced in some instances by different views of the best way to move forward. These differences, intrinsic to any healthy debate, are remarkably slight in our view, considering the multi-faceted complexity of the issues that must be addressed as Africa takes its rightful place as a dominant force in the global economy in decades to come.

PART I

The Future of the Multilateral Trading System: Perspectives from African Policy-Makers and Partners

2

African Union Priorities at the WTO

FATIMA HARAM ACYL

Abstract

The African Union's (AU) priorities at the WTO reflect the priorities of the WTO's African member states that the multilateral trading system should contribute to the economic development of their economies through the elaboration of equitable, fair and development-friendly rules. The position of the AU is consistent with the recently adopted United Nations Sustainable Development Goals (SDGs), which also see trade as being critical to achieving the goal of eradicating extreme poverty everywhere. The AU's priority is, therefore, to see WTO outcomes that serve to facilitate the structural economic transformation and development of developing and least-developed African countries in line with the vision of the African Union's Agenda 2063.

The African Union (AU) is made up of its constituent member states, and as such the African Union's priorities at the WTO are African priorities, as reflected in various declarations and decisions issued from African ministers of trade and heads of state through the years. These same decisions reflect the commitment of Africa to multilateralism. The AU sees that a strong multilateral trading system, as advocated by the WTO, is in the best interest of African economies, which are, by and large, small, developing and least-developed economies. A strong, effective and sustainable World Trade Organization is the best way to protect the interests of developing countries in the multilateral trading system.

The overriding priority for Africa is economic development and the creation of high-quality jobs for its growing population. African policy-

This chapter is an adapted version of a presentation made at the Fourth China Round Table, Nairobi, Kenya, on 13–14 December 2015.

makers believe that trade can be a tool towards this end. African economies therefore do not see trade merely as an end in itself, but rather as an
opportunity to grow their economies and lift their people out of poverty.
Consequently, the AU pushes for an acknowledgement that development
through trade is a legitimate and critical objective of the WTO.
Therefore, there should be a more concerted effort to ensure that the
multilateral trading system contributes to the development of developing
and least-developed economies.

The 2030 Agenda for Sustainable Development, which was adopted by
heads of state at the United Nations Headquarters in New York in
September 2015, contains the Sustainable Development Goals (SDGs).
The very first goal of the SDG is to eradicate extreme poverty for all
people everywhere by 2030. As a key institution in the global community,
it is appropriate to reflect on how the WTO will contribute to this
laudable goal.

Even more specifically, the SDGs have a number of targets related to
trade and the WTO. One of the targets of Goal 17 of the SDGs, which is
'Strengthen the means of implementation and revitalize the global partnership for sustainable development', is to 'Promote a universal, rules-
based, open, non-discriminatory and equitable multilateral trading system under the World Trade Organization, including through the conclusion of negotiations under its Doha Development Agenda'. It is not
clear that the outcomes of Nairobi significantly contribute towards this
target. Assertions about the conclusion of the Doha Development
Agenda are therefore premature until it delivers on 'a universal, rules-
based, open, non-discriminatory and equitable multilateral trading
system'.

In addition, under Goal 17 of the SDGs, there is a target to 'Significantly
increase the exports of developing countries, in particular with a view to
doubling the least-developed countries' share of global exports by 2020' as
well as a target to 'Respect each country's policy space and leadership to
establish and implement policies for poverty eradication and sustainable
development'.

How do the WTO and the current negotiations contribute towards this
target of increasing the proportion of exports from developing countries
in global exports? Do the current rules provide enough flexibility for
developing countries to achieve their development objectives? These are
some of the critical questions to think through in determining how the
WTO can contribute to Africa's development.

The goals and targets outlined above reflect global consensus in their adoption as part of the SDG targets. The AU's expectations and priorities from the multilateral trading system are consistent with these goals and targets. A multilateral trading system that actively and proactively facilitates growth and development is critical for the attainment of the AU's Agenda 2063, which envisages 'an integrated, prosperous and peaceful Africa, driven by its own citizens and representing a dynamic force in the global arena'.

In order to actualize the AU's Agenda 2063, African countries must be able to use trade as a tool to develop their economies. A WTO system that is committed to development outcomes will facilitate this. This commitment to development outcomes should be reflected in the critical issues of the day that are being negotiated, including agriculture and market access for non-agricultural products, services, development, special and differential treatment and other issues currently being negotiated.

Any movement towards discussions of new issues should include discussions on how the WTO can help to achieve the adopted SDG goals. The WTO must reflect the thinking of its members that trade is for economic development, and its rules should address this need. There must therefore be coherence and consistency in our approach to multilateralism, and it is time for the WTO system to take a more proactive approach to how its rules can help countries to develop.

In concluding, the African Union priority at the WTO is simple. It wants a strong and equitable multilateral trading system that actively facilitates the economic development and growth not only of African states, but of all developing and least-developed economies.

3

Economic Diversification in Africa's Number One Economy

OKECHUKWU E. ENELAMAH

Abstract

Nigeria is the largest economy in Africa, with a GDP in excess of US$ 500 billion, dependent on oil and gas exports for the bulk of government revenues as well as foreign exchange. Its growth – which averaged about 7 per cent in the decade between 2005 and 2014 – has in recent years been driven by the non-oil sectors: services, agriculture and manufacturing. The principal challenge for the President Buhari administration, which took office in May 2015, is to build on this trend, by diversifying export income and the sources of government revenues, as well as kickstarting the long-overdue task of industrializing the Nigerian economy. One of the goals of this approach is to achieve robust, stable and predictable growth, free from short-to-medium-term cycles of boom and bust.

The strategy for Nigerian economic diversification is based on sustained domestic institutional and structural reforms, the Nigeria Industrial Revolution Plan (NIRP), a sectoral focus on core services (finance, telecommunications, transportation, energy), investment in infrastructure, support for manufacturing and for small and medium-sized enterprises and access to enlarged markets through integration into regional and global value chains.

Coupled with these priorities is the premium accorded to high-quality governance, plugging fiscal leakages and frontally addressing the systemic challenge of corruption. Successful implementation will require buy-in and ownership by Nigerians, support from Nigeria's external partners and patience from investors in ongoing reforms.

This chapter is an adapted version of a presentation made at the Fourth China Round Table, Nairobi, Kenya, on 13–14 December 2015.

Background of the Nigerian Economy

Nigeria is the largest economy in Africa, with a GDP greater than US$ 500 billion. Its growth averaged 7 per cent per annum between 2005 and 2014, but has slowed since 2015. This growth was driven primarily by the non-oil sectors, such as financial services, telecommunications and entertainment. Foreign direct investment (FDI) inflows have been strong, averaging about US$ 2 billion per quarter since 2013, with more than 70 per cent of this in the non-oil sectors. Nigeria's economy is actually more diversified than it seems, with the oil sector contributing only about 14 per cent of GDP. Nevertheless, considering the significant natural and human resources with which Nigeria is blessed, it should be possible to reduce the longstanding dependence on oil to finance government spending and foreign exchange. While oil has contributed substantially to Nigeria's revenue since its discovery in 1956, and particularly since 1970, when its price was rising, the management of these earnings has challenged the government profoundly over time. Deeper economic diversification is necessary in order for Nigeria to undertake structural transformation, buffer the domestic economy from externally transmitted shocks and accelerate growth accompanied by job creation.

Current Diversification Efforts

Diversification is a priority for Nigeria. The task ahead to diversify the economy further and expand exports is enormous, and should be approached strategically.

Encouraged strides have been made in some sectors already. Three sectors or categories stand as examples:

- First, the telecommunications sector. The Nigerian economy has experienced an increase in the number of telephone lines available in the country from about 400,000 lines in 2001 to over 140,000,000 lines currently, because of the government's deregulation policy. According to the Nigerian Communications Commission, operators in the sector have created, directly and indirectly, more than one million jobs and have helped attract over US$ 25 billion. Today, the sector contributes about one-tenth of GDP and has helped spur the development of ancillary sectors like e-commerce and the domestic entertainment industry, for example, Nollywood, Nigeria's home-grown film industry. Nigeria currently has one of the highest mobile phone usages per capita in the global economy. Increased mobile phone user density and the increased telecommunication platform have produced leap-frog effects in connectivity, including the increased digitization of the economy. Furthermore, the use of telecommunication, particularly through mobile telephony, is key platform in retail sales and distribution of Nollywood products (see *Financial Times*, 2015). Nollywood has gained world-class recognition, as evidenced by its use by the World Trade Organization as part of the programme advertisement for the Nairobi Fourth China Round Table for African Trade Ministers and their least-developed country (LDC) counterparts. The Nigerian Government will continue to provide appropriate encouragement for the entertainment industry and other service sectors to grow and diversify the economy. This is through an improved regulatory environment for competitiveness, as in the Nigeria Industrial Revolution Plan (NIRP). Subsidies are not being provided, neither financially nor in other forms. The entertainment services sector has become so successful that operators in developed economies have begun to invest in it (see *Financial Times*, 2015).

- Second, the financial services sector. The economy has witnessed the strong growth of this sector since the liberalization exercise that started in the 1990s. The exercise continued in 2005, with the guidance of the financial regulatory body, the Central Bank of Nigeria (CBN). Market-led mergers and acquisitions reduced the number of banks from eighty-nine to twenty-four. The banks emerged from the exercise bigger and with better corporate governance, and have now started to operate across Africa, financing larger transactions. The market-led business combinations served as a catalyst for the growth of the stock exchange, which has grown to market capitalization in excess of US$ 50 billion.
- Third, the cement industry. Until recently, despite the abundant domestic supply of limestone, the major constituent for making cement, Nigeria primarily imported limestone for the economy's building needs. The efforts of the government to improve the business environment and encourage backward integration – allowing the purchase or internal production by the industry of segments of its supply chain – introduced in the early 2000s, have since borne fruit, transforming the country from one of the world's leading importers to one that produces in excess of domestic demand, and that now has the potential to be a major exporter. Production capacity, which stagnated throughout the 1980s and 1990s, has grown nine-fold since 2002, and continues to grow, with more than 10 million tonnes of new capacity due to be added by 2017.

The successes that have been recorded in growing these three industries have some basic underlying elements in common: the right enabling environment, including appropriate regulation; policy consistency; and fostering competition among the industry operators. Nigeria will build on these elements to develop sectors where Nigerians have a comparative advantage in order to foster more diversification of the economy. The task of further diversifying the economy is herculean, but Nigeria's short- and medium-term prospects remain favourable and are driven by strong fundamental advantages. Four of the strongest advantages are the large domestic market and labour force, abundant natural resources and a favourable climate, a developing financial sector with strong management teams and the ability to partner with international banks to fund businesses and growing democratic institutions with the political will to build the foundation for the future.

Building the Future

The plan for continuing to foster the diversification of the economy is predicated on three major underlying elements: implementation of the Nigerian industrialization plan, improvement of the ease of doing business and the building of both hard and soft domestic infrastructure.

The Nigeria Industrial Revolution Plan (NIRP) was launched in 2012 under the auspices of the Federal Ministry of Industry, Trade and Investment. It provides a strategic and integrated roadmap towards industrialization across three sectors: agro-allied products, solid minerals, and the oil- and gas-related industries, where Nigeria's comparative and competitive advantages are apparent. Nigeria will build upon, review and update the NIRP, while implementing the plan pragmatically and adapting it as necessary as the economy forges ahead. The plan also proposes to focus on science and technology, without which further industrialization will not be sustainable, relevant or up-to-date.

The Nigerian government proposes to work assiduously to improve the operating environment for small, medium and large corporate businesses to thrive. This will require inter-ministerial coordination and elimination of the bottlenecks that impede doing business in Nigeria. This is a high priority for the government, which is committed to change at all levels. The government is keen to remove the inhibitions and obstacles impeding investment in Nigeria. Trade and investment policies, laws and incentives are being reviewed in order to bring them in line with global best practices. Technology will be used to improve the speed and efficiency of business procedures and to ensure transparency.

Modern, efficient infrastructure is key to promoting diversification and economic growth. Industries require a steady supply of electricity to function optimally, just as agricultural and mining products require robust, efficient and cost-effective transport networks to reach markets. The government is creating an ambitious national infrastructure fund to complement the existing infrastructure component of Nigeria's Sovereign Wealth Fund. This is consistent with the national infrastructure master plan, aimed at catalysing economic activity. It is not only a question of hard infrastructure – i.e. a reliable electricity supply and transport networks – but also soft infrastructure, the intangibles that all too often account for the difference between success and failure: for example, a culture of coherent policy-making and instinctive collaboration among government agencies and officials, to replace the 'silo' mentality that all too often characterizes bureaucratic operations.

There is no better time than now to start the journey along the path of diversification. None of the outlined plans will be easy. An economic system long used to behaving in a certain way and responding to certain types of incentives cannot be reformed overnight. It is important to ensure that, in the critical intervening period between the implementation of reform and the harvest of the fruits of that reform, all citizens are carried along and no one is left behind. Indeed, the best insurance for the achievement of long-term reform goals is a simultaneous focus on measures designed to tackle poverty head-on. For this reason, the government is rolling out a phased series of social intervention programmes – including conditional cash transfers, micro-credit schemes and a school feeding initiative – aimed at the poorest and most vulnerable members of the Nigerian population.

Conclusion

Diversification is a priority for Nigeria. No nation grows without developing and expanding its productive base. The current administration will strive to create a conducive environment for domestic and foreign trade and investment, focusing especially on the non-oil economy. The government is committed to improving the ease of doing business in Nigeria by painstakingly dismantling the many obstacles that entrepreneurs, businesses and investors have long complained about. Active efforts will be made in the context of industrial policy to learn from

Nigeria's own experiences and those of other economies. Policy partnerships with other economies and international organizations like the WTO will continue to be deepened to achieve win-win economic growth, improve the welfare of Nigerians and contribute to global economic health and growth.

Reference

Financial Times (2016). 'Smart Africa: Nigerian groups target "100% mobile-first market"', 28 January 2016, *Financial Times*. Retrieved from http://www.ft.com /cms/s/0/0ad2bbe4-c044-11e5-846f-79b0e3d20eaf.html#axzz4ExwRLCG6

4

Trade, Investment and Development

ROB DAVIES

Abstract

Structural transformation is imperative for Africa's economies. An unprecedented policy unanimity has emerged amongst African government and business leaders that to achieve sustained growth and development, Africa must industrialize and secure a greater share of the benefits of its participation in global value chains. This requires further advances in a programme for 'development integration' that simultaneously combines market integration with purposeful industrial development intervention and cooperation to strengthen regional value chains, underpinned by efforts to develop and rehabilitate cross-border infrastructure for greater connectivity across Africa.

The recent, generalized decline in global commodity prices has underscored not only the need to reduce Africa's over-dependence on lower value-added commodity exports, but also the importance of leveraging growing African markets for Africa's industrialization. Already, the shares of intra-African trade in African countries' total exports makes Africa by far the second most important export market for most African countries. More importantly, around half of total intra-African trade, primarily within regional blocs, comprises manufactured goods, again highlighting the vital importance of current regional integration programmes for African industrialization.

Africa's external engagements in the multilateral arena and in bilateral trade and investment must be (re-) designed to support this agenda. At the heart of the argument is the need to secure policy for industrialization, economic diversification and structural transformation. Investment and trade partners that participate positively in this effort will help to initiate a virtuous cycle of trade and investment, growth and development from which they can benefit while also contributing to sustained growth and development across the continent.

This chapter is an adapted version of a presentation made at the Fourth China Round Table, Nairobi, Kenya, on 13–14 December 2015.

In 2015, Kenya hosted the first WTO ministerial conference (15–19 December) and South Africa co-chaired and hosted the first summit of the Forum on China-Africa Cooperation (FOCAC) (4–5 December) to take place on African soil. The Fourth China Round Table, which took place back-to-back with the Tenth WTO Ministerial Conference in Nairobi, provided an excellent opportunity to discuss, from an African perspective, some of Africa's needs, and to enable Africa to understand more clearly what it seeks in the Nairobi Ministerial Declaration. The economic challenge facing Africa is *not* that it is not integrated into the world economy; it is *how* it is integrated into the world economy. Under colonialism, African economies were drawn into the world economy as producers and exporters of primary products, such as mineral and agricultural commodities. African economies were largely importers of finished goods exported from the colonizing economies. That pattern of integration by and large persists, and the problem for Africa, underscored in statements by President Uhuru Kenyatta of Kenya and the Minister of Industry, Trade and Investment Okechukwu E. Enelamah of Nigeria,[1] is that Africa's economies are not sufficiently diversified and Africa is not in the best place in the global division of labour.

What is striking, at this point in time, is the degree of convergence amongst African leaders in governments, businesses and civil society on the imperative to promote the structural transformation of African economies through regional integration and industrialization. The most authoritative and definitive statement on this is contained in the African Union document entitled "Agenda 2063: The Africa We Want" that was released in April 2015.

The challenge faced by Africa can be illustrated by a few statistics. A few years ago, KPMG, a firm that provides audit, tax and advisory services, offered evidence that Africa produces and exports coffee beans to the value of US$ 6 billion. But coffee beans are then turned into different products through blending, mixing, branding and other processes, outside the borders of Africa, in a value chain which totals US$ 100 billion. In other words, US$ 94 billion of the value chain does not lie in the primary production of that particular product. Another example is that Italy earns more from the production of gold-based jewelleries than South Africa does from the production of gold.

---

[1] These statements were made by the Nairobi China Round Table. See https://www.wto.org /english/thewto_e/acc_e/chinaround2015_e.htm

Placing this in a wider perspective, over the period 2000–10, the average annual growth rate of real output in Africa accelerated to over 5.3 per cent. While Africa was not immune to the global economic crisis of 2008–09, its average growth rate in the post-crisis period remained at around 2 per cent above that of the world economy. During the same period, Africa also saw its share of world trade grow from 2.1 per cent in 2000 to 3.5 per cent in 2015. These somewhat positive indicators do not reveal that most of the trade growth can be attributed to price increases, and that imports grew faster than exports. More importantly, Africa became increasingly dependent on low value-added exports during this period.

The reality is that, in a global value chain, the producer and exporter of primary commodities is at the least income-generating developmental position in that chain. To compound the problem, Africa is confronted with rapid and dramatic declines in mineral commodity prices. One of the largest multinationals recently announced that it would be down-sizing and would reduce its workforce across the world by 65 per cent.

What does this all mean? It means that, as President Kenyatta of Kenya stated at the opening of the Fourth China Round Table, and as a number of African leaders stated at the recently concluded FOCAC, the economic future of the African Continent requires industrialization: that is, Africa must move up the value chain and diversify. Diversification is linked to a very important trade policy process that is ongoing in Africa. Policy-makers have all agreed with regard to the need to broaden regional integration and establish large free trade areas that reach beyond existing regional economic communities. The first is the SADC-COMESA-EAC (Southern African Development Community–Common Market for Eastern and Southern Africa–East African Community) Tripartite Free Trade Area, launched on 15 June 2015. Eventually, this should culminate into a free trade agreement covering the whole of the continent of Africa.

A closer examination at intra-African trade is instructive. Intra-African trade as a proportion of total trade grew from 10 per cent in 2010 to 14 per cent in 2014. While this is comparatively low, we should not lose sight of the fact that for most African countries, intra-African trade is already considerably more important than the aggregate figures suggest. For instance, a 2009 UNCTAD Report, 'Strengthening Regional Economic Integration for African Development', showed that the shares of intra-African trade in African countries' total exports makes Africa by far the second most important export market for most African countries. Seven African countries count Africa as their main export market and twenty-five count it as their second most important market. Five African countries have exports to Africa that are larger than half of their total exports, while a further fourteen countries export more than a quarter of their exports to Africa.

Thus, Africa represents a significant export market for many African countries, and more than three quarters of intra-African trade takes place within regional trading blocs. Perhaps most importantly, the Report by the UN Economic Commission for Africa (ECA), 'Economic Report on Africa 2015: Industrializing through Trade', shows that while Africa's exports to the rest of the world are dominated by raw materials and commodities, value-added products make up a large proportion of the content of intra-African trade, as 46 per cent of intra-African trade consists of manufactured products.

To take full advantage of the opportunities that arise from more open regional and global markets, African economies must build their productive capacities to supply those markets with diversified value-added products. *Africa must industrialize.* Economic history shows that all countries that have succeeded in breaking out of poverty and underdevelopment have done so by nurturing a cluster of industrial activities characterized by increasing, rather than diminishing, returns. This nurturing has involved the identification and targeting of appropriate value-added activities and the deployment of public and private resources to support innovation, entrepreneurship and infrastructure development, as well as the judicious use of tariffs and other forms of protection.

Although this is an era of freer trade than at any time since the Second World War, we do not live in an environment characterized by literally 'free' trade. Industries and sectors which advanced economies have either identified as areas where they can progress or else as areas that are vulnerable to competition from others are subject to nurturing or protection, not just through financial support and tariffs, but also and increasingly through a range of more sophisticated barriers to trade. In such an environment, an intelligent and strategic approach to tariff policy is needed.

The ECA 2015 Report draws attention to a 'highly selective' trade policy framework for industrializing Africa. At the heart of this is the understanding that trade policy must serve industrial development. A selective trade policy also means proper sequencing: African economies should be opening their markets to each other in order to build competitiveness at a regional and continental level that, over time, will serve as a platform for global competitiveness. Further, Africa's overriding interest in negotiations with third parties will preserve already narrowed policy space. Africa needs to be able to deploy tariffs in a responsible manner that supports industrial development and the development of regional value chains across Africa.

Africa should approach these objectives through development integration, recognizing that in many cases it is not the trade rules that cause problems in Africa, but the lack of hard and soft infrastructure (i.e. of functional physical networks and of human and social institutions and services) and of economic capacity to produce competitive products that Africa can trade across these big regions. This is the journey upon which Africa has embarked. This is the African mega-regional trade agreement that will, among other things, allow for the possible emergence of regional value chains by means of which several countries could participate in the production of value-added products that could initially find markets on the continent and might eventually also find export markets beyond.

What does this mean for Africa's stance on global issues? The ideas surrounding global value chains involve both a description of an evident reality and a much more debatable set of policy prescriptions. No one can deny that the production of manufactured goods takes place across national borders. Manufactured goods are indeed 'made in the world' rather than in individual countries. Also, no one can deny that much of international trade – the part of international trade that is growing – is trade in intermediate goods, including trade in intermediate/semi-finished goods that may be moved several times across national borders before the final product is traded.

The policy prescription that arises from this suggests openness to the import of inputs to which value would be added. This is correct and the right approach. However, to apply that prescription more generally to the import of finished goods is to fundamentally undermine the policy space that African countries need in order for them to allow the growth and emergence of regional value chains within Africa. In other words, the import of finished goods from outside the continent could overwhelm the development of regional value chains on the continent. Africa needs policy space to pursue industrialization and to build its own regional value chains. Africa must also retain the policy space to deploy important instruments that every industrial economy around the world – whether acknowledged or not – is applying right now. These include rules for localization under government procurement decisions.

So what does this mean? It means that Africa must have a global trade stance that allows African economies the policy space to deploy the tools that will allow the continent to industrialize and to use the very instruments that every industrialized country has used. Africa must also achieve the removal of barriers in one of the value chains where the African continent has a strong competitive advantage, namely agriculture and agro-processing. African economies should continue to work towards removing distortions, such as subsidies, that prevent African agricultural and agro-processed products from finding their place in global markets.

Africa needs also to support productive investments coming into the continent, particularly in manufacturing. This was one of the major outcomes that emerged from FOCAC. The Chinese government identified particular ways in which they could cooperate with the African continent to support industrial development, skills development for industrialization, special economic zones and infrastructure, through investment within the African continent. An announcement of the new programme, made by China at the Second Summit of the "Forum on China-Africa Cooperation" in Johannesburg, South Africa, on 4 December 2015, is a good example of the kind of cooperation that Africa would like to see from other development partners on the African continent.

African economies need to stand up for their right to industrialize. If they do not, they will condemn themselves to remain in their existing position in the global division of labour – and this will be at a time when the challenges of that position are only going to become greater.

5

Integration into Global and Regional Value Chains – How Is It Done? The Experience of Lesotho in the Textiles and Apparel Sector

JOSHUA SETIPA

Abstract

Lesotho is a landlocked, least-developed economy and a member of the Southern African Customs Union (SACU), the oldest customs union (CU) in the global economy. Forty per cent of the population lives under the poverty line. The economic base is narrow, reliant on the textiles and apparel industry (for 59 per cent of total exports), subsistence agriculture, remittances, regional customs revenue and a degree of manufacturing. The apparel industry and agriculture constitute the backbone of the economy and the main employer. Faced with Lesotho's geo-economic circumstances and development challenges, the trade and economic response of government has been strategic. Domestic economic policy and structural reforms, accompanied by a policy of economic diversification, trade openness and integration, have been pursued. A trade development plan was carefully designed for active integration into regional and global value chains. These measures have yielded significant welfare gains and economic livelihood dividends. Trade and economic policies are reviewing the next generation of reforms, inter alia in the sectors of mining, electricity and tourism, which face challenges, but have potential for growth. This chapter identifies and discusses the specific steps in the trade policy plan for Lesotho's successful integration into the textile and apparel value chain, specifically, and more broadly, into a global value chain.

Introduction: Lesotho's Economic and Trade Profile

In recent years, Lesotho has achieved solid economic growth, with the average real GDP growth rate of 4.5 per cent between 2010 and 2014, led

This chapter is an adapted version of a presentation made at the Fourth China Round Table, Nairobi, Kenya, on 13–14 December 2015.

by the mining and construction sectors, before dropping to a lower estimated rate of 2.6 per cent in 2015. Lesotho's economy relies mainly on agriculture and the textile and clothing industry, with agriculture being the backbone of the rural economy and the country's main employer. In 2013, agriculture accounted for 7.9 per cent of Lesotho's GDP, behind the construction sector (9.6 per cent), and was followed by textiles and clothing (7.7 per cent) and mining and quarrying (6 per cent).

Textiles and clothing constitute Lesotho's main manufacture and exporting industry, accounting for 45 per cent of its total exports in 2014, followed by diamonds (28 per cent). Outside the South African Customs Union (SACU), whereby South Africa absorbed 47.3 per cent of Lesotho's exports in 2012, the United States is the largest destination of Lesotho's exports (43.9 per cent), followed by the European Union (3.7 per cent). The US market is the main destination for Lesotho's textiles and clothing exports, while exports to the European Union consist mainly of rough diamonds. Recently, the African market (outside the SACU) became the third largest destination for Lesotho's exports, accounting for 1.6 per cent in 2012. On the import side, South Africa accounted for 89 per cent of the total, followed by Chinese Taipei (4.7 per cent) and China (2.8 per cent) in the same year.

Lesotho is a net importer of services. The travel industry is Lesotho's leading sector in services, both for exports and imports, accounting for about 70 per cent and 59 per cent of the total, respectively, in 2013. The other main exports were other business services (20.7 per cent of total exports in 2013), telecommunications (5.3 per cent) and transport services (3.7 per cent). On the import side, travel services were followed by transport (17 per cent of total imports in 2013), insurance services (6 per cent) and telecommunications (3 per cent).

Investment Trends and Challenges

Since 2009, Lesotho has taken steps to improve its investment climate, notably through the establishment of a trade and investment facilitation centre to serve as a one-stop-shop to speed up the processing of trading and manufacturing licenses. Nonetheless, in general, foreign direct investment (FDI) in Lesotho has been inhibited by structural constraints, such as high transport costs, an underdeveloped legal, judicial, and regulatory framework, labour market rigidities, limited access to bank financing and limitations on land ownership by foreigners. Lesotho ranks 128th (out of 178 economies) in the World Bank's Ease of Doing Business 2014 Index. The World Bank's ongoing Private Sector Competitiveness and Economic Diversification Project, of which the Ministry of Trade, Industry, Cooperatives and Marketing is one of the implementing agencies, seeks to facilitate increased private sector investment by improving the business environment and diversifying sources of growth, including reducing the cost of doing business and enhancing Lesotho's regional and global competitiveness.

In order to attract more FDI inflows as well as to promote domestic investment, a number of measures are under way, including further reducing administrative impediments for investors, providing a water supply and other basic infrastructure, improving workers' productivity and labour stability, and identifying industries other than textiles and clothing (e.g. agri-business, mining and tourism), to add value to local products and diversify the economy.

About 90 per cent of Lesotho's FDI inflows have gone into export-oriented manufacturing industries, notably textiles and clothing. The telecommunications subsector has also attracted FDI.

The Economic Diversification Strategy and the Global Value Chain Strategy

Following the 2008 economic and financial crisis, which revealed the vulnerabilities of the Lesotho economy as a result of its overdependence on a few export markets and a limited range of export products, a decision to re-double diversification efforts was taken by the Government of Lesotho. However, Lesotho, like other countries at a similar level of development, has very limited choices given its industrial capacity, resource endowment, human resources capacity and limitations attributable to its being landlocked.

A decision was taken to pursue a strategy that would focus primarily on exploiting the opportunities presented by being landlocked within South Africa, which has the most diversified economy in Africa. An obvious option was to pursue a regional value chain strategy whereby Lesotho would form part of the South African manufacturing sector's value chain, with an emphasis on labour-intensive sectors including agro-processing, light assembly, manufacturing and business process outsourcing.

To mitigate the limitations of a narrow skills base, it was also decided that focus should be on pursuing FDI opportunities in sectors where the skills and experience gained from the more than twenty years of apparel manufacturing could be leveraged.

The auto sector has been identified as offering the best opportunities, given that South Africa has a thriving auto industry. The first investments secured were in the car seat manufacturing sector in 2012, and car seat covers for brands like BMW, Nissan and Ford began to be produced as part of the South African auto sector value chain. The labour-intensive nature of these operations also began to address the urgent need to create jobs and the high levels of unemployment, one of the challenges faced by Lesotho.

The auto sector strategy represented the first effort by Lesotho to integrate into the regional value chain, and thus initiated a structured approach to a broader value chain strategy.

Lesotho's over-dependence on the apparel sector, coupled with declining terms of trade in traditional export markets, and particularly in the US market, highlighted the need for a structured national effort to adopt a comprehensive global value chain strategy.

The initial experience of launching a strategy to integrate Lesotho into the South African auto industry value chain highlighted a number of key issues that are critical to a successful value chain strategy. Among these are the following:

- The critical importance of an efficient and competitive trade facilitation framework – in the case of Lesotho, this involved examining behind-the-border inefficiencies, particularly on customs operations and logistics systems, and determining that upgraded port facilities and customs systems were required.
- Alignment of the tax regime with the aforementioned strategy to ensure that critical inputs towards component manufacturing are not undermined by rigid tax provisions and tariff measures.
- A review of the existing investment regime to ensure that incentives are sector-specific.
- The imperative for a comprehensive incentive regime to encourage the development of small and medium-sized enterprises (SMEs) and thereby support the growth of a competitive supply chain network among local SMEs.
- A critical review and upgrade of the skills development framework to direct resources towards developing non-traditional technology-based skills, such as process engineering.

Since 2013, the World Bank, through its Trade and Competitiveness Global Practice, has been helping Lesotho to undertake reforms and modernize key aspects of its value proposition in order to enhance its investment climate and improve its trade competitiveness.

In particular, the experience of Lesotho has highlighted the following as being key to a successful value chain strategy;

- A clear vision and mandate to improve coordination among government departments and ensure private sector involvement.
- Investment in trade facilitation to accelerate FDI flows, which can contribute significantly to entry into regional and global value chains.
- Identification and implementation of strategies to maximize the potential of domestic economic players to be absorbed into value chains, enhancing the possibility of linkages with regional and global value chains.
- Improved integration of diverse policy areas that affect the success of a regional and global value chain. These include, among others, trade policy, logistics and trade facilitation, regulation of business services, investment, business taxation, innovation, industrial development, conformity to international standards and encouraging the wider business environment to foster entrepreneurship.

The intervention and support of cooperating partners, particularly the World Bank, is beginning to deliver positive results. Since the launch of the auto sector strategy, new investments have been secured from manufacturers that supply auto manufacturers in Europe and elsewhere outside South Africa.

There has also been success in securing opportunities in the aquaculture sector, particularly trout farming to supply markets in Asia and the Gulf Region.

Lesotho shall remain firmly committed to the active implementation of economic diversification and a global value chain strategy. This approach will be consistent with the commitment to a modern trade and economic agenda that is compatible with a rapidly changing global economy. In this approach, Lesotho will remain in active engagement with key development partners and multilateral institutions.

6

From Marrakesh to Nairobi: Africa – A Force for the World Trading System: From the Past Twenty Years to the Next Twenty Years

MOULAY HAFID ELALAMY

Abstract

Morocco's membership of the GATT and WTO has been part of an overall strategy of the Government of the Kingdom of Morocco, at the instigation of the late King Hassan II, to introduce a package of institutional and socio-economic reforms, which sought mainly to modify and diversify the structure of the national economy, optimize the allocation of its resources and ensure its integration into the world economy. Being a Member of the Multilateral Trading System is also an expression of the government's wish to integrate more fully into the world economy by anchoring its reforms in the legal primacy of an international agreement, rather than just in domestic legislation, as reaffirmed by the Constitution adopted in 2011. In doing so, Morocco made opening up its economy a firm and irreversible commitment.

Through the WTO and its wide network of free trade agreements, Morocco is moving to the next phase of its trade and investments policies, focusing on value-added exports and world-class infrastructures as well as on renewable energy. Twenty years after Marrakesh, the system still carries value for Morocco and Africa and will certainly be a tool for trade and investments in the next two decades. Africa's role needs to be strengthened. While Africa's share in world trade has improved considerably over the past decade, it is difficult to accept that a continent which represents more than the 15 per cent of the world's population should still account for only 3 per cent of world trade. The legitimate objective that we should probably all be pursuing over the next few decades is matching Africa's share in world trade with its share in the world's population.

We have come a long way since the Marrakesh Conference in 1994 – not only the WTO, but Morocco and Africa as well. In 1994, Morocco crowned a decade of structural reforms begun in the early 1980s by organizing the Marrakesh Conference that marked the end of the Uruguay Round and gave birth to the WTO.

Thus it was that Morocco, which had joined the GATT in 1987, became one of the founding members of the Marrakesh Agreement establishing the WTO. As His Majesty King Hassan II pointed out during the closing session of the Marrakesh Conference, 'by bringing into being the World Trade Organization today, we are enshrining the rule of law in international economic and trade relations, thus setting universal rules and disciplines over the temptations of unilateralism and the law of the jungle'.

He was absolutely right: the Marrakesh Conference represents an historical turning point in international trade relations. In Marrakesh in 1994, the objective that the founding fathers of the multilateral system as we know it today had been promoting ever since the end of the Second World War was put into practice. Not only did the Marrakesh Conference mark the end of the Uruguay Round, it also marked the end of an interim agreement, the General Agreement on Tariffs and Trade (GATT), and the realization of one of the objectives of the San Francisco Conference and the Havana Charter.

It is therefore with great pride and honour that in April 2015, on the occasion of the WTO's 20th anniversary celebration, I was able to invite my African colleagues, the trade ministers, together with a number of African Parliamentarians and the WTO Director-General, Mr Roberto Azevêdo, to join me at the very place where the agreement establishing this Organization was signed. The agreement has since that date carried the name of the wonderful city of Marrakesh.

This celebration of the WTO's 20th anniversary was an opportunity to reflect on what had been achieved over the past twenty years in the field of international trade, to examine the possibilities and challenges offered by the Tenth Ministerial Conference, held in Nairobi in December 2015, and, more generally, to look ahead to the direction of the multilateral trading system over the next twenty years and discuss the possible role of each one of our countries and of the African continent in that mechanism.

If we were to reflect upon some messages coming out of that discussion in Marrakesh, we would conclude that the WTO has become an indispensable component of countries' trade and economic policies. Indeed, WTO membership is among the leading criteria in the decision-making process of many investors.

Another key message is that, given the proliferation of free trade agreements (FTAs) among economies today, the WTO, with its balance of rights and obligations and the flexibilities it can guarantee according to the level of development of each one of its members, offers significant advantages for developing and least-developed economies. These advantages must be preserved.

At the same time, it is important to try to achieve greater complementarity between the WTO system and the preferential systems known as regional trade agreements (RTAs).

It is only through this balancing act that Africa can hope to play its rightful role in world trade, by combining greater involvement in the rules and operation of the WTO with ambitious regional and sub-regional integration projects.

While Africa's share in world trade has improved considerably over the past decade, it is difficult to accept that a continent which represents more than 15 per cent of the world population should still account for only 3 per cent of world trade. The legitimate objective that we should probably all pursue over the next few decades will be to match Africa's share in world trade with its share in the world's population.

Here we have one of the components of a true vision for Africa's role in the future of world trade. Africa is already a land of trade and investment opportunities. Many African economies are growing at rates comparable to those of the most rapidly growing economies in Asia, and several of these economies are among the IMF's top twenty most dynamic economies of the world. Foreign investment flows, coupled with the exponential growth in South–South trade, have given birth to a true African middle class which, with the significant increase in domestic demand, could very well drive growth.

In spite of all these very positive signals, we need to combine our efforts and do more for Africa. Inclusive development is a necessity for the millions of young Africans entering the labour market each year. Environmentally friendly and sustainable development is also a necessity, in keeping with the United Nation's Sustainable Development Goals (SDGs), adopted by the international community in New York in September 2015.

In this context, the Kingdom of Morocco has made a number of important economic choices, and thanks to those choices, it is able to look to the future with a certain amount of serenity. However, it has been a bumpy ride.

The early 1980s was a time of severe crisis for the Kingdom of Morocco. The country's economy, weakened by its own opacity, was dominated by the informal sector and dependent on agricultural production, itself vulnerable to climatic variations. All this was set against a gloomy and unfavourable international backdrop following two successive oil shocks and a slow-down in world growth that had led to a drop in international phosphate prices, a surge in the value of the dollar and a rise in interest rates.

To address this crisis, the Government of Morocco, at the initiative of the late King Hassan II, introduced a package of institutional and socio-economic reforms, which sought mainly to modify and diversify the structure of the national economy, optimize the allocation of its resources and ensure its integration into the world economy.

Direct action was taken in a number of areas over the course of several years. Basic texts were adopted, relating to public finance, monetary policy, foreign trade, price policy and the restructuring of state economic intervention instruments. In this context, on 8 March 1985, Morocco submitted its request to join the then-multilateral trading system – the General Agreement on Tariffs and Trade – and subsequently began negotiating its terms of accession with the contracting parties. The Protocol for the Accession of Morocco was adopted on 19 February 1987, thus paving the way for Morocco's accession to a rules-based multilateral trading system on 17 June 1987. This step was also an expression of the government's wish to integrate more fully into the world economy by anchoring its reforms in the legal primacy of an international agreement, rather than just in domestic legislation, as reaffirmed by the Constitution adopted in 2011.

Thus, Morocco made the opening up of its economy a firm and irreversible strategic commitment. Since then, the different economic policy measures implemented by Morocco have been the logical result of that choice.

In an effort to promote foreign trade, tariff protection and quantitative restrictions were rescheduled and drastically reduced. At the same time, other reforms were introduced, in particular the exchange rate policy reform, designed to provide for foreign capital transfer operations in addition to current account transactions and thus to enable Moroccan companies access to the international financial market.

In order to complete the transition to a market economy, state intervention in the economy was restricted. State control of the prices of goods and services was for the most part abolished and a vast privatization programme undertaken with a view to establishing the status of the private sector, improving business management and attracting foreign investors as well as stimulating domestic investment.

Thanks to the implementation of this ambitious reform programme, it was possible to rehabilitate and stabilize the macroeconomic framework. During the period 1983–94, the economy grew at an average annual rate of 4.1 per cent, while inflation was reduced from 10.5 per cent to 5 per cent. On the public finances front, the external-debt-to-GDP ratio was reduced from 128 per cent in 1985 to about 70 per cent in 1994. In addition, the balance-of-payments current account deficit, which stood at 12.3 per cent of GDP in 1982, was brought down to 2 per cent in 1993. Although these reforms were successful in strengthening and stabilizing the macroeconomic balances, they were not able to generate enough employment to absorb the substantial and steady increase in the active population.

These different reforms laid the foundations for a genuine economic take-off at the instigation of King Mohammed VI, who, since acceding to the throne in 1999, has presided over a stable economy driven by domestic demand and public investment, a steady annual growth of 4.7 per cent during the period 2001–13, a low inflation rate of about 2 per cent and a progressive decrease in unemployment, although poor harvests and economic problems in Europe have tended to affect economic growth. A number of additional and innovative structural reforms have been implemented under the guidance of King Mohammed VI in order to stimulate exports. They involved the mobilization of the state and of economic operators with a view to creating the wealth and jobs needed to provide Moroccans with better opportunities for human development through improvement of the business environment.

To that end, Morocco has launched a number of large-scale projects over the past decade to upgrade its infrastructure and bring it into conformity with international standards. The Tanger-Med port entered into service in 2007 with an initial overall capacity of 3 million containers (8 million in 2016) and more than 2,000 hectares worth of business premises, completing the port system which already consisted of eleven ports built to international standards.

With the implementation of the highway extension and improvement programme, the total highway network reached 1,800 km in 2015 and now links all of the cities with a population of over 400,000. With 15 international airports served by numerous international airlines and linked to the world's main economic centres and business hubs, Morocco ranks first in the region in terms of airport infrastructure. At the same time, its passenger and cargo railway network was extended to 2,110 km and modernized by equipping 93 per cent of the network with long welded rails. Morocco is currently building the first high-speed railway line in Africa.

With the opening up of the telecommunications sector in Morocco, there are currently three global operators (each offering telephone, mobile, and Internet and data services) with an infrastructure that meets international standards. Business is active and sustained from year to year: the mobile penetration rate is 129 per cent.

In order to build up a balanced and homogenous industrial network throughout the country's territory, a vast national network of economic zones has been developed, with integrated industrial platforms, a free zone and agricultural parks.

Last but not least, the first Moroccan solar power plant, the largest in the world, was officially inaugurated by King Mohammed VI in February 2016 in the framework of a national renewable energy plan, the objective of which is to produce 42 per cent of the country's electricity from renewable resources by 2020.

In keeping with its historical tradition as a trading nation open to the world, and to its African partners in particular, Morocco introduced a series of sectoral plans. This development process involves an innovative approach to contracting and public/private partnerships that calls for increased and concerted participation of the private sector in the development of sectoral strategies and policies and in project financing, enabling the state to refocus on its regulatory role. These plans seek both to modernize traditional sectors such as agriculture, fisheries and mining, while at the same time developing innovative sectors such as renewable energies, logistics, the automobile industry, aviation and the high-value-added services for which Morocco has a real competitive advantage.

In fact, the development of exports would appear to justify this dual approach of strengthening exports and traditional industries while investing in high-value-added products and services. Today, Moroccan exports account for important shares in the international horticultural, phosphate, automotive and aeronautic markets. On the occasion of the fifth Trade Policy Review of the Kingdom in February 2016, WTO members were unanimous to highlight the importance of Morocco's economic and trade choices as well as the important results of its foreign trade.

Morocco's use of WTO rules to modernize and adapt its trade policy in several areas, such as tariffs, sanitary and phytosanitary measures, trade defence measures and intellectual property protection, serves to illustrate the country's strong commitment to the system.

This commitment continues to be an important component of the country's trade policy. If we take, for instance, the new WTO Agreement on Trade Facilitation, Morocco was among those that anticipated the provisions of the Agreement: as early as 2009, Morocco adopted new measures to streamline customs procedures, including the introduction of a computerized clearance system (called the 'Base Automatisée des Douanes en Réseau' (BADR), i.e. an automated base for networked customs).

At the same time, the introduction of a virtual single window (i.e. for the electronic exchange of trade information) for foreign trade was considerably speeded up, contributing to the simplification of formalities and the move towards a paperless process.

The PortNet system currently functions as a virtual single window for foreign trade transactions, connecting more than 15,000 importers with different government agencies, banks and private operators and enabling several formalities to be carried out remotely simply by connecting to the PortNet platform.

While Morocco's accession to the GATT in 1987 and the establishment of the WTO in 1995 played crucial roles in strengthening the structural reform process pursued by the country since the 1980s, it was accompanied by a reorganization of Morocco's international trade relations, with the signature of some fifty-six free trade agreements, making Morocco one of the countries best connected to global value chains. This network of agreements also strengthens the country's strategic and geographical position as a platform for world trade.

The reorganization consists chiefly of: (1) deepening the country's existing economic and trade relations with the European Union; (2) establishing secure economic and trade relations alongside the political relations that have existed between Morocco and the United States for centuries; and (3) promoting relations with Arab, African and Mediterranean economies, and in particular West African economies, Arab economies and with Turkey.

With Morocco's main trading partner, the European Union, Morocco has patiently built up a relationship based on reciprocity and concessions. This has involved the progressive dismantling of tariffs which, although it exposed our productive sector to a number of hardships, generally led to increased competitiveness in several areas of the economy. Efforts have now turned to the negotiation of the Deep and Comprehensive Free Trade Agreement (DCFTA) securing Morocco's advanced status in its relations with the European Union.

Morocco concluded a free trade agreement with the United States in 2006, and is the only North African country to have such a comprehensive framework for trade and investment with the United States. Trade and investment flows between the two countries are strengthening daily.

Morocco's close ties with Africa in general and West Africa in particular are well known, and are among economy's strategic priorities. The historical, cultural, religious and economic relations are numerous and date back to centuries, providing a firm foundation for economic development based on an innovative approach to South–South trade and investment flows. Long before the WTO initiative on duty-free and quota-free market access for least-developed countries (LDCs), Morocco had unilaterally decided to provide this preferential access to all of the LDCs in Africa. Morocco also ranks second among African investors in Africa.

For the Kingdom of Morocco, opening up to the world by playing a more active role within the WTO, strengthening economic and trade relations with several key partners and consolidating historical and multi-dimensional relations with Africa are very much a part of King Mohammed VI's vision for the country.

In this connection, I would like to make an important observation regarding Morocco as a member of that large Middle East and North African community that faces considerable political and socio-economic challenges: it is probably the only country in the vicinity to have held firm in its tireless and irreversible effort to reconcile substantial constitutional, political and socio-economic reforms with real and sustained economic development.

It is encouraging to note, in this connection, that the Kingdom's gross domestic product has more than doubled in the last fifteen years. The same applies to the population's purchasing power, although it is true that unemployment and the unequal distribution of growth remain a reality and pose a challenge which Morocco is determined to tackle energetically and proactively.

For Morocco, sustaining a major role within the WTO is an integral part of that strategy.

7

Building Capacity in Africa to Facilitate Integration into Global Value Chains: Contributions from the ITC

ARANCHA GONZÁLEZ

Abstract

While Africa's share of global value-added trade has increased significantly during the past 20 years, connecting African small and medium-sized enterprises (SMEs) to value chains and turning the support for greater intra-African trade into a reality remains challenging. Ensuring that the trade discourse is fully integrated into this development story is critical and countries, especially those that have recently acceded, have to be supported to recognise and take advantage of the global trading system and their WTO membership. To place a spotlight on trade-led growth for SMEs, the International Trade Centre (ITC) launched its SME Competitiveness Outlook in 2015. This flagship publication identified three key determinants of SMEs' ability to integrate into value chains: their ability to compete, connect and change. The ITC's capacity-building interventions, which have a strong focus on African countries, are centred on helping SMEs become more competitive and connect to value chains to drive the continent's sustainable economic development.

Africa's fifty-four countries are deeply committed to the multilateral trading system and to using trade, both within the continent and externally, as an engine for economic development. This was most recently symbolized by Kenya's hosting of the WTO's Tenth Ministerial Conference in Nairobi and the active participation of African countries in the WTO negotiations.

This chapter is an adapted version of a presentation made at the Fourth China Round Table, Nairobi, Kenya, on 13–14 December 2015.

Enabling African countries – many of which have small economies or are landlocked – to take advantage of market-led growth is at the heart of the support provided by the International Trade Centre (ITC). Openness, smart reforms and connectivity are central priorities guiding this work. ITC, a joint agency of the World Trade Organization and the United Nations, focuses in particular on interventions in Sub-Saharan Africa, least-developed countries (LDCs), post-conflict countries, small and vulnerable economies and small-island developing states (SIDS), with work in Africa representing close to 70 per cent of the ITC's activities.

A significant part of ITC interventions is aimed at supporting initiatives for small and medium-sized enterprises (SMEs). A productive and robust SME sector will enable African economies to deepen their integration into international value chains while also creating much-needed jobs. But it is not just international value chains that are important; helping the continent to strengthen regional value chains is a clear precursor to greater global competitiveness, as it offers local producers opportunities to access fast-growing markets across Africa and creates a strong basis for dismantling regional barriers to trade. At the same time, the ITC has focused its efforts on building strong relationships with the regional economic communities and with the African Union Commission (AUC), to ensure that they can continue to deliver for their membership and the business communities within these countries.

Africa's Participation in International Value Chains

With the changing economic and social landscape, this is a promising time for the African continent. Education has seen tremendous progress. Growth rates have averaged more than 5 per cent over the last fifteen years, and look set to continue, albeit in the context of a more fragile global economic environment.

These developments are taking place within a context of expanding participation in value chains, particularly by SMEs. Although Africa still has a relatively small share of global value-added trade (2.2 per cent in 2011), this has increased by almost 60 per cent since 1995 and looks set to expand further.

In addition, the growing importance of services and the seamless integration of services and manufacturing across borders also create new opportunities. Technological advances, such as e-commerce, have a strong positive impact on many SMEs by lowering the barriers to entering new export markets and facilitating access to low-cost imported inputs.

But considerable challenges remain. Africa continues to be largely agrarian, with economies fuelled by resource-driven growth and a large and expanding informal sector. Productivity across all sectors of the region's economy – agriculture, manufacturing and services – remains low. As a result, Africa's participation in global trade and investment flows remains low when compared with other regions.

Intra-African trade also remains low. As noted in the African Union's 'Boosting Intra-African Trade' agenda, African economies have a tendency to trade more with countries outside the region than among themselves. The ITC's research on trading trends in the African Caribbean and Pacific Group of States (ACP) supports this assertion. This suggests that countries in Africa could take greater advantage of trading with their neighbours to benefit from geographical proximity and to develop export competitiveness in a regional context. Furthermore, Africa's regional participation in value chains is driven by Southern and North Africa, which together account for the lion's share of the continent's total value chain trade at 78 per cent, while West Africa accounts for only 14 per cent, East Africa for 5 per cent and Central Africa for 3 per cent.

Integrating Africa's SMEs into Value Chains

The key now is to move from diagnostics – on which there is broad consensus – to solutions. Drawing from our extensive work in Africa, including domestic policy and regulatory reforms related to WTO accession in countries such as Liberia, Comoros, Sudan and Ethiopia, we know that reforms related to WTO accession can go a long way towards creating a business environment conducive to integration into value chains.

In October 2015, the ITC launched its first-ever flagship publication, the *SME Competitiveness Outlook*, which, using the ITC's applied research, has illustrated many of the constraints that SMEs face in reaching the levels of competitiveness needed to participate in value chains. The report identifies three key determinants of SMEs' competitiveness necessary to participate in value chains: the ability of SMEs to compete, to connect and to change. Within this triple 'c' lie the 'solutions agenda'. The ITC's technical assistance projects are aimed at addressing these determinants.

SMEs deserve policy-makers' attention because they represent more than 98 per cent of the economic tissue of any African country. We need to think of them as important actors in agro-processing, in manufacturing and, increasingly, in services, which are a solid engine for competitiveness. And we need to think of them as vectors for inclusive and sustainable growth, given the large number of women and young people employed in SMEs.

1   SMEs' Ability to Compete

An SME's ability to compete – that is, to supply quality goods in a timely and cost-effective manner – does not depend only on the firm's own talents. It depends on access to an open trading system and on macro-level considerations like swift customs procedures and a functional product quality certification system. This is what we call a 'good business environment'. While tariffs are important, policy-makers must also ensure that product and service regulations are clear and transparent. This is particularly relevant for e-commerce, as weak regulatory frameworks and payment systems are limiting the ability of SMEs to e-connect.

The African Union's 'Boosting Intra-African Trade' initiative, including the Continental Free Trade Area (CFTA), will result in overall reduction in tariff barriers to trade, which is an important precondition for engagement in value chains. The ITC is in the process of collaborating with the African Union Commission (AUC) to establish a Pan-African Trade Observatory, which will capture important information about trade flows and barriers and make that information available to policy-makers and the private sector. Accurate and timely trade and market intelligence is a *sine qua non* for a competitive SME and, by extension, for a competitive economy. The ITC has also supported the AUC in their efforts to structure an African Business Council that would bring private sector views into the process.

The ITC also actively supports Africa's regional economic communities, working in close collaboration with the West African Economic and Monetary Union (WAEMU), the Central African Economic and Monetary Community (CEMAC), the Economic Community of West African States (ECOWAS), the Economic Community of Central African States (ECCAS), and the Common Market for Eastern and Southern Africa (COMESA). In Nairobi, on the margins of the WTO's Tenth Ministerial Conference in December 2015, the ITC and the East African Community (EAC) signed a memorandum of understanding to strengthen their partnership. Again in East Africa, the ITC assisted a leading regional trade and investment support institution (TISI) – the East African Business Council – which is pushing for deeper services integration and for mutual recognition of professional service suppliers. And in the first quarter of 2016, we will also launch a joint publication with the COMESA Business Council on 'Services in COMESA: An industry perspective'.

Key to the ability of SMEs to compete is the facilitation of cross-border trade, starting with the implementation of the WTO Trade Facilitation Agreement. This has to be driven at the national level but carefully coordinated at the regional level, to support building regional markets. Effective trade facilitation is no longer a policy choice. It is a policy necessity for any country wanting to support a stronger business sector connected to value chains.

The ITC assisted twenty-five African countries in assessing their needs and prioritizing their reforms with a view to accelerating the notification of their Category A commitments and the ratification of the Protocol of Amendment. In 2016, the ITC will deepen its interventions and support countries in establishing and strengthening their national trade facilitation committees, enhancing the efficiency of their single-window mechanisms (i.e. a single entry point through which traders can submit relevant documents and/or data requirements and be notified of decisions to release goods from border control) and improving SMEs' capacity to comply with cross-border requirements. In order to promote a coordinated and harmonized approach to the implementation of the WTO Trade Facilitation Agreement, the ITC is working with African regional economic communities, an approach that will result in a more homogenous and predictable business environment for traders across the continent.

Given the potential for value addition with the agro-processing sector in Africa, support for product quality enhancement is essential. Supporting SMEs' capacity to meet technical requirements in export markets and to overcome technical barriers to trade, including sanitary and phytosanitary measures, will be key. The ITC helps enterprises to comprehend sanitary and phytosanitary requirements that are often difficult to understand and even more challenging to meet. We provide hands-on assistance to SMEs to apply and certify to international standards such as the HACCP system (Hazard Analysis Critical Control Point) and ISO 22000 (food safety management systems). For example, under one of the ITC's interventions, a pool of ITC-trained local advisers supported Kenyan SMEs to be certified against HACCP standards, in turn enabling those SMEs to gain important footholds in regional and international markets. In the Gambia, the ITC helped the Gambian Bureau of Standards to prepare the first ten national standards based on international Codex Alimentarius and ISO 22000 standards.

Since in many developing countries there are no accredited testing laboratories, or what laboratories are present lack necessary equipment and trained personnel, we help to upgrade those laboratories for accreditation and international recognition. For example, the Standards Association of Zimbabwe has been refurbished with state-of-the-art laboratory equipment and training. Trained analysts now provide analyses of aflatoxins, pesticides residues and some vitamins found in water, fruits, vegetables and other food samples, which will help open the door to foreign markets for local agricultural producers.

2   SMEs' Capacity to Connect

'SMEs' capacity to connect' refers to the way SMEs absorb and exploit information to better understand and target customers, and is another important determinant of participation in value chains.

Access to trade and market intelligence tools helps SMEs understand the best opportunities for internationalising. The ITC has a set of market analysis tools which helps more than half a million users, both SME suppliers and sourcing managers in value chains, to research market trends and requirements and connect with each other. These tools are global public goods and are free to access. In essence, these tools can help reduce the costs and burdens for SMEs of finding market opportunities, developing export potential and connecting to value chains.

In 2015, the ITC launched the Blue Number Initiative. The concept is straightforward: farmers are provided with a global location number – the Blue Number – which is issued by GS1, a not-for-profit global standards organization. The Blue Number is part of a profile that contains the farmer's name, gender, product and email address or mobile phone number. Once the farmer is in the registry, he or she can e-connect on a sustainability marketplace with other trading partners and share sustainability achievements with them. It might be compared to an online networking platform, a Facebook or LinkedIn for farmers.

Having a Blue Number gives farmers a voice and access to sustainability resources. It increases their visibility and allows them to connect more effectively with global buyers. This initiative will also help buyers improve the traceability of their value chains and enable them to make informed purchasing decisions, such as identifying farms owned by women with which they may wish to trade. Today, more than 60,000 farmers have already accepted the invitation to receive a Blue Number. The registry is already online and the marketplace site is fully functional.

The ITC's Supporting Indian Trade and Investment for Africa (SITA) project works to improve the competitiveness of selected value chains in East Africa, through partnerships with India. For example, in Ethiopia, crop rotation is not commonly practiced by spice farmers, which has been one of the causes for the spread of a bacterial wilt disease that has destroyed nearly 80 per cent of production in an export sector once worth more than US$ 24 million. Through the SITA project, the ITC brought in Indian spice experts to assess the situation, and are now introducing good agricultural practices, such as crop rotation and the use of organic materials on demonstration ginger farms, which will help increase crop resistance to the disease. The project is further building capacity by connecting potential Indian investors with African businesses in these sectors, by making them aware of the investment opportunities and facilitating business and institutional contacts on both sides.

3   SMEs' Ability to Change

SMEs' ability to change, i.e. to adapt constantly to shifting market forces, depends to a great extent on the education level of the work force and on access to credit in the economy, not just on the internal dynamism of a given company.

It is about accessing finance, which is why the ITC is supporting SMEs in Comoros, Kenya, Rwanda, Tanzania, Uganda and Zambia with pre- and post-finance coaching through local business development services providers trained and certified as financial management counsellors. The ITC also builds the capacity of TISIs and financial service providers to develop appropriate instruments for SMEs in given sectors, such as agriculture. Finally, the ITC facilitates the mobilization of credit guarantee facilities and/or credit lines from national, regional and international development financing institutions to provide a measure of comfort to would-be financiers contemplating potentially risky investments that could possibly yield large economic and employment dividends.

It is also about entering the right industry sectors. As Africa progressively enters the international fashion industry, this has resulted in the creation of sustainable opportunities for local micro-producers who have been enabled to grow their businesses and improve their livelihoods. The ITC's Ethical Fashion Initiative has contributed to this by focusing intensively on the insertion of African micro-producers into this value chain. Today, bags made in Kenya for Vivienne Westwood are showcased on catwalks in London and Paris, while cotton textiles hand-woven in Burkina Faso or dyed in Mali are distributed in the hippest stores of United Arrows in Tokyo.

It is also about knowledge gains. The ITC has been helping farmers, particularly in Africa, to integrate into value chains, for example under the ITC's project on the Integration of Horticulture Supply Value Chains into Tourism. Under the United Nations Development Assistance Plan (UNDAP), it is anticipated that in Tanzania, by the end of 2015, knowledge gains will allow 17,500 SMEs to improve the supply of good quality fresh fruit and vegetables to the market by at least 75 per cent, leading to a 40 per cent increase in those SMEs' incomes. From sustainable vertical linkages and enhancement practices, at least 70,000 people are positively impacted by development activities incorporating these ITC project outputs. Similar approaches can be seen in Ghana, where the ITC has helped improve the competiveness of women in the yam value chain, and in Ethiopia, where the ITC has supported the inclusive value chain development of natural gum and resins.

Services, especially tourism services, are the next frontier for many African countries. The ITC is growing its portfolio in this area and partnering with other agencies to ensure greater impact. The ITC, the United Nations World Tourism Organization (UNWTO) and the Ministry of Tourism, Transport and Meteorology of Madagascar are collaborating on an inclusive and sustainable tourism project for the country which aims to position Madagascar in the niche tourism market, using the sector as an engine for the sustainable growth of local communities that will actively participate and benefit. The project sets out to help build a branding strategy for Madagascar and conduct an economic analysis of the country's economy to define its main strengths and weaknesses with a view to improving the business environment. The ITC and UNWTO will be conducting a wide variety of training activities for people across the sector, including training in management, tourism development policies and branding. By improving the performance of SMEs in the sector, this partnership will build capacity along the value chain and create a strong and robust tourism offer for Madagascar. The hope is that similar projects could also be put together in other countries in Africa, such as Seychelles and Liberia, where tourism has been identified as a priority.

Conclusions

SMEs participating in value chains can accelerate African economic transformation and have economy-wide benefits. The ITC's *SME Competitiveness Outlook* clearly demonstrates the catalytic role that SMEs have, particularly when empowered and equipped through effective market access, good market and trade intelligence, e-connectivity, supportive national policies, conducive infrastructure and purposeful capacity building. SMEs are also essential to fostering more inclusive growth that supports women's economic empowerment and youth employment.

Accelerating the implementation of regional trade agreements should help African SMEs, since they are more likely to succeed first in regional markets, which they can then use as a stepping stone to international value chains.

The multilateral trading system and the governance function of the WTO are important pieces in this puzzle, as they provide transparency on trade rules. The recent outcome of the WTO's Tenth Ministerial Conference in Nairobi has emphasized the importance of building a multilateral trade architecture to support regional and national growth. The accessions of Afghanistan and Liberia – two countries where the ITC has been active and where it will continue to work intensively in their post-accession phase – to the WTO are also important signals that multilateralism remains a viable path for development. The challenge is to ensure that market opportunities translate into actual trade and development results.

The ITC's growing partnerships with African countries at the national, regional and continental levels is, in sum, about empowering African SMEs to tap into the full potential of value chains. Building on the outcomes of the Nairobi Ministerial Conference, the ITC will continue to play a part in this process via its network of policy-makers, SMEs and trade and investment support institutions. Through this work and the work of other international organizations, countries can learn from each other to design and implement better policies, which should ultimately translate into higher living standards for African citizens.

8

Investment and Trade Rules: Increasing the Stock of African Foreign Direct Investment Flows

JOAKIM REITER

Abstract

Trade can be a powerful engine for development. But harnessing trade for development in Africa requires investment to foster lasting economic transformation. Investment, therefore, is key to unlocking the potential of trade-led growth. While flows of foreign direct investment (FDI) into Africa paint a familiar picture of the dominance of extractive industries, the reality is more nuanced and promising. The fact that FDI stocks in Africa are geared towards the burgeoning services sector offers immense potential for countries in Africa to access and climb regional and global value chains; however, unless interrelated policy challenges are addressed, Africa will not be able to optimize the benefits of FDI. Combined with efforts at national and regional levels, the WTO should be better used by African countries to properly exploit the trade-investment nexus for the achievement of the United Nations' Sustainable Development Goals.

The United Nations' 2030 Agenda for Sustainable Development outlines a promising future that is as ambitious as it is daunting. The challenges for least-developed countries (LDCs) – most of which are African – are formidable. To put things bluntly, if LDCs are to meet the UN's Sustainable Development Goals (SDGs), they will have to out-perform China's top fifteen years of growth performance. Moreover, they will have to do so in a far more fragile global economic environment.

Africa needs to tap into every available source of growth to fuel its progress towards the SDGs. Trade is one of them. Trade is an engine that has powered the emergence of many developing countries, and it can play

This chapter is an adapted version of a presentation made at the Fourth China Round Table, Nairobi, Kenya, on 13–14 December 2015.

the same role in Africa. Putting trade at the service of development would entail increasing Africa's share of trade flows in total global trade flows (which have edged up to 3 per cent from 2.3 per cent in 2000,[1] but remain far below the peaks of 5–6 per cent achieved in the 1960s and 1970s[2]).

But quantity (exporting more) is not enough. In fact, during the peak period of global trade growth, in the years preceding the financial crisis, LDCs experienced double-digit export growth, fuelled largely by commodity price hikes and a soaring demand for natural resources by China. Yet, despite often-record export earnings, poverty levels remained high in most of these countries. Diversification remained limited and manufacturing, in many LDCs, contracted as a share of GDP.

For the future, therefore, harnessing trade for development in Africa will need to entail adding greater value to the goods and services exported within the continent. This requires economic transformation, which in turn, requires ample levels of investment. UNCTAD has estimated the annual investment gap for the SDGs to be around US$ 2.5 trillion annually. Without an agenda laying out concrete action for closing this investment gap,[3] the odds of achieving the Sustainable Development Goals would be insurmountable. Multiple sources of financing – ranging from commercial lending to development assistance to foreign direct investment (FDI) – are possible, but this chapter focuses on the source of financing that has the greatest potential to nurture structural transformation, namely foreign direct investment (FDI).

FDI is a key component in the growth of regional and global value chains and the investment–trade know-how nexus that they represent. FDI can build productive capacity, enhance competitiveness and create new job opportunities, helping the poor lift themselves out of poverty. And FDI can fuel trade and promote new export opportunities, contributing to economic diversification.

Therefore, FDI is key to Africa's future transformation and, specifically, to its ability to unlock the full potential of trade-led growth and development. What is more, the face of Africa is already changing, and at times faster than what we may perceive. FDI has played, and will continue to play, an important role in this story.

Five observations are worth making to uncover the powerful story of FDI-induced change that is happening in Africa, but also to identify gaps and find ways forward.

---

[1] WTO (2015) [2] Hartzenberg (2011) [3] UNCTAD (2014)

First, FDI inflows to Africa have increased dramatically in the last fifteen years. In fact, FDI flows in 2014 (US$ 54 billion) were more than five times their level in 2000 (US$ 10 billion). In addition, Africa's share in global FDI increased to 4.4 per cent in 2014, from 0.7 per cent in 2000. Africa's share of global investment flows is today – by a wide margin – bigger than its share of global trade. This underscores the rising appeal of the region for foreign investors. The world is anticipating a brighter African future and investing accordingly.

Second, notwithstanding this increase in FDI, FDI inflows to Africa can and should be higher. They are still below – in some case, far below – their potential. Recent figures reveal the vulnerability of FDI flows to Africa. There are also big regional variations in FDI inflows, which reflect remaining challenges. Some of these are of a domestic economic nature. But there are also challenges negatively affecting African FDI inflows arising from both the overall global economic environment and non-economic reasons (like health or political stability) in some regions and countries.

Third, there have been large increases of FDI flows into smaller, more vulnerable or poorer African economies, even if the large and/or commodity-rich countries still dominate the inflows.

Fourth, there has been diversification of the source of Africa-bound FDI. Investment from multinational enterprises from Asian emerging economies, mainly China, Singapore, Malaysia and India, has increased rapidly. This is good news as it broadens the base from which Africa attracts investments, reducing its vulnerability to shocks in the individual home economies of large multinational enterprises.

Fifth, there has been an increase in FDI facilitating deeper regional integration. Intra-African investments are on the rise, driven by a continuous rise in South African FDI, as well as by increases from Kenya, Nigeria and Northern African countries. In fact, between 2009 and 2014, the share of the announced cross-border greenfield investment projects – creating new facilities for business where no facilities currently exist – originating from within Africa rose to nearly 20 per cent of the total, from less than 10 per cent between 2003 and 2008.

Ultimately, however, a real chance for better future in Africa hinges on whether investments lead to lasting transformation. In this respect, the answer is unclear. The lion's share of FDI flows to Africa is still in the natural resources sector. Announcements of greenfield investment confirm the preponderance of natural resources in these trends.

But this is not the whole story. Looking at FDI stocks in Africa, almost half (48 per cent) of them are geared to services, compared to 31 per cent to the primary sector.

This means that services-related FDI has been more stable than investment in natural resources, which tend to react to changes in international commodity markets. And this fact reveals two important – and positive – features of Africa's ongoing transformation.

First, and contrary to some expectations, many African countries are increasingly services-driven economies. We see the emergence of the African middle class – estimated to have expanded by 30 per cent over the past decade, to 120 million people. This is shown by the fact that investors target more and more consumer products such as food, information technology, tourism, finance and retail.

And second, the recent growth story in Africa is due to the dynamism and development of the services sector. In thirty-four out of all African countries, services have been driving growth over the last few years.[4]

Africa is showing immense potential in some services sectors. And the benefits of this transformation are not confined to the services sector alone. Many services sectors, especially infrastructure services, are the backbone of trade in goods, be it manufacturing or agriculture. In that way, services enhance countries' capacity to access, as well as to climb, value chains. For example, Botswana has generated higher benefits from its diamond industry by promoting downstream linkages with cutting and polishing industries; similarly, the Nigerian oil industry has pursued upstream linkages in the form of project management and exploration services.[5]

Services can also be increasingly traded in their own right. Long gone are the days when services were seen as a non-tradable sector. This is already happening in Africa. Some African countries have even developed their services beyond national confines, offering these services to other African countries, in sectors such as banking, telecoms and air transport. This regional experience is a platform for developing regional value chains (RVCs), which in many cases are stepping-stones for global value chains (GVCs).

Still, despite these encouraging signs, much more can be done to stimulate additional growth and trade by African services providers. So far, many positive developments – also reflected in FDI stocks – seem to have been achieved rather despite governments than thanks to

[4] UNCTAD (2015)   [5] UNCTAD (2015)

governments. Domestically, inadequate attention has often been given to promoting services, including important infrastructural services (such as transport, distribution, logistics, financial services, insurance, telecoms, energy, water and sanitation) that yield high dividends for the performance of the economy as a whole. The regulatory environment, and the independent role of regulators, should be improved. At a regional level, services still tend to be relegated to a secondary (or tertiary) role in integration schemes, trailing far behind the traditional issues of border protection for agriculture and industrial goods, despite the critical role performed by services as a lubricant for all forms of trade and investment. Finally, at a global level, very few African countries have translated the growing importance of their services sectors domestically into a forward-looking and active negotiating stance on services within the WTO.

So what about manufacturing? In the end, with the possible exception of a few island economies, services will not be enough to precipitate transformation. A healthy manufacturing sector is essential to industrial transformation in Africa. And FDI tells us something about this opportunity, as well the challenges ahead.

On the positive side of the ledger, there has been a sharp increase in the number of Asian manufacturers engaging in Africa, as well as new investments from North America and Europe. For example, in Nigeria, Nissan, Peugeot and Hyundai all began auto assembly in 2014. Ethiopia is becoming a hub for multinational enterprises producing garments and textiles.

But Africa needs to do far more, and better, in promoting productive capacity in manufacturing. Industrialization is struggling, and in some parts of Africa, manufacturing has even been shrinking as a percentage of GDP. Africa is still capturing a relatively limited share of global FDI flows within manufacturing. In fact, only 21 per cent of African FDI stocks are in this sector.

This is where the link to trade policy also comes in. In order for FDIs to be able to effectively promote the capacity of African countries to access and climb regional and global value chains, investment and trade policies must go hand in hand. In this respect, much more can be done to lower trade costs more generally, and specifically to foster regional integration.

Regional integration in Africa is very low. Only 17.7 per cent of African trade is intra-regional, compared to rates of 50.2 per cent and 68.5 per cent for North America and Europe, respectively. High trade costs are part of the problem. In fact, African nations can pay 40 to

70 per cent more on average for the international transport of their imports than developed countries. According to some estimates, shipping a car from Japan to Abidjan would cost US\$ 1,500, whereas shipping the same car from Addis Ababa to Abidjan would cost US\$ 5,000.[6] To this it must be added that non-tariff measures are estimated to represent 60 to 90 per cent of the trade costs faced by African businesses.

Africa needs regional integration with a much higher level of ambition, and the proposed Pan-African Continental Free Trade Area (CFTA) offers a unique opportunity for this. Regulatory convergence, at a regional level, should be promoted. At national level, better pro-competitive regulations are necessary to ease the cost of doing business and to allow policy-makers to factor in fully the cost of trade with neighbouring countries. Modernized customs and soft and hard infrastructure (i.e. human and social institutions or services and functional physical networks) should also be pursued.

Attending to trade costs regionally, and thereby ensuring proper connectivity between markets, between businesses and between people, would allow African countries to promote a manufacturing base that is more productive, competitive and able to exploit economies of scale. As such, it would offer a stepping stone for entering into global production networks and a strategy for climbing value chains.

As mentioned above, FDI flows reveal the potential of increased regional integration. Africa is already witnessing increases in intra-regional flows, strengthening the efforts of deeper integration. By unlocking this potential further, African countries can help expand consumer markets and economies of scale, which in turn attracts more FDI, creating a positive and upward spiral.

But it does not end there. If African countries are serious about becoming a new global manufacturing hub, including by attracting some of the investments that arise from outsourcing from China as production costs there increase, its trade costs with regard to the rest of the world must also be tackled. Again, as exemplified by the WTO Trade Facilitation Agreement (TFA), the WTO provides a critically important forum in which Africa can pursue such objectives. Africa could learn from this experience, including the innovative ways in which the TFA addresses capacity constraints, and apply that new knowledge to tackle other areas of high domestic, regional and global costs to its trade.

---

[6] Hartzenberg (2011)

Conclusion

The face of Africa is changing dramatically. FDI has contributed to these changes. In order to achieve the 2030 Agenda for Sustainable Development, more FDI will need to be harnessed in the future, partly in order to more effectively unleash the power of trade for development. Understanding and exploiting the mutually supportive linkages between trade and investment will be critical in this regard. This calls for a pro-active trade agenda for African countries domestically, regionally and globally, in which WTO should play a central role.

References

Hartzenberg, T. (2011), 'Regional Integration in Africa', Geneva: WTO, Staff Working Paper.

UNCTAD (2014), *World Investment Report 2014. Investing in the SDGs: An Action Plan*, Geneva: United Nations Conference on Trade and Development (UNCTAD).

UNCTAD (2015), *Economic Development in Africa Report 2015: Unlocking the Potential of Africa's Services Trade for Growth and Development*, Geneva: United Nations Conference on Trade and Development (UNCTAD).

WTO (2015), *International Trade Statistics 2015*, Geneva: WTO.

9

Deepening African Integration: Intra-African Trade for Development and Poverty Reduction

ANABEL GONZÁLEZ

Abstract

The obstacles to deeper African integration are great, but the potential gains for development and poverty reduction warrant a sustained effort to overcome these challenges. High trade barriers between countries have been reflected in trade that is more oriented toward distant markets than neighbouring African countries – it is often easier for Africans to trade with the rest of the world than with each other. The potential exists for greater intra-African trade in ways that would have significant, positive impacts on the lives of millions living in poverty. Barriers to intra-regional trade need to be tackled, along with complementary efforts to ensure that the poorest people can access the opportunities created. The World Bank Group is working in a number of different areas to support this effort and is ready to do more.

Regional integration in Africa is of critical importance for development and poverty reduction. This chapter examines the topic through three key points. First, there are great challenges, but consequently there is enormous untapped potential through regional integration in Africa to deliver poverty reduction and development gains. Second, we must take a fresh look and reinvigorate some regional integration initiatives if the continent is to become better integrated. Finally, the World Bank Group is ready to intensify its support for the continent's governments and regional communities in this effort.

This chapter is an adapted version of a presentation made at the Fourth China Round Table, Nairobi, Kenya, on 13–14 December 2015.

1   The Challenges Being Faced – And the Opportunities That Exist if These Challenges Can Be Overcome

Regional trade integration has long been a strategic objective for Africa, yet, despite some success in eliminating tariffs within regional communities, the African market remains highly fragmented. A range of non-tariff and regulatory barriers still raise transaction costs and limit the movement of goods, services, people and capital across borders throughout Africa.

These barriers exist in all African regional groupings. By imposing unnecessary costs on exporters, they raise prices for consumers, undermine the predictability of trade regimes and reduce investment.

Two concrete examples highlight the impact of these costs:[1]

- If the residents of San Francisco faced the same charges in crossing the Bay Bridge to Oakland as do residents crossing the Congo River between Kinshasa and Brazzaville, a similar distance, the cost would be more than US$ 1,200 for a return trip. The high cost of the Kinshasa–Brazzaville crossing means that passenger traffic at this obvious focal point for cross-border exchanges between the Democratic Republic of the Congo and Congo is around five times smaller than that between East and West Berlin in 1988. This is, of course, before the dismantling of the Berlin Wall!
- In Southern Africa, licences and other requirements mean that a truck serving supermarkets across a border may need to carry up to 1,600 documents. The cost for transporters is compounded by slow and costly customs procedures and delays caused by agencies operating at the border. For example, one supermarket chain in Southern Africa reports that each day one of its trucks is delayed at a border costs US$ 500, and it spends US$ 20,000 per week on import permits to distribute meat, milk and plant-based goods to its stores in one country alone.

It is estimated that intra-African trade costs are around 50 per cent higher than in East Asia, and are the highest of intra-regional costs in any developing region.[2] The result of these high costs is that Africa has integrated with the rest of the world faster than with itself, with many

---

[1] Drawn from Brenton and Isik (2012).
[2] Based on the WB-UNESCAP Trade Costs Database. See Chapter 2 in OECD/WTO (2015).

export-oriented efforts focused on trade with distant markets rather than neighbouring countries in the region.

A reflection of this greater focus on extra- than on intra-regional trade is that recent export growth in Africa has been driven primarily by commodities, with limited impacts on employment and poverty. This is of particular concern now that traditional markets in Europe are stagnating and the relative slow-down in the Chinese economy has heralded the end of the commodity price super cycle.

These 'negative' reasons for a greater focus on intra-African trade are supplemented by many 'positive' ones. Some of the opportunities that could come about through greater regional integration include:

- Bringing staple foods from areas of surplus production across borders to growing urban markets and food-deficient rural areas. Africa does have the potential to meet its own food demand, but at present only 5 per cent of Africa's imported cereals come from other African countries.
- A significant amount of cross-border trade takes place on a small scale between African countries and is not measured in official statistics. Allowing small traders, many of them women, to flourish and gradually integrate into the formal economy, would boost trade as well as the private sector base for future growth – and would also have a swift impact on poverty.
- With rising incomes in Africa, there are emerging opportunities for cross-border trade in basic manufactured goods such as metal and plastic products that are relatively costly to import from the global market.
- The potential for regional production chains to drive global exports of manufactured goods, as is done in East Asia, has yet to be exploited. There are also opportunities to develop regional value chains around mineral commodities such as phosphates for fertilizers and regional processing of nickel and copper.
- Cross-border trade in services offers untapped opportunities for exports as well as better access for consumers to critical services such as health and education and access for firms to professional services such as accountancy that boost productivity.

The potential is clear. With the right policies, with political will and with strong support from the World Bank Group and other partners, a great deal could be done to boost African integration.

2   Taking a Fresh Look at African Integration in Terms of Poverty Impact

Tackling barriers to intra-African trade can have positive effects on the poorest people. This makes greater African trade integration central to the World Bank Group's goal of ending poverty by 2030, and to the aspirations of African governments and communities.

To end extreme poverty, policies to increase the contribution of intra-regional trade to growth will need to be matched with a new effort to maximize the gains of trade for the poorest. This entails tackling constraints faced by the extreme poor – including those generated by rural poverty, gender inequality, fragility and conflict, and the nature of the informal economy. These issues were explored in detail in the joint flagship publication by the World Bank Group and World Trade Organization, published in June 2015.[3]

Regional integration can play a key role in maximizing the benefits of trade opportunities for the extreme poor in a number of ways:

- By linking rural communities to markets to improve access to new technologies or the results of new technologies, such as higher-yielding seeds, and to markets for the goods and services they produce.
- By leveraging trade and cross-border exchange to generate solidarity between communities in fragile states and enhance opportunities for sharing the benefits of growth and increasing prosperity.
- By providing a route for small firms to grow and increase their capacity to leave the informal sector and thrive in the economy.
- By assisting women in dealing with poverty by providing more opportunities for jobs and better returns from cross-border trading activities.[4]

The extent to which trade leads to increased economic activity in the areas and sectors in which poor people earn their livelihoods is critical for poverty reduction. Rather than exporting minerals and fuels to distant markets, greater intra-African trade of goods and services would support more employment-intensive activity than has been the case for exports from extractive industries. For example, greater intra-African trade is likely to have a more direct impact on poverty by creating opportunities for the poor who both produce and trade the basic foodstuffs dominating intra-regional trade.

[3] World Bank Group/WTO (2015).
[4] For further detail see Brenton, Gamberoni and Sear (2013).

Currently, trade barriers mean that poor farmers in rural areas are denied access to markets in neighbouring countries that would deliver higher returns. The opportunities for them to raise their productivity by using higher-yielding seeds and through the greater application of fertilizers are stymied by restrictions which prevent the emergence of more efficient regional markets in these crop inputs.[5] Barriers at borders particularly affect small-scale traders, preventing them from earning a better living by catering to local markets across borders, where they have a comparative advantage. Most of these small-scale poor traders are women and their trading activities provide an essential source of income for their households. Their profit margins are small and are reduced by every delay or extra charge they face. They are also vulnerable to abuse.

Given the central importance of agriculture for poverty reduction, facilitating greater intra-African trade would not only boost trade performance and increase food security, it would also have strong impacts on poverty reduction. The same is true for greater intra-African trade in each of the other areas listed in the preceding section – including services, regional value chains and manufactured goods.

In addition to renewing the focus on poverty reduction, our experience and analysis at the World Bank Group also point to a number of ways in which policy makers and the regional communities can increase the impact of regional integration efforts. There are a number of key ideas that could guide the next phase of implementation of regional agreements in Africa:[6]

- Moving **beyond tariffs**. Making regional integration more effective requires a focus on addressing the on-the-ground challenges that small-scale producers and traders face on a daily basis. Thus, more effective regional integration entails a more holistic process focusing on the wider range of trade costs that prevent growth in new areas like agro-processing, manufacturing and services.
- Focusing **on regulatory reform and building the capacity of regulatory agencies**. Effective integration requires the reform of regulations that create non-tariff barriers to trade and segmented markets in Africa. It is critical that this happen at the national level, with the institutions responsible for enforcing regulations, and not just with the regional institutions promoting integration (see below).

[5] World Bank (2012)   [6] Brenton and Hoffman (2015)

- Addressing **services as well as goods**. Policy makers have traditionally focused more on goods than on services integration. This needs to change. Services are not just important for trade in their own right; they are critical to the competitiveness of almost all other economic activities. They create jobs and boost productivity and have special importance for firms seeking participation in regional and global value chains.
- Balancing **action at both supra-national and national levels**. Regional communities have a critical role to play by providing the framework for reform, but the responsibility for implementing regional commitments lies at the national level. For example, a regional community can bring together national regulators to define harmonized standards or frameworks for mutual recognition, but it is the national regulators of each country that must implement the required reform to make this work in practice.

3   The Role of the World Bank Group

The World Bank Group is a key partner for regional integration in Africa. We have been scaling up our work and are committed to doing even more on trade integration in the region. Some key areas of our support are:

- **Supporting implementation of regional trade agreements.** A key priority is working with regional secretariats, the African Union (AU), the United Nations Economic Commission for Africa, the African Development Bank, and others to support the effective implementation of regional trade agreements such as the Tripartite Free Trade Area Agreement (TFTA) of the Common Market for Eastern and Southern Africa (COMESA), the East African Community (EAC) and the Southern African Development Community (SADC), and the Continental Free Trade Area championed by the AU. The World Bank Group's support spans technical advice on demand for regional governments and other partners, as well as large-scale financing instruments, operating at both national and regional levels. For example, we are using a new instrument called a 'Regional Development Policy Operation' to provide support for groups of countries that decide jointly to implement policies that will result in trade integration.

- **Regional integration.** We are also working with our partners to better **monitor** the impacts of regional integration. Improved monitoring is critical for allowing policy makers to better assess progress and fine-tune the regional integration reform agenda where necessary.
- **Trade facilitation.** This is a strong focus of the World Bank Group's work, with more than half of our trade-related assistance devoted to trade facilitation. We are also supporting efforts to proceed with implementation of the WTO Trade Facilitation Agreement. Africa is central to this work. Simplifying customs procedures, improving their speed and efficiency, and improving transparency – all central features of the Agreement – are central to the integration agenda in Africa. In 2014, we launched a Trade Facilitation Support Program – a five-year, US$ 36 million technical assistance package dedicated to supporting developing countries' efforts to reform their trade facilitation practices. Approximately one-third of the forty-seven countries we are working with through this programme, as of December 2015, are in Sub-Saharan Africa.
- Physical **infrastructure investments.** Working together with our clients, we are designing our operations to target investments in trade-related infrastructure to benefit the poorest, and to ensure that these investments are accompanied by the necessary policy and procedural reforms that will allow trade to flourish along this new infrastructure. For example, the Great Lakes Trade Facilitation Project is constructing essential infrastructure at borders shared by the Democratic Republic of the Congo, Rwanda and Uganda, with a specific focus on the needs of small-scale traders, while simplifying procedures and improving management of the agencies operating at these borders.

Of course, these investments are not just about boosting intra-African trade – they are providing the basis for integrating the continent into the global economy, and maximizing the gains of participation in the multi-lateral trading system. Kenya's hosting of the Tenth WTO Ministerial Conference in December 2015 was widely seen as a reflection of Africa's growing importance in the global economy and in international trade. The WTO continues to be of central importance to Africa, by providing a bedrock of international trade rules and transparency for trading partners large and small, giving voice in a multilateral setting to African interests, and providing a forum for resolving disputes. This co-exists with efforts to deepen regional integration in Africa, aimed at opening new trade opportunities to reduce poverty.

But we also need to recognize that, while trade openness and deeper regional integration are critical, they need to be complemented with a more wide-ranging agenda if the maximum positive impact on poverty is to be achieved. A range of complementary policies helps maximize the gains from trade integration for the poor – including policies related to human and physical capital, access to finance, governance and institutions, and macroeconomic stability. People living in extreme poverty in Africa also face particular risks that may prevent them from taking advantage of trade opportunities. We need to do more to identify and mitigate these risks. Achievement of this goal will require deeper cooperation across sectors, better coordination across government ministries and agencies, and more effective work among a wide range of stakeholders. In Africa, the World Bank Group is working to support our clients in providing the environment in which trade can drive the elimination of extreme poverty reduction as it has done in other regions.

References

Brenton, P., E. Gamberoni and C. Sear (eds) (2013), *Women and Trade in Africa: Realizing the Potential*, Washington, DC: World Bank.

Brenton, P., and B. Hoffman (eds) (2015), *Political Economy of Regional Integration in Sub-Saharan Africa*, Washington, DC: World Bank.

Brenton, P., and G. Isik (eds) (2012), *De-Fragmenting Africa: Deepening Regional Trade Integration in Goods and Services*, Washington, DC: World Bank.

Organisation for Economic Co-operation and Development (OECD)/World Trade Organization (WTO) (2015), *Aid for Trade at a Glance 2015: Reducing Trade Costs for Inclusive, Sustainable Growth*, Paris: OECD Publishing. https://www.wto.org/English/res_e/aid4trade15_e.pdf

World Bank (2012), *Africa Can Help Feed Africa: Removing Barriers to Regional Trade in Food Staples*, Washington, DC: World Bank.

World Bank Group/WTO (2015), *The Role of Trade in Ending Poverty*, Geneva: WTO.

PART II

Africa's Participation in the Rules-Based Multilateral Trading System

10

Rising Africa in World Trade? A Story of Traditional Commodities and New Products

MICHAEL FINGER

Abstract

International trade provides ample opportunities for the economic development of countries and regions. The fall in trade costs – communication and transportation costs, greater access to international capital markets, regional cooperation and, last but not least, the decrease in trade barriers – has supported global trade and output expansion over the last decades. Emerging opportunities and challenges resulting from technological, economic and political developments differ, however, from region to region. Historical experience shows that much of the progress in economic growth and development also depends on the readiness of local business and governments to rapidly adapt and seize opportunities.

This chapter examines a range of questions. How has Africa's trade evolved since 1995? Did Africa's trade expand in line with global trade, or faster? Did the region's exports become more diversified in terms of product structure and market destinations? Did Africa's trade increase its share relative to GDP? Some observers might argue that an analysis of a large region at an aggregate level can only be of limited value. More than 1 billion people live in Africa, populating over fifty economies that differ considerably in size, resource endowments, governance and openness. Nevertheless, a shared history, combined with common economic experiences and a shared evolving destiny justify a continent-wide analysis of certain trends in trade. This approach should not, however, detract from the reality of Africa's rich diversity.

But there is also focus on a number of country experiences. The results of analysis indicate that, while they may not be representative, selected countries have recorded an above-average economic and trade growth record over the last decades, although they were broadly representative of the

A preliminary version of this chapter was presented at the Fourth China Round Table, Nairobi, Kenya, on 13–14 December 2015.

starting baseline for most African countries in 1995, with their exports dominated by agricultural products. The analysis examines what has changed in product and market structure, and factors that contributed to their above-average trade and growth performance.

Africa's Trade Performance in the 1995–2014 Period: A Broad View

Africa's trade expansion over the twenty years since 1995, when the WTO entered into force, has been strong but uneven. International and domestic factors, both economic and political, have left their mark on the expansion and structure of Africa's trade. Improvements in the macroeconomic situation provided the basis for a strong trade performance. Somewhat surprisingly to many observers, economic growth in Africa exceeded that of the global economy by a large margin in the first decade of the twenty-first century. Looking at the 1995–2014 period, Africa's share in world GDP[1] rose from 2.4 per cent to 3.1 per cent (Table 10.1). This strong growth was broadly based and could be observed across Africa's five major regions (Appendix Table 10.3). Many low-income countries recorded strong output growth and were labelled the 'African lion economies', a reference rooted in the characterization decades earlier of the Asian tigers.

What triggered this strong growth? Although explanations vary from country to country, the major factors seem to be improved governance, increased political stability, debt reduction and trade. The vigorous expansion of Africa's trade was supported by favourable price and demand developments in the fuels and mining sector and foreign direct investment (FDI) inflows.

The importance of relative price developments on the structure and growth of African exports is very obvious in the case of crude oil and products, Africa's major export group. According to World Bank data, real crude oil prices deflated by the prices of manufactured goods increased by a factor of 4.5 from the average of the 1995–99 period to the average in 2010–14. The increase in real prices for non-fuel commodities rose by 50 per cent between these two periods.[2]

---

[1] Measured at current prices and exchange rates.

[2] Price developments in 2015 have dramatically reversed the situation. As a result, Africa's merchandise exports will decline sharply in dollar terms and the share of Africa in world merchandise is expected to decrease.

Table 10.1 *Africa in the world economy, 1995 and 2014*
(Selected indicators)

	Africa	World	Africa's share in world	
	2014	2014	1995	2014
				(per cent)
Population (million)[a]	1,137	7,244	12.5	15.7
Labour force (total million)[a]	444	341	10.2	13.0
Agricultural labour force (million)[a]	237	1,334	13.3	17.8
GDP (billion US$, current)[a]	2,426	77,450	2.4	3.1
Crude oil production (million MT)[b]	392.2	4,221	10.3	9.3
Gas production (million MTOE)[b]	182.4	3,127	4.0	5.8
Gold output (MT)[c] (2012)	527	2,690	29.2	19.6
Merchandise exports (billion US$)[d]	555	18,495	2.2	2.9
Merchandise imports (billion US$)[d]	642	18,641	2.4	3.4
Commercial services exports (billion US$)[d]	100	4,939	2.2	2.0
Commercial services imports (billion US$)[d]	172	4,782	3.0	3.6
FDI inflows (billion US$)[a]	53.9	1,228	1.7	4.4
FDI outflows (billion US$)[a]	13.1	1,354	0.8	1.0
FDI inward stock (billion US$)[a]	709	24,603	2.6	2.9
Personal remittances (billion US$) (2012)[e]	57.8	488.1	9.4	11.8
Official development assistance (ODA) total net (billion US$) (2013)[f]	55.8			

Sources:
[a] UNCTAD, UNCTADSTAT (http://unctadstat.unctad.org/wds/ReportFolders/reportFolders.aspx).
[b] BP (2015).
[c] US Geological Survey, http://minerals.usgs.gov/minerals/pubs/commodity/gold/
[d] WTO, International Trade Statistics (various years).
[e] World Bank, World Bank Data Base, World Development indicators.
[f] OECD (2015).

Improved governance included more market-friendly investment regimes and trade policies. The combination of high commodity prices, in particular for fuels and other mining products, a more welcoming foreign investment regime, and a lower external debt that freed domestic resources for infrastructure investments, are all factors contributing to a sharp rise in foreign direct investment and a marked increase in inflows of personal remittances. FDI inflows and personal remittances were much smaller than aid flows[3] in the 1990s, while in 2012–13, FDI inflows exceeded aid flows, and remittances nearly matched them (Table 10.1).

The financial integration of African economies also picked up, helped by regional integration efforts and the spread of information and communication technology.

As regards trade policy, improvements are less easy to quantify. In 2013, average applied most-favoured nation (MFN) rates (i.e. treating all trading partners equally and without discrimination) are still well above 10 per cent, and the share of tariff peaks (i.e. rates above 15 per cent) exceeded 40 per cent (median value) of all tariff lines in a sample of forty-five African countries, according to WTO tariff statistics. The World Bank provides indicators that point to improvements in customs administration, as regards imports. The number of documents and days needed to import goods decreased between 2005 and 2014. The national indicators vary among African countries but remain on average well above those in more advanced economies.

Africa's Trade and Investment Openness

The growth of imports exceeded that of exports of goods and services over the 1995–2014 period, and both flows expanded faster than GDP. Consequently, Africa's trade-to-GDP ratio (average of exports and imports divided by GDP) is estimated to have risen from 25 per cent in 1995 to 30 per cent in 2014.[4]

A more attractive investment regime for foreign investors has stimulated investment inflows in many African countries. A large part of this inflow took place only after the year 2000. The mining and tourism sectors benefitted greatly from these investment inflows, which contributed to expanded exports. According to UNCTAD statistics, the share of Africa in the stock of global FDI (inward) rose from 2.1 per cent in 2000 to 2.9 per cent in 2014. FDI inflows in the latter year reached US\$ 54 billion or 4.4 per cent of world flows, and the stock of FDI in Africa is estimated to have reached US\$ 709 billion.

---

[3] Total ODA net flows.   [4] Measured at current prices and exchange rates.

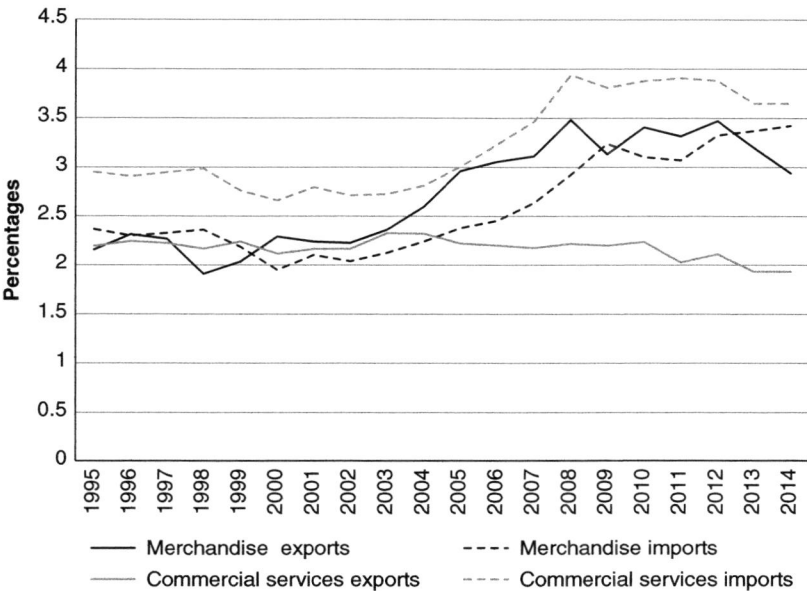

Figure 10.1   Share of Africa in world trade, 1995–2014

Trade Participation (Shares in World Trade)

Africa's shares in world merchandise exports and imports stagnated or decreased slightly between 1995 and 2002, increased thereafter sharply up to 2008 and were then levelling off until 2012. The share of merchandise exports decreased in 2013 and 2014, while the share of merchandise imports increased slightly (Figure 10.1). Africa's share in world imports of commercial services evolved in a broadly similar manner to that of merchandise exports, while the share of Africa's commercial services exports departed from this general evolution from 2002 onwards, as the share did not follow the rise and eroded rather steadily thereafter. The main reason for this development can be attributed to Africa's very low and decreasing share in services exports other than transportation and travel. This group of commercial services is not only the most heterogeneous but also the fastest growing.

Looking at Africa's share in world merchandise exports by major product groups, one notices that the shares for agricultural products, fuels and mining products (and in particular that of fuels) have been decreasing moderately (0.2 per cent each) between 1995 and 2014. These decreases are entirely due to developments after 2010. For manufactured goods, the share is estimated to have increased slightly, reaching 1 per cent in 2014. Despite this increase, Africa's share in world exports of manufactured goods continues to be much smaller than the corresponding share in agricultural products (3.6 per cent) or that of fuels and other mining products (9.2 per cent). Although the share of Africa decreased in the two product groups for which it has an above average share, it nevertheless recorded an increase in its global share of total merchandise exports. Its most prominent export group (fuels and other mining products) recorded the strongest trade expansion of all product groups at the global level.

Developments in commercial services are in some major aspects the opposite of those of merchandise exports. In the two most important services categories for Africa, transportation and travel, their respective shares in world exports increased between 1995 and 2014. However, because other services are the most important and fastest-growing categories globally and because Africa's already small shares decreased between 1995 and 2014, the overall share for Africa in world commercial services exports decreased from 2.2 per cent in 1995 to 2 per cent in 2014. However, the long-term view obscures some interesting developments. First, Africa's transportation services have grown faster than global transportation services since the year 2000. Africa's travel services exports also gained in global market share up to 2010, but in large part these gains were lost because of political instability in some North African countries, which are major travel destinations. Despite this unfavourable development, Africa's share in world travel exports (3.4 per cent) exceeded that of transportation (3.1 per cent) in 2014. Africa's share in what is, in global terms, the fastest growing residual category of other services is estimated to have slipped to 0.9 per cent in 2014 (Table 10.2).

Trade Structure

The structure of Africa's merchandise and services trade has changed little over the 1995–2014 period if one looks only at the six broad merchandise and services categories. For merchandise trade exports, the group 'fuels and mining products' has increased, while the shares of both manufactured and agricultural goods decreased. In services exports, travel services remains the largest category in Africa's commercial services exports. The share of travel rose markedly between

Table 10.2 *Share of Africa in major categories of world merchandise and services trade, 1995–2014*
(Percentages)

	1995	2000	2005	2010	2014
Merchandise					
Exports (total)	**2.3**	**2.4**	**3.0**	**3.5**	**3.0**
Agricultural products	3.8	3.3	3.3	3.8	3.6
Fuels and mining products	9.4	10.2	11.4	11.3	9.2
Fuels	11.5	11.7	13.0	12.5	9.7
Manufactured goods	0.8	0.8	0.9	1.0	1.0
Commercial services					
Exports (total)	**2.2**	**2.1**	**2.2**	**2.2**	**2.0**
Transportation	2.6	2.3	2.6	2.8	3.1
Travel	2.7	3.0	4.1	4.4	3.4
Other services	1.5	1.4	1.0	1.0	0.9

Source: WTO International Trade Statistics.

1995 and 2005 and exceeded half of Africa's services exports, but under the impact of political unrest in North Africa, the share fell back sharply to 43 per cent, a similar level to that of 1995. The categories 'transportation' and 'other services' accounted for 30 per cent and 27 per cent respectively of Africa's services exports in 2014, roughly unchanged from the level in 1995.

Africa was consistently a net exporter of travel services and a large net exporter of fuels and mining products throughout the 1995–2014 period, as well as a net importer of the other four categories (agricultural products, manufactured goods, transportation and other commercial services). Africa's merchandise trade balance recorded large variations in the review period but has been positive in most years. In contrast, the commercial services trade balance has always been negative and has widened.

Real Merchandise Developments

The following three sections of the report focus on the evolution of Africa's merchandise exports in dollar value by product group, destination and country. As has been flagged earlier, price developments had a major impact on the trade flows in the period under review, and for this reason some estimates on real or volume changes of Africa's merchandise exports would be helpful.

The dollar value of African merchandise exports rose from US\$ 112 billion in 1995 to US\$ 555 billion in 2014, an increase that corresponds to an annual average rate of growth of 8.8 per cent. According to the author's calculation, the volume or real rise in African merchandise exports accounted (at 2.6 per cent) for only one-third of this value increase, while two-thirds of it are attributable to price changes (6.2 per cent). Looking at merchandise imports, the rise was from US\$ 127 billion to US\$ 642 billion, an annual average increase of 8.9 per cent. In contrast to exports, less than one-third of this increase can be attributed to price changes (2.2 per cent) and more than two-thirds are real or volume changes (6.7 per cent). Over the two decades from 1995 to 2015, a marked deceleration occurred in the real expansion of exports, starting with an average rate of 5 per cent in 1995–2000, slowing to 4.5 per cent in 2000–05, and decreasing further to about 1.5 per cent in 2005–10 before turning slightly negative (−1.5 per cent) for the period 2010–14.

Africa's Merchandise Exports by Product, 1995 to 2014

More than half of Africa's fast-growing labour force is still employed in the agricultural sector, but only 10 per cent of Africa's merchandise exports are agricultural products (average 2012 to 2014). Although exports of agricultural products nearly tripled in value terms between 1995 and 2014 and amounted to US\$ 64 billion in 2014, the rate of expansion since 1995 was well below that of manufactured goods and fuels and other mining products. While at the aggregate level the share of agricultural products in merchandise trade is small and has decreased in relative terms over the last two decades, these products remain very important for many African economies. Moreover, since 2005 agricultural exports from Africa recorded faster growth than mining and manufactured goods. The more vigorous growth of agricultural exports has contributed to a recovery of Africa's share in world exports of agricultural products since 2005. However, the share of Africa in world exports in 2014 was still slightly lower (at 3.6 per cent) than in 1995 (Table 10.2).

Developments have differed significantly by product group within the agricultural sector. Exports of tropical beverage crops (coffee, tea and

Table 10.3 *Major product categories in African merchandise exports, 2014*

Product (SITC)	Export value (billion US$)	Share in African exports (per cent)	Growth 1995–2014 (per cent)
Crude oil and products (333–335)	249.0	45.0	10.5
Natural gas (342–344)	43.5	7.9	14.9
Coal (321–325)	4.8	0.9	5.2
Metalliferrous ores (27,28)	25.2	4.6	9.9
Non-ferrous metals (68)	22.3	4.0	7.7
Of which copper (682)	*9.4*	*1.7*	*12.0*
Pearls, precious stones (667)	13.8	2.5	4.8
Gold (971)	12.9	2.3	10.9
Coffee, tea, cocoa (07)	14.0	2.5	5.6
Vegetables, fruits (05)	13.1	2.4	7.9
Fish, fish preparations (034–037)	6.6	1.2	4.1
Wood, pulp (24,251)	5.3	1.0	4.3
Textile fibres (26)	3.8	0.7	3.3
Tobacco, tobacco products (121,122)	3.5	0.6	6.3
Oilseeds (222,223)	2.6	0.5	12.9
Clothing (84)	11.1	2.0	3.4
Road motor vehicles (78)	10.0	1.8	8.4
Electrical machinery (77)	9.8	1.8	11.4
Iron and steel (67)	7.8	1.4	4.7
Inorganic chemicals (522–25)	5.5	1.0	6.0
Manufactured fertilizer (562)	4.7	0.8	7.4
Textiles (65)	3.3	0.6	4.2
Ships, boats, floating structures (793)	3.0	0.5	13.3
Total of above	475.6	86.0	. . ..
ALL PRODUCTS	553.0	100.0	8.8
Total less fuels (3)	254.3	46.0	7.1

Source: UNCTADSTAT (http://unctadstat.unctad.org/wds/ReportFolders/reportFolders.aspx).

cocoa), traditionally the major category in Africa's agricultural exports, expanded only moderately over the period (Table 10.3). Not only did this group of products expand less than total agricultural exports from the region, it also expanded less than global exports in these categories. Relatively weak growth and a loss in global market share could also be observed for fish and fish preparations. Faster than average growth occurred in vegetable and fruit products, as well as in tobacco and tobacco products. In these two categories, African exporters have also gained market share in the global market. In the case of a number of agricultural exports, which accounted for a small share in African exports in the 1990s, the growth in shipments was spectacular. Among these non-traditional exports are oilseeds, cut flowers, fresh vegetables and live animals. While these categories still represent a small share in the region's agricultural exports, they have become major export items in a number of African countries.

Africa's export value of manufactured goods has risen nearly fourfold between 1995 and 2014, and amounted to US$ 118 billion in 2014. In 2014, the share in total African exports exceeded one-fifth of and corresponded to about 1 per cent in world exports, marginally higher than in 1995. The structure of manufactured goods exports from Africa has changed remarkably. The most important product groups in 1995 were other semi-manufactures (mainly diamonds, pearls and other precious stones), clothing and chemicals. By 2014, exports of machinery and transport equipment had become the major category, followed by chemicals and other semi-manufactures, estimated to amount respectively to US$ 40 billion and US$ 24 billion. The marked rise in machinery and transport equipment exports is accounted for both by transport equipment and electrical machinery and appliances.

According to WTO estimates, African exports of automotive products exceeded those of clothing for the first time in 2014 (respectively, US$ 11.6 billion and US$ 10.6 billion) (Appendix Table 10.4). Although African exports of clothing nearly doubled in value terms between 1995 and 2014, the expansion remained well below the expectations of many observers. Africa's share in world clothing exports fell from 3.9 per cent in 1995 to 2.2 per cent in 2014. In recent years African clothing exports were adversely affected by civil unrest in major clothing exporting countries in North Africa, but the decline in Africa's share in world markets started in 2005 (when the final restrictions on China's exports to developed markets were lifted).

Fuels and mining products remain the mainstays of African merchandise exports. With the exception of the years 1995 and 1998, the share of fuels and mining products accounted for one-half to two-thirds of African merchandise exports. Africa's share in world exports of fuels and mining products rose slightly between 1995 and 2010 but eased thereafter, mainly due to civil unrest in the North African region. Africa's share of 9.2 per cent in 2014 was only marginally different from that in 1995. At US$ 300 billion in 2014, fuels exports were by far the largest subgroup in this sector. Ores and minerals accounted for some US$ 25 billion to US$ 27 billion, as did non-ferrous metals.

For the 1995–2014 period, the three subgroups (fuels, ores and minerals, and non-ferrous metals) expanded at a similar average annual growth rate of about 10 per cent (Appendix Table 10.4). Despite a similar overall rate of expansion of these three subgroups, Africa's share in world exports increased significantly between 1995 and 2014 for non-ferrous metals and for ores and minerals, but decreased slightly for fuels. The rise in Africa's share in mining products (excluding fuels) occurred during the period 2005–14, when increased investment in Africa's mining sector started to bear fruit and prices were strong. Thanks to the FDI inflows, the concentration of Africa's mining sector exports on a few major suppliers was reduced as small and new suppliers significantly increased their share in Africa's mining output and exports.

Given the prominent role of fuels in Africa's merchandise exports, a closer look at this trade segment is of interest. As noted above, Africa's share in world fuels exports decreased slightly between 1995 and 2014. This can be attributed largely to developments in the oil trade and to a lesser extent to the evolution of coal exports. For oil and coal, Africa's share in world exports decreased from 12.5 per cent to 9.5 per cent and from 8.2 per cent to 4.5 per cent, respectively. African natural gas exports, however, increased their share in world exports from 6.7 per cent in 1995 to 11 per cent in 2014.[5] Natural gas exports rose at an annual average rate of nearly 15 per cent between 1995 and 2014, and stood at US$ 43.5 billion in 2014. Much of this strong expansion of gas trade was made possible through large infrastructure investments (pipelines, liquefaction plants, port facilities and gas tankers). At US$ 1.4 billion, exports of electric current are still a minor element in the region's fuels exports,

---

[5] The increase in Africa's share of natural gas exports corresponds to an increased African share in world gas production, which rose from 4 per cent in 1995 to 5.8 per cent in 2014 (see Table 10.1).

but have more than doubled in the last five years, and have gained importance in a number of countries.

The breakdown of African fuels exports by origin shows a marked shift from North to Sub-Saharan Africa between 1995 and 2014, a development that was accentuated by the increased civil and political unrest in the North after 2010.

In international trade statistics, gold is not included in mining products nor in manufactured goods, but is treated as a separate category. Africa has always been a major gold producer, although its share has decreased over the last decades to about one-fifth of world output. Nevertheless, gold exports remain a major export product of the region. UNCTAD estimates that African gold exports amounted to US$ 12.9 billion in 2014 and roughly matched those of the two largest agricultural product groups in the 2013–14 period. Mainly as a result of price developments, Africa's gold exports also rose faster than total merchandise exports between 1995 and 2014. International statistics on the gold trade are not always reliable, as national trade statistics are often not complete and accurate. Nevertheless, available information points to the emergence of a number of new African gold exporters which have contributed in a significant way to the rise in African gold exports.[6]

In sum, the data presented above show that the already prominent share of fuels and mining products in Africa's merchandise exports increased in the review period at the expense of both manufactures and agricultural products. In 2014, the respective shares were 63 per cent for fuels and mining products, 21 per cent for manufactures and 12 per cent for agricultural products. In addition, within these broad groups, important changes also occurred. In fuels exports, natural gas became more important. Among non-ferrous metals, copper exports rose much faster than the other metals combined. In agricultural products, exports of vegetables and oilseeds excelled, and in manufactured goods, exports of machinery and transport equipment expanded much faster than those of clothing and textiles.

Africa's Merchandise Exports by Destination

The strong expansion of African exports between 1995 and 2014 was not uniform across major destinations. Looking at the evolution between the

---

[6] The combined gold exports of two new gold suppliers (Burkina Faso and Tanzania) alone amounted to US$ 3.1 billion in 2013.

start and the end of the period, the most striking developments are the relative decline of shipments to Europe and North America (the two major markets in 1995) and the relative rise of Asian and intra-African trade. The share of Europe and North America, combined, exceeded two-thirds in 1995 and fell to 43 per cent in 2014. Shipments to Asia and Africa, combined, accounted for less than one quarter (23.6 per cent of the total in 1995) and reached 45 per cent in 2014, thus exceeding for the first time the value of exports to Europe and North America.

Europe remains Africa's largest regional export market. More than one half of African exports went to Europe in both 1995 and 2000. Thereafter, Europe's share decreased to 40 per cent in 2005, slipping further to 36 per cent in 2014. Within Europe, the share of the EU(15) slightly exceeded half in 1995, and fell to one-third for the (larger) EU(28) in 2014.

Asia has become the second largest regional destination for Africa. Its share in African exports has been rising steadily since 2002, surpassing that of North America in 2009 and reaching a peak level of 27 per cent in 2014. The increase in Asia's share can be attributed largely to two countries, China and India. In 1995, Japan was, at 3.6 per cent, still the largest destination in Asia for African exports, but it was overtaken by China in 2000 and by India in 2002. In 2014, Africa's combined exports to China and India exceeded six times those to Japan. African exports to India surpassed those to the United States for the first time in 2014 (Figure 10.2).

North America was the second-largest market for African merchandise exporters between 1995 and 2009. Its share peaked at 22 per cent in 2007 but fell steeply thereafter, to reach a new low of 7 per cent in 2014. Much of this decline is related to the expansion of the shale oil industry in the United States, which led to a steep fall of US imports of African oil. Between 2008 and 2014, the share of the United States in African fuels exports decreased from 26 per cent to 7 per cent, which corresponds to a value decline of US$ 72 billion.

South America's share more than doubled between 1995 and 2014 (from 2 per cent to 5 per cent). The increase is concentrated in the 2010 to 2014 period. More than half of these exports were destined for Brazil.

The share of the Middle East in Africa's exports has increased somewhat since 1995, and is estimated still to be below 4 per cent in 2014. The share of the CIS region remains modest at one-half of one per cent.

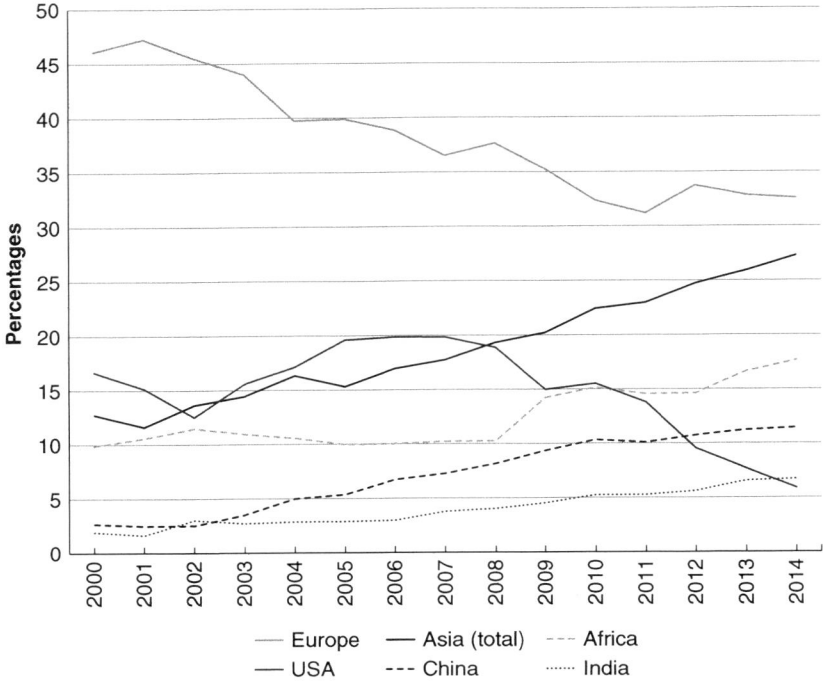

Figure 10.2   Shift in Africa's merchandise exports by destination, 2000–14

Intra-African trade, which accounted for about 10 to 12 per cent of Africa's exports throughout the 1995–2008 period, rose sharply thereafter and reached a record high of nearly 18 per cent in 2014.[7] A part of this increase is due to a change in the statistical reporting of South African exports, which from 2010 onwards include exports to Southern African Customs Union (SACU) members. South Africa's exports to

---

[7] According to UNCTAD data the peak reached is 15 per cent. The measurement of intra-African trade poses a number of challenges. Unrecorded informal trade flows are most likely more important for intra-African trade than for trade with other destinations, leading to an under-recording of the importance of intra-African trade. Informal border trade usually flourishes when regulated prices differ sharply between neighbouring countries (e.g. gasoline in West Africa) or official exchange rates depart in a major way from market rates. Although tariff rates have come down, the remaining tariff peaks and surcharges, as well as export taxes, can contribute to the rise in informal trade. Smuggling of gold, precious stones and rare metals are often reported in the press, together with illicit trade in animals and animal products. However, the final destinations of these products are usually outside Africa and should not lead to an underreporting of intra-African trade.

SACU ranged from US$ 11 billion to US$ 12 billion, or nearly 2 per cent of intra-African trade, in the 2010–14 period. While this change corrects for underreporting intra-African trade in the past, it also results in a discontinuity of the historic time series.

In 2014, intra-African trade amounted to US$ 98 billion, a small decrease from the peak level in the preceding year. The broad product composition of intra-African trade has fluctuated with the relative price of fuels, but probably did not change much between 1995 and 2014. In 2014, manufactured goods recorded the largest share, at 43 per cent, followed by fuels and mining products (30 per cent) and agricultural products (18 per cent). Among manufactured goods the three largest categories are machinery and transport equipment (16.4 per cent) followed by chemicals (9 per cent) and other semi-manufactures (8 per cent).

According to WTO data, South Africa is by far the largest single source of intra-African trade, accounting for about 30 per cent of total exports and more than 50 per cent of all manufactures exports in 2014.[8] The combined exports of all other African countries to each other amounted to about US$ 48 billion, or about 10 per cent of their total exports, and about one half of total Africa's intra-trade. African countries' exports to South Africa, worth US$ 21 billion in 2014, accounted for about one-fifth of intra-African trade. Slightly more than one half of this amount originates from South Africa's SACU partners.

There is a great variation in African countries' share of merchandise exports shipped to other African countries. The lowest shares[9] (below 5 per cent) are typically found for oil exporting countries (such as Algeria, Angola, Congo, Equatorial Guinea, Gabon and Libya), while the largest shares (20 per cent to 50 per cent) are generally found for landlocked agricultural exporters (such as Burundi, Malawi, Rwanda, Uganda, Zambia and Zimbabwe in Eastern and Central Africa, and Mali and Niger in West Africa). In recent years, intra-trade shares in excess of 20 per cent of exports are also found for all five SACU member countries.

Regional integration agreements have received much attention over the last decades and one might ask how much they have contributed to the expansion of intra-African trade. The answer is not straightforward, but

---

[8] In recent years (2012–14), Nigeria's exports accounted for about 10 per cent of Africa's intra-trade, followed by Ghana, Côte d'Ivoire and Egypt, each with a share of about 5 per cent.

[9] Based on UNCTAD (2014) Table 3 for the period average 2007–11.

a few indicators can be given. One indicator could be that the rise of intra-trade of African regional trade agreements (RTAs) expands more quickly than that of total African exports or total intra-African trade. Among the African RTAs, South African Development Community (SADC) and Economic Community of West African States (ECOWAS) stand out with the largest trade volume. Unfortunately, due to changes in South African statistics no consistent data exist for the intra-trade of SADC and SACU. However, it is possible to report on the evolution of ECOWAS' intra-trade and that of the smaller RTAs such as the West African Economic and Monetary Union (UEMOA) and East African Community (EAC). According to UNCTAD data, the share of intra-trade in ECOWAS exports hardly changed between 1995 and 2014. (The share actually decreased slightly, by one percentage point to 9 per cent.) The same observation can be made for UEMOA, for which the share of 15.3 per cent in 2014 is also slightly lower than that observed in 1995. The share of intra-trade in the EAC increased somewhat from 17.2 per cent in 1995 to 18.4 per cent in 2014. These partial observations do not support the view that the RTAs in Africa contributed in a prominent way to the expansion of Africa's intra-trade.

The main changes in the destination of Africa's merchandise exports is the sharp rise in the share of Asia, especially of China and India, at the expense of the shares of both Europe and the United States. South and Central America also gained in importance, thanks mainly to the fast growth in exports to Brazil. The rise of Asia, and in particular China, tends to favour African exporters of fuels and mining products in particular, as these products account for a much larger share in shipments to Asia (89 per cent) compared to those to North America (69 per cent) or Europe (64 per cent).

UNCTAD and WTO trade data both report a marked increase in the share of intra-African trade since 2008. However, there are questions about the origins of this increase. One explanation is falling oil prices, which tend to adversely affect extra-trade more than intra-trade. This factor played a major role in 2009 when oil prices declined sharply. The rise in 2009–10 could be partly accounted for by a change in statistical reporting. Apparently, South Africa started to include trade with SACU members from 2010 onwards. The strong oil prices throughout 2010–13 should have lowered the share of intra-African trade, but instead it continued to increase. One possible partial explanation could be that the steep fall in Libyan (and Tunisian) exports, with their low level of intra-trade, increased the share of all other African countries, which recorded on average a higher level of intra-trade than these two North African countries that were affected by civil unrest.

African Merchandise Exports by Country

Between 1995 and 2014 the majority of African countries recorded an export growth in excess of the global average, partly due to favourable price developments for fuels and other commodities (Appendix Table 10.2). Among the smaller exporters (thirty-seven countries with exports of less than US$ 5 billion in 2014) a majority (i.e. twenty-two countries) also achieved an export expansion above the global average. Only two of the smaller exporters sold less in 2014 than in 1995: the Central African Republic and the Republic of Liberia. Despite strong export growth in the majority of small exporters, the region's exports remain relatively concentrated on some major exporters. Throughout the observation period, nine countries accounted for more than three-quarters, seven for more than two-thirds, five for more than one-half, and two (Nigeria and South Africa) for more than one-third of African merchandise exports (Appendix Table 10.1). Among these major exporters, performance differed greatly over the 1995–2014 period, with average growth rate ranging from less than 5 per cent for Libya to more than 16 per cent for Angola. The latter tripled its share in African merchandise exports (11.2 per cent in 2014) and became the region's fourth largest exporter, thanks to a dramatic increase in oil output.[10] Nigeria's exports rose on average by more than 11 per cent and exceeded those of South Africa for the first time in 2014. Nigeria, the region's largest oil producer, benefitted not only from additions to its oil output but even more so from the strong development of its gas output and exports. The sharp decline in South Africa's share from 25 per cent in 1995 to about 17 per cent in 2014 occurred entirely between 1995 and 2005.

Trade Performance of Selected African Exporters

A number of African countries have recorded outstanding GDP and export growth (in dollar values) over the last two decades. The six selected countries covered in what follows are among them. For the

---

[10] Crude oil production rose from 31.2 million MT in 1995 to 83 million MT in 2014.

Table 10.4 *Macro-economic indicators for selected African countries*

	Burkina Faso	Chad	Ethiopia	Mozambique	Rwanda	Tanzania
Population (million, 2014)	17.4	13.2	96.5	26.5	12.1	50.8
GDP (billion US$, 2014)	13.1	11.3	54.2	16.8	8.0	50.1
GDP per capita (2014)	757	862	562	634	662	988
GDP real growth (1995–2014)	6.3	6.5	7.7	8.8	8.1	6.2
Export growth (current US$) (1995–2014)	12	15	11	19	15	11
Import growth (current US$) (1995–2014)	12	13	16	16	13	11
Trade balance/GDP (2013)	−11	−21	−24	−46	−17	−11
Current account/ GDP (2013)	−4	−11	−7	−38	−7	−14
FDI inflows to GDP (2010–2014)	2	4	2	29	3	5

Sources: UNCTAD Country profiles.

1995–2014 period, they recorded average annual GDP growth between 6 per cent and 9 per cent, which was two to three times faster than the world economy. The dollar value of their exports rose over the reference period between 11 per cent and 19 per cent. These 'star performers' are Burkina Faso, Chad, Ethiopia, Mozambique, Rwanda and Tanzania. All are low-income economies with a per capita income in current dollars ranging from US$ 560 to US$ 1,000 in 2014. Their population size ranges from 12 million (Rwanda) to 97 million (Ethiopia) (Table 10.4). They were all exporting mainly agricultural products in 1995, with shares ranging from 80 per cent to 90 per cent of total exports (Table 10.5).

Despite the rapid growth, their combined merchandise exports of US$ 21 billion only accounted for 4 per cent of African exports in 2014. While

Table 10.5 *Selected African countries' merchandise export structure, 1995–2014*

	Year	Million US$ total	Agricultural products	Fuels	Mining products including gold, precious stones	Manufactures
					Share	
Burkina Faso	1995	276	78.3	1.2	12.0	8.2
	2005	468	90.8	0.1	2.5	6.3
	2014	2,489	42.0	9.0	39.0	8.0
	2014(a)	2,846	...	9.0	54.4	...
Chad	1995	243	91.5	0.0	0.0	6.1
	2005	3,081	0.0	90.6	0.1	2.2
	2014	3,600	4.0	94.0	...	2.0
Ethiopia	1995	422	85.9	2.9	0.1	11.2
	2005	926	88.8	0.0	5.8	5.1
	2014	4,437	81.0	5.0	5.0	9.0
Mozambique	1995	174	78.8	2.7	5.6	12.1
	2005	1,745	18.2	12.7	65.2	3.9
	2014	4,725	23.0	27.0	42.0	9.0
Rwanda	1995	52	83.0	0.2	7.4	8.1
	2005	125	47.1	1.8	37.5	10.1
	2014	736	34.0	4.0	51.0	10.0
Tanzania	1995	685	88.3	0.3	3.9	7.1
	2005	1,672	51.5	4.1	33.6	10.4
	2014	4,645	44.0	3.0	40.0	17.0

Sources: UNCTAD (2014), UNCTAD Country profiles (http://unctadstat.unctad.org/CountryProfile/148/148GeneralProfile.pdf)
(a) UNSTAT Country profiles

this chapter focuses on developments on the export side, it should not be overlooked that these countries recorded very strong import growth, resulting in sizeable trade and current account deficits. UNCTAD estimated that the trade deficits had been in excess of 10 per cent of GDP for all the six 'star performers' in 2014 (Table 10.4). It should be noted that trade deficits are a natural accompaniment to rapid growth in these circumstances and are ideally financed through FDI and other non-debt financial flows.

The highlights of their merchandise export performances are summarized below.

Burkina Faso averaged a real growth rate of 6.3 per cent per annum from 1995 to 2014, and current (dollar) export and import growth rates of 12 per cent.

Burkina Faso's merchandise exports consisted largely of agricultural products (mainly cotton) in 1995. In 2014, agricultural products accounted for about 30 per cent (cotton, oilseeds and coconuts) of exports, a sharp decline from a nearly 80 per cent share in 1995. Fuels and mining products have become the predominant exports, accounting for nearly two-thirds of total exports in 2014 (up from 13 per cent in 1995). Exports of oil products rose from small amounts in 1995 to US$ 275 million in 2014, accounting for nearly 10 per cent of merchandise exports. The major change in Burkina Faso's export structure occurred when the industrial production of gold started to take off in 2007. With the start of industrial mining, gold production rose from small artisanal operations to thirty-two tonnes per year by 2011 and kept to roughly that level up to 2013. Exports of gold amounted to US$ 1.4 billion, or slightly more than 50 per cent of total exports, in 2014. Zinc exports started in 2013 and accounted for 3 per cent of exports in 2014. The emergence of industrial gold production was made possible through major foreign direct investments. In most of the gold mining companies, the Government of Burkina Faso holds a minority stake.

Chad averaged a real growth rate of 6.5 per cent per annum from 1995 to 2014, and current (dollar) export and import growth rates of 15 per cent and 13 per cent, respectively. The export story of Chad is quickly told. In 1995 agricultural products accounted for more than 90 per cent of exports, and in 2014 oil exports had a share in excess of 90 per cent. Oil production in Chad started in 2003 and rose sharply up until 2008. Production fell sharply thereafter and oil export volumes suffered but remained the predominant export product at about US$

3 billion. The exports of crude oil by landlocked Chad required the construction of a 1,070 kilometre pipeline, with the largest segment in neighbouring Cameroon. The Chad–Cameroon oil pipeline was financed through a (largely foreign) private-public ownership project. The development of the oil fields, the pipeline and the offshore floating storage and offloading vessels called for investments likely to have exceeded US$ 3 billion. The International Finance Cooperation and the World Bank helped to establish a monitoring process to ensure that the gains from these investments contribute to the welfare of the local population. In addition to the benefits accruing in Chad, there have also been significant earnings from transportation services for neighbouring Cameroon.[11]

Ethiopia averaged a real growth rate of 7.7 per cent per annum from 1995 to 2014, and current (dollar) export and import growth rates are at 11 per cent and 16 per cent, respectively.

Among the six selected countries, Ethiopia has by far the largest population and economy. A very strong export performance has been achieved with agricultural products, which accounted for more than 80 per cent of Ethiopian merchandise exports in both 1995 and 2014. However, the dynamic performance was achieved with non-traditional agricultural exports such as cut flowers, fresh vegetables, oilseeds, meat and live animal exports, and not with the traditional agricultural exports such as coffee and raw and tanned animal skins. This can be best illustrated by the fact that the share of coffee accounted for more than one-half (54 per cent) of Ethiopian exports in 1995 and for less than one-fifth (19 per cent) in 2013. The corresponding shares for skin (raw and tanned) exports are 17 per cent and 4 per cent. More recently, gold and petroleum oil also gained in importance, accounting for 5 per cent and 7 per cent, respectively, in 2014.

Linked to the change in the export product structure was also a shift in export destinations. The share of Europe decreased markedly, while that of the Middle East recorded the largest gains over the 1995 to 2013 period.

FDI inflows in the form of joint ventures facilitated the emergence of cut flower exports through know-how transfer covering production, transportation, marketing and distribution channels. The emergence

---

[11] Transportation services exports of Cameroon rose sharply from US$ 120 million in 2002 to US$ 335 million in 2004. It is estimated that revenues from pipeline transport services amounted to US$ 400 million annually in the years 2007–13.

of non-traditional exports was strongly supported by various govern-
ment policies, which targeted sectors with a high export potential.
Special tariff exemptions and preferences contributed to the rise of
FDI inflows.

Mozambique averaged a real growth rate of 8.8 per cent per annum
from 1995 to 2014, and current (dollar) export and import growth rates
of 19 per cent and 16 per cent, respectively.

In 1995, Mozambique mainly exported agricultural products (nearly
80 per cent of merchandise exports). Mining products and fuels combined accounted for nearly 70 per cent of merchandise exports in 2013,
a dramatic change from the small share in 1995 (less than 10 per cent).
Among the various fuels exported, coal and crude oil have become far
more important than exports of electric current. The shift from being an
agricultural exporter to a mining exporter started in 2000 when aluminium exports started to take off and accelerated when mineral fuels and
coal exports developed from 2010 onwards.

Since 2009 FDI inflows have risen sharply, reaching a record US$
6.2 billion in 2013, and promising a further rise in mining exports.
Among the six countries reviewed, Mozambique has attracted the largest
FDI inflows, both in dollar-value terms and in relative terms, as percentages of GDP (Table 10.5).

Rwanda averaged a real growth rate of 8.1 per cent per annum from
1995 to 2014, and current (dollar) export and import growth rates of
15 per cent and 13 per cent, respectively.

Predominantly an exporter of agricultural products in 1995, Rwanda
became a more diversified exporter by developing its (non-fuel) mining
industry. In 1995 agricultural exports are estimated to have exceeded
80 per cent of total exports. Tea and coffee were the major export
commodities. In 2014, exports of metal ores alone accounted for one-
third of exports, and the larger group of metal ores, metals and precious
stones for slightly more than one-half of merchandise exports.

Tanzania averaged a real growth rate of 6.2 per cent per annum from
1995–2014, and current (dollar) export and import growth rates of
11 per cent.

Merchandise exports from Tanzania largely comprised agricultural
products (88 per cent) in 1995. Food exports alone represented about
two-thirds of the country's exports. Major products were coffee
(21 per cent), textile fibres (15 per cent) and tobacco (14 per cent).
In 2014, the situation was quite different, with gold being a major new

export item. The group ores, metals, precious stones and non-monetary gold accounted for nearly 40 per cent of exports in 2014. In 1995, the share of this group was below 4 per cent. The decline in the share of food products in Tanzania's exports does not imply that all agricultural exports experienced below average growth. Cashew nuts, a traditional export item, accounted for 2 per cent of total exports in 2005 and for 7 per cent in 2014. Sesame seed exports rose from US$ 10 million in 1995 to US$ 172 million in 2013. A rise in output combined with strong prices contributed to this outcome. A number of non-traditional agricultural exports emerged after 2000, such as fish and fish products and vegetables and flowers. However, the expansion of these two export categories slowed sharply after 2008.

The change in the product structure also caused a shift in the destination of exports. Europe lost dramatically in importance as its share decreased sharply while that of Africa, in particular South Africa, rose sharply. Asia was always a major destination but its share evolved little, although China and India became more prominent destinations.

A major change in the FDI regime contributed to the rise of the mining and tourism sectors. In 2014, Tanzania's exports of travel services amounted to US$ 2 billion and exceeded slightly her exports of fuels and mining products.

The exports of the six countries above consisted to a very large extent of agricultural commodities. The share of agricultural products in their exports ranged from 79 per cent to 95 per cent in 1995. Two decades later, the situation is very different.

In five of the six countries, the share of agricultural products has declined and that of (broadly defined) mining products has increased sharply. In the case of Chad's exports, the change is perhaps the most dramatic. From exclusively exporting food (91 per cent) in 1995, it largely exported crude oil (94 per cent) in 2014.

Burkina Faso exported agricultural raw materials and food but by 2013 gold had become its major export item. Mozambique was mainly an exporter of food in 1995 and exported primarily fuels and non-ferrous metals in 2014.

For Tanzania and Rwanda, the importance of agricultural products (mainly food) was also reduced, but in a less dramatic way than in the case of Mozambique and Chad. Nevertheless, the share of agricultural products was matched (Tanzania) or surpassed (Rwanda) by mining products (including fuels) in 2014.

Ethiopia stands out in this country sample, as its high export growth was underpinned by a substitution among agricultural products. Ethiopian exports seem to have taken a different path than those of the great majority of the nearly thirty African economies that exported primarily agricultural products in 1995. Almost two decades later, the latter had markedly diversified their exports into other product sectors, mainly mining products and fuels.

It is striking that the relative decline in agricultural exports was not accompanied by a general rise in the share of (labour-intensive) manufactured goods. Among the six sample countries, only Tanzania records an increase in the share of manufactured goods in its merchandise exports. The manufactures that increased their share in Tanzania's exports include chemicals (fertilizer, soap and other cleaning materials), textiles, and machinery and transport equipment. A decrease in shares was observed for exports of clothing and footwear for the 1995–2014 period.

In all six countries, foreign capital (FDI inflows, debt conversion) and transfers (especially personal remittances) played a major role in export expansion and in the financing large trade deficits. The sharp fall in fuel and other commodity prices in 2015 will be an unwanted 'stress test' for the sustainability of Africa's merchandise export expansion. In the short run, lower export earnings and lower FDI inflows will adversely affect government revenues and the decline in external debt levels will be reversed. The already large trade and current account deficits will increase further, and their sustainability could in some cases be called into question. The financial sector, which was supportive of export growth, may generate headwinds against the trade expansion in the six sample countries, but also in Africa as a whole.

Appendix Tables

Appendix Table 10.1 *African merchandise exporters, 2014*

	Million US$	Growth average rate	Percentage share				
	2014	1995–2014	1995	2000	2005	2010	2014
Africa	554,916	8.8%	100	100	100	100	100
Nigeria	97,000	11.5%	11.1	14.2	16.2	16.1	17.5
South Africa	91,047	6.4%	24.9	20.3	16.6	17.5	16.4
Algeria	62,956	10.0%	9.2	14.9	14.8	10.9	11.3
Angola	62,400	16.1%	3.3	5.4	7.7	9.7	11.2
Egypt	27,091	11.5%	3.1	3.6	4.2	5.1	4.9
Morocco	23,663	6.7%	6.2	5.0	3.6	3.4	4.3
Libya	21,000	4.6%	8.0	8.6	10.1	9.3	3.8
Tunisia	16,756	6.1%	4.9	4.0	3.4	3.2	3.0
Ghana	13,216	11.3%	1.5	1.1	0.9	1.5	2.4
Côte d'Ivoire	12,783	6.7%	3.3	2.6	2.5	2.2	2.3
Equatorial Guinea	12,600	27.3%	0.1	0.7	2.3	1.9	2.3
Zambia	9,696	12.5%	0.9	0.6	0.6	1.4	1.7
Gabon	8,926	6.5%	2.4	1.8	1.6	1.7	1.6
Congo	8,263	10.8%	1.0	1.7	1.5	1.8	1.5
Botswana	7,800	7.0%	1.9	1.8	1.4	0.9	1.4

Appendix Table 10.1 (*cont.*)

	Million US$	Growth average rate		Percentage share				
	2014	1995–2014	1995	2000	2005	2010	2014
Democratic Republic of the Congo	6,900	8.1%	1.4	0.5	0.8	1.0	1.2
Kenya	6,115	6.4%	1.7	1.2	1.1	1.0	1.1
Cameroon	4,853	5.9%	1.5	1.2	0.9	0.7	0.9
Mozambique	4,725	19.2%	0.2	0.2	0.6	0.6	0.9
Tanzania	4,645	10.6%	0.6	0.5	0.5	0.8	0.8
Namibia	4,441	6.2%	1.3	0.9	0.7	0.8	0.8
Ethiopia	4,437	13.2%	0.4	0.3	0.3	0.4	0.8
Sudan	4,350	...	0.5	1.2	1.6	2.2	...
Chad	3,600	15.2%	0.2	0.1	1.0	0.7	0.6
Mauritius	3,107	3.8%	1.4	1.1	0.7	0.4	0.6
Zimbabwe	3,064	2.0%	1.9	1.3	0.6	0.6	0.6
Senegal	2,812	5.6%	0.9	0.6	0.5	0.4	0.5
Burkina Faso	2,489	12.3%	0.2	0.1	0.2	0.3	0.4
Uganda	2,274	8.8%	0.4	0.3	0.3	0.3	0.4
Madagascar	2,126	7.8%	0.5	0.6	0.3	0.2	0.4
Mali	2,100	8.6%	0.4	0.4	0.4	0.4	0.4
Benin	2,010	8.6%	0.4	0.3	0.2	0.2	0.4
Mauritania	1,946	7.5%	0.4	0.2	0.2	0.4	0.4

Swaziland	1,918	4.3%	0.8	0.6	0.6	0.3	0.3
Sierra Leone	1,886	22.1%	0.0	0.0	0.1	0.1	0.3
Niger	1,500	9.1%	0.3	0.2	0.2	0.2	0.3
Guinea	1,400	3.7%	0.6	0.5	0.3	0.3	0.3
Malawi	1,374	6.6%	0.4	0.3	0.2	0.2	0.2
Togo	1,350	6.9%	0.3	0.2	0.2	0.2	0.2
Lesotho	925	9.7%	0.1	0.1	0.2	0.2	0.2
Eritrea	766	12.2%	0.1	0.0	0.0	0.0	0.1
Rwanda	736	15.0%	0.0	0.0	0.0	0.1	0.1
Republic of Liberia	583	–1.8%	0.7	0.2	0.0	0.0	0.1
Seychelles	539	13.0%	0.0	0.1	0.1	0.1	0.1
Somalia	510	6.0%	0.2	0.1	0.1	0.1	0.1
Guinea-Bissau	162	10.6%	0.0	0.0	0.0	0.0	0.0
Djibouti	139	13.0%	0.0	0.0	0.0	0.0	0.0
Burundi	125	0.9%	0.1	0.0	0.0	0.0	0.0
Gambia	108	10.5%	0.0	0.0	0.0	0.0	0.0
Central African Republic	90	–3.3%	0.2	0.1	0.0	0.0	0.0
Cabo Verde	81	12.3%	0.0	0.0	0.0	0.1	0.0
Comoros	25	4.5%	0.0	0.0	0.0	0.0	0.0
Sao Tomé and Principe	17	6.6%	0.0	0.0	0.0	0.0	0.0

Source: WTO, International Trade Statistics.

Appendix Table 10.2 *African merchandise exporters ranked by export growth, 1995–2014*

	Million US$	Percentage growth at annual rate				
	2014	1995–2014	1995–2000	2000–2005	2005–2010	2010–2014
World	18,495,000	7.1	4.5	10.2	7.8	5.6
Africa	554,916	8.8	5.8	16.0	10.9	1.6
Equatorial Guinea	12,600	27	54	45	7	6
Sierra Leone	1,886	22	−21	65	17	53
Mozambique	4,725	19	17	37	11	12
Angola	62,400	16	17	25	16	5
Chad	3,600	15	−6	76	3	0
Rwanda	736	15	0	19	19	25
Ethiopia	4,437	13	3	13	21	17
Djibouti	139	13	18	5	17	13
Seychelles	539	13	30	12	3	8
Zambia	9,696	13	−3	15	32	8
Cabo Verde	81	12	4	10	20	16
Burkina Faso	2,489	12	−5	17	28	12
Eritrea	766	12	−16	−21	3	177
Egypt	27,091	11	9	20	15	1
Nigeria	97,000	11	11	19	11	4

Ghana	13,216	11	−1	11	23	14
Congo	8,263	11	16	14	15	−3
Tanzania	4,645	11	1	18	19	3
Guinea-Bissau	162	11	21	8	7	6
Gambia	108	10	0	−14	56	12
Algeria	62,956	10	17	16	4	2
Lesotho	925	10	7	24	6	1
Niger	1,500	9	0	12	19	7
Uganda	2,274	9	−3	15	15	9
Benin	2,010	9	−1	8	17	12
Mali	2,100	9	4	15	13	1
Democratic Republic of the Congo	6,900	8	−12	24	17	7
Madagascar	2,126	8	10	1	6	17
Mauritania	1,946	8	−6	12	27	−2
Botswana	7,800	7	5	11	1	14
Togo	1,350	7	−1	13	8	8
Morocco	23,663	7	2	9	10	7
Côte d'Ivoire	12,783	7	1	15	8	3
Malawi	1,374	7	−1	6	16	7
Sao Tomé and Principe	17	7	−10	18	10	12

Appendix Table 10.2 (*cont.*)

	Million US$	Percentage growth at annual rate				
	2014	1995–2014	1995–2000	2000–2005	2005–2010	2010–2014
Gabon	8,926	6	–1	14	11	1
South Africa	91,047	6	1	11	12	0
Kenya	6,115	6	–2	15	9	4
Namibia	4,441	6	–1	9	14	2
Tunisia	16,756	6	1	12	9	0
Somalia	510	6	3	5	12	3
Cameroon	4,853	6	2	9	6	6
Senegal	2,812	6	–2	11	6	7
Libya	21,000	5	7	20	9	–19
Comoros	25	4	4	–2	11	5
Swaziland	1,918	4	1	14	0	2
Mauritius	3,107	4	0	7	1	8
Guinea	1,400	4	–1	5	12	–1
Zimbabwe	3,064	2	–2	–1	12	–1
Burundi	125	1	–14	3	12	5
Sudan	…	…	27	22	19	…
Republic of Liberia	583	–2	–17	–17	11	27
Central African Republic	90	–3	–1	–4	2	–10

Source: WTO, International Trade Statistics.

Appendix Table 10.3 *Real GDP growth in Africa, 1970–2014*
(Average annual growth)

	1995–2014	1995–2000	2000–2010	2010–2014
World	**2.8%**	**3.4%**	**2.6%**	**2.4%**
Africa	**4.4%**	**3.5%**	**5.3%**	**3.2%**
Eastern Africa	**5.4%**	3.8%	5.6%	7.1%
Middle Africa	**5.5%**	2.9%	7.3%	4.5%
Northern Africa	**3.6%**	4.1%	4.8%	0.1%
Southern Africa	**3.1%**	2.9%	3.5%	2.5%
Western Africa	**5.8%**	3.4%	7.1%	5.3%
Africa excluding South Africa	**4.8%**	3.7%	5.8%	3.4%
Sub-Saharan Africa	**4.7%**	3.3%	5.6%	4.1%
Sub-Saharan Africa excluding South Africa	**5.5%**	3.6%	6.6%	4.9%
COMESA (Common Market for Eastern and Southern Africa)	**3.8%**	3.5%	5.3%	0.5%
EAC (East African Community)	**5.4%**	3.8%	6.0%	5.8%
ECCAS (Economic Community of Central African States)	**5.5%**	2.8%	7.3%	4.5%
ECO (Economic Cooperation Organization)	**4.3%**	3.9%	4.9%	3.6%
ECOWAS (Economic Community of West African States)	**5.8%**	3.4%	7.1%	5.3%
Selected African countries				
Burkina Faso	**6.3%**	6.5%	5.9%	7.0%
Chad	**6.5%**	2.7%	9.0%	5.3%
Ethiopia	**7.7%**	4.6%	8.6%	9.4%
Mozambique	**8.8%**	11.5%	8.1%	7.4%
Rwanda	**8.1%**	10.2%	7.7%	6.6%
Tanzania	**6.2%**	4.4%	6.5%	7.5%

Source: UNCTADSTAT (http://unctadstat.unctad.org/wds/ReportFolders/
reportFolders.aspx), accessed on 23 September 2015, and author's calculations.

Appendix Table 10.4 *Product structure of Africa's merchandise exports, 1995–2014*

	Million US$	% Share	% Share	% Share	% Growth	% Growth
	2014	2014	1995		1995–2014	2000–2014
Agriculture	**63,608**	**11.5**	**19.6**		**5.8**	**9.3**
Food	51,240	9.2	14.2		6.4	9.8
Fish	5,853	1.1	…		…	5.3
Other food products	45,387	8.2	…		…	10.7
Raw materials	12,368	2.2	5.4		3.9	7.4
Fuels and mining products	**349,195**	**62.9**	**44.6**		**10.8**	**10.5**
Ores and minerals	26,780	4.8	3.5		10.6	15.4
Fuels	297,817	53.6	37.3		10.9	10.1
Non-ferrous metals	24,599	4.4	3.8		9.8	10.5
Manufactures[a]	**118,292**	**21.3**	**27.7**		**7.3**	**8.9**
Iron and steel	8,875	1.6	3.3		4.8	7.1
Chemicals	23,672	4.3	4.5		8.5	11.4
Pharmaceuticals	1,258	0.2	…		…	12.6
Other chemicals	22,414	4.0	…		…	11.4
Other semi-manufactures[a]	23,624	4.3	…		…	7.3
Machinery and transport equipment	39,813	7.2	…		…	12.8
Office and telecom equipment	4,810	0.9	…		…	11.3
Electronic data processing and office equipment	695	0.1	…		…	10.8

Telecommunications equipment	3,261	0.6	...	...	16.6
Integrated circuits and electronic components	854	0.2	...	...	3.5
Transport equipment	17,755	3.2	...	...	13.6
Automotive products	11,599	2.1	...	...	13.5
Other transport equipment	6,155	1.1	...	...	13.6
Other machinery	17,248	3.1	...	...	12.6
Textiles	3,481	0.6	1.4	4.2	6.9
Clothing	10,608	1.9	5.5	2.9	2.9
Other manufactures	8,219	1.5	...	...	8.7
Personal and household goods	2,601	0.5	...	...	6.1
Scientific and controlling instruments	1,419	0.3	...	...	12.9
Miscellaneous manufactures	4,199	0.8	...	...	9.6
Residual[b]	24,331	4.4	8.1	5.3	8.6
Total merchandise exports	**555,426**	**100.0**	**100.0**	**8.8**	**9.9**

[a] Including pearls and precious stones
[b] Including non-monetary gold
Source: WTO, International Trade Statistics.

Appendix Table 10.5 *Intra-Africa merchandise exports by product, 2000–14*

	Million US$				Percentage share			
	2000	2005	2010	2014	2000	2005	2010	2014
Agriculture	**3,336**	**5,373**	**12,862**	**17,135**	**22.7**	**17.3**	**16.3**	**17.5**
Fuels and mining products	**4,133**	**10,619**	**22,654**	**29,577**	**28.2**	**34.3**	**28.7**	**30.2**
Fuels	3,671	9,215	18,980	26,298	25.0	29.7	24.0	26.8
Manufactures	**5,805**	**11,892**	**33,866**	**42,016**	**39.6**	**38.4**	**42.9**	**42.8**
Iron and steel	365	1,180	2,473	2,907	2.5	3.8	3.1	3.0
Chemicals	1,463	2,732	6,737	8,713	10.0	8.8	8.5	8.9
Other semi-manufactures	1,144	2,524	6,953	8,123	7.8	8.1	8.8	8.3
Machinery and transport equipment	1,612	3,277	11,653	16,056	11.0	10.6	14.8	16.4
Office and telecom equipment	217	336	870	1,453	1.5	1.1	1.1	1.5
Transport equipment	638	1,522	5,506	8,116	4.4	4.9	7.0	8.3
Other machinery	757	1,419	5,278	6,487	5.2	4.6	6.7	6.6
Textiles	288	351	756	1,040	2.0	1.1	1.0	1.1
Clothing	190	421	856	1,010	1.3	1.4	1.1	1.0
Other manufactures	742	1,406	4,438	4,166	5.1	4.5	5.6	4.2
Residual	1,397	3,104	9,578	9,350	9.5	10.0	12.1	9.5
Total exports	**14,670**	**30,988**	**78,960**	**98,078**	**100.0**	**100.0**	**100.0**	**100.0**

Note: Product breakdown is based partly on estimates.
Source: WTO, International Trade Statistics.

Appendix Table 10.6 *Prices, FDI and debt developments in Africa, 1995–2014*

A. Favourable price developments

Period averages	Crude oil US$ per barrel	Nominal price index 2010=100	Real (a)	Real (a) non-fuel commodity price index
1995–99	17.6	22.4	25.8	65.4
2000–04	28.8	36.8	45.8	64.0
2005–09	69.5	88.0	92.4	84.0
2010–13	97.7	123.8	116.9	100.4
2015 est.	58	73	71	84

(a) Deflated by the 'world' export unit value index of manufactured goods.
   Source: World Bank.

B. Strong investment flows and personal remittances

| | FDI inflows into Africa | | Remittances | African FDI | |
| | Billion US$ | Share in world | Billion US$ (b) | Outflow billion US$ | Share in world |
Period averages					
1995–99	9.1	1.5	10.9	2.5	0.4
2000–04	15.9	1.9	14.5	0.6	0.1
2005–09	46.7	3.1	39.4	6	0.4
2010–13	51.9	3.5	53.3	9.5	0.6

(b) Referring to 2010–12 instead of 2010–13.
   Source: UNCTADSTAT (http://unctadstat.unctad.org/wds/ReportFolders/reportFolders.aspx).

C. Debt reduction in Sub-Saharan Africa

Period averages	External debt Stocks as % Exports of goods and services	External debt Stocks as % Gross National Income	Total debt Service as % Exports of goods and services
1995–99	232.3	68.6	15.0
2000–04	171.3	60.0	10.2
2005–09	73.5	28.4	6.3
2010–13	71.0	23.2	4.7

Source: World Bank, International debt service statistics, accessed on 24 September 2015 at http://data.worldbank.org/data-catalog/international-debt-statistics

References

BP (2015), *Statistical Review of World Energy*, London: BP.

OECD (2015), *Geographical Distribution of Financial Flows to Developing Countries*, Paris: OECD.

UNCTAD (2014), *Handbook of Statistics*, Geneva: UNCTAD.

UNCTAD Country profiles http://unctadstat.unctad.org/CountryProfile/148/148GeneralProfile.pdf

WTO (1995–2014), *International Trade Statistics*, Geneva: WTO. https://www.wto.org/English/res_e/its_e.htm

11

Trade Policy Trends in Africa: Empirical Evidence from Twenty Years of WTO Trade Policy Reviews

MAIKA OSHIKAWA, UKAMAKA ANAEDU AND VICKY CHEMUTAI

Abstract

Trade liberalization has been a key component of economic development and transformation in the global economy since the middle of the last century and is a leading force in fostering globalization and connectivity in the twenty-first century. Trade reform has been on the agenda of African economies, first under the IMF-supported structural adjustment programmes of the 1980s and the early 1990s, and subsequently pursued within the multilateral legal and policy framework of the WTO. Following two decades of rapid trade growth in Africa, the evidence suggests that significant barriers to trade remain within Africa, impeding its integration to regional and global value chains. Considerable scope exists for the use of trade policy to accelerate and deepen sustained economic development and transformation. African economies should embark on the next generation of trade and associated structural reforms more aggressively and ambitiously.

This chapter examines the evolution of trade policy reforms in Africa across the twenty-year period from 1995 to 2015. It addresses the three following questions: What have been the broad patterns and the substantive factors in African trade policy in the twenty-year period from 1995 to 2015? What factors have influenced African trade policy-making and implementation? What factors enhance our understanding of the evolution of African trade policy in this period? In answering these questions, the authors analyse 107 WTO Trade Policy Reviews (TPRs) conducted for forty-two African members. The results of the analysis show that, overall, Africa

Maika Oshikawa, Ukamaka Anaedu and Vicky Chemutai work in the Accessions Division of the WTO. A preliminary version of this paper was presented at the Fourth China Round Table, Nairobi, Kenya, on 13–14 December 2015. The authors are grateful for guidance and comments received from Chiedu Osakwe, as well as research assistance provided by Nannan Gao, Masa Lekic, Ghulam Reza Mohammady and Tatiana Yanguas.

continued trade liberalization under the WTO, building on its earlier trade reforms, although the pace of reforms varied in different countries and different parts of the continent. Analysis focused, inter alia, on the use of selected trade policy instruments by African members, principally tariffs, 'other' border duties and taxes, non-tariff measures, such as import restrictions, measures related to customs procedures, state trading, export measures and trade in services. Drawing on quantitative and qualitative information extracted from the TPR reports and other WTO data, specific attention is accorded to policy developments at the regional level, which has accounted, in part, amongst the drivers for trade liberalization in Africa, although the pace and degree of such liberalization varied greatly among the sub-regions and from one country to another, including some cases of policy reversal and back-sliding registered in the use of particular trade policy instruments.

Key findings suggest that most African members used the WTO system below potential to support their trade and wider structural reforms and leverage for governance. It is argued that the influence of the origin of their inherited, rather than negotiated, GATT/WTO membership, a disproportionate focus on the Doha Development Agenda negotiations and inadequate technical capacity explain, in part, Africa's under-utilization of the multilateral framework for trade-driven development growth. It is suggested that African policy-makers, in future participation in the organization, would benefit from the following: strengthened bindings and commitments in the goods and services schedules; embarking on the next generation of structural reforms of which the WTO accession template remains relevant, addressing implementation gaps; maintaining a proactive utilization of regular WTO bodies for implementation of trade rules and the TPR oversight peer review mechanism; and, finally, a robust engagement for plurilateral initiatives in the wake of the WTO's Tenth Ministerial Conference in Nairobi in 2015.

1 Introduction

Africa's trade performance has gone through a dynamic transformation over the last two decades. Between 1995 and 2014, the volume of Africa's goods exports grew by 500 per cent or at an annual average growth rate of 8.8 per cent. During this period, Africa's share in world trade grew from 2.3 per cent in 1995 to 3.0 per cent in 2014, while on the import side its share grew from 2.4 per cent to 3.4 per cent. The destination of trade also substantially changed: the share of Africa's trade with Europe and North America, its two major markets in 1995, decreased from more than two-thirds to 43 per cent in 2014, while trade between Asia and Africa soared from 23.6 per cent to 45 per cent during the same period. Trade within Africa rose, reaching 18 per cent of the region's total exports in 2014 compared with only 10 per cent in 1995. Increased trade has been a powerful engine for growth, although this increase largely reflects favourable commodity price developments (see more detail in Chapter 10 by Finger). However, evidence also points to the increasing growth from non-commodity exports and services which would help cushion the boom-and-bust cycles that had characterized Africa's economic developments in the past.

Trade policies play an increasingly critical role in influencing Africa's trade performance, as the continent undertakes structural transformation to diversify its commodity-based economies. Africa's international trading environments, including reciprocal and non-reciprocal trading arrangements, have offered valuable opportunities and instruments to harness Africa's trade potential. While acknowledging the positive export performance of the last twenty years, the bulk of trade is still overwhelmingly made up of unprocessed raw materials that have minimal to no value added and make nominal contributions to sustained growth and development. The recent sharp decline in oil and other commodity prices further cast a shadow on the future outlook of Africa's trade performance. Trade preferences have addressed little in the way of practical impacts on the structure of narrowly based African economies. Implementation of the decisions from the follow-up to the WTO's Tenth Ministerial Conference in Nairobi in December 2015 on the Doha Development Agenda (DDA) and non-DDA tracks provides a platform to deepen the dividends from Africa's membership of the multilateral trading system and the use of trade as an engine for growth. At the same time, the proliferation of preferential trade arrangements in general, and the negotiation of mega-regional agreements among large trading partners in particular, have increased the level of competition for African economies, specifically for producers in these markets. African trade and economic policy-makers urgently need to reflect on various options for trade policy goals so that trade policy can serve to establish a platform for structural transformation, promote sustainable economic development, industrialization and integration into global and regional value chains.

This chapter examines the evolution of trade policy reforms over the past two decades. In doing so, a content analysis is undertaken of 107 WTO Trade Policy Reviews (TPRs) which were conducted for forty-two African members between 1995 and 2015. A number of central questions are addressed:

- How have trade policy instruments, such as tariffs, other border duties and taxes, non-tariff measures (such as import licensing, restrictions, customs measures), as regulated by the WTO Agreements, evolved over the last twenty years?
- How effectively were they implemented?
- What were the forces behind the evolution of trade policies?
- Looking ahead, how can Africa effectively use trade policy reforms to expand and maximize gains from the multilateral trading system?

We shall argue the advantages that the multilateral trading system can offer Africa to support and foster its trade policy reforms and afford it critical instruments to facilitate the realization of the continent's integration agenda on the basis of global rules and best practices.

2 Framework for Analysis

We shall examine 107 TPRs between 1995 and 2015. These reviews were conducted by the WTO's TPR Body, based on reports prepared by the WTO Secretariat and the government under review, and questions and comments from other WTO members, to monitor the evolution of members' trade policies and instruments for the purpose of transparency (Annex 11.1). All African members are examined as part of a six-year cycle (i.e. they are not on the list of the twenty largest traders which are reviewed either as part of a two- or four-year cycle). At the end of 2015, of the forty-three WTO African members, forty-two had been reviewed at least once, while thirty-six members had been reviewed twice, twenty-one members three times, and eight members (Cameroon, Mauritius, Uganda and the Southern African Customs Union (SACU)-5, i.e. Botswana, Lesotho, Namibia, South Africa and Swaziland) four times. Seychelles, which joined the WTO in 2015, is scheduled to be reviewed in 2021. These TPRs provide comprehensive information on African members' trade policy framework, instruments and implementation, covering trade in goods and services, as well as other trade-related policies, such as investment, intellectual property rights (IPRs), government procurement, competition and privatization. This study largely relies on the information contained in the reports by the Secretariat, which are collected in a standardized manner, based on materials directly provided by the members under review, complemented by publicly available information and reports by other multilateral institutions such as the International Monetary Fund (IMF). This study also draws on each chairperson's concluding remarks, which reflect WTO members' assessments of the trade policies of the African members under review.

Despite the wealth of information contained in the TPR reports, several drawbacks need to be noted up-front, as they define some limitations for the analysis in this chapter.

First, the six-year review cycle results in gaps in updated information, monitoring and evaluation of trade policy developments, particularly in the fast-moving global economy. Only half of the African members were reviewed, based on the mandated periodicity. In other words, half lagged behind their mandated periodic reviews. As a result, each review often provides a snapshot of trade policy developments at the time of a review, rather than an evolution of trade policy between reviews, especially for those non-regulars. Moreover, the (more than) six-year review cycle makes cross-country comparison challenging as, on an average, only five African members were reviewed each year.

Second, the qualitative information on trade policy measures makes the analysis difficult, as such information is not always up to date or comprehensive. The WTO Secretariat frequently relies on the goodwill of the government to provide accurate information. The only quantitative information that is provided and analysed on a consistent and coherent basis in the TPR reports are tariffs. As a result, this study places greater emphasis on tariff analysis, as the information in the TPRs can be supplemented by the data available in the Integrated Data Base (IDB), independent of the TPRs.

Third, the TPRs are a 'transparency' exercise driven by WTO members. As a result, they do not impose any penalty, other than peer pressure, to direct trade policy in a certain direction. The level of engagement by WTO members varies significantly from one review to another. In the case of Africa, given its small share in world trade, the value of this TPR exercise is recognised as a tool for internal transparency, rather than external transparency *vis-à-vis* other members.

3 Trade Policy Reform in Africa, 1995–2015

Trade Policy Reform before the Establishment of the WTO in 1995

Of the current forty-three African members of the WTO, forty-one are original members, meaning that they were contracting parties to the General Agreement on Tariffs and Trade (GATT) 1947 when the WTO was established in 1995. Two African countries, Cabo Verde and Seychelles, joined the WTO in 2008 and 2015, respectively. Of the forty-one GATT contracting parties, two (South Africa and Zimbabwe) were original Contracting Parties since 1948, while the other 39 countries acceded to GATT between 1957 and 1994, with more than half of them joining in the 1960s soon after their independence (Table 11.1). In all cases except for four, independent African states joined the GATT under sponsorship or succession as provided in Article XXVI:5(c) of the GATT 1947,[1] which provided for former colonies to become contracting parties without negotiations, provided they offered the same concessions to other contracting parties as applied before independence. Only the Democratic Republic of the Congo (1971), Egypt (1970), Morocco (1987) and Tunisia (1990) gained their GATT membership under Article XXXIII of GATT 1947,[2] through negotiations on terms of entry that had to be agreed with the contracting parties.[3] Such accessions through GATT Article XXXIII negotiations were rare at the time, so that on the occasion of the accession of the Democratic Republic of the Congo in September 1971, the GATT Secretariat issued a press release stating that:

> The Democratic Republic of the Congo is acceding to GATT under Article XXXIII of the General Agreement. In doing so, it is following a path different from that of other developing countries which have joined GATT in recent years. The Government of the Democratic Republic of the Congo preferred to negotiate a fresh basis for its adherence to the General Agreement, and has successfully done so.[4]

[1]   GATT 1947 Article XXVI – Acceptance, Entry into Force and Registration:
    '5. (c) If any of the customs territories, in respect of which a contracting party has accepted this Agreement, possesses or acquires full autonomy in the conduct of its external commercial relations and of the other matters provided for in this Agreement, such territory shall, upon sponsorship through a declaration by the responsible contracting party establishing the above-mentioned fact, be deemed to be a contracting party.'
[2]   GATT 1947 Article XXXIII – Accession:
    'A government not party to this Agreement, or a government acting on behalf of a separate customs territory possessing full autonomy in the conduct of its external commercial relations and of the other matters provided for in this Agreement, may accede to this Agreement, on its own behalf or on behalf of that territory, on terms to be agreed between such government and the CONTRACTING PARTIES. Decisions of the CONTRACTING PARTIES under this paragraph shall be taken by a two-thirds majority.'
[3]   Out of 128 Contracting Parties to GATT 1947, a total of sixty-four, including thirty-five from Africa, acceded to the GATT through Article XXVI:5(c).
[4]   GATT Press Release, 'Democratic Republic of the Congo to join GATT', GATT/1086, 12 August 1971.

Table 11.1 *Africa's membership in WTO and GATT*

No.	Member	Date of WTO membership	Date of GATT contracting party	Accession to GATT/WTO through	Date of independence
1	Angola	23/11/1996	08/04/1994	GATT1947 Art. XXVI:5(c)	11/11/1975
2	Benin	22/02/1996	12/09/1963	GATT1947 Art. XXVI:5(c)	01/08/1960
3	Botswana	31/05/1995	28/08/1987	GATT1947 Art. XXVI:5(c)	30/09/1966
4	Burkina Faso	03/06/1995	03/05/1963	GATT1947 Art. XXVI:5(c)	05/08/1960
5	Burundi	23/07/1995	13/03/1965	GATT1947 Art. XXVI:5(c)	01/07/1962
6	Cabo Verde	23/07/2008	N.A.	WTO 1994 Article XII	05/07/1975
7	Cameroon	13/12/1995	03/05/1963	GATT1947 Art. XXVI:5(c)	01/10/1961
8	CAR	31/05/1995	03/05/1963	GATT1947 Art. XXVI:5(c)	13/08/1960
9	Chad	19/10/1996	12/07/1963	GATT1947 Art. XXVI:5(c)	11/08/1960
10	Congo	27/03/1997	03/05/1963	GATT1947 Art. XXVI:5(c)	15/08/1960
11	Côte d'Ivoire	01/01/1995	31/12/1963	GATT1947 Art. XXVI:5(c)	07/08/1960
12	DRC	01/01/1997	11/09/1971	GATT 1947 Article XXXIII	30/06/1960
13	Djibouti	31/05/1995	16/12/1994	GATT1947 Art. XXVI:5(c)	27/06/1977
14	Egypt	30/06/1995	09/05/1970	GATT1947 Art. XXXIII	28/02/1922
15	Gabon	01/01/1995	03/05/1963	GATT1947 Art. XXVI:5(c)	17/08/1960
16	The Gambia	23/10/1996	22/02/1965	GATT1947 Art. XXVI:5(c)	18/02/1965
17	Ghana	01/01/1995	17/10/1957	GATT1947 Art. XXVI:5(c)	06/03/1957
18	Guinea	25/10/1995	08/12/1994	GATT1947 Art. XXVI:5(c)	02/10/1958
19	Guinea-Bissau	31/05/1995	17/03/1994	GATT1947 Art. XXVI:5(c)	24/09/1973
20	Kenya	01/01/1995	05/02/1964	GATT1947 Art. XXVI:5(c)	12/12/1963
21	Lesotho	31/05/1995	08/01/1988	GATT1947 Art. XXVI:5(c)	04/10/1966
22	Madagascar	17/11/1995	30/09/1963	GATT1947 Art. XXVI:5(c)	26/06/1960

Table 11.1 (*cont.*)

No.	Member	Date of WTO membership	Date of GATT contracting party	Accession to GATT/WTO through	Date of independence
23	Malawi	31/05/1995	28/08/1964	GATT1947 Art. XXVI:5(c)	06/07/1964
24	Mali	31/05/1995	11/01/1993	GATT1947 Art. XXVI:5(c)	22/09/1960
25	Mauritania	31/05/1995	30/09/1963	GATT1947 Art. XXVI:5(c)	28/11/1960
26	Mauritius	01/01/1995	02/09/1970	GATT1947 Art. XXVI:5(c)	12/03/1968
27	Morocco	01/01/1995	17/06/1987	GATT1947 Article XXXIII	02/03/1956
28	Mozambique	26/08/1995	27/07/1992	GATT1947 Art. XXVI:5(c)	25/06/1975
29	Namibia	01/01/1995	15/09/1992	GATT1947 Art. XXVI:5(c)	21/03/1990
30	Niger	13/12/1996	31/12/1963	GATT1947 Art. XXVI:5(c)	03/08/1960
31	Nigeria	01/01/1995	18/11/1960	GATT1947 Art. XXVI:5(c)	01/10/1960
32	Rwanda	22/05/1996	01/01/1966	GATT1947 Art. XXVI:5(c)	01/07/1962
33	Senegal	01/01/1995	27/09/1963	GATT1947 Art. XXVI:5(c)	04/04/1960
34	Seychelles	26/04/2015	N.A.	WTO 1994 Article XII	29/06/1976
35	Sierra Leone	23/07/1995	19/05/1961	GATT1947 Art. XXVI:5(c)	27/04/1961
36	South Africa	01/01/1995	13/06/1948	Original GATT1947	31/05/1910
37	Swaziland	01/01/1995	08/02/1993	GATT1947 Art. XXVI:5(c)	06/09/1968
38	Tanzania	01/01/1995	09/12/1961	GATT1947 Art. XXVI:5(c)	09/12/1961
39	Togo	31/05/1995	20/03/1964	GATT1947 Art. XXVI:5(c)	27/04/1960
40	Tunisia	29/03/1995	29/08/1990	GATT1947 Art. XXXIII	20/03/1956
41	Uganda	01/01/1995	23/10/1962	GATT1947 Art. XXVI:5(c)	09/10/1962
42	Zambia	01/01/1995	10/02/1982	GATT1947 Art. XXVI:5(c)	24/10/1964
43	Zimbabwe	05/03/1995	11/07/1948	Original GATT1947	18/04/1980

Source: Information compiled by the WTO Secretariat.

After the establishment of the WTO, Cabo Verde and Seychelles became WTO members through accession negotiations pursuant to Article XII of the Marrakesh Agreement Establishing the WTO, which is similar to Article XXXIII of GATT 1947.[5]

Although Africa made up nearly one-third of the GATT membership by the end of the Uruguay Round that ended in 1995, the impact of their GATT membership on trade reform was minimal, in particular for Sub-Saharan Africa. While the Uruguay Round of 1986–94 was hailed as the largest multilateral trade negotiations with far-reaching implications on trade policy reforms at the global level, Africa's participation was limited, and consequently, few benefits accrued to the continent. For instance, a study by Wang and Winters (1997)[6] documented that under the Uruguay Round, African economies undertook little liberalization and in return received fewer benefits. Yeo (2005)[7] further argued that African countries achieved very little in the Round because they failed to liberalize their trade policies, and because neither their trade policy communities nor their public were convinced that liberal trade policies were the right policies. Evidence for Africa's reluctance to undertake trade policy reforms was provided by a review of trade reforms in Africa in the 1980s by Dean, Desai and Riedel (1994),[8] who observed that trade reforms had progressed gradually and had been full of interruption and reversals. Additionally, Rodrik (1997) analysed Africa's resistance to trade reforms and pointed to the institutional weakness of African countries in terms of their ability to deal with the distributional effects, as highlighted in the dynamic inconsistency of policy-making and the lack of credible commitment to policies. Some have argued that the limited participation of Africa in the Uruguay Round is due to a lack of comprehension of the role of GATT as an instrument for opening its own and others' markets, as the African nations' trade was largely defined by non-reciprocal, preferential arrangements with current or former colonial powers, that operated outside the GATT framework.[9] Whatever the reasons for their

---

[5] In December 2015, the Republic of Liberia completed its accession negotiations under Article XII of the WTO Agreement. In addition, the following African countries are in the process of accession to the WTO (application date in parentheses): Algeria (June 1987), Comoros (February 2007), Equatorial Guinea (February 2007), Ethiopia (January 2003), Libya (June 2004), Sao Tomé and Principe (January 2005), Somalia (December 2015) and Sudan (October 1994). Eritrea and South Sudan are the only African countries which have no status in the WTO.

[6] Wang and Winters (1997)   [7] Yeo (2005)   [8] Dean, Desai and Riedel (1994)

[9] See for instance, Hudec (1987), Ohiohenuan (2005) and Kessie and Apea (2004).

limited participation, the GATT membership of African members had little direct impact on the evolution of their trade policies.

Major trade policy reforms started under the IMF's structural adjustment programmes (SAPs) in the 1980s and the early 1990s, as documented in trade reform episodes of individual African members in Annex 11.2. The main rationale for trade reform, under the SAPs, was to improve economic efficiency by creating a transparent and neutral system of incentives that eliminated anti-export bias, direct impediments to trade and economic distortions caused by the trade regime. Thus, IMF-supported trade reform involved removing export barriers, quantitative restrictions and other non-tariff measures (including quotas, bans, restrictive licensing requirements, restrictive foreign exchange practices, state trading monopolies, restrictive technical and phytosanitary standards, and restrictive customs procedures); reducing tariff dispersion by introducing low and relatively uniform tariffs administered in a transparent and even-handed manner; and establishing neutral treatment of imports under domestic economic policies.[10] These were also the central focus of the transparency exercise of the TPR Mechanism, the implementation of which started in 1989 as an early result of the Uruguay Round.

Trade Policy Reforms under the WTO

An overall message from the 107 trade policy reviews of forty-two African members in the period from 1995 to 2015 is the acknowledgement of trade liberalization efforts taken by African members. Despite a few instances of policy reversals, African members continued to liberalize their trade regimes as they had started to do under the IMF-supported SAPs, as tariffs and non-tariff measures were reduced across the continent. Tariffs are the main trade policy instrument used by African members, first to protect domestic industry and second to generate revenues, although the relative significance of the latter decreased over time for most members. Non-tariff measures such as quantitative restrictions, import restrictions and licensing, which were still widely used by some members in the 1990s, were removed and reduced to a minimum with the exception of their use for public policy reasons. At the same time, in line with global trends, behind-the-border-measures have gained more attention from trade policy-makers; in particular, customs-related

---

[10] Sharer (1997)

issues, along with trade in services, have topped the trade policy agenda of African members in more recent years.

The evolution of trade policy has not been uniform across the African continent, as trade policy is largely, though not solely, country-specific. The formation and implementation of trade policy falls under the competence of national governments, in most cases led by the Ministry of Trade/Commerce. However, it is worth noting that the delegation of certain competences to the secretariats or commissions of Africa's Regional Economic Communities (RECs) or regional trade agreements (RTAs), as part of deepening regional integration across the continent, is one of the key features observed in the evolution of African trade policy developments over the last two decades.

While the overall trade regime has moved towards further opening for most African members, policy reversals and backsliding were registered at the reviews of some members. For example, the 2015 TPR for Angola noted an increase in the most-favoured nation (MFN), or non-preferential, applied tariff from 7.4 per cent to 11.5 per cent in the period of 2013 to 2014 in order to encourage local production. Similar increases in the MFN applied tariffs were observed in the cases of Madagascar, where the rate increased from 3.5 per cent to 12.5 per cent in the period of 2004–05 (see Table 11.2); Ghana, where the re-introduction of a special import tax of 20 per cent in 2000, covering 7 per cent of tariff lines, increased the rate on many consumer goods to 40 per cent, well above their previous 25 per cent (TPR 2001); and Nigeria, where the increase from 23.5 per cent 29.1 per cent in the period between 1998 and 2003 was accompanied by increased tariff dispersion and peaks, as well as a ten-fold increase in the number of items subject to import bans (TPR 2005). In the latter two cases, the backsliding was partly redressed in subsequent reviews. It is also worth noting that there was a duality of the trade strategy, which combined export promotion and import substitution, in Mauritius (2001, 2008) and Tunisia (2005), and this limited the impact of trade liberalization by distorting the allocation of resources between the domestic and export sectors.

Box 11.1 provides a non-exhaustive summary of the main conclusions from the 107 TPRs, based on the chairpersons' concluding remarks. While several WTO-related issues referred to in Box 11.1 are analysed in detail in Section 4 of this chapter, a few observations should be noted. First, there have been minimal changes, from the baseline of the 'Concluding Remarks', which are the collective appreciation by WTO members of an African member's trade policy review. While there is

BOX 11.1: NON-EXHAUSTIVE SUMMARY OF CHAIRPERSONS CONCLUDING REMARKS AT TRADE POLICY REVIEWS, 1995–2015

I   General Observations

a)   Overall Legal, Institutional and Administrative Reforms

Many African Members were urged to rationalize and modernize their trade and investment regimes in order to improve the business environment with a view to making these regimes more conducive to the countries' economic development ambitions.

b)   Heavy Dependence on Border Taxes

Many governments sourced their revenues from border taxes and thus, further trade liberalization through reduction of border taxes was met with reluctance. In light of this, the trade policy advice provided was on the need to broaden the internal tax base, integrate the informal sector and mobilize private savings.

c)   High Dependence on Agriculture and Natural Resources

High dependency on agriculture such as cotton exports was raised as one of the main concerns of African countries' trade performance. This dependency, accompanied by developed countries' cotton subsidies, had distorting effects on the domestic economy as well as world markets. Also, dependence on natural resources such as oil and minerals was pointed out. Diversification of economy was, therefore, underscored consistently as a key for development on a sustainable basis.

d)   Infrastructural Inefficiencies and High Production Costs

Numerous supply-side constraints were mentioned as inhibitors to optimally benefitting from the multilateral trading system (MTS). Poor infrastructure, high trade costs and inefficiency in transport, electricity and fixed-line telecommunications services added to the high costs of doing business and ultimately constituting obstacles to growth.

e)   Overwhelming Informal Sector

In some countries, many large-scale businesses operated in the informal sector, which accounted for three-quarters of all economic activity. A proper framework was required to incorporate these activities into a formal and accountable economic regime.

f)   Political Instability

Members that were characterized by prolonged civil strife and political upheavals are not able to fully implement agreements and integrate into the MTS. There was an imminent need to sort out internal questions of governance, stability and predictability.

BOX 11.1: (*Cont.*)

g) Public Health Challenges

Diseases like Ebola and Malaria continued to generate serious public health concerns resulting in negative economic and trade repercussions. Inadequate measures to address and curb the diseases institutionalized poverty, narrowed the skills gap, stalled trade and limited market access.

h) Minimal Outward Investment

Insufficient capital and market access limitations maintained on foreign investment led to minimum foreign direct investment (FDI) outflows. More specifically, investment in the industrial sector tended to stagnate for long periods.

i) High Foreign Debt

Several members were plagued with large foreign-debt-to-GDP ratios that were unsustainable, and whose servicing posed major constraints on the members' purchasing power and infrastructural development.

II WTO-Related Observations

j) Low Level of WTO Participation

Low participation of African Members in the day-to-day work of the WTO was highlighted. Attempts to justify this were made by pointing out the lack of resources and capacity building. Nonetheless, observers and analysts continued to point out that lack of participation would hamper African countries from benefitting substantially from the MTS and impede the implementation of their WTO obligations, e.g. inadequate use of the WTO Dispute Settlement Mechanism (DSM).

k) Lack of Notifications and Transparency

Lack of transparency was another challenge against predictability of African countries' markets. In particular, businesses had faced certain unexpected delays and extra technical procedures due to lack of an efficient notification system.

l) Delayed Implementation of WTO Agreements

The implementation of several WTO Agreements, such as those on customs valuation, anti-dumping, subsidies and countervailing measures and safeguards, had been delayed in most countries. There was emphasis on the benefits of actual implementation.

m) Misused or Underutilized Technical Assistance

Despite constant requests for technical assistance in various trade-related areas from international organizations, there were reports of misuse and gross underutilization, eventually allowing the skills gap to grow.

n) Overlapping Preferential Arrangements

There were repeated concerns by business on the application of certain key trade measures, such as rules of origin, customs procedures and other duties charged on

BOX 11.1: *(Cont.)*

production within the different regional agreements *vis-à-vis* the WTO Agreements. A lack of harmonization within the regional/bilateral arrangements and duplication of activities posed a risk to WTO non-compliance.

III   Observations in Specific Trade Policy Instruments

o)   Complicated border regimes

Concerns were raised over the complicated tariff regimes and overlap of technical controls at the borders. A simplification of custom procedures and tariff system reform were key for those countries' competitiveness and for the attraction of foreign investments.

p)   Binding Overhang

There was an observed large disparity between bound and applied rates. In several cases, the applied MFN tariffs exceeded the bindings, and this was not addressed between reviews over time.

q)   National Treatment Concerns

In some countries, the application of internal taxes on specific like products was discriminated between imported and domestic goods, and therefore inconsistent with the WTO provisions.

r)   Preshipment Inspection Concerns

Observations were made on the high costs and delays in procedures for preshipment inspection. High costs and delays were reflected in increased trade costs and made the economies in question uncompetitive.

s)   Establishment of the Single Window System

Some African economies had been successful in establishing a single window system, i.e. a platform for the electronic exchange between trading partners of trade information, in a bid to simplify formalities, promote transparency and predictability, and prevent bureaucratic rigidity in international trade. Others were encouraged to emulate those that had set up such single windows and implement them.

t)   Clarification on Sanitary and Phytosanitary (SPS) and Technical Barriers to Trade (TBT) Measures

There was repeated emphasis on the absence of harmonized SPS and TBT measures in compliance with international standards. There were many requests for clarification in respect of measures being applied transparently and predictably.

u)   Protection of Intellectual Property Rights and Competition Policies

Huge gaps were observed in the implementation of the Agreement on Trade-Related Aspects of Intellectual Property Rights (TRIPS) obligations, as well as the Bangui Agreement on Intellectual Property of reviewed African Members.

BOX 11.1: (Cont.)

African Members were encouraged to establish competition policies in order to foster a healthy and robust growth in a predictable environment.

v)   Government Procurement and Corruption
Corruption concerns in government procurement were continuously raised. Corruption was particularly illustrated in the arrangement of generous income tax concessions and exemptions for certain national companies and state-owned enterprises. Corruption costs jeopardized the free play of competition and dissuaded investors.

w)   Further liberalization in Services
It was noted that despite notable liberalization in some services sectors, there was room to increase the binding coverage to cover other sub-sectors, as this would enhance predictability and signal openness for foreign investments. This was highlighted in the areas of energy, transport, finance and telecommunications.

Source: These observations are those of the authors. They are non-exhaustive and are largely derived from the circulated concluding remarks by the chairpersons ex officio of the WTO Trade Policy Body on Trade Policy Reviews of African Members, 1995–2015.

---

acknowledgement of progress made between reviews, the list of concerns expressed by members is often on the same set of issues for any African member. Second, as evident in 'General Observations', WTO members have used the TPRs to raise concerns that go beyond trade policy and the WTO Agreements. While the number of issues and concerns listed in the summary does not indicate any magnitude of significance, these factors nonetheless weigh in assessing the overall conduciveness of trade policies in Africa. These factors include the complexity of the trade and investment regimes that are not conducive to business, both in their design and implementation; the lack of diversification that hinders economic development on a sustainable and equitable basis; infrastructure deficiencies that raise overall production costs, despite relatively low labour costs; the presence of the informal sectors that impede the role of the state in managing the economy; political instability and public health challenges that can, when they occur, nullify trade activities; and corruption that adds to already high business operational costs in Africa.

What are the factors that have influenced African trade policy-making and policy implementation over the two decades? Based on the conclusions from the TPRs, it is evident that African members continued to implement the standard template of reform measures that had been introduced under the IMF-supported SAPs. A study by Sharer (1997), which reviewed IMF-assisted trade reform programmes in thirteen African countries over the period 1990 to 1996, concluded that the factors implementing trade reform were primarily linked to balance-of-payments and fiscal consideration. The study also found that the implementation of multilateral commitments under the WTO 'did not appear to have an impact on trade liberalization in the Sub-Saharan African countries', while there was some evidence that participation in RTAs 'may have promoted trade liberalization in some countries', such as Zambia. However, what was equally important, if not more, was 'the authorities' commitment to trade reform'.

The analyses of selected trade policy instruments in Section 4 below, together with trade policy summary reform narratives of individual African members in Annex 11.2, suggest that regional integration has been influential as the driving force for the evolution of trade policy and the extent of associated trade liberalization in Africa during the last two decades. Today, on average, African members belong to 2 or more RTAs/ RECs within the region that may be at different levels of integration. In addition, they also maintain or are negotiating economic partnership agreements (EPAs) or free trade agreements (FTAs) with the European Union, for Sub-Saharan and North Africa, respectively (see Annex 11.3). Mauritania, Morocco and Tunisia are the only African countries that do not belong to any RTAs, but they do belong to two of the eight African Union RECs,[11] as well as EPAs/FTAs with the European Union. While the RTAs within the region have provided platforms to facilitate tariff reduction and harmonization of non-tariff measures (NTMs) and regulations among members, to a degree, concerns are expressed about the complexity and overlapping nature of these agreements, in terms of tariff structures, preferences, rules of origin and customs procedures

---

[11] The African Union commission officially recognizes only eight RECs as building blocks for continental integration namely; Arab Maghreb Union (UMA), Common Market for Eastern and Southern Africa (COMESA), Community of Sahel–Saharan States (CEN–SAD), East African Community (EAC), Economic Community of Central African States (ECCAS), Economic Community of West African States (ECOWAS), Intergovernmental Authority on Development (IGAD) and Southern African Development Community (SADC). See Annex 11.4. See more at: http://www.au.int/en/ organs/recs#sthash.Z4ThZVT5.dpuf.

(see Annex 11.4 for detailed descriptions of major RTAs in Africa). In recent years, in order to rationalize and streamline these overlapping agreements, a Continental Free Trade Area[12] and a Tripartite Agreement that would merge the East African Community (EAC), Southern African Development Community (SADC) and the Common Market for Eastern and Southern Africa (COMESA) have been launched (see Chapter 12 by Karingi, Pesce and Mevel in this book). In the WTO, in order to accommodate the growing importance of RTAs and provide broader regional economic contexts, the TPRs of individual African members have been increasingly grouped for regional communities and conducted as integrated regional reviews (see Annex 11.1).[13]

4 Evolution of Selected Trade Policy Instruments

This section analyses the trends in selected trade policy instruments used by African members. The following instruments are examined:

- tariff and other border taxes;
- other import measures affecting trade in goods, including customs procedures (CVA, PSI), import restrictions and trade remedies;
- other measures affecting trade in goods, including state trading and export measures; and,
- trade in services.

The selection of trade policy instruments in this section does not represent the entirety of trade policy instruments used by African members; indeed, there is greater scope to increase the coverage in future studies.

---

[12] As part of the African Union's efforts for continental integration, the 18th Ordinary Session of the Assembly of Heads of State and Government of the African Union, which was held in Addis Ababa, Ethiopia in January 2012 took a decision (Assembly/AU/Dec.394 (XVIII) to establish a Continental Free Trade Area (CFTA) by an indicative date of 2017. See more at http://au.int/en/sites/default/files/newsevents/workingdocuments/12582-wd-update _on_the_report_on_the_continental_free_trade_en.pdf.

[13] TPR joint reviews include: the Southern African Customs Union (SACU, i.e. Botswana, Lesotho, Namibia, South Africa and Swaziland in 1998, 2003, 2009 and 2015); the East African Community (EAC, i.e. Kenya, Tanzania and Uganda in 2006 and all five members of the EAC in 2012); the Western African Economic and Monetary Union (WAEMU; selected two to three members of the WAEMU in 2003, 2004, 2009 and 2012); the Central African Economic and Monetary Community (CEMAC; Cameroon and Gabon in 2007, and all five WTO members of the CEMAC in 2013); and the Common Market for Eastern and Southern Africa (COMESA, Djibouti and Mauritius in 2014).

Evolution of Tariff Regimes (Including Other Duties and Charges)

Tariffs

One of the main messages emerging from the TPRs during the period under study is that tariffs are one of the main instruments for African trade policy. Due to the nature of data, tariffs are the only trade policy instrument that the study has been able to analyse and evaluate over the period of twenty years across African members. However, the data availability of tariffs for African members is limited before 2002, when less than a half of them are available in the sample (see Annex 11.5 for the availability of tariff information for African members). While all WTO members are required to submit tariff data annually to the WTO Secretariat, out of forty-three African members, only twenty-nine have ten or more years of data available; and even among these, nine countries have three or more years of data missing within the available range. Hence there are tariff data limitations for the analysis.

Figure 11.1 indicates that the simple average of tariffs was reduced from 16.4 per cent in 2002 to 11.4 per cent in 2014, based on the available tariff information on forty-three African members from the WTO IDB. Tariff protection was consistently higher on agricultural products than on non-agricultural products. Overall, agriculture is the most protected sector, with rates usually higher than those in place for non-agricultural products, excluding petroleum products. The highest protection is given to essential foods such as wheat flour, vegetables, meat offal, fish, fruits, milk, coffee, tea, nuts and spices. Numerous TPR reports suggest that the rationale for these high tariffs was to protect and encourage domestic

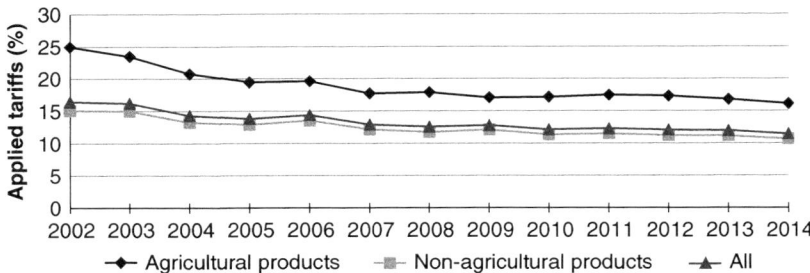

Figure 11.1   Evolution of applied tariffs in Africa, 2002–14, based on available data
Source: Author's construction from WTO IDB

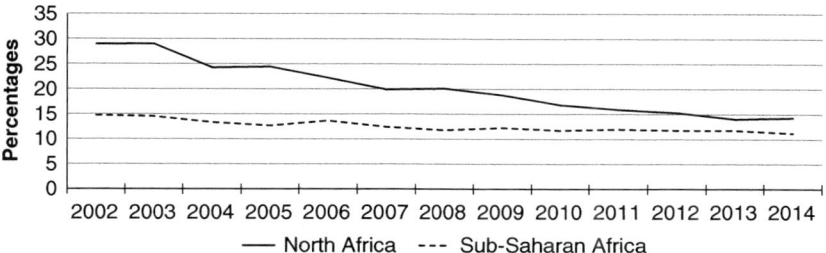

Figure 11.2   Evolution of simple averages of applied tariffs – North and Sub-Saharan Africa, 2002–14, based on available data
Source: Author's construction from WTO IDB

production, although there have been cases where local agro-food producers who use these products as inputs complain that this tariff structure drives up their production costs.[14]

Manufacturing is the sector subject to the second-greatest levels of protection from external competition. The analysis shows that the highest tariffs are on alcoholic beverages and spirits, tobacco, fabrics, clothing and other textile articles and fisheries. The extractive industries (mining/quarrying) are the least-protected sectors, although many of them are subject to export duties (see the section on the 'Evolution of trade policy instruments affecting trade', below). In most countries, a broad range of essential items which are duty-free include pharmaceutical goods, agricultural equipment, fertilizers, electricity, certain mineral fuels, most capital goods and educational materials. The tariff structure for African members displays either positive escalation, whereby duty rates increased with the degree of processing, or a mixed escalation, with negative escalation from the first stage of processing to semi-finished products and then positive escalation to fully processed goods.

Figure 11.2 compares the level of simple average tariff protection in North and Sub-Saharan Africa for the same period. North Africa, which, for the purposes of this study, consists of Egypt, Morocco and Tunisia, three of the six leading trading nations on the African continent, had higher levels of effective tariff protection; this was particularly true in 2002 when the tariff protection was twice as high in North Africa as in Sub-Saharan Africa, i.e. 28.9 per cent compared to 14.7 per cent, mainly due to high protection in the former's agricultural sector. However, such a gap was significantly narrowed over time, although higher tariffs

---

[14] For instance, see Madagascar TPR 2015.

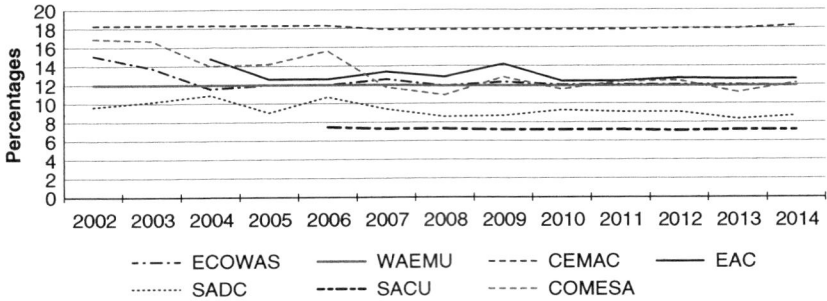

Figure 11.3 Evolution of simple averages of applied tariffs of regional groups in Africa, 2002–14, based on available data
Source: Author's construction from WTO IDB

remained on agricultural products in North Africa. Figure 11.3 (as well as Annex 11.6) shows the evolution of simple averages of applied tariffs among regional groups for the same period. All the regional groups with varying degrees of integration demonstrated a downward trend of tariff protection between 2002 and 2014, with larger drops between 2002 and 2006. In 2014, SACU was the most liberal among the regional groups in Africa at 7.2 per cent, followed by SADC at 8.7 per cent, the Economic Community of West African States (ECOWAS) and the Western African Economic and Monetary Union (WAEMU) at 11.9 per cent, the Common Market for Eastern and Southern Africa (COMESA) at 12.2 per cent, the East African Community (EAC) at 12.6 per cent and the Central African Economic and Monetary Community (CEMAC) at 18.3 per cent, bearing in mind the overlapping nature of memberships of some of these groupings.

Table 11.2 provides the tariff information for forty-three African members for the 1995–2015 period, based on combined data from the IDB and TPRs. Among African WTO members, Mauritius stands out in its tariff liberalization, as the simple average tariff rate was reduced from 29 per cent in 1995 to 0.8 per cent in 2015; it is interesting to note that Mauritius is one of the most competitive economies on the African continent. While the tariff information before 2002 is limited, large African trading members[15] maintained tariff protection at high rates in

---

[15] In 2014, the ten largest merchandise exporters were (1) Nigeria, (2) South Africa, (3) Algeria, (4) Angola, (5) Egypt, (6) Morocco, (7) Libya, (8) Tunisia, (9) Ghana and (10) Côte d'Ivoire.

Table 11.2 Tariff information of African members, 1995-2015

Tariff information of African members,

1995–2015	1995	1996	1997	1998	1999	2000	2001	2002	2003	2004	2005	2006	2007	2008	2009	2010	2011	2012	2013	2014	2015
SACU*			**15.0**			**12.8**	**12.0**	**11.4**						**8.1**	**8.1**					**7.6**	**7.2**
Botswana								5.9			7.5		7.3	7.3	7.2	7.2	7.2	7.1	7.2	7.2	7.2
Lesotho											7.5		7.3	7.3	7.2	7.2	7.2	7.1	7.2	7.2	7.2
Namibia								5.9			7.5		7.5	7.3	7.3	7.2	7.2	7.1	7.2	7.2	7.2
South Africa		13.1	9		6.1	5.9	5.8	5.9	5.6		7.5		7.3	7.3	7.2	7.2	7.2	7.1	7.2	7.2	7.2
Swaziland								5.9			7.5		7.3	7.3	7.2	7.2	7.2	7.1	7.2	7.2	7.2
EAC																					
Kenya					18.0		15.4	14.8		14.8	12.6	12.6	13.2	13.2	13.2	12.5	12.5	12.7	12.6	12.6	12.6
Tanzania					16.1				13.5		12.6	12.6	13.6	12.5	12.5	12.5	12.4	12.7	12.6	12.6	12.6
Uganda	17.1						9.0				12.6				12.5	12.4	12.4	12.7	12.6	12.6	12.6
Burundi								31.2	23.5			19.8	17.5	16.3	15.6	12.4	12.4	12.7	12.6	12.6	12.6
Rwanda						10		19.2	17.4	18.0					18.7	12.4	12.4	12.7	12.6	12.6	12.6
CEMAC																					
Cameroon	18.8					18.3	18.1	18.3	18.3	18.3	18.1	18.3	19.1	17.9	17.9	17.9	17.9	18.0	18.0	18.2	
Central African Republic						18.3		18.3	18.3	18.3	18.3	18.1	18.2	17.9	17.9	17.9	17.9	18.0	18.0	18.0	
Chad								18.3	18.3	18.3	18.3	18.3	18.4	17.9	17.9	17.9	17.9		18.0	18.0	
Congo								18.3	18.3	18.3	18.3	18.3	17.9	17.9	17.9	17.9	17.9		18.0	18.1	
Gabon						18.0	18.3	18.3	18.3	18.3	18.3	18.3	18.2	17.9	17.9	17.9	17.9	17.8	18.1	17.7	

Table 11.2 (*cont.*)

Tariff information of African members, 1995–2015

	1995	1996	1997	1998	1999	2000	2001	2002	2003	2004	2005	2006	2007	2008	2009	2010	2011	2012	2013	2014	2015
WAEMU																					
Benin			13.7						12	12	12	12	12	11.9	11.9	11.9	11.9	11.9	11.9	11.9	12.1
Burkina Faso			31.1						12	12	12	12	12	11.9	11.9	11.9	11.9	11.9	11.9	11.9	12.1
Côte d'Ivoire									12	12	12	12	12	11.9	11.9	11.9	11.9	11.9	11.9	11.9	12.1
Guinea-Bissau					11.2				12	12	12	12	12	11.9	11.9	11.9	11.9	11.9	11.9	11.9	12.1
Mali		16.8	16.8	16.8					12	12	12	12	12	11.9	11.9	11.9	11.9	11.9	11.9	11.9	12.1
Niger			20.0					12.1	12	12	12	12	12	11.9	11.9	11.9	11.9	11.9	11.9	11.9	12.1
Senegal	23.5							14.7	12	12	12	12	12	11.9	11.9	11.9	11.9	11.9	11.9	11.9	12.1
Togo		12	13.3	13.4	13.4	12	12	12	12	12	12	12	12	11.9	11.9	11.9	11.9	11.9	11.9	11.9	12.1
ECOWAS only																					
Cabo Verde												10.3	10.3	10.3	10.3	10.1	10.1	10	10	10	9.9
Gambia						13.6			12.9				19.1		18.7	14.1	14.1	14.1	14.1	14.1	
Ghana				16.4		14.7	13.2	13.2	13.2				13.1	13.1	13.1	13.1	13.1	13.1	13	12.9	12.1
Guinea				16.4						14.9					11.8		12.0	11.9			
Nigeria		24.4	24.5	23.5	26	26.1	26	29.1	29.0		11.9	12		12	12.0	11.7	11.7		11.7	11.9	12.8
Sierra Leone										14.9		13.5			11.9			11.9			
OTHERS																					
Angola										8.8	7.4	7.4			7.4	7.4	7.4	7.4	7.4	11.5	11.5
Egypt				28.1	29	29	27.7	27.7	27.4	20.0	20.2	20.2	17.7	17.6	17.4	17.4	17.4	17.4	17.2	17.4	17.4
Djibouti				30.7	30.7					28.3		30.3			21		21.1	21.1			
Democratic Republic of the Congo															11.9	11.3				10.9	
Madagascar		6.6	6.6	6.2		5.6	4.6	5.1	4.6	3.5	12.5	13.2	12.4	12.4	11.6	11.6	11.6	11.8	11.7	11.7	
Malawi			21.0	16.0	13.4	13.4	13.6	14.0	13.2				13.1	13.1	13.1	12.7	12.7	12.8		12.6	
Mauritius	29.0	28.5		26.4	26.4	18.8	19.1	17.6	17.5		6.2	3.1	3.2	1.1	1.1	1.1	0.9	0.9	0.8	0.8	0.8

Country																
Mauritania						10.6	10.6		9.7	11.8	9.7	9.7	9.7	12.1	10	10	12
Mozambique							13.8		10.1	10.1	10.1	10.3	10.1	10	10	10.1	10.1
Morocco	23.5	30.5	33.9	32.1	31	31	33.4	30.5	26.1	24.3	22.2	23.8	18.1	16.9	14.4	13.1	11.2	11.2
Seychelles				32.1													11.5	2.9
Tunisia					31.9		28.7	29.2	33.0	32.0	21.4	20.9	16.2	15.9	15.4	13.8	14.1
Zambia	13.6				14		13.4	13.9	13.9	14	13.8	13.7	13.4	13.4	13.5	13.8	13.2	13.5
Zimbabwe	18.9	19.2	20.2	21.4	18.5	16.9	16.9		14.5	13.9	13.9	13.7	13.9	13.5	13.5	13.5	10.9

Source: WTO Integrated Database (IDB) and TPRs.

Notes: The above table contains the data extracted from the IDB; where the information is not available in the IDB, the tariff information contained in the TPRs is used. In most cases, with the exception of SACU countries, the tariff information in the IDB and the TPRs is identical or approximately the same.

* There are discrepancies between tariff information from the TPR and the IDB for SACU, especially for the period 1997–2002. These discrepancies are due to the existence of non-*ad valorem* rates (specific, mixed, compound, formula duties and their combinations) in the SACU, or South African tariffs which were not calculated in the IDB. In TPRs, *ad valorem* equivalents (AVEs) are calculated and included in the tariff analysis (for additional details, see the South African TPR 1998).

the 1990s (e.g. 23.6 per cent in Côte d'Ivoire in 1994; 28–29 per cent in Egypt in 1998–99; 17.0 per cent in Ghana in 1991; 23.5–33.9 per cent in Morocco in 1995–99; 24.5–26.0 per cent in Nigeria in 1996–99; 31.9 per cent in Tunisia in 2000); by 2014, most of these countries came closer to the African average of 11.4 per cent, except Egypt, for which the simple average rate stood at 17.4 per cent in 2014 (and 2015). In 2014, the highest tariff protection among all African members was afforded by Djibouti, with the simple average rate of 21 per cent in 2014 (down from 30.7 per cent in 1998, the earliest data available). This is also one of the three members (along with Mauritania and Mauritius) which afford higher tariff protection to non-agricultural products than agricultural products in the continent, as shown in Table 11.3. Table 11.3 also shows that, in spite of tariff liberalization over the last two decades, Africa's tariff protection is still far higher than that of other developing countries, as the average tariff rates were 11.4 per cent for African members and 8.3 per cent for developing countries in 2014.

Tariff liberalization in Africa was undertaken unilaterally and regionally. Tariff information contained in Table 11.2 for all African members between 1995 and 2015 indicates that the introduction of a common external tariff (CET) in the regional groups, i.e. CEMAC in 1998, WAEMU in 2000 and EAC in 2005, contributed to reductions in their tariff regimes, as the CET rate in each group was consolidated at a lower rate for all members of the group. For instance, in the EAC, the average individual rates of Kenya (18.0 per cent), Tanzania (16.2 per cent) and Uganda (9.0 per cent) in 1999 to 2001 were unified at 12.9 per cent with the introduction of a CET in 2005, which was later joined by Burundi (23.5 per cent in 2003) and Rwanda (18.0 per cent in 2004) in 2009. Similarly, the simple average rates of the eight-member WAEMU, ranging from 13.7 per cent to 31.1 per cent in 1995 to 1999, were unified to a lower simple average of 12.1 per cent, with the introduction of a WAEMU CET in 2000. Moreover, together with tariff reduction, the tariff structure was also simplified as the number of tariff bands was consolidated at a lower number for all. It is important to note, however, that while the introduction of a CET harmonized and lowered tariffs in these regional groups, there was little further reduction on tariffs after the CET adoption. For instance, in 2015, the simple average rate of the EAC CET was 12.8, only 0.1 per cent lower than that of 2005, while the WAEMU CET was on average at 11.9 per cent, only 0.2 per cent lower than in 2000. Interestingly, with the introduction of the ECOWAS CET along with an additional tariff band, the average rate went up to

Table 11.3 *Tariff profile and binding coverage of African and WTO members in for the years of most recent data, 2014–15*

No.	Member	Most-favoured nation applied rate (%)			Final bound rate (%)			Binding coverage (%)	
		All products	Agricultural products	Non-agricultural products	All products	Agricultural products	Non-agricultural products	All products	Non-agricultural products
SACU									
1	Botswana	7.6	8.5	7.4	18.7	37.9	15.7	96.1	95.5
2	Lesotho	7.6	8.5	7.4	78.3	199.0	60.1	100	100
3	Namibia	7.6	8.5	7.4	19.0	40.4	15.7	96.1	95.5
4	South Africa	7.6	8.4	7.4	19.0	40.4	15.7	96.1	95.5
5	Swaziland	7.6	8.5	7.4	19.0	40.4	15.7	96.1	95.5
EAC									
6	Burundi	12.8	20.2	11.5	67.1	94.4	26.5	22.0	10.2
7	Kenya	12.8	20.3	11.5	95.1	100.0	57.0	14.8	2.0
8	Rwanda	12.7	20.0	11.5	89.4	74.0	91.7	100	100
9	Tanzania	12.8	20.3	11.5	120.0	120.0	120.0	13.3	0.3
10	Uganda	12.7	20.2	11.5	73.1	77.5	51.0	15.7	3.0
CEMAC									
11	Cameroon	18.2	22.5	17.5	79.9	80.0	67.1	13.3	0.2
12	Central Africa Republic	18.0	21.8	17.4	36.1	30.0	37.7	62.0	56.2
13	Chad	18.0	21.8	17.4	79.9	80.0	76.3	13.4	0.4

Table 11.3 (*cont.*)

No.	Member	Most-favoured nation applied rate (%)			Final bound rate (%)			Binding coverage (%)	
		All products	Agricultural products	Non-agricultural products	All products	Agricultural products	Non-agricultural products	All products	Non-agricultural products
14	Congo	18.1	22.2	17.4	27.2	30.0	15.1	16.2	3.5
15	Gabon	17.7	21.5	17.1	21.2	59.7	15.4	100	100
WAEMU									
16	Benin	11.9	14.6	11.5	28.3	61.8	11.3	39.1	29.9
17	Burkina Faso	11.9	14.6	11.5	42.1	98.1	13.8	39.1	30.0
18	Côte d'Ivoire	11.9	14.6	11.5	11.1	14.9	8.5	33.3	23.3
19	Guinea-Bissau	11.9	14.6	11.5	48.7	40.1	50.0	97.7	97.4
20	Mali	11.9	14.6	11.5	28.5	59.2	13.4	39.9	30.9
21	Niger	11.9	14.6	11.5	44.7	85.7	38.2	96.7	96.2
22	Senegal	11.9	14.6	11.5	30.0	29.8	30.0	100	100
23	Togo	11.9	14.6	11.5	80.0	80.0	80.0	13.9	0.9
ECOWAS only									
24	Cabo Verde	10.1	12.2	9.8	15.8	19.3	15.2	100.0	100.0
25	Ghana	12.9	17.2	12.2	92.5	97.1	39.7	14.3	1.3
26	Guinea	11.9	14.1	11.5	20.1	39.7	10.1	38.7	29.5
27	Nigeria	11.9	15.6	11.4	118.3	150.0	49.2	19.1	7.0
28	The Gambia	14.1	16.9	13.7	102.8	104.6	60.5	13.7	0.7
29	Sierra Leone	11.9	15.3	11.4	47.4	40.4	48.5	100	100

OTHERS

#									
30	Angola	11.4	23.2	9.5	59.2	52.8	60.1	100	100
31	Democratic Republic of the Congo	10.9	10.9	10.9	96.1	98.1	95.8	100	100
32	Djibouti	20.9	14.3	21.8	41.3	50.4	39.9	100	100
33	Egypt	16.8	60.6	9.5	36.8	98.3	27.5	99.3	99.2
34	Madagascar	11.7	14.6	11.3	27.3	30.0	25.2	30.0	19.5
35	Malawi	12.6	18.8	11.5	74.7	121.2	42.2	31.9	21.6
36	Mauritania	12.0	11.1	12.2	19.8	38.1	10.6	39.3	30.1
37	Mauritius	1.0	0.9	1.1	97.8	119.6	27.6	17.2	4.7
38	Morocco	11.2	27.4	8.7	41.3	54.4	39.3	100	100
39	Mozambique	10.1	13.8	9.5	97.4	100.0	22.8	13.6	0.5
40	Seychelles	2.9	2.4	5.6	9.5	16.9	8.3	100	100
41	Tunisia	14.1	24.6	12.3	57.9	116.0	40.8	58.0	51.6
42	Zambia	13.5	18.9	12.6	106.0	123.3	44.0	16.8	4.2
43	Zimbabwe	16.3	23.7	15.0	88.0	141.1	10.9	22.2	10.4
	Africa	**11.4**	**15.9**	**10.4**	**56.0**	**74.0**	**38.2**	**56.5**	–
	Developed	**4.7**	**18.6**	**2.4**	**10.4**	**40.1**	**5.8**	**99.0**	–
	Developing	**8.3**	**13.3**	**7.5**	**31.7**	**48.8**	**26.6**	**87.5**	–
	LDCs	**11.5**	**14.8**	**11.0**	**59.2**	**72.8**	**42.2**	**60.5**	–

Source: WTO Integrated Data Base.

12.3 per cent in 2015, slightly higher than the 2014 WAEMU CET of 11.9 per cent.[16]

Despite the two decades of a downward trend in tariffs, the complexity of tariff regimes of African members is frequently cited as an impediment to the transparency and predictability at borders (see Box 11.1). In this regard, the existence of numerous tariff exemptions and concessions was one area of concern in peer review assessments. Exemptions and concessions compromise the transparency and predictability of any trade regime by opening the window for abuse by the officials who grant these concessions and exemptions. This has led to a significant amount of revenue being foregone, ranging from 24.7 per cent to 40.9 per cent for the period of 2009–14 for Angola (TPR 2015), 25 per cent for Ghana (TPR 2014), one-third to 50 per cent for Guinea in 2002 and 2010 (TPR 2006, 2011), 42 per cent for Tanzania in 1999 (TPR 2000), and in West Africa, CFAF 3 billon for Burkina Faso, CFAF 35.8 billon for Mali in 2003, CFAF 14.8 billion in Niger and CFAF 56 billon in Senegal in the period of 2002–03. Apart from these exemptions and concessions, the tariff structure of African members is largely dominated by *ad valorem* rates, which are more transparent than other types of duties. However, peer review commentary has repeatedly expressed concerns about the complexity of the SACU tariff regime, which is characterized by the use of different types of duties, including *ad valorem*, specific, mixed, compound, formula duties and their combinations, although the share of these non-*ad valorem* rates decreased from 25 per cent in the 1998 TPR to 3.8 per cent in the 2015 TPR. Another concern that emerged in the peer reviews that adds to the complexity of tariff regimes is the application of other duties and charges (ODCs).

Tariff Bindings

Tariff binding is one of the most powerful expressions of transparency and predictability, which are amongst the core principles enshrined in the GATT and WTO Agreements. This is also a unique feature of WTO tariff negotiations which is not found in other trade agreements. In the case of Africa, every TPR emphasizes the value of tariff binding as an instrument to improve transparency and predictability of the trade regime and to provide credibility for trade reforms in African economies in spite of their opening-up measures. However, as Figure 11.4 illustrates, there is a large overhang (or 'water') between applied and bound rates.

---

[16] TPR Cabo Verde (2015)

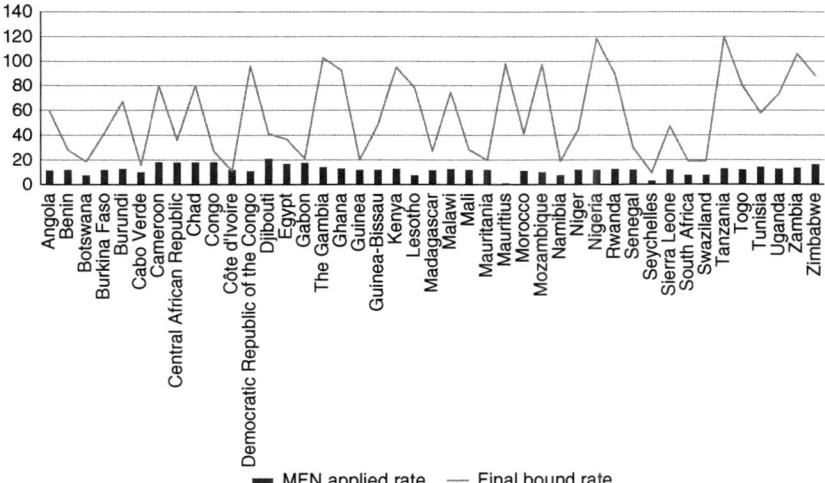

Figure 11.4   Tariff profiles of 43 African members in 2014 – tariff overhang (latest available year)

Table 11.3 shows the tariff profiles and binding coverage of all African members in 2014. Even in comparison with other developing WTO members, Africa's low binding coverage and its tariff overhang stand out. In 2014, the average binding coverage of forty-three African members stood at 56.5 per cent, while that of developing countries was 87.5 per cent. The gap between the applied and bound rates was five times for Africa, compared to 3.8 times for developing countries, leaving a huge scope for tariff increases and possible reversals by policy-makers, at their discretion.

It is interesting to note that there is a high degree of heterogeneity in the binding coverage of individual members throughout Africa (Table 11.3). Such divergent rates are evident regardless of the size of the economy even when they are within the same regional groups. As shown in Table 11.3, while sixteen members, including Morocco and seven LDCs, had a binding coverage of 100 per cent, the other fourteen members, including Ghana, Kenya, Mauritius, Nigeria and nine LDCs, had a binding coverage of less than 25 per cent. The latter is a result of very low levels of binding on non-agricultural products: Cameroon (0.2 per cent), Chad (0.4 per cent), Congo (3.0 per cent), The Gambia (0.7 per cent), Ghana (1.3 per cent), Kenya (2.0 per cent), Mauritius (4.7 per cent), Mozambique (0.5 per cent), Nigeria

(7.0 per cent), Tanzania (0.3 per cent), Togo (0.9 per cent), Uganda (3.0 per cent) and Zambia (4.2 per cent). The binding coverage for agricultural products is 100 per cent for all African members, as a result of the tariffication process of all agricultural products during the Uruguay Round. Wide variations exist within regional groups, both for the level of final bound rates and binding coverage, except in the case of SACU, where all members (except Lesotho, which is an LDC) have almost identical tariff concessions.

Despite the overall low tariff binding coverage and the wide gap between applied and bound rates, the TPRs observed several instances of binding breach whereby applied rates exceeded bound rates. Table 11.4 indicates that the incidence of tariff breach was observed for twenty-nine African members during their TPRs, and in most cases, such breaches were not redressed between reviews. A tariff binding breach involves, in many cases, a small number of tariff lines (TLs), but in some cases it involves up to 40 per cent of TLs for Gabon and 18.5–35 per cent of TLs for Morocco, where both members have 100 per cent binding coverage; and 27 per cent of the bound TLs for Benin, Burkina Faso and Mali (2002 and 2010), which accounted for about 40 per cent of their total TLs. In the latter case, their tariff bindings reflect the concessions inherited from the colonial era, which France had made on behalf of French colonies in West Africa. The issue is being addressed as part of the harmonization of tariff bindings by WAEMU members. Also, Gabon has recently made efforts to rectify its tariff concessions through GATT Article XXVIII. In the case of the SACU members, non-compliance with binding commitments was due to their tariff concessions expressed in *ad valorem* rates in the Goods Schedules, while they imposed non-*ad valorem* duties.

Other Duties and Charges

In addition to tariffs, African members levy other duties and charges (ODCs) on imports at the borders. ODCs are a source of government revenue as well as a tool to protect domestic production, and therefore, like customs duties, they directly affect access to markets. Depending on the country, ODCs consist of multiple taxes and duties, either across the board or on specific products. ODCs are levied nationally or regionally; while regional community ODCs are imposed in Central and West Africa, there is no harmonization of nationally imposed ODCs in the RTAs/RECs, except in East Africa. Annex 11.7 provides a non-exhaustive

Table 11.4 *Incidence of breach of tariff/ODC commitments and of national treatment in internal taxation identified in TPR Reports, 1995–2015*

| | Member | Binding breach | | National treatment breach – internal taxation |
		Tariff commitments	ODC commitments	
1	Angola	X	–	–
2	Benin	X	–	–
3	Botswana	X	–	–
4	Burkina Faso	X	–	X
5	Burundi	X	–	X
6	Cabo Verde	X	–	–
7	Cameroon	X	–	X
8	Central African Republic	X	X	–
9	Chad	X	X	X
10	Congo	X	X	X
11	Côte d'Ivoire	–	–	–
12	Democratic Republic of the Congo	–	–	–
13	Djibouti	X	–	–
14	Egypt	X	–	–
15	Gabon	X	–	X
16	The Gambia	–	–	–
17	Ghana	X	X	–
18	Guinea	X	–	–
19	Guinea-Bissau	–	–	–
20	Kenya	–	X	–
21	Lesotho	X	–	–
22	Madagascar	X	–	X
23	Malawi	–	–	–
24	Mali	X	X	–
25	Mauritania	X	–	–
26	Mauritius	X	X	X
27	Morocco	X	X	X
28	Mozambique	–		–

Table 11.4 (*cont.*)

| | Member | Binding breach | | National treatment breach – internal taxation |
		Tariff commitments	ODC commitments	
29	Namibia	X	–	–
30	Niger	–	–	–
31	Nigeria	–	–	X
32	Rwanda	X	X	–
33	Senegal	X	–	–
34	Sierra Leone	–	–	–
35	South Africa	X	–	X
36	Swaziland	X	–	–
37	Tanzania	X	X	–
38	Togo	–	–	–
39	Tunisia	–	–	–
40	Uganda	X	X	X
41	Zambia	–	–	–
42	Zimbabwe	X	–	X

Source: TPRs, various years.
Notes: "X" indicates an incidence whereby a beach, whether tariff or ODC commitments, or with respect to national treatment in internal taxation, was reported in the TPRs. "–" means no such incidence was reported.

list of ODCs levied by African members on imported goods, as identified during the TPRs. ODCs increase the complexity of customs border regimes and the level of protection beyond tariffs, which can be considerable. For instance, the additional level of protection provided by six types of ODCs in Ghana amounted to 5.4–6.4 per cent additional points to the tariff (TPR 2014). In the case of Madagascar, the simple average of customs tariffs including ODCs (specifically, import taxes) was 16.2 per cent in 2000, which was ten percentage points higher than the simple average tariff without ODCs of 6 per cent in the same year (TPR 2001). In the case of the Democratic Republic of Congo, which charges up to 113 ODCs, the largest number in Africa, the additional protection could amount to more than 30 per cent on the customs value of imported goods (TPR 2010).

ODCs are more extensively used in West and Central Africa than in the rest of Africa. Regionally levied ODCs include those by ECOWAS, WAEMU, CEMAC and the Economic Community of Central African States (ECCAS), charged at rates ranging from 0.05 per cent to 1 per cent on imports outside the regional blocs to support regional integration processes or directly fund the operation of the respective regional commissions and organizations. Many of the charges employed by Western and Central African members are labelled as administrative charges and mandatory contributions to national bodies/schemes, such as the Chamber of Commerce and Industry of Burkina Faso, a comprehensive import supervision scheme in Nigeria and an export development and agricultural investment fund in Ghana. Countries by the sea such as Benin and Nigeria have several port charges. Goods in transit through some countries are subjected to additional charges, including in Guinea-Bissau and Cameroon. In addition, a statistical fee of varying rates (0.2 per cent–3 per cent) charged on all imports, irrespective of origin, is prevalent in all these regions.

Southern Africa applies fewer charges, mostly as fuel duties and import surtaxes on particular products such as sugar and cement. Some temporary charges are justified by the infant industry argument, e.g. Article 26 of the SACU Agreement, which allows members to provide temporary protection to infant industries for a maximum of eight years through the imposition of additional duties. Under this provision, Botswana has levied an additional duty of 40 per cent on imports of ultra-heat-treated (UHT) milk since 2008, which is to be eliminated by end of 2016. In the case of the EAC, the Customs Management Act provides for ODCs applicable on imports, including overtime fees, fees for cautionary visits, licence fees, and fees for services to the public, which were harmonized at the regional level in 2012.

African members have bound ODCs in their Goods Schedules at varying degrees. Sixteen members bound ODCs at 0 per cent (with six members making exceptions on some tariff lines and selected items), seven members bound between 0.1 per cent and 10 per cent, nine members bound between 15 per cent and 30 per cent, and eleven members bound their ODCs between 50 per cent and 250 per cent. During TPRs, the incidence of breach in ODC commitments was registered for eleven African members (see Table 11.4). The members that bound their ODCs at 0 but imposed numerous charges as detailed above were in breach of ODC commitments, deepening the complexity of their customs regimes and, subsequently hampering trade flows.

Internal Taxation on Imports

Internal taxation on imports is covered by GATT Article III (National Treatment on Internal Taxation), as they have economic effects that are similar, if not equivalent, to tariffs and other border taxes. According to Daly (2011), however, over the past twenty years, direct and indirect taxation has become less distorting as far as trade and investment are concerned. This trend is largely the consequence of unilateral tax reforms, although WTO Agreements have played a role too.[17] Over the last decades, in Africa, the importance of revenues from tariffs and other border measures has decreased as tax reforms have focused on broadening the tax base, including through the introduction of value-added tax (VAT) and excise taxes.

VAT was introduced throughout Africa starting in the 1990s, replacing, *inter alia*, sales tax, turnover tax, general business tax and tourism accommodation tax.[18] The VAT rate ranges between 10 per cent and 18 per cent.[19] Excise duties are charged at specific or *ad valorem* rates on certain goods, including alcohol and non-alcoholic beverages, cigarettes and passenger motor vehicles.[20] Harmonization of VAT and excise taxes is underway in some RECs, such as WAEMU and SACU.[21] VAT, and, to

---

[17] Daly (2011)

[18] The general sales tax (South Africa TPR 1998), turnover tax (Guinea TPR 1999), general business tax (Togo TPR 1999), sales tax (Tanzania TPR 2000) and the tourism accommodation tax (Mozambique TPR 2001).

[19] Standard VAT rates are lower in Djibouti, Nigeria and Ghana, whereas Kenya, with 16 per cent, and Uganda, Tanzania and Rwanda apply 18 per cent. Throughout Africa, VAT exemptions are made on basic food and necessities include the following: deliveries of medicines and pharmaceuticals, unprocessed and staple food products, banking operations and insurance and reinsurance services, exports and international transport.

[20] These include, for instance, 5 per cent on perfumes and cosmetics, non-alcoholic beverages and fruit juices, soaps and detergents, spaghetti and noodles, telephone recharge cards, corrugated paper and paper board, and on toilet paper and cleansing tissues (Nigeria TPR 2011); 5 per cent on tobacco products and on alcoholic and non-alcoholic beverages, 5 per cent on malt drinks, 50 per cent on beer, 25 per cent on other alcoholic beverages, 20 per cent on mineral water and 140 per cent on tobacco products (Ghana TPR 2014); 7 per cent on mobile phone services, 10 per cent on saloon cars, station wagons and four-wheel-drive vehicles with engine capacity exceeding 2,000 cc, 120 per cent on plastic shopping bags and 30 per cent on mostly 'luxury goods', e.g. cigars, hard drinks (Tanzania TPR 2006).

[21] On VAT, the WAEMU regulations provide for a single rate of VAT of 18 per cent, with a provision of common exemptions. However, the SACU agreement does not provide for harmonization of VAT, and each SACU member continues to set its own VAT, ranging from 14 per cent in Lesotho, South Africa and Swaziland, 12 per cent in Botswana and 15 per cent in Namibia. On excise taxes, in WAEMU, they are mandatorily imposed on tobacco, tobacco products, alcoholic and non-alcoholic beverages (excluding water); in

some extent, excise taxes, constitute a large source of government revenue in Africa. VAT is generally neutral with respect to international trade, as it is imposed on domestically produced and imported goods alike. However, in some cases, excise taxes have been used as *de facto* tariffs to discriminate against imports.

As GATT Article III stipulates that WTO members must not accord discriminatory treatment between imports and 'like' domestic products (with the exception of the imposition of tariffs, which is a border measure), the majority of the excise duties and VAT are applied non-discriminatorily. However, there have been instances where internal taxes on particular products have not been applied equally on imported and domestic goods. While the incidence of national treatment breach – whereby domestically produced goods and imported goods are taxed at different rates – has been observed for fourteen members (see Table 11.4), especially in the 1990s, it has reduced over time.

Evolution of Other Selected Trade Policy Instruments Affecting Imports

While tariffs and related measures serve as the main trade instrument for African members, other measures that affect imports are widely used, as covered in the WTO Secretariat's reports of the TPRs. These measures include:

- customs procedures and valuation, including preshipment inspection (PSI);
- import prohibitions, restrictions and licensing; and
- anti-dumping, countervailing and safeguard measures.

These measures are described without being quantified, as in the case of tariffs, and the level of restrictions cannot be compared over time or across members. Thus, this section provides a broad overview of developments of the usage of these instruments by African members.

Customs Procedures and Valuation, Including PSI

Despite Africa's efforts in opening trade, the costs of trading remain high on the continent. The Trading Across Borders data of the World Bank

addition, four products selected from a common list of nine products – coffee, cola, wheat flour, edible oils and fats, perfumery and cosmetics products, tea, arms and ammunition – may also be subject to excise duty. However, each member state is free to fix the excise duty within the ranges determined. In SACU, excise duties are already harmonized.

Table 11.5 *World Bank Doing Business – Trading Across Borders, 2015*

Region	Trading Across Borders DTF	Border compliance		Documentary compliance	
		Time to import: (hours)	Cost to import: (US$)	Time to import: (hours)	Cost to import: (US$)
East Asia and Pacific	68.67	59.3	420.8	69.7	148.1
Europe and Central Asia	82.42	23.2	202.4	27.4	108.1
Latin America and Caribbean	66.02	106.8	665.1	93.3	128.1
Middle East and North Africa	54.2	119.7	594.3	104.7	384.6
OECD high income	93.33	9.4	122.7	3.9	24.9
South Asia	57.75	113.9	652.8	108.1	349.3
Sub-Saharan Africa	48.96	159.6	643	123	351.3

Source: World Bank Doing Business 2015 at: http://www.doingbusiness.org/data/exploretopics/trading-across-borders

Doing Business 2015, in Table 11.5, which measures the time and cost, excluding tariffs, associated with three sets of procedures – documentary compliance, border compliance and domestic transport – within the overall process of exporting or importing a shipment of goods, ranked most African countries at the bottom of 189 countries in the dataset. For instance, for border compliance, the average time and cost of importing in Sub-Saharan Africa were 159.6 hours and US$ 643, respectively, and for documentary compliance, the average time and cost were 123 hours and US$ 351.3, respectively. These are highest in comparison to other regions of the world, in most instances. During the last two decades, nonetheless, trade facilitation measures to simplify customs procedures, such as automation and computerization, including the ASYCUDA (Automated SYstem for CUstoms DAta), have been introduced across Africa. In this regard, the new WTO Trade Facilitation Agreement, which focuses on the expeditious movement, release and clearance of goods, including goods in transit, can contribute to Africa's improvement of trade facilitation challenges. As of the end of 2015, eight African members (Côte d'Ivoire, Kenya, Lesotho, Mauritius, Botswana, Niger, Togo and Zambia) had ratified the TFA and deposited their Instruments of Acceptance. Additionally, seventeen African members have made notifications in Category A provisions that they would implement by the time the Agreement enters into force.

Before the adoption of the new TFA, the WTO Agreement on Customs Valuation provided WTO members with tools for improving customs procedures. TPRs track the efforts by African members to adopt the Customs Valuation Agreement (CVA), for which the timetable for implementation was for the year 2000. While the CVA-consistent legislation was introduced by many African members, its implementation has been challenging.[22] The WTO Secretariat's TPR reports have registered that reference prices or minimum prices were still being used for the valuation purpose of particular products in a number of countries, including Angola, Morocco, the Democratic Republic of the Congo, Mauritania and Sierra Leone, as well as members of the CEMAC, EAC and the WAEMU. Moreover, the notifications by African members are also lacking in this area.[23]

In the 1990s, preshipment inspection (PSI) was widely used by African members (see Annex 11.8), except in North and Southern Africa, as well as Mauritius, as a service provided by specialized private companies to verify shipment details such as price, quantity and quality of goods ordered overseas, in order to compensate for inadequacies in customs administration. With the introduction of customs and revenue reforms, PSI was gradually terminated in a number of African members, including EAC members (except Burundi), Ghana, Madagascar, Mozambique and Nigeria between 2001 and 2005.[24] However, according to the latest available TPRs, PSI is still being used by CEMAC members (except Gabon), WAEMU members (except Guinea-Bissau), the Democratic Republic of the Congo, Guinea, Mauritania and Sierra Leone, indicating a capacity deficit in verification of customs-related information. In some cases, such as in Guinea, the PSI had to be re-introduced after the initial removal. When the PSI is employed, a preshipment inspection fee is charged, in the range of 0.6–1.5 per cent of the customs values, often with

---

[22] At the end of 2015, no African member maintained delayed application of the provisions of the Agreement in accordance with the provisions of Article 20.1 of the Agreement.

[23] Sixteen African members (Angola, Benin, Burundi, Cameroon, Central African Republic, Chad, Congo, the Democratic Republic of the Congo, Djibouti, Ghana, Guinea-Bissau, Mauritania, Niger, Seychelles, Sierra Leone and Togo) were yet to make notifications on national legislation on customs valuation and responses to the checklist of issues.

[24] Djibouti and Zambia terminated the use of PSI in 1997 and 1998, respectively.

a fixed minimum charge, which is imposed on top of customs duties paid on imported goods.

Import Prohibitions, Restrictions and Licensing

The use of non-tariff measures, including quantitative restrictions (QRs), import prohibitions and restrictions, has been reduced over the last two decades. Most QRs were abolished as part of the IMF SAPs. Only few QRs on particular products were registered in the TPR Reports. These include potatoes (Guinea 1999; Mauritius 2001, 2008; Togo 1999), table salt (Mauritius 2001, 2008), black tea (South Africa 1998, Mauritius 2008), carpets and other craft products (Tunisia 2005), wheat flour (Congo 2006, 2013; Gabon 2013) and sugar (Gabon 2001, 2007, 2013; Congo 2006, 2013; Central Africa Republic 2007 and 2013), coffee (Central Africa Republic 2007) and poultry (Namibia 2015), and some of them have been converted to import licensing. It is worth noting that in 2015 Angola issued an executive decree to impose quotas for the import of certain products when domestic production covered over 60 per cent of domestic consumption, although the decree was yet to be implemented at the time of the TPR meeting in September 2015.[25] Tariff quotas on agricultural products have been used by only two African members, South Africa and Morocco, although the introduction of a tariff quota for horse mackerel was registered for Angola for the first time in its 2015 TPR. Among all African members, Nigeria maintains the largest list of import prohibitions, covering a number of food items, minerals and manufactured products, which have been used mostly to protect domestic industry, although it has been reduced steadily over the past few years.

Anti-Dumping, Countervailing and Safeguard Measures

At the time of the establishment of the WTO, many African members did not have legislation related to trade remedies: anti-dumping duties, countervailing duties and safeguards. Over the last two decades, only a few African members have developed legislation on anti-dumping, countervailing and safeguard measures. According to the latest notifications made to the relevant bodies in Table 11.6, only thirteen African members have anti-dumping legislation, eleven members have legislation

---

[25] Goods subject to import quota, in Joint Executive Decree No. 22/15 of 23 January 2015, were edible oil, wheat flour, maize flour, salt, rice, sugar, water, non-alcoholic aerated beverages, beer, juices and nectars, eggs, potatoes, garlic and onions (TPR 2015).

Table 11.6 *Trade remedies legislation, notified by African members, 2015*

	Member	Anti-dumping duty	Countervailing duty	Safeguards
1	Angola	X*	No notification	No notification
2	Benin	X*	X*	X*
3	Botswana	X*	No notification	X*
4	Burkina Faso	X*	X*	X*
5	Burundi	X*	X*	X*
6	Cabo Verde	No notification	No notification	No notification
7	Cameroon	X	X	X
8	Central African Republic	No notification	No notification	No notification
9	Chad	X*	X*	X*
10	Congo	X*	X*	X*
11	Côte d'Ivoire	X*	X*	X*
12	Democratic Republic of the Congo	No notification	No notification	No notification
13	Djibouti	No notification	No notification	No notification
14	Egypt	X	X	X
15	Gabon	X*	X*	X
16	The Gambia	X*	X*	X*
17	Ghana	X*	X*	X*
18	Guinea	X*	X*	X*
19	Guinea-Bissau	No notification	No notification	No notification
20	Kenya	X	X	X*
21	Lesotho	No notification	No notification	X*
22	Madagascar	X*	No notification	X*
23	Malawi	X	X*	X*
24	Mali	X*	X*	X*
25	Mauritania	No notification	No notification	No notification
26	Mauritius	X	X*	X*
27	Morocco	X	X	X
28	Mozambique	No notification	No notification	No notification
29	Namibia	X*	X*	X*
30	Niger	No notification	No notification	No notification
31	Nigeria	X	X	X*
32	Rwanda	No notification	No notification	No notification
33	Senegal	X	X	X*
34	Seychelles	No notification	No notification	No notification

Table 11.6 (*cont.*)

	Member	Anti-dumping duty	Countervailing duty	Safeguards
35	Sierra Leone	No notification	No notification	No notification
36	South Africa	X	X	X
37	Swaziland	X*	No notification	No notification
38	Tanzania	No notification	No notification	No notification
39	Togo	X*	X*	X*
40	Tunisia	X	X	X
41	Uganda	X	X	X*
42	Zambia	X	X	X
43	Zimbabwe	X	X	X*
	TOTAL Members with	**30**	**26**	**29**
	notification			7
	– With legislation (X)	13	11	
	– Without legislation (X*)	17	15	22
	Members without	**13**	**17**	**14**
	notification			

Note: * Notification of no relevant legislation. X Indicator incidence reported in TPRs.
Source: 2015 Annual Reports of the Committee on Anti-Dumping Practices (G/AD/22), the Committee on Subsidies and Countervailing Measures (G/SCM/146) and the Committee on Safeguards (G/SG/141).

on countervailing measures and seven on safeguards legislation, while seventeen, fifteen and twenty-two members notified that they did not have relevant respective legislation. About a third of the African members have yet to make any notification in this area. Only three African members, South Africa, Egypt and Morocco, have used trade remedies measures to date.

Evolution of Trade Policy Instruments Affecting Trade

State Trading

Annex 11.9 provides an evolution of state trading in Africa, based on information in the TPRs and notifications made to the WTO Working Party on State Trading Enterprises (STEs). Over the last two decades, several members have abolished the operations of STEs which were either privatized or whose monopoly or exclusive rights to purchase/sell and import/export were dismantled. Fourteen African members have notified the Working Party that no STEs within the meaning of Article XVII:4(a) of GATT 1994 are maintained. Twenty-two African members have not made notifications to date. Annex 11.9 also indicates some gaps in the information collected during the TPRs and submitted to the Working Group, i.e. while the operation of STEs was reported by the WTO Secretariat for members under review, those members notified that they did not maintain any STEs. The operation of remaining STEs can be found on agricultural products (beef, cocoa, coffee, tea, sugar, garlic, cotton, rice and tobacco), mining products (petroleum, diamonds) and pharmaceuticals; many of them also appear on the list of products subject to export taxes.

Export Taxes

Export measures, including export taxes and restrictions, were liberalized as part of the overall trade policy reform. Like import taxes, export taxes were levied mainly for revenue purposes, often on a wide range of products, but their significance declined over time. For instance, in Côte d'Ivoire, export taxes collected on certain raw materials amounted to 18 per cent of government revenues in 1994 (TPR 1995). In Ghana, the share of export taxes in total government revenue was 11.4 per cent in 1998, but was significantly decreased to 2.3 per cent in 2005 (TPR 2008). The remaining export taxes, which are imposed on a few selected products, including some that were re-introduced in recent years, are aimed at encouraging domestic processing and value-addition activities for primary commodities in the African economies involved. Annex 10 lists export taxes, duties and charges identified by the TPRs of African members.[26] The most commonly taxed products include agricultural products (e.g. cotton, coffee, cocoa, cashew nuts and livestock), fish, minerals (diamonds, gold and gemstones), petroleum, logs and woods, and hides and skin.

Unlike import duties, export taxes have not been harmonized among members of the RTAs, leaving each member to set rates. Nonetheless, as in the case for other duties and charges imposed at borders, Western and Central African members employ a greater number of duties, charges and

---

[26] Based on the last available information, seven (Burundi, Cabo Verde, Egypt, Malawi, Morocco, Rwanda and Swaziland) reported that they did not impose any export taxes, duties or charges.

fees often linked to the administration and services for their exports. These include a statistical fee (Angola, Benin, Chad, Mauritania, Niger), a preshipment/customs clearance fee (Cameroon, Madagascar, Nigeria), a computer/automation fee (Cameroon, CAR, Congo) and various taxes supporting specific boards/funds/communities (Burkina Faso, Chad, Cote d'Ivoire, Guinea, Guinea-Bissau, Uganda). In the case of Niger and Togo, a levy of 1–7 per cent is collected on the exports as an advance payment for income or profit tax on the exporters.

Evolution of Trade Policy Developments in Services

Throughout Africa, services constitute a large and growing share of contribution to GDP. The share of services in African output stood at 49 per cent in the period 2009–12, ranging from a low around 20–30 per cent (Congo, Nigeria, DRC and Sierra Leone) to a high around 70–80 per cent (Djibouti, Mauritius, Seychelles and South Africa).[27] During the same period, the services sector accounted for more than 50 per cent of real economic growth in more than a half of African countries.[28] The services sector accounted for 32.4 per cent of total employment in Africa during the same period, again with its importance at varying degrees. Moreover, the significance of services in the economy cannot be restricted to its contribution to GDP and employment, as they are necessary inputs for all stages along the production chains.

TPRs over the last two decades reveal that African members have made tremendous progress in opening up their services sectors. African economies are being strongly encouraged to pursue further liberalization to improve the efficiency not only of these sectors but also of other sectors, such as manufacturing and agriculture. Also, further opening of infrastructure-related services, particularly financial services, telecommunication and transport sectors, would allow better access to high-quality services which would benefit the whole economy. At the global level, however, Africa remains a marginal player in services exports and imports, accounting for 1.2 per cent and 0.7 per cent of the total services trade, respectively, in 2014.[29] Overall, Africa is a net importer of services, with only ten of the forty-three African members operating consistently as net services exporters.[30]

---

[27] UNCTAD (2015)   [28] UNCTAD (2015)   [29] WTO (2015b)
[30] These include Cabo Verde, Djibouti, Egypt, Kenya, Mauritius, Morocco, Namibia, Seychelles, Tunisia and Tanzania (UNCTAD, 2015).

Africa's liberalization efforts in services over the last two decades have been well documented and welcomed in the peer review. In the early 1990s, most of services sectors had been predominately in the hands of the state. Starting in the late 1990s, several service sectors, including banking, telecommunications and air transport sectors, were opened to the private sector, to both domestic and foreign investors, registering dynamic growth rates. However, the TPRs also reveal that the state, in some countries, has retained control, wholly or partly, over selected services sectors, including postal services, electricity and other transport services. Moreover, there have been very minimal instances of policy reversal, as in the case of Chad, where the role of the state was reinstated in the banking sector after the initial liberalization through the nationalization of the *Banque agricole et commercial*, increasing the government's stake in the equity of Commercial Bank of Chad (Chad TPR 2013). While most of the opening in services sectors has been unilateral in nature and led by national governments, it has also taken place at the regional level, albeit at a slower pace than for trade in goods. Financial services (banking and insurance) and air transport, as well as movement of natural persons, are some examples of regional approaches to the harmonization of services policies and services liberalization.

Table 11.7 shows that, compared to other regions, Africa made a low level of commitments in services schedules, with an average of twenty-seven services sub-sectors, as compared to the average for developing members of fifty-three, and for developed members, of 106. Figure 11.5 illustrates the country-specific number of services commitments: The Gambia and Sierra Leone have the highest at 110 and 107 sub-sectors,

Table 11.7 *Services profiles of African members*

	Average number of services commitments	Range (lowest/highest number of specific commitments in sub-sectors per schedule)
Developed	106	87 – 117
Developing	53	1 – 149
LDCs	24	1 – 111
Africa	27	1 – 110

Source: WTO Secretariat.

Note: Total number of services sub-sectors is approximately 160.

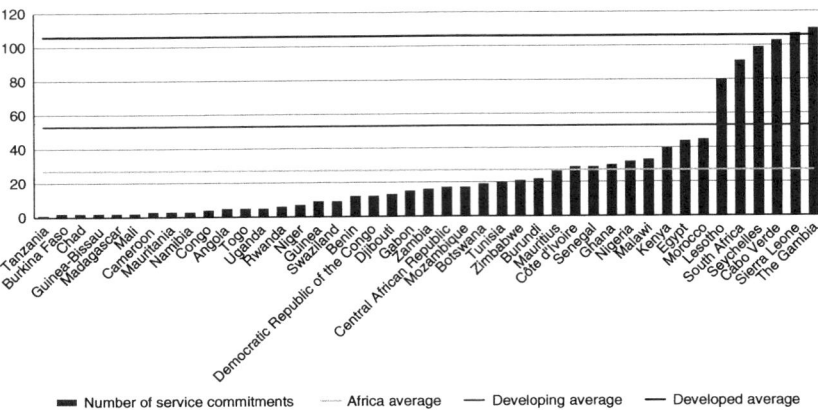

Figure 11.5   Services profile of African members
Source: WTO

respectively, even above the average for developed countries, while more than one-third of African WTO members have commitments in less than ten sub-sectors, including only one commitment for Tanzania (tourism and travel-related services). Yet the level of commitments did not reflect the actual regime that underwent autonomous liberalization during the last two decades. The peer reviews conclude with encouragement for African members to improve multilateral commitments under the General Agreement on Trade in Services (GATS) in order to increase transparency, predictability and credibility of their reforms, thus signalling their open services regimes for foreign investments.

The financial services sector, and in particular the banking sector, has undergone extensive liberalization throughout Africa over the past two decades. Both the banking and insurance sectors had been dominated by a few state-owned institutions in the 1990s. After deregulation (including deregulation through the granting of new licences and the privatization of government shares in banks and insurance companies), the number of institutions providing financial services increased dramatically. For instance, in Angola, the number of banks increased from a handful of state-owned banks to twenty-four, only three of which were government banks, in 2014, while the number of insurance companies increased from one state-owned insurer in 2000 to seventeen companies in 2014.[31] Along with deregulation, measures to strengthen regulatory oversight were

---

[31] Angola TPR 2015

introduced and tightened, particularly after the global financial crisis of 2008 to 2009, for instance, by increasing the minimum capital requirements (e.g. Ghana, Uganda)[32] and adopting the Basel III measures (e.g. Mauritius, Nigeria, South Africa, Tanzania).[33] In other, smaller African members, despite the deregulation in the sector, the markets are still dominated by a few institutions, particularly in the insurance sector, which remains under-developed in the African continent. Efforts towards harmonizing the licencing requirements are advanced in WAEMU and CEMAC, where only a single banking licence, issued by the Central Bank of West African States (BCEAO) and the Bank of Central African States (COBAC), respectively, is required for operation within the region. In the insurance sector, the Insurance Code of the Inter-African Insurance Conference (CIMA) has provided the regular framework for all direct terrestrial insurance for members of the WAEMU and CEMAC. Generally, foreign ownership is not heavily restricted, as a majority of African economies have no limits on foreign equity ownership in their commitments. Mauritius is especially open, as it allows foreign ownership of slightly over 50 per cent. South Africa, on the other hand allows only 10 per cent. Out of the forty-three African members, twenty-one have commitments in the banking sector, while sixteen made commitments in the insurance sector (see Annex 11.11). Eight African members (Egypt, Ghana, Kenya, Mauritius, Nigeria, Senegal, South Africa and Tunisia) participated in the 1997 negotiations for financial services.

The rapid growth of the telecommunications sector in Africa over the last two decades can be attributed to the advancement of global mobile technology and a massive wave of liberalization. This sector had originally been monopolized by the state but gradually opened up, first in mobile telephony and then in fixed telephony, to allow mergers and acquisitions, including those by foreign operators. Opening the sector promoted fierce competition which led to higher-quality services and lower rates that undercut (or put out of business) the uncompetitive, state-owned mobile companies. On average, there are at least three mobile telecom operators per African country, with Mobile Telephones Network (MTN), Vodafone, MobiNil, Vodacom, Airtel, Glo Mobile, Orange and Safaricom ranking the highest among the top mobile companies in Africa. In fixed telephony, the share of which has decreased in

---

[32] Ghana TPR 2014 and Uganda/EAC TPR 2012
[33] Mauritius TPR 2014, Nigeria TPR 2011, South Africa TPR 2015 and Tanzania/EAC 2012

light of the rapid growth in mobile telephony, the statutory monopoly ended in many if not most African members between 2003 and 2010, while the sector still remained in the statutory or *de facto* monopoly in some countries (e.g. Burundi, the Central African Republic, the Democratic Republic of the Congo, Djibouti, The Gambia, Malawi, Mozambique, Togo, Zambia and Zimbabwe).[34] It is worth noting that even where countries maintain state control on fixed telephony and telex services, other communications services, such as electronic mail, voice mail, online information and electronic data interchange (EDI), are mostly open to the market. Despite the significant liberalization measures undertaken by African members, fewer than half of them (i.e. eighteen) made commitments in the telecommunications services in their services schedules (see Annex 11.11). Eight African members (Egypt, Côte d'Ivoire, Ghana, Mauritius, Morocco, Senegal, South Africa and Tunisia) participated in the 1997 negotiations on market access for basic telecommunications service.

The transport sector (maritime services and air, rail and road transport) is of critical importance for a well-functioning economy, and is fundamental for trade facilitation. Maritime transport is the most dominant mode of transport for moving freight to and from Africa, accounting for more than 90 per cent of Africa's external trade. With a total coastline of 30,725 km, Africa has ninety major ports handling 6 per cent of global traffic, although ports in South Africa (Durban and Cape Town) and Egypt (Said and Alexandria) handle about 50 per cent of Africa's container traffic. Other major ports handling container traffic, including traffic for the sixteen landlocked African countries, include Morocco (Tangier), Tanzania (Dar es Salaam), Côte d'Ivoire (Abidjan), Angola (Port Luanda), Kenya (Mombasa) and Djibouti.[35] In several African economies, the provision of port services and cargo handling are

---

[34] Based on the latest information available in the TPRs, the statuary or *de facto* monopoly ended in Benin in 2005, Burkina Faso in 2005, Cote d'Ivoire in 2003, Egypt in 2005, Gabon in 2012, Ghana in 2008, Guinea in 2005, Kenya in 2007, Madagascar in 2008, Mali in 2004, Mauritius in 2003, Morocco in 2007, Niger in 2004, Rwanda in 2005, Senegal in 2004, Tanzania in 2005 and Togo in 2010. However, the privatization of the state operator was postponed indefinitely or suspended in Burundi (TPR 2012), Djibouti (TPR 2014), Malawi (TPR 2000) and Mozambique (TPR 2009) and remains in state monopoly in the Central African Republic (TPR 2013), the Democratic Republic of the Congo (TPR 2010), the Gambia (TPR 2010), Togo (WEAMU 2012), Zambia (TPR 2009) and Zimbabwe (TPR 2010).

[35] An extensive assessment of the status and usability of African ports is made in Foster and Briceño-Garmendia (2010).

dominated by the state-controlled authority (Cote d'Ivoire, Egypt, Kenya, South Africa and Tanzania) or through concession arrangements (Angola, Djibouti and Morocco).

The railway sector remains largely state-owned in most countries (e.g. South Africa, Morocco and Ghana).[36] However, in a bid to improve the efficiency of their railway system following operational management inadequacies, other countries initiated privatization efforts. For instance, Kenya Railways and Uganda Railways jointly signed a concession agreement in 2006 with a South Africa-led consortium which was later amended in 2010 when 49 per cent was acquired by the Egyptian Citadel Capital, and the Railway Systems of Zambia, which were purchased by a consortium of two South African companies.[37] In contrast, the Tanzania Railway Corporation, which had previously been privatized, performed very poorly, leading the government to buy it back in 2011, exhibiting a policy reversal.[38] Other privatization concessions include the Abidjan-Ouagadougou railway linking Côte d'Ivoire and Burkina Faso in 1995, and railways in Malawi, Gabon and Cameroon towards the close of the 1990s. The air transport sector, which had been largely state-dominated, has moved towards liberalization, albeit at a slow pace, on both the national and regional fronts, starting in the early 2000s. Several national airlines, such as Kenya Airways, Air Malawi and Tunis Air, were partly sold to the private sector, while other airlines remain under state control, including the largest ones in Africa such as Egypt Air, Air Mauritius, Royal Air Maroc and South African Airways, as well as others (TAAG Angola Airlines, Air Botswana, Madagascar, Air Mozambique, Air Namibia and Air Tanzania). Some other national airlines, such as Ghana Airways, Nigerian Airlines and Air Afrique, owned by eleven Western African states,[39] were liquidated. The airport services, including its associated services, such as ground handling and catering airport services, are provided by the state bodies or through concession arrangements. Air services have been governed by a number of bilateral air transport agreements.[40] At the regional level, forty-four African

---

[36] South Africa TPR 2015, Morocco TPR 2009, and Ghana TPR 2014
[37] Kenya TPR 2006 and Zambia TPR 2009   [38] Kenya TPR 2012
[39] Air Afrique was owned by Benin, Burkina Faso, the Central African Republic, Chad, Cote d'Ivoire, Mali, Mauritania, Niger, Congo, Senegal and Togo at the time of liquidation in 2002.
[40] For instance, Tanzania had bilateral air services agreements with forty-eight economies in Africa, Asia, Europe and the Americas (TPR 2012); Morocco had bilateral air services agreements with eighty-two countries (TPR 2009); and Ghana signed with forty-seven countries, which normally covered the first four freedoms of the air (TPR 2014).

members in 1999 signed the Yamoussoukro Declaration with the aim of full liberalization of the African skies for African airlines, and aimed to establish a single African air transport market by avoiding market restrictions imposed by bilateral air service agreements.[41] Moreover, in 2004, seven West African members (Cabo Verde, Gambia, Ghana, Guinea, the Republic of Liberia, Nigeria and Sierra Leone) signed the Banjul Accord Group Agreement in order to harmonize their policies on aviation. The TPRs noted that the implementation of these agreements has been slow, and the envisioned benefits are yet to be realized.

Accounting for nearly 9 per cent of the continent's GDP, Africa's travel and tourism industry has potential to help generate growth, create jobs and enable development in Africa. South Africa, Seychelles, Mauritius, Morocco, Namibia, Kenya, Egypt, Cabo Verde, Botswana and Tanzania are ranked the highest in the continent on the list of the World Economic Forum Travel and Tourism Competitiveness Index Ranking in 2015. This sector has undergone significant liberalization, which is often linked with developments in the air transport sector. While most African countries have no foreign equity restrictions on hotels and restaurants, countries such as Tunisia (1 per cent–49 per cent) and Kenya (50 per cent–99 per cent) maintain them. Also, restrictions remain in the movement of persons through mandatory visa requirements for people from certain countries by immigration offices. This sector represents the largest number of commitments made by African members under the GATS. As Annex 11.11 illustrates, with the exception of Madagascar and Mozambique, all African members made commitments in tourism and travel-related services, forty-one members have commitments in hotels and restaurants, thirty-two in travel agencies and tour operator services, twenty-two in tourist guide services and seven in other services.

Throughout Africa, services are generally open to foreign investment, except for limitations on the movement/presence of foreign natural persons (Mode 4), as reflected in African members' GATS commitments. Restrictions take the form of specificities on the type of person and skills required for those that can enter the market (e.g. technicians, specialists or executives) and/or the purpose of the entry, as seen in the schedules of Egypt, Cote d'Ivoire and Zambia.[42] However, notable efforts are under

---

[41] New Report Confirms Significant Benefits of Liberalized African Air Markets, International Air Transport Association (2014) http://www.iata.org/pressroom/pr/Pages/2014-07-07-01.aspx.

[42] For instance, Egypt's GATS Schedule restricts the entry and temporary stay of foreign natural persons, limiting the number of foreigners to 10 per cent of the total personnel

way at the regional level. For instance, the introduction of the ECOWAS Travel Certificate, EAC and COMESA passports have facilitated movement of people within these regions. Moreover, Article 23 of the SADC Trade Protocol underscores the significance of liberalization of trade in services and, by extension, promotes free movement of natural persons within the SADC region.

An Assessment of Trade Policy Reforms in Africa in the Last Twenty Years

The main conclusions from TPRs over the last twenty years acknowledge the substance of the trade reforms undertaken at various fronts by African members. These have included the reduction of the overall tariff protection and non-tariff measures, improvement of customs procedures and administration, and the liberalization and deregulation of key services sectors, although there is still much room for further opening, particularly when compared with other parts of the world. While tariffs, one of the main trade policy instruments used by African members, were reduced from the simple average rate of 16.4 per cent in 2002 to 11.4 per cent in 2014, the tariff regime remains complex for many African members due to the existence of a large number of exemptions and concessions as well as multiple layers of other duties and charges imposed on top of tariffs. Overall, progressively, the role of the state in trade and economy has been reduced, although the state still retains control over key segments of the economy, employing selected trade instruments. Trade policy instruments for protection that have been applied include high tariff protection on agriculture in order to protect local production; state trading and export taxes to promote the production and export of strategic agricultural and mineral products; and state control over selected services sectors, including postal, electricity and transport services. Moreover, while commodity price booms contributed to an unprecedented growth of trade expansion over the last twenty years, on the policy front, regional integration, through the harmonization of policy instruments that reduced their trade-restricting impact, has

employed by a company, as provided under the Labour Code (TPR 1999); Zambia's commitments exclude the presence of foreign natural persons except where entry and temporary stay is for management purposes for expert tasks relating to the implementation of foreign investment (TPR 1996); and Côte d'Ivoire bound access to foreign investment in the energy and mining sectors by foreign suppliers for a number of activities including exploration, drilling and related activities (TPR 1999).

been a driving force of African trade policy, setting the trade and economic agenda for the continent.

On the multilateral front, an unchanged central message from the conclusions of 107 TPRs is that scope exists for African WTO members to use the legal and policy framework of trade multilateralism in rules and accompanying binding schedules to anchor and lock in domestic trade reforms. More specifically, they have not maximized the rules-based multilateral trading system, including through notifications, to improve transparency and predictability of their trade policy and close gaps in implementation. There is a strong relationship between transparency, certainty and investment flow. The facts indicate that investment flow to African economies has been affected negatively by degrees of uncertainty, lack of transparency and the governance questions in particular African economies.

With twenty years of tariff liberalization undertaken unilaterally or regionally, there are risks that require control and elimination. For instance, as the applied MFN tariffs have been reduced, gaps between the applied and bound tariffs are widening. Closing these gaps will provide and consolidate the much-needed predictability in the tariff regime. Allowing the expansion and continued existence of tariffs will undermine the gains from trade. Binding breaches on tariffs and ODCs, as well as national treatment in internal taxation, identified widely across African members during TPRs, would have to be corrected. Failures to notify, and lagging submission of notifications, would also have to be addressed urgently. Lack of resources and capacity, as frequently cited by African members, cannot by themselves justify twenty years of non-compliance with some of the core principles of the organization that bind all members and on agreements reached in good faith and voluntarily entered.

What reasons account for the under-utilization of the multilateral trading system by African members? First, the origin of GATT/WTO membership of African members, which was granted, rather than acquired through negotiations and the specific acceptance of the rights and obligations of membership, has impacted their sense of ownership and functional role in the organization. This has been further reinforced by general lack of penalties for non-compliant behaviour by African members. The peer review mechanism in the TPR process has played a critical role, but it requires deepening and real-time follow-up with the members in question. In this regard, the differences in WTO membership that are the most striking are between original members and Article

XII members. The latter, having negotiated terms of WTO membership and explicitly accepted commitments that balance rights and obligations, have to explain to and persuade domestic stakeholders of the benefits of WTO membership for integrated domestic economies. For instance, the Republic of Liberia, the most recently concluded accession from the African continent, said that one goal from its WTO membership was to 'ensure that the Liberian market is one that is transparent, predictable and that business is structured in such a way that it supports its domestic private sector while accommodating the foreign investor'.[43] As part of its entry into the WTO, the Republic of Liberia has made commitments to bind all tariff lines at an average rate of 26.7 per cent, far lower than the average of 56.0 per cent of forty-three African members that only bind 56.5 per cent of their tariff lines, on average. A similar level of discrepancy can be observed for services commitments; the Republic of Liberia made commitments in 102 services sub-sectors, while the average of services commitments made by forty-three African members stands at twenty-seven. The evidence indicates that WTO commitments made by Article XII members reflect closer alignment of their trade regime to WTO rules, ensuring competitiveness and using WTO accession commitments as an instrument for domestic reforms.[44]

Second, while Africa's participation in the WTO has increased over the last two decades, it has disproportionately focused on the DDA negotiations, seeking trade reforms for other members rather than for its own. Among the three core pillars of the work of the WTO – regular work, negotiations and dispute settlement – majority efforts and resources of African members were poured into the DDA negotiations, starting from the preparation of the Third Ministerial Conference in Seattle in 1999. The main platform for trade policy reforms falls within WTO regular committees and the Trade Policy Review Body. According to Apecu (2014), low levels of participation of African members in WTO regular committees led to missed opportunities to learn from other members about various usages of trade policy instruments that the WTO system offers to protect or pursue domestic commercial interests, including in areas where African members drew clear linkages to their ability for market access (SPS, TBT) and development (trade-related investment measures/TRIMs, local content requirements). Combined with limited resources, the disproportionate focus of African engagement in the DDA negotiations, with the emphasis on opening others' markets rather than

[43] Addy (2015) [44] WTO (2016)

ones' own, based on the Doha principle of less-than-full reciprocity, led to further misalignment between their domestic reform agenda and their participation in the WTO. This was evident in Africa's participation, for instance, in the non-agricultural market access (NAMA) negotiations, in which most African members, except those from North Africa, only agreed to increase their binding coverages, rather than to make tariff reductions through a formula, or were simply exempted from reductions for LDCs.[45]

Third, after twenty years of WTO membership, a lack of technical capacity, combined with limited resources, in handling the work of the WTO continues to be cited as a reason for under-utilization. Such capacity problems have been met by the provision of technical assistance (TA) and capacity-building by the WTO Secretariat, as well as by other multilateral and regional institutions and development partners. Indeed, Africa has been the biggest beneficiary of WTO technical assistance.[46] However, although demand for TA exceeds supply, there have been incidences of misappropriation and/or underutilization of these facilities. This issue requires reflection on the design, products and mode of technical assistance and its delivery by the providers, on the one hand, and the structure and resource allocation for participation in the WTO by African members on the other hand. Apecu (2014), in reviewing the institutional aspects of the African participation in the WTO, noted that trade negotiators from systems with fragile democracies and weak governance structures tended to be tentative, largely inactive, inconsistent in participation and ineffectual in engagement. However, she also argued that the degree of engagement and participation could be impacted by the levels of personal commitment and professional engagement of individual negotiators, regardless of capacity constraints and weaknesses.

---

[45] According to the 2008 Draft NAMA modalities, African members with a low binding coverage, i.e. 35 per cent of NAMA tariff lines and subject to the exemption from tariff reductions under the draft NAMA modalities of 2008, were Cameroon, Congo, Côte d'Ivoire, Ghana, Kenya, Mauritius, Nigeria and Zimbabwe. Under the draft modalities, these members were expected to increase their tariff coverage to 75 to 80 per cent at an average level not exceeding 30 per cent. Special provisions were available for SACU and Gabon. Moreover, twenty-five of the forty-three African members are LDCs, which were exempt from tariff reductions, although, as part of their contribution to the DDA, they were expected to substantially increase their level of tariff binding commitments.

[46] See WTO (2015a). In 2014, Africa represented the largest share in the geographical distribution of TA, in terms of the number of activities, participants, days of training and expenses.

Conclusions: Trade Policy for Africa in the Next Decades

This chapter has reviewed the developments of trade policy in Africa since the establishment of the WTO in 1995. During its twentieth anniversary in 2015, the Organization held its Tenth Ministerial Conference, and its first in Africa, in Nairobi, Kenya. The Nairobi Conference and its outcome provided an opportunity for African members to reflect on their participation in the WTO. Nairobi delivered on some long-standing demands on the African DDA agenda, such as the elimination of agricultural export subsidies, international food aid, LDCs' services waivers and preferential rules of origin, public stockholding for food security purposes, the special safeguard mechanism, and cotton. Nairobi also opened a new window for new issues and approaches in multilateral negotiations. All of this provides an opportune moment for African members, individually and as a group, to further reflect on two questions, post-Nairobi:

- How can Africa derive more value from its WTO membership in order to pursue its goal of the use of trade policy for a development agenda?
- What is the interface between Africa's trade agenda and its participation in the WTO, particularly in the post-Nairobi period?

Based on findings from twenty years of trade policy developments, a range of policy options are worthy of consideration by African policymakers.

Improving Bindings and Commitments: Linking Trade Policy Reforms to the Goods and Services Schedules

Elimination of trade barriers and restrictions to improve competitiveness, accelerate growth and augment the gains from trade are warranted, regardless of what others do. A major advantage of WTO membership is the 'right' to legally challenge breaches and violations in the trade measures by other members. No other multilateral institution offers the unique WTO advantage of a legal and policy balance of rights and obligations. Economic literature provides ample evidence that the largest gains from trade liberalization come from unilateral opening, before reciprocal arrangements. In the case of Africa, trade opening took place unilaterally and on a regional basis, whereas the multilateral agreements have made fewer direct contributions to their opening efforts, except through harmonization with international rules and practices, despite their decade-long GATT/WTO membership. However, the WTO framework is best-placed to add value to the liberalization efforts of African members by increasing the level of tariff-binding coverage and reducing the gaps between the bound and applied tariffs, as well as increasing services commitments which would reflect the actual level of liberalization. Bindings through the goods and services schedules, and their associated rules in the GATT 1994 and GATS, have proven to be effective tools for locking in trade reforms. Individual African members may wish to consider the use of the WTO binding mechanisms on a unilateral basis to support their trade reforms. Based on evidence and experience from thirty-six accessions since the establishment of the WTO, the greatest benefits of participation in the WTO accrue from domestic reform agendas. These can be leveraged when there is a coincidence between the national and multilateral agendas for domestic policy, institutional and structural reforms. The WTO framework provides one of the most powerful and credible instruments available in global economic governance for locking in domestic reforms and reducing the chances of policy reversals.

Better Utilization of Regular WTO Committees and the TPRB: Linking Trade Policy to the Participation in the WTO

Trade policy instruments covered by the WTO Agreements are monitored through the WTO's regular work, which represents a large part of members' participation in the organization. Regular work is carried out by some forty bodies under the WTO's General Council. While each body has a specific mandate, they all operate towards managing the multilateral trade regime through the exchange of information, the collection of data and the review of notifications on the implementation of WTO obligations. It is important to note that the interactions of regular committees sometimes lead to an exchange of views on best practices and eventually to the elaboration of new norms in trade regulation. Africa's engagement in regular work has been low so far, particularly during the DDA negotiations. As the role of regular committees is expected to increase in the post-Nairobi work programme, Africa could scale up its participation in regular work across the board. In doing this, there will be a lot to learn from other members on the strategic use of trade policy instruments, which could generate economy-wide efficiencies and improved welfare. Moreover, a better and more proactive use of the Trade Policy Review Mechanism (TPRM) should be explored by African members, as a form of technical assistance that would assist them in improving domestic transparency and inter-governmental coordination and in evaluating the effectiveness of their policies. In particular, greater emphasis should be placed on addressing issues and concerns raised by the TPR Body, with the assistance of the WTO Secretariat, for follow-up between reviews.

Post-Nairobi Engagement in the WTO: Linking Domestic Reforms to Plurilateral Initiatives

Nairobi opened a window for the WTO to explore new ideas, approaches and issues that could be considered for future negotiations, building on the earlier understanding reached at the Eighth Ministerial Conference in 2011 on the need to explore 'different negotiating approaches'. One of the approaches tested by WTO members since 2011 is plurilateral negotiations on specific issues, with the involvement of a limited number of members.[47] So far, three issue-specific plurilateral negotiations have been launched: the Information Technology Agreement (ITA-II) launched in 2012 and concluded at the Nairobi Ministerial Conference in 2015; the Trade in Services Agreement (TISA), launched in 2013; and the Environmental Goods Agreement (EGA), launched in 2014. Since the Nairobi Conference, several new ideas are being floated amongst members. These include investment, competition policy, e-commerce and the digital economy, and value chains. It is advisable that African members be in lock-step with negotiations in the WTO in all formats and configurations, including plurilaterals.[48] The WTO was established as a permanent negotiating forum. Although members have a sovereign choice of which negotiations they participate in, interests are best served by a comprehensive negotiating engagement in a permanent negotiating forum which evolves with the business reality. Engagement in plurilateral

---

[47] There are different types of plurilateral agreements. The WTO Agreement contains two plurilateral agreements on Government Procurement and Trade in Civil Aircraft in Annex 4, and commitments made by participating members would be applicable only to themselves. The ITA and EGA are so-called critical mass agreements, whereby commitments made by participating members are extended to non-participating members on a MFN basis. As for TISA, a decision is yet to be taken by participating members on whether their commitments would be extended to non-members.

[48] As of December 2015, the only African member which participates in these plurilateral negotiations is Mauritius, in TISA.

agreements would be consistent with ongoing domestic reforms in these areas, including services liberalization and the deregulation of government procurement (as part of good governance).[49] Moreover, goods negotiated under the ITA and EGA are often key inputs to the African economic policy agenda of integration into global value chains, the green economy and sustainable development. Given the ongoing domestic efforts on handling 'new issues', consideration may be given to advance the reform agenda by locking in these domestic efforts through plurilateral initiatives under the multilateral framework, in addition to the participation in rules-making on new issues of Africa's strategic trade agenda.

Tackling Corruption: WTO as a Good Governance Organization

There are constraints, challenges and opportunities in Africa's trade policy regime. One area of challenge, underlined in TPRs, is weak governance. As many neo-institutional scholars such as Douglass North have re-asserted, trade policy reforms without the enabling factor of good governance are futile.[50] Several cross-national empirical studies have found a positive relationship between the quality of institutions and governance structures and economic growth.[51] Africa is set to be the next growth frontier. If trade policy is to contribute to Africa's growth potential, the issue of corruption, which imposes huge political, economic and social costs, must be addressed by African policy-makers up-front.[52] For instance, in Africa, corruption in trade in the form of mis-invoicing or under-invoicing at customs, according to one estimate, resulted in a loss of revenue in the range of 7.14 per cent to 12.7 per cent of the total tax revenues.[53] While political and business grafts impose the largest direct financial cost on a country, petty bribes serve as a pervasive and

---

[49] As of December 2015, no African members participate in the Annex 4 plurilateral agreement on Government Procurement, although Cameroon is an observer to the agreement.

[50] North (1991)   [51] See Knack and Keefer (1995).

[52] For instance, Hanson (2009) highlights the grandiose nature of African corruption. She asserts that, according to Transparency International, of the ten countries considered most corrupt in the world, six come from Sub-Saharan Africa. In the same vein, a 2002 African Union study estimated that corruption cost the continent an outrageous amount of US$ 150 billion a year.

[53] According to the study by Global Financial Integrity (2014), the estimates of lost tax revenues due to corruption in the form of mis-invoicing and under-invoicing in 2002–11 were 12.7 per cent in Uganda, 11 per cent in Ghana, 10.4 per cent in Mozambique, 8.3 per cent in Kenya and 7.14 per cent in Tanzania.

destructive force that undermines public trust in governance and erodes the effectiveness of basic institutions of governance.[54]

The WTO, while the regulator and adjudicator of multilateral trade rules, is *ipso facto* a good governance institution, embracing the principles of non-discrimination, openness and transparency at the heart of its work. Transparency, through shared information and knowledge, levels the playing field. Rules reduce arbitrariness and opportunities for corruption. They can shield governments from lobbying pressure by narrow interest groups. Therefore, trade reforms pursued under the WTO umbrella can provide a rule-of-law-based platform on the basis of which African governments can tackle the political, economic and institutional structures that perpetuate corruption in many of African economies. In doing so, governance challenges such as low levels of accountability and transparency can be improved by the effective and optimal utilisation of WTO instruments, such as the schedules, notifications, regular committees and the TPRM, to promote trade policy reforms.

Since its establishment in 1995, the multilateral trading system has supported Africa's trade reforms, although the WTO can improve on this support across the board. Trade reform will continue to play a critical role in the agenda for economic transformation and development. There is wide scope for Africa's active and deeper integration in regional and global value chains. Africa should accord priority and invest resources in all three pillars of the rules-based multilateral trading system to maximize the gains from trade in an interdependent global economy and harness its boundless trade potential.

References

Addy, M.A. (2015), 'An Agenda for Transformation: We Talk to Liberia's Minister of Commerce and Industry'. Retrieved 23 January 2016, from OURS Magazine: http://ours-mag.com/2015/12/03/an-agenda-for-transformation-we-talk-to-liberias-minister-of-commerce-and-industry-axel-m-addy/

Andoh, D. (2014), 'Common ECOWAS Tariff Set for 2015 as Govt Targets GH986 m Revenue'. Retrieved 16 January 2016, from Delegation of German Industry and Commerce in Ghana (AHK): http://ghana.ahk.de/news/single-view/artikel/common-ecowas-tariff-set-for-2015-as-govt-targets-gh986 m-revenue/

---

[54] Hanson (2009)

Apecu, L.J. (2014), *African Participation at the World Trade Organization: Legal and Institutional Aspects, 1995–2010*. Graduate Institute of International and Development Studies; Volume 13, M. Nijhoff Publishers, 2014.

Daly, M. (2011), 'Evolution of Asia's Outward-Looking Economic Policies: Some Lessons From Trade Policy Reviews', WTO Staff Working Paper ERSD-2011–12, WTO.

Dean, J., S. Desai and J. Riedel. (1994), 'Trade Policy Reform in Developing Countries since 1985: A Review of the Evidence', World Bank Discussion Paper 267.

Erasmus, G. (2014), 'Namibia and the Southern African Customs Union'. Retrieved 21 January 2016, from: http://www.kas.de/upload/Publikationen/2014/namibias_foreign_relations/Namibias_Foreign_Relations_erasmus.pdf

Foster, V. and C. Briceño-Garmendia (2010), 'Ports and Shipping: Landlords Needed'. Retrieved 19 January 2016, from World Bank: http://www.infrastructureafrica.org/system/files/Africa's%20Infrastructure%20A%20Time%20for%20Transformation%20CHAPTER%2012%20PORTS.pdf

GATT, (1971), 'Democratic Republic of the Congo to Join GATT', Press Release, *GATT/1086*.

Global Financial Integrity (2014), 'Hiding in Plain Sight, Trade Mis-invoicing and the Impact of Revenue Loss in Ghana, Kenya, Mozambique, Tanzania, and Uganda: 2002–2011'. Retrieved 18 January 2016, from GFIntegrity: http://www.gfintegrity.org/wp-content/uploads/2014/05/Hiding_In_Plain_Sight_Report-Final.pdf

Hanson, S. (2009), 'Corruption in Sub-Saharan Africa'. Retrieved 21 January 2016, from: http://www.cfr.org/africa-sub-saharan/corruption-sub-saharan-africa/p19984

Hudec, R.E. (1987) (edited by C. Thomas and J.P. Trachtman in 2009), *Developing Countries in the GATT/WTO Legal System*, Oxford University Press.

International Air Transport Association (2014), *New Report Confirms Significant Benefits of Liberalized African Air Markets*. Retrieved 28 January 2016, from IATA: http://www.iata.org/pressroom/pr/Pages/2014-07-07-01.aspx

International Trade Centre (2015), 'Tunisia: Country Brief'. Retrieved 23 January 2016, from: http://www.intracen.org/country/tunisia/#sthash.E0y45lux.dpuf

Kessie, E. and Y. Apea (2004), 'The Participation of African Countries in the Multilateral Trading System', African Yearbook of International Law.

Knack and Keefer (1995), *Institutions and Economic Performance: Cross-country Tests using Alternative Institutional Measures*: http://homepage.ntu.edu.tw/~kslin/macro2009/Knack&Keefer_1995.pdf

Martijn, J.K. and C.G. Tsangarides (2007), 'Trade Reform in the CEMAC: Developments and Opportunities'. Retrieved 18 January 2016, from International Monetary Fund: https://www.imf.org/external/pubs/ft/wp/2007/wp07137.pdf

Mpande, S and A. Kannan (2015), 'Seychelles' from *African Economic Outlook 2015*. Retrieved 12 January 2016, http://www.africaneconomicoutlook.org/fileadmin/uploads/aeo/2015/CN_data/CN_Long_EN/Seychelles_GB_2015.pdf

North, D.C. (1991), 'Institutions'. Retrieved 18 January 2016, from *The Journal of Economic Perspectives*, Vol. 5, No. 1. (Winter, 1991), pp. 97–112: http://kysq.org/docs/North_91_Institutions.pdf

Ohiohenuan, J. (2005), 'Capacity Building Implications of Enhanced African Participation', from *Africa and the World Trading System, Selected Issues of the Doha Agenda*, Volume I, edited by A. Oyejide and W. Lyakurwa, Africa World Press.

Rodrik, D. (1997), 'Why Is Trade Reform so Difficult in Africa?', in *Trade Reform and Regional Integration in Africa*, edited by Z. Iqbal and M. Khan (1998), IMF.

Sharer, R. (1997), 'Trade Liberalization in Sub-Saharan Africa', in *Trade Reform and Regional Integration in Africa*, edited by Z. Iqbal and M. Khan (1998), IMF.

UNCTAD (2015), *The Economic Development in* Africa Report 2015: Unlocking the Potential of *Africa's Service Trade for Growth and Development*. Retrieved 28 January 2016, from United Nations Conference on Trade and Development: http://unctad.org/en/PublicationsLibrary/aldcafrica2015_en.pdf

UNECA (2012), *Assessing Regional Integration in Africa – Towards an African Continental Free Trade Area*. Retrieved 18 January 2016, from United Nations Economic Commission for Africa: https://www.unece.org/fileadmin/DAM/trade/TF_JointUNRCsApproach/ECA_RegionalIntegrationInAfrica.pdf

Wang, Z. and A. Winters (1997), 'Africa's Role in Multilateral Trade Negotiations: Past and Future', in *Trade Reform and Regional Integration in Africa*, edited by Z. Iqbal and M. Khan (1998), IMF.

World Bank (2015), *World Bank Doing Business*. Retrieved 5 January 2016, from: http://www.doingbusiness.org/data/exploretopics/trading-across-borders

WTO (2015a), *Annual Report on Technical Assistance and Training 2014*, (official document WT/COMTD/W/209, available at www.wto.org), World Trade Organization.

WTO (2015b), *International Trade Statistics 2015*. Retrieved 19 January 2016 from World Trade Organization: https://www.wto.org/english/res_e/statis_e/its2015_e/its2015_e.pdf

WTO (2016), *Post-Accession Best Practices*, World Trade Organization (*forthcoming publication*).

Yeo, S. (2005), 'Trade Policy in Sub-Saharan Africa: Lessons from the Uruguay Round Experience' in *Africa and the World Trading System*, Volume 1, edited by T. Ademola Oyejide and W. M. Lyakurwa, Africa World Press.

Annex 11.1 *Trade Policy Reviews of African members, 1995–2015*

	Member	1st TPR	2nd TPR	3rd TPR	4th TPR
1	Angola (2)	14+16/02/2006	22+24/09/2015		
2	Benin (3)	15+16/11/1997	28+30/06/2004*	04+06/10/2010*	
3	Botswana (4)	21+23/04/1998*	23+25/04/2003*	04+06/11/2009*	04+06/11/2015*
4	Burkina Faso (3)	18+20/11/1998*	28+30/06/2004*	04+06/10/2010*	
5	Burundi (2)	02+04/04/2003	21+23/11/2012*		
6	Cabo Verde	06+08/10/2015			
7	Cameroon (4)	13+14/02/1995	18+20/07/2001	01+03/10/2007*	29+31/07/2013*
8	Central African Republic (2)	11+13/06/2007	29+31/07/2013*		
9	Chad (2)	22+24/01/2007	29+31/07/2013*		
10	Congo (2)	03+05/07/2006	29+31/07/2013*		
11	Democratic Republic of the Congo (1)	24+26/11/2010			
12	Côte d'Ivoire (2)	04+ 05/07/1995	02+04/07/2012*		
13	Djibouti (2)	27/02+01/03/2006	22+24/10/2014*		
14	Egypt (2) [+]	24+25/06/1999	26+28/07/2005		
15	Gabon (3)	26+28/06/2001	01+03/10/2007*	29+31/07/2013*	
16	The Gambia (2)	04+06/02/2004	14+16/09/2010*		
17	Ghana (3) [+]	26+28/02/2001	28+30/01/2008	26+28/05/2014	
18	Guinea (3)	25+26/02/1999	12+14/10/2005	28+30/09/2011*	
19	Guinea-Bissau (1)	02+04/07/2012*			

No.	Country				
20	Kenya (3) [+]	26+28/01/2000	25+27/10/2006*	21+23/11/2012*	04+06/11/2015*
21	Lesotho (4)	21+23/04/1998*	23+25/04/2003*	04+06/11/2009*	
22	Madagascar (3)	19+21/02/2001	02+04/04/2008	14+16/07/2015	
23	Malawi (2)	06+08/02/2002	09+11/06/2010		
24	Mali (3)	18+20/11/1998*	28+30/06/2004*	04+06/10/2010*	
25	Mauritania (2)	11+13/09/2002	28+30/09/2011*		
26	Mauritius (4)	17+18/10/1995	02+0/11/2001	23+25/04/2008	22+24/10/2014*
27	Morocco (3) [+]	17+18/01/1996	16+18/06/2003	24+26/06/2009	
28	Mozambique (2)	24+26/01/2001	22+24/04/2009		
29	Namibia (4)	21+23/04/1998*	23+25/04/2003*	04+06/11/2009*	04+06/11/2015*
30	Niger (2)	22+24/09/2003*	11+13/11/2009*		
31	Nigeria (3) [+]	23+24/06/1998	11+13/05/2005	28+30/06/2011	
32	Rwanda (2)	28+30/09/2004	21+23/11/2012*		
33	Senegal (2) [+]	22+24/09/2003*	11+13/11/2009*		
34	Seychelles				
35	Sierra Leone (1)	09+11/02/2005			
36	South Africa (4) [+]	21+23/04/1998*	23+25/04/2003*	04+06/11/2009*	04+06/11/2015*
37	Swaziland (4)	21+23/04/1998*	23+25/04/2003*	04+06/11/2009*	04+06/11/2015*
38	Tanzania (3)	02+03/03/2000*	25+27/10/2006*	21+23/11/2012*	
39	Togo (3)	27+28/01/1999	03+05/07/2006	02+04/07/2012*	
40	Tunisia (1)	05+07/10/2005			
41	Uganda (4)	27+28/07/1995	19+21/12/2001	25+27/10/2006*	21+23/11/2012*

Annex 11.1 (*cont.*)

	Member	1st TPR	2nd TPR	3rd TPR	4th TPR
42	Zambia (3)	09+10/09/1996	23+25/10/2002	27+29/07/2009	
43	Zimbabwe (1) [+]	19+21/10/2011			
	TOTAL:107	**42**	**36**	**21**	**8**

Note: The first TPR for Seychelles is scheduled for 2021.

[+] TPRs were held for nine African economies under the GATT 1947: Egypt (1992), Ghana (1992), Kenya (1993), Morocco (1989), Nigeria (1991), Senegal (1994), South Africa (1993), Tunisia (1994) and Zimbabwe (1994).

[*] Joint reviews of regional groups were held for SACU-5 (21+23/04/1998; 23+25/04/2003; 04+06/11/2009; and 04+06/11/2015); EAC (Kenya, Tanzania and Uganda on 25+27/10/2006, and Burundi, Kenya, Rwanda, Tanzania and Uganda on 21+23/11/2012); WAEMU (Burkina Faso and Mali on 18+20/11/1998, Benin, Burkina Faso and Mali on 28+30/06/2004 and 04+06/10/2010, Niger and Senegal on 22+24/09/2003 and 11+13/11/2009 and Côte d'Ivoire, Guinea-Bissau and Togo on 02+04/07/2012); CEMAC (Cameron and Gabon on 01+03/10/2007 and Cameron, the Central African Republic, Chad, Congo and Gabon on 29+31/07/2013); COMESA (Djibouti and Mauritius on 22+24/10/2014).

Annex 11.2 Trade policy reforms in Sub-Saharan African economies, based on Lanre (2013) and WTO Trade Policy Reviews

Member	Selected trade reform
	South African Customs Union (SACU) Horizontal Note
	Under the SACU agreement, the oldest customs union in the world, member countries apply import duties, excise duties, tariff exemptions, anti-dumping and safeguard duties and other customs related laws set by South Africa, the largest trading partner in the union. SACU trade reforms significantly started in 1994 following the end of the Apartheid in South Africa. Import permits are only maintained to administer quotas on health, sanitary, phytosanitary and environmental grounds. Tariff reforms have reduced the applied MFN common external tariff from 15 per cent in 1997 to 11.4 per cent in 2002, although the tariff structure remains complex, comprising *ad valorem*, specific, mix, formula (variable) and their combination. By 2015, the rate had further dropped to 7.2 per cent, while the share of non-*ad valorem* decreased from 25 per cent in 1997 to 3.8 per cent in 2015. Some SACU members apply export taxes (e.g. Namibia and South Africa on rough diamond). All SACU members are engaged in the Southern African Development Community (SADC). As of 2015, SACU's common trade regime had remained broadly unchanged since 2009; and the areas so far harmonized are in general customs related, including tariffs, other border taxes and trade remedies. See more information on SACU in Annex 11.4.
Botswana **SACU, SADC**	Botswana does not have an independent trade policy. The extent of its openness to the outside world is dependent on the trade policies adopted by SACU. Botswana maintains an export monopoly on the export of beef. Additionally, see SACU Horizontal Note.
Lesotho **SACU, SADC**	Trade liberalization started in Lesotho in 1994. Additionally, see SACU Horizontal Note.

Annex 11.2 (*cont.*)

Member	Selected trade reform
Namibia **SACU, SADC**	Trade reforms started in Namibia in 1994. Additionally, see SACU Horizontal Note.
South Africa **SACU, SADC**	Trade reforms started in South Africa in 1994. Being the largest country, South Africa's trade policies influenced others in the region. It maintained highly protectionist tendencies during the Apartheid period. The tariff regime remained highly complicated with a broad range of numerous charges. However, from the 2000s, regional harmonization was pursued and tariff rates were reduced. Additionally, see SACU Horizontal Note.
Swaziland **SACU, SADC, COMESA**	Trade liberalization started in Swaziland in 1994. Additionally, see SACU Horizontal Note.

East African Community (EAC) Horizontal Note

Pioneer members (Kenya, Uganda and Tanzania) adopted the EAC CET in January 2005. Rwanda and Burundi adopted the CET in 2009 as they joined the Customs Union in 2008. The CET consists of three bands of 0 per cent, 10 per cent and 25 per cent, with the exception of fifty-eight tariff lines of sensitive products. The tariff has averaged at 12.6 per cent for the previous five years. All countries are engaged in the Common Market for Eastern and Southern African (COMESA). Regional efforts towards the elimination of non-tariff barriers (NTBs) are facilitated by the NTB Monitoring Mechanism. See more information on the EAC in Annex 11.4.

Burundi **EAC, COMESA, ECCAS**	Originally, trade reforms in Burundi began in 1986 with the dismantling of QRs on most goods and the rationalization of the tariff structure. However, the civil war between 1993 and 2002 resulted in a break in the reform process. During this period, there were ten tariff rates, ranging from 0 per cent to

100 per cent. The 10 per cent modal rate and 100 per cent maximum rate applied to 38 per cent and 12 per cent of tariff lines, respectively. Also, an import licensing system was applied. Trade reforms resumed in January 2003 and the maximum tariff rate fell to 40 per cent with five tariff bands – 0 per cent, 10 per cent, 12 per cent, 15 per cent and 40 per cent. The import licensing system was abolished and import bans only applied to products such as ivory, narcotic drugs, weapons and ammunition. In the same year, export taxes on coffee, tea and cotton were all eliminated. Although recent trade policy commitments at the regional level, coupled with legislative and regulatory developments, demonstrate the government's commitment to improving the country's trade performance, the sustainable and effective implementation of the reform package remains a major challenge for Burundi, whose institutional and human resource capacities are still limited. In 2009, Burundi adopted the EAC CET. Additionally, see EAC Horizontal Note.

Kenya
EAC, COMESA

In May 1993, Kenya began liberalizing its trade and foreign exchange regime after years of inward-looking policies and policy reversals. In the same year, the Kenyan shilling was devalued three times; the maximum duty rate reduced to 50 per cent from 135 per cent in 1988; import licences were abolished except those maintained for conservation, environmental and national security purposes; and the export compensation scheme was abolished. In 1994, the maximum duty rate fell to 25 per cent with five bands (0 per cent, 5 per cent, 10 per cent, 15 per cent and 25 per cent), while a managed floating exchange rate system was adopted. In 2004, an export tax of 25 per cent on hides and skins was introduced in order to encourage local processing. The country applies neither voluntary export restraint nor export quotas. In January 2005, the EAC CET entered into force. Additionally, see EAC Horizontal Note.

Rwanda
EAC, COMESA

Rwanda undertook significant trade reforms to rebuild its economy after the 1994 genocide. The country abolished all quantitative restrictions (QRs) except those imposed on goods for health and security reasons. Between 1997 and 2004, thirty-seven enterprises were privatized while export taxes were fully eliminated in 1999. In 2009, Burundi adopted the EAC CET. Additionally, see EAC Horizontal Note.

Annex 11.2 (*cont.*)

Member	Selected trade reform
Tanzania EAC, SADC	The reforms that Tanzania has undertaken since 1985 – and at a more accelerated pace in the past decade – have resulted in a trade policy framework that has been significantly liberalized. Export restrictions have been eliminated as have foreign exchange controls. As of 2000, Tanzania's customs duties were simplified to a five-tier structure with tariff rates of 0 per cent, 5 per cent, 10 per cent, 20 per cent, and 25 per cent. When the EAC CET entered into force on January 2005, Tanzania made provisional exemptions on its wheat and barley imports. Additionally, see EAC Horizontal Note.
Uganda EAC, COMESA	Trade reforms started in Uganda in 1987 under the Economic Recovery Programme. In 1990, export licensing requirements were replaced by a less restrictive export certificate but export taxes were abolished. By 1994, all QRs were dismantled except for those maintained for moral, health, security and environmental reasons. The simplification of the tariff structure led to the reduction of tariff bands from five in 1995 to three in 2000 (0 per cent, 7 per cent and 15 per cent), while the maximum tariff rate also dropped from 60 per cent in 1995 to 15 per cent 2000. In January 2005, the EAC CET entered into force. Also, Uganda does not apply export voluntary restraints or export subsidies. Additionally, see EAC Horizontal Note.

Central African Economic and Monetary Community (CEMAC) Horizontal Note

The CEMAC CET, introduced in 1994, consists of five rates, all of which are *ad valorem*: 0 per cent on pharmaceutical preparations, books and brochures and aviation-related goods, 5 per cent on staple goods, 10 per cent on raw materials and capital goods, 20 per cent on intermediate goods and 30 per cent on wage goods with an average of 18.2 per cent in 2014 (without any notable change since 2006). All the CEMAC countries also belong to the Economic Community of Central African States (ECCAS), which was established in 1983 but whose integration process has been slow to take off (see more information on CEMAC and ECCAS in Annex 11.4).

Cameroon
CEMAC, ECCAS

Cameroon's trade liberalization and fiscal reform were part of a larger market-oriented economic reform programme aimed at reversing the prolonged economic downslide triggered by the halving of world petroleum prices in 1986. Import-substitution policies commenced. In 1989, the number of goods subject to QRs was reduced, the special import authorization system was abolished and export taxes on coffee and cocoa were eliminated. In 1994, the CFA Franc was devalued by 50 per cent in order to raise the level of exports and restore Cameroon's competitiveness. Also, the exports of logs of certain species are prohibited for economic reasons. Cameroon's tariff structure is based on the CEMAC CET. Additionally, see the CEMAC Horizontal Note.

Central African Republic
CEMAC, ECCAS

The numerous armed conflicts in the country have undermined its economic and trade liberalization efforts. The Central African Republic applies the CEMAC's Customs Code. Apart from a few exceptions, its customs tariff is based on the CEMAC's CET. Additionally, see CEMAC Horizontal Note.

Chad
CEMAC, ECCAS

Trade liberalization started in Chad in the early 90s. As part of CEMAC, it adopted the group's common external tariff (CET) in 1994. However, the tariff applied by Chad in 2012 contains exceptions to the CET for forty-five tariff lines. For twenty-six lines, tariffs are higher than the CET (58 per cent of the exceptions). The exceptions do not introduce new rates but the products are mostly reclassified in another tariff category. They no longer target a specific group of products, apart from man-made staple fibres (HS 2007, section 55), covered by over half the exceptions (twenty-eight tariff lines). Additionally, see CEMAC Horizontal Note.

Congo
CEMAC, ECCAS

After decades of political turmoil, the government in 2006 initiated a wide-ranging programme of structural reforms and enhanced governance to consolidate peace and promote the Congo's economic and social development in a bid to increase trade. The Congo applies but has not yet ratified the Kyoto Convention on the Simplification and Harmonization of Customs Procedures. Like all the other CEMAC member countries, since 2001 the Congo has applied the Community Customs Code to the importation, exportation and re-exportation of goods. Additionally, the Congo applies the acts of the

Annex 11.2 (*cont.*)

Member	Selected trade reform
	CEMAC with regard to the general preferential tariff (GPT), and internal taxes. Additionally, see CEMAC Horizontal Note.
Gabon **CEMAC, ECCAS**	Economic reform started in Gabon in 1986 under the first SAPs. It gathered pace with the 1994 devaluation of the CFA franc as part of a renewed sub-regional integration process. By 1996, QRs had been dismantled on all goods except sugar and mineral water. Foreign trade had been liberalized, VAT and excise taxes had been introduced, the turnover tax had been updated and new systems created for regulating and supervising financial services. By 2013, Gabon had abolished most of its export duties and taxes. However, manganese remains subject to an export tax of 3.5 per cent of its reference value. Also, Gabon banned all log exports in 2010 to promote the local processing of wood. Additionally, see CEMAC Horizontal Note.

Western African Economic Monitoring Union (WAEMU) Horizontal Note

In 2000, WAEMU adopted a CET which had four bands of duties: 0 per cent on essential goods, 5 per cent on staple goods, 10 per cent on intermediate goods and inputs and 20 per cent on final consumer goods from all non-WAEMU countries, including ECOWAS countries, with a simple average import tariff of about 12 per cent. All members of the WAEMU are part of the ECOWAS, and therefore the introduction of the ECOWAS CET and a fifth band affected the overall CET for WAEMU countries by increasing it marginally. See additional information in the ECOWAS Horizontal note.

Benin **WAEMU, ECOWAS**	Benin started liberalizing its trade regime in 1988 with the elimination of all quantitative restrictions (QRs) on imports and exports. In 1991, import licences were abolished together with the import price lists. The tariff reforms in 1991 and 1994 led to a drop in the number of import taxes to two and the range of duty rates decreased from 16 to 5 (i.e. 0 per cent, 5 per cent, 10 per cent, 15 per cent and 20 per cent). Although, export taxes were eliminated in 1993, a fiscal exit duty of 3 per cent free-on-

board (f.o.b) still applies to cocoa beans, crude oil and precious metals. The national currency was devalued by 50 per cent in 1994 while all forms of export subsidization schemes and domestic support measures were abolished in 1997. From 31 January 2000, Benin's tariff structure was based on the WAEMU CET. Additionally, see WAEMU Horizontal Note.

Burkina Faso
WAEMU, ECOWAS

Trade liberalization in Burkina Faso started in 1991 under the SAPs supported by the World Bank and IMF. Between 1991 and 1994, QRs were abolished on all imports except those relating to health and security (e.g. asbestos-based products), the arithmetic average of import duties fell to 31.1 per cent with a minimum of 6 per cent and a maximum of 37 per cent and the CFA Franc was devalued by 50 per cent. Within the same period, all export duties were banned with the exception of a special levy on the export of livestock. Furthermore, state monopoly is maintained on sectors such as electricity, water and rail transport, which the government describes as 'strategic'. Just like Benin, Burkina Faso also adopted the WAEMU CET on 1 January 2000, which reduced its average applied MFN tariff rate to 12.1 per cent. Additionally, see WAEMU Horizontal Note.

Côte d'Ivoire
WAEMU, ECOWAS

Côte d'Ivoire began to liberalize its trade regime in 1994 with the devaluation of the CFA Franc. By the end of the year, QRs on imports had been lifted except for those levied on security, sanitary and phytosanitary grounds, while the average *ad valorem* import duty fell to 23.5 per cent. In January 2000, Côte d'Ivoire adopted the WAEMU CET along with a 10 per cent special import tax on products such as soya bean and palm oil. There are duties levied on the exports of cocoa and coffee (raw or processed), while key productive sectors are still under government control. Additionally, see WAEMU Horizontal Note.

Guinea-Bissau
WAEMU, ECOWAS

In the context of almost uninterrupted political instability that the country has experienced over the years, trade and investment policies have not been a major government priority. The country is lagging behind significantly with the modernization of its regulatory framework for trade in general but there have been recent efforts to change this. As of 2012, the overall direction of Guinea-Bissau's economic policy is focused on increasing productivity by strengthening basic infrastructure and processing cashew nuts locally, in the hope of eventually diversifying into fisheries and mining. Therefore,

Annex 11.2 (*cont.*)

Member	Selected trade reform
	Guinea-Bissau has given the WAEMU Commission exclusive authority over several areas of its third-country trade policy. Additionally, see WAEMU Horizontal Note.
Mali **WAEMU, ECOWAS**	Trade reforms started in Mali in 1988 under the IMF and World Bank sponsored SAPs. In the same year, import monopolies were abolished while in 1990, all QRs and import licencing requirements were eliminated. In 1991, a value-added tax of 10 per cent and 15 per cent was introduced while price controls on goods were terminated in 1992. The CFA franc was devalued in 1994 and by the end of 1997, twenty state enterprises had been dissolved while forty had been wholly or partially privatized. Mali adopted the WAEMU CET in January 2000. Consequently, its average applied MFN tariff rate fell from 22.1 in 1997 to 14.6 per cent in 2003. As of 2010, exports of gold and cotton were subject to a levy of 3 per cent *ad valorem* under the ISCP. Additionally, see WAEMU Horizontal Note.
Niger **WAEMU, ECOWAS**	Niger gradually liberalized its trade policy through the SAPs in the 1980s and regional efforts after joining WAEMU in 1994. However, trade policy liberalization within WAEMU was hampered by political upheavals that took place up until 1999. Quantitative import restrictions were abolished in 1990. The CFA franc was devalued in 1994. Tariffs were streamlined and lowered following the gradual introduction of the WAEMU CET between 1998 and 2000. As a result, the simple average of MFN customs duties fell from 20 per cent to 12.1 per cent between 1997 and 2000. Additionally, see WAEMU Horizontal Note.
Senegal **WAEMU, ECOWAS**	Trade reforms started in Senegal in 1986 under the medium and long-term SAP. Between 1986 and 1989, QRs on imports and import licensing systems were largely abolished; while by mid-1993, twenty-six enterprises had been privatized. It is worth noting that Senegal maintains some of these prohibitions, quantitative restrictions and licensing, whose notification to the WTO, which dates back to 1997, has not been updated. In 1994, the CFA franc was devalued while QRs on exports and export licencing

systems were dismantled except those levied on gold, hides and skins and petroleum products. In 1997, Senegal notified the WTO that no direct export subsidies were granted. In 1999, Senegal adopted the WAEMU CET, which lowered its average applied MFN tariff rate from 37 per cent in 1994 to 14.7 per cent in 2002. Additionally, see WAEMU Horizontal Note.

Togo
WAEMU, ECOWAS

Togo originally began trade reforms in the late 1980s; however, the social and political crises between 1991 and 1993 undermined these reforms. In 1994, the CFA franc was devalued by 50 per cent as trade reforms resumed under the second SAP. By August 1995, import licensing only applied to goods on health, sanitary and environmental grounds while exports of coffee, cocoa and cotton fibre were no longer subject to licensing and price controls by 1996. The average applied MFN tariff rate was 16.5 per cent in 1998; however, the introduction of WAEMU common external tariff lowered the tariff rate to 12.1 per cent. It is worth noting that in 1999, the Togolese economy was already quite liberal in comparison with those of other WAEMU countries. As of 2010, export costs were to be paid on the export of precious and semi-precious mineral substances. Additionally, see WAEMU Horizontal Note.

Economic Community of West African States (ECOWAS) Horizontal Note

Regional liberalization in ECOWAS has been fostered by the ECOWAS Trade Liberalisation Scheme (ETLS), which has been in place since 1990 albeit exhibiting slow progress. Its essential features included free movement of transport, goods and persons within ECOWAS and the removal of all tariff and non-tariff barriers to trade. The ECOWAS CET was introduced in 2015 and built on WAEMU's four bands by introducing a fifth band (35 per cent for specific goods for economic development) and at the time, tariffs on products from non-ECOWAS members were expected to increase.

Cabo Verde
ECOWAS

Cabo Verde became the 153rd Member of the WTO on 23 July 2008. The CET was not adopted in Cabo Verde on 1 January 2015 as originally planned, but may be implemented with a delay of approximately one year. According to the Cabo Verdean authorities, the simple average applied MFN tariff is set to rise from 10.3 per cent to 12.3 per cent with full implementation of the CET. As of May 2015, Cabo Verde had not yet formalized a new target date for its implementation of the ECOWAS CET. Cabo Verde does not use tariff quotas to regulate imports. Additionally, see ECOWAS Horizontal Note.

Annex 11.2 *(cont.)*

Member	Selected trade reform
The Gambia ECOWAS	Since the introduction of the Economic Recovery Programme in 1986, The Gambia has been implementing significant trade reforms. Import prohibition was abolished on all goods except for those maintained for environmental, health, security and morality reasons. Also, export licences and quotas were completely eliminated. In 2000, the 1998 tariff structure with thirty rates ranging from 0 per cent to 90 per cent was replaced with six rates running from 0 per cent to 18 per cent. As of 2010, the Gambia applied export duties to waste and scrap of precious metals, taxed at 5 per cent. Additionally, see ECOWAS Horizontal Note.
Ghana ECOWAS	Extensive trade reforms started in Ghana in 1983 under the Economic Recovery Programme. From that year to the end of 1986, the Ghanaian Cedi was devalued and a dual exchange rate system was introduced along with a new import licensing system which allowed for the import of non-consumer goods by the private sector without restriction. In 1987, the dual exchange rate was unified, while in 1989, import licencing, prohibitions and foreign exchange rationing were fully abolished. The average MFN tariff rate was 17 per cent in 1999, a figure which fell to 14.7 per cent in 2000 and 12.9 per cent in 2014. Export taxes were levied on cocoa, oil and aviation jet fuel. The most-favoured nation (MFN) tariff was modified frequently between 2007 and 2013. In particular, Ghana abolished non-*ad valorem* tariffs which applied to petroleum products and replaced them with *ad valorem* rates. Additionally, see ECOWAS Horizontal Note.
Guinea ECOWAS	The reforms carried out by Guinea since 1985 have enabled it to significantly liberalize its economy and its trade. Quantitative restrictions were abolished on most products, with the exception of potatoes, the import of which was prohibited from February to June each year in order to allow local production to be sold. Other restrictions were also maintained for health, security or moral reasons or under international conventions to which Guinea is a signatory. Since 1986, price controls were progressively streamlined in Guinea. In practice, only petroleum products were regulated. In 2011, agricultural

products were protected more than non-agricultural products (11.7 per cent on average). Before the adoption of the ECOWAS CET in 2015, Guinea's MFN tariff was aligned to the WAEMU's CET from 2005. Additionally, see ECOWAS Horizontal Note.

Nigeria ECOWAS

Trade reforms in Nigeria commenced in 1986 under the SAPs sponsored by the IMF. In the same year, QRs on imports were eliminated except those maintained for health and safety reasons; export taxes and import licensing systems were removed; six marketing boards were abolished and sixteen public enterprises, mainly in agro-industries, were privatized. In 1991, duty suspension schemes, which permitted Nigerian manufacturers to import duty-free raw materials for the production of exports, were introduced, while in 1992 the first export processing zone (EPZ) was established. In 1994, a value-added tax of 5 per cent on most imported goods and services was introduced, while all excise duties levied on domestically produced goods were abolished in 1998. The average applied MFN tariff in Nigeria fell from 28.6 per cent in 2003 to 11.9 per cent in 2009. Nigeria generally imposed import restrictions during times of economic crises. As of 2011, many important pieces of legislation were still at the draft stage and had not been implemented in areas such as public utilities, competition policy, the petroleum industry, and contingency measures. Additionally, see ECOWAS Horizontal Note.

Sierra Leone ECOWAS

Trade liberalization in Sierra Leone started in 1989 under the SAPs sponsored by the IMF. Tariff reforms reduced rates ranging from 0 per cent to 100 per cent in the 1980s, to between 5 per cent and 40 per cent in 1994. The average MFN tariff was 13.9 per cent in 2005 with seven tariff bands: 0 per cent, 5 per cent, 10 per cent, 15 per cent, 20 per cent, 25 per cent and 30 per cent. Import and export restrictions were still maintained on goods for health, safety and environmental reasons. Most export taxes were eliminated in 1993; however, exports of cocoa and coffee products remained subject to a levy of 2.5 per cent of the f.o.b. export value. Also, Sierra Leone abandoned export subsidies. Additionally, see ECOWAS Horizontal Note.

Annex 11.2 (*cont.*)

Member	Selected trade reform
OTHER AFRICAN MEMBERS	
Angola SADC, ECCAS	Since the end of the civil war in 2002, and even before that, Angola revised its trade- and investment-related legislation. In 2003, new foreign investment legislation was introduced. In 2005, a new customs code was adopted and the customs tariff was revised. A revised tariff, introduced in February 2005, reduced the maximum applied rate to 30 per cent, with six tariffs levels ranging from 2 per cent, and the simple average MFN rate from 8.8 per cent to 7.4 per cent. More recently, in order to diversify its economy, Angola took several import substitution measures, including an increase of tariffs to an average of 10.9 per cent in 2015.
Democratic Republic of the Congo SADC, COMESA, ECCAS	After decades of economic downturn owing to, *inter alia*, irrational economic decisions and political crises, the Democratic Republic of the Congo embarked on a series of uninterrupted reforms aimed at liberalizing its economy in 2001. Among the reforms was the introduction of an *ad valorem* MFN tariff system comprising four rates: 0 per cent, 5 per cent, 10 per cent and 20 per cent. The simple average tariff was 11.3 per cent while the modal rate and standard deviation were 5 per cent and 6.1 per cent, respectively. Export duties, ranging from 1 per cent to 10 per cent, apply to goods such as green coffee, mineral oil, electric power and fresh water. For economic reasons, there were still restrictions on unrefined mineral ores and logs. As of 2010, imports were subject to numerous other levies which, for the most part, were unjustified or disproportionate in comparison with the services provided, in addition to the tariff.
Djibouti COMESA	Djibouti is part of the COMESA Free Trade Area, which was established on 1 November 2000. As of 2006, the absence of domestic production of goods in Djibouti justified the lack of a customs tariff *stricto sensu*. However, the internal consumption tax (TIC), introduced primarily for fiscal reasons, served a very similar purpose, as Djibouti's limited local production is solely and generally TIC-free. The TIC is solely *ad*

valorem and comprises six rates: 0, 5, 8, 10, 20 and 33 per cent. The average of these rates was 28.2 per cent in 2005, with mixed escalation. In 2008, Djibouti adopted its first legislation introducing value-added tax (VAT), intended gradually to eliminate the TIC in such a way that domestic fiscal pressure remained unchanged. Additionally, import prohibitions are generally governed by the international conventions to which Djibouti is party. The only products specifically banned for import are right-hand drive vehicles and non-biodegradable plastic bags. Djibouti has been using ASYCUDA World since January 2013 and all import declarations have been made electronically since 2005.

Egypt
COMESA

Egypt's economic stabilization programme was launched in 1990–91. Much progress has been made in reducing trade barriers: most NTMs have been removed and tariff protection has been sharply reduced – MFN duties currently average about 27 per cent compared to 42 per cent in 1991. In early 1993, the tariff range was further narrowed to a maximum rate of 80 per cent with a short list of exceptions. Between 1996 and 1998, various tariff amendments were made, e.g. Egypt reduced tariffs across the board by 10–15 percentage points, lowering the maximum tariff from 70 per cent to 55 per cent. As of 2005, the number of tariff bands had reduced to twelve. Additionally, the removal of export bans and reduced domestic restrictions on pricing and distribution reduced the anti-export bias in the economy. In 2011, there was an increase in the incentives offered in the free economic zones in order to encourage exportation. Egypt generally does not require any export approval requirements nor does it apply any export taxes, charges or levies although in 2015, an export tariff of 2,000 Egyptian pounds (US$ 255.43) a tonne was imposed on the staple food (rice) in order to replace the lift of the export ban which had been imposed earlier in the year.

Madagascar
SADC, COMESA

Even though trade liberalization was part of the objectives of the economic reform initiated in 1982, efforts to liberalize trade did not start until the late 1980s. All QRs on imports were eliminated, except

Annex 11.2 (*cont.*)

Member	Selected trade reform
	for prohibitions maintained on health, phytosanitary and security grounds. In 1996, a privatization programme was launched which led to the deregulation of several state-owned enterprises. In the same year also, most marketing boards in agriculture were liquidated, while price controls were abolished on virtually all products. The simple average applied MFN tariff rate is 12.2 per cent (2015) and there are no tariff quotas. Also, Madagascar does not impose any export tax. As of 2015, Madagascar has a simple import tax structure, with the customs tariff being the only duty levied exclusively on imports.
Malawi **SADC, COMESA**	Trade liberalization in Malawi began in 1988 under the auspices of IMF-sponsored SAPs. The maximum tariff rate dropped from 45 per cent in 1988 to 40 per cent and 35 per cent respectively in 1996 and 1997. In 1991, a negative list of imports requiring foreign exchange approval was introduced, but later abolished in 1994. The government embarked on a privatization programme in 1996, while all licencing requirements on imports were eliminated in 1997, except those maintained for health, safety, security and environmental purposes. Export surrender requirements were abolished in February 1994 except for traditional products such as tobacco, tea and sugar, while all export taxes were fully terminated in April 1998. Export licences apply only to a few products such as war materials, wildlife, maize and maize meals, atomic energy materials and unmanufactured tea and tobacco. As of 2010, Malawi prohibits the export of scrap metal and petroleum products as the latter is a strategic product for Malawi.
Mauritius **SADC, COMESA**	Mauritius started liberalizing its foreign trade in 1985 with the dismantling of QRs, reduction of export tax on sugar and lowering of the number of items subject to price control. In 1991, import licensing, which hitherto applied to majority of imports, was eliminated except for those maintained for health

and sanitary reasons. In 1993, the remaining export taxes were fully terminated while a value-added tax of 10 per cent replaced the sales tax in 1998. The simple average applied MFN tariff rate fell from 19.9 per cent in 2001 to 6 per cent in 2007 which consisted of only four bands: 0 per cent, 10 per cent, 15 per cent and 30 per cent. Mauritius is considered to be the most open economy in Africa as it underwent significant liberalization which culminated in a simple average applied MFN tariff of 0.8 per cent in 2015.

Mozambique
SADC

Mozambique has undertaken important reforms since 1987, and at a more accelerated pace in the past few years. The reforms resulted in a significantly liberalized trade regime that was essentially based on tariffs. Most export restrictions were eliminated, as were foreign exchange controls. As of 2001, Mozambique had simplified the structure of its customs duties; the tariff rates ranged from 0 to 30 per cent. The tariff structure was modestly escalatory. The simple average applied MFN tariff was 13.8 per cent, among the lowest import duties in southern Africa. Between 2001 and 2009, Mozambique lowered its maximum tariff from 30 per cent to 20 per cent. Its 2008 MFN applied tariff comprises rates of zero, 2.5 per cent, 5 per cent, 7.5 per cent and 20 per cent; all tariffs continue to be *ad valorem*. As a result of the reductions, the simple average applied MFN tariff rate declined from 13.8 per cent in 2001 to 10.1 per cent in 2008.

Seychelles
SADC, COMESA

Liberalization was under way in the early 1990s. The Government of Seychelles applied for accession to the WTO on 8 May 1995, signalling a desire for multilateral liberalization. After years of negotiations, it joined the WTO in April 2015. Seychelles is also a member of COMESA, the Indian Ocean Commission (IOC) and SADC. Seychelles has been operating under the COMESA Free Trade Area since 2009. Furthermore, Seychelles submitted its accession to the SADC FTA in May 2014 (respecting

Annex 11.2 (*cont.*)

Member	Selected trade reform
	its COMESA obligations). Being a services-based economy, Seychelles has an open trade regime: 98 per cent of imports enter at a 0 per cent rate (increased from 94 per cent in 2013). While the country has six tariff bands, only 0.13 per cent of tariff lines are taxed at a rate of over 25 per cent (mainly beverages and alcohol, fish and fish products), with the average applied tariff rate of 1.73 per cent. The country has very few non-tariff barriers, which are largely for food security and biosecurity purposes.
Zambia **SADC, COMESA**	Zambia started liberalizing its trade regime in 1991 under the IMF's SAPs. The goal of opening up the economy was mainly to diversify exports in order to reduce the dependence on copper. By the end of 1991, QRs and all export taxes had been abolished; import controls only applied to goods for health and safety reasons while all direct consumer and producer subsidies were eliminated. In 1992, price regulations and controls were abolished for all goods and services except transportation, electricity and petroleum products, while Zambia completed the dismantling of import licensing in 1995. Between 1992 and 1996, the maximum tariff fell from 100 per cent to 25 per cent with tariff bands dropping from 12 to 4, i.e. 0 per cent, 5 per cent, 15 per cent and 25 per cent. The simple average applied MFN tariff rate has only dropped slightly from 13.6 per cent in the late 1990s to 13.4 per cent in 2009.
Zimbabwe **SADC, COMESA**	Comprehensive trade reforms in Zimbabwe started in 1991 under the Economic SAP supported by the World Bank. In the same year, the Export Retention Scheme (ERS) was established, under which exporters were granted 15 per cent of the revenues from export. In 1993, an export subsidy available to manufacturers was eliminated while a dual foreign exchange market which had an ERS and an official exchange rate was introduced. In 1994, all goods except those on a published negative list became importable without a licence, while the dual exchange rate was unified. Even though there is provision

for imposing export taxes in its legislation, Zimbabwe levies none. The simple average MFN tariff rate was 15.4 per cent in 2011.

Mauritania

Mauritania's trade regime underwent liberalization in the late 1990s with a simplification of customs procedures, rationalization of customs duties and abolishing of most non-tariff measures. As of 2001, the applied tariff is entirely *ad valorem*, with a relatively simple four-rate structure (0, 5 per cent, 13 per cent and 20 per cent). In June 2002, Mauritania amended its customs valuation legislation and now uses the transaction value as the basis for valuing imported goods. Furthermore, Mauritania raised its customs duty on non-agricultural products, which meant higher prices for consumers of these imported goods, i.e. the average applied rate raised from 10.6 per cent in 2001 to 12.1 per cent in 2011. Mauritania was a Member of the ECOWAS until the end of 1999, when it withdrew for political and economic reasons.

Morocco

Morocco's trade regime in the early 1990s combined progressive import liberalization with the promotion of industrial exports and heavy protection for certain agricultural staples. On the import side, domestic production was protected by a number of measures such as the licences required for a few products (10.2 per cent of total merchandise imports in 1994 as against 8.4 per cent in 1993), import duties, the fiscal import levy and a para-fiscal tax. Subsidies were granted in order to encourage the consumption of certain locally produced agricultural products. However, in 1996, Morocco took several strides towards liberalization. There was an end to the imposition of quantitative import restrictions on the majority of products. The leaps in the simplification of customs procedures substantially reduced the time taken and enhanced transparency. Subsidies were abolished for the majority of products. In 2009, tariffs were higher (an average of 44.5 per cent) on agricultural products than on non-agricultural products (16.3 per cent, excluding petroleum). Between 2009 and 2015, Morocco revised/amended much of its legislation on trade and international investment with emphasis on trade facilitation through computerization of customs procedures and the development of transport and telecommunications. In 2015, there remains a duality of the VAT system and imposition of

Annex 11.2 (*cont.*)

Member	Selected trade reform
	numerous ODCs. Morocco also still has numerous pending WTO notifications, especially regarding state aid and state trading enterprises.
Tunisia	Under its SAP, the Tunisian government launched an ambitious trade liberalization plan, with the initial objective of removing all import restrictions by the end of 1991, while achieving uniform effective protection of around 25 per cent. Accordingly, tariffs were reduced and the coverage of import restrictions progressively reduced, starting with liberalization on goods not locally produced. The pace of reform slowed as the liberalization process moved into more sensitive areas of imports competing with locally produced goods; the initial completion date of 1991 was postponed to 1994 and the removal of non-tariff barriers was offset by the introduction of higher tariffs in the form of surtaxes. Quantitative import restrictions were largely removed. However, in 2001, efforts were steered towards trade facilitation with special emphasis on documentation and the implementation of the WTO Agreement on Customs Valuation. Despite substantial reforms, Tunisia's trade regime remains more restrictive than that of its neighbours in the Middle East and North Africa as well as other lower-middle -income economies, especially in the agricultural sector.

Sources: ITC (2015), Lanre (2013), Mpande and Kannan (2015) and TPRs.

Annex 11.3 *African membership in Regional trade agreements and Regional Economic Communities, 2015*

	SACU*	SADC*	EAC*	CEMAC*	ECCAS	COMESA*	ECOWAS*	WAEMU*	UMA	CEN-SAD	IGAD	Total	EPA with EU** and FTA
Angola		X			X	X						3	
Benin							X	X		X		3	X
Botswana	X	X										2	X
Burkina Faso							X	X		X		3	X
Burundi			X		X	X						3	X
Cabo Verde							X					1	X
Cameroon				X	X							2	X
Central African Republic				X	X					X		3	
Chad				X	X					X		3	
Congo				X	X							2	
Côte d'Ivoire							X	X		X		3	X
Democratic Republic of the Congo		X			X	X						3	
Djibouti						X				X	X	3	
Egypt						X				X		2	FTA
Gabon				X	X							2	
The Gambia							X			X		2	X
Ghana							X					1	X
Guinea							X			X		2	
Guinea-Bissau							X	X				2	X

Annex 11.3 (cont.)

	SACU*	SADC*	EAC*	CEMAC*	ECCAS	COMESA*	ECOWAS*	WAEMU*	UMA	CEN-SAD	IGAD	Total	EPA with EU** and FTA
Kenya			X			X					X	3	X
Liberia							X					1	X
Lesotho	X	X										2	X
Madagascar		X				X						2	X
Malawi		X				X						2	X
Mali							X	X		X		3	X
Mauritania									X	X		2	X
Mauritius		X				X						2	X
Morocco									X			1	FTA
Mozambique		X										1	X
Namibia	X	X										2	X
Niger							X	X		X		3	X
Nigeria							X			X		2	X
Rwanda			X		X	X						3	X
Senegal							X	X		X		3	X
Seychelles		X				X						2	X
Sierra Leone							X					1	X
South Africa	X	X										2	X
Swaziland	X	X				X						3	X
Tanzania		X	X									2	X

												Total	
Togo		X						X		X		3	X
Tunisia			X							X		2	FTA
Uganda	X					X					X	3	X
Zambia						X	X					2	
Zimbabwe						X	X					2	X
Non-WTO members													
Algeria			X									1	FTA
Comoros						X				X		2	
Equatorial Guinea				X	X							2	
Eritrea						X					X	2	
Ethiopia						X					X	2	
Libya			X			X				X		3	
Sao Tomé and Principe					X							1	
Somalia										X	X	2	
Sudan						X				X	X	3	
TOTAL	5	15	5	6	11	19	15	8	5	20	7		

Source: Author's compilation.

Notes: "X" indicates membership.

⋆ These are RTAs which were notified under the WTO. ⋆⋆ Some members are still undertaking negotiations.

Economic Community of Central African States (ECCAS), Arab Maghreb Union (UMA), Community of Sahel–Saharan States (CEN-SAD) and Intergovernmental Authority on Development (IGAD) are RECs.

Annex 11.4 *Regional trade agreements in Africa*

RTA	Description
South African Customs Union (SACU)[55] South Africa Botswana Lesotho Namibia Swaziland	SACU, the oldest RTA in Africa, dates back to the 1889 Customs Union Convention between the British Colony of Cape of Good Hope and the Orange Free State Boer Republic. An agreement was later signed on 29 June 1910, to extend coverage to the Union of South Africa and the British High Commission Territories (HCTs), which were Lesotho, Botswana and Swaziland. South West Africa (Namibia) "was a *de facto* member, since it was administered as part of South Africa" before it became a *de jure* member. South Africa was the sole administrator of the common SACU revenue pool, setting SACU import duties and excise policy. An assessment of *Namibia and the SACU* by Erasmus (2014) noted that the 1969 Agreement provided for a CET for trade with third parties, while South Africa retained the sole decision-making power. With the Independence of Namibia and the end of Apartheid in South Africa, negotiations commenced again in 1994, which culminated in the SACU 2002 agreement of 15 July 2004, that effectively dealt with the joint decision-making process, revenue-sharing formula and the question of external (outside SACU) trade. The 2002 Agreement established an independent administrative Secretariat to oversee SACU with its headquarters in Windhoek, Namibia. The implementation of the new Revenue Sharing Formula as contained in the 2002 SACU Agreement began in 2004, and has the following components: customs, excise and development. As at the end of 2015, harmonized areas include applied customs tariff; excise duties; duty rebates, refunds and drawbacks; customs valuation; non-preferential rules of origin; and contingency trade remedies. Areas yet

---

[55] See more from the official Secretariat website at: http://www.sacu.int/.

Annex 11.4 (*cont.*)

RTA	Description
	to be fully harmonized include: customs procedures, value-added tax (VAT), standards, technical regulations, SPS measures, competition, agricultural and industrial policies and non-tariff measures. All SACU countries are members of SADC. In the African Economic Community (AEC), SACU countries are represented through the SADC group, being one of the eight pillars of African Economic Community.
Southern African Development Community (SADC)[56] SACU states: Botswana Lesotho Namibia South Africa Swaziland Angola Democratic Republic of the Congo Mauritius Mozambique Malawi Madagascar Seychelles Tanzania Zambia Zimbabwe	SADC was established in August 1992, originating from the Southern African Development Coordinating Conference (SADCC) established in April 1980. The SADC Free Trade Area was achieved in August 2008, but maximum tariff liberalization was attained by January 2012, when the tariff phase-down process for sensitive products was completed. The Secretariat, which facilitates the implementation of its programmes, is located in Gaborone, Botswana. It was established by the Treaty of 1992 and was re-established by the SADC Treaty Amendment of 2001 upon transitioning from a coordination conference to a Commission. The guiding frameworks for SADC Regional Integration are the Regional Indicative Strategic Development Plan (RISDP) and the Strategic Indicative Plan for the Organ (SIPO). Advancements have been made in pursuing a Monetary Union as the ultimate goal of SADC is to become an Economic Union by 2018. The Real Time Gross Settlement System has been developed to modernise cross-border payment settlements and has been implemented in twelve SADC member states; fourteen member states have implemented an application to harmonize banking supervision processes, developed by the ICT sub-committee of

[56] See more from the official Secretariat website at: http://sadc.int/.

Annex 11.4 (*cont.*)

RTA	Description
	the SADC Sub-Committee on Bank Supervision; and in 2009, the SADC ministers of finance developed and approved the Model Central Bank Law, which was designed to set harmonized frameworks for control of exchange policies, bank procedures and systems. SADC harmonization efforts have been in the areas of custom procedures and instruments, nomenclature of common tariffs; rules of origin; and trade facilitation software. Additionally, a task force formed by EAC, SADC and COMESA is working on a draft protocol of trade in services which includes regional qualification frameworks and a harmonization of education systems (UNECA 2012).
East African Community (EAC)[57] Burundi (2007)Kenya Tanzania Rwanda (2007) Uganda	Kenya, Tanzania, and Uganda have a long history of regional integration that dates back to the creation of the original EAC (in 1917), which collapsed for a variety of political and economic reasons by 1977. The current EAC, which entered into force on 7 July 2000, is set to become an Economic Area (including a customs and monetary union, with harmonized macroeconomic policies) and ultimately a political federation. The EAC CET between the three countries entered into force in January 2005 and for Rwanda and Burundi in 2009. In January 2010, its fully fledged CU and Common Market Protocol entered into force. The protocol for the establishment of a Monetary Union was signed in November 2013. The Secretariat is based in Arusha, Tanzania. Regarding revenue management, partner states adopted a destination principle where assessment and collection of revenue is at the first point of entry and revenue remitted to the destination partners subject to a fulfilment of key pre-conditions. Ongoing harmonization efforts have been successful

[57] See more from the official Secretariat website at: http://eac.int/.

Annex 11.4 (*cont.*)

RTA	Description
	in syncing cargo-tracking systems and streamlining customs procedures and documentation requirements; duty and tax exemptions, concession schemes; and export promotion instruments (manufacturing under bond, export processing zones, and duty remission schemes). Also, while technical regulations issues remain country-specific, some 1,200 (voluntary) standards have been harmonized for uniform application by EAC members. Further harmonization is yet to occur in areas such as customs-related issues, national export regimes, competition issues, sanitary and phytosanitary requirements, rules of origin, sectoral policies, import procedures – goods for direct home use, warehousing, transit and temporary importation. Regarding infrastructure, progress has been made on the East African Road Network Project, in particular the Northern and Central Corridor, which have reached the implementation stage. The EAC passport has been operational since 1999 and allows free multiple entries to citizens of partner states for up to six months. Member states agreed to develop a framework for mutually recognizing professional qualifications. It is now possible for legal practitioners to operate in any EAC country, without having to sit new bar examinations (UNECA 2012).
Central African Economic and Monetary Community (CEMAC)[58] Cameroon Central African Republic Chad	CEMAC was created in 1994 to replace the largely neglected customs union, the Union Douanière et Economique de l'Afrique Centrale (UDEAC), following the countries' independence in the 1960s. The CEMAC introduced (i) a common external tariff (CET), (ii) the gradual removal of tariffs on intra-regional trade (completed in 1998), (iii) the harmonization of indirect taxation (with the introduction of a VAT in 1999); and (iv) the

[58] See more from the official Secretariat website at: http://www.cemac.int/.

Annex 11.4 (*cont.*)

RTA	Description
Congo Equatorial Guinea* Gabon	replacement of quantitative import barriers by temporary import surcharges (Martijn and Tsangarides, 2007). CEMAC's two main pillars are the Monetary Union (UMAC) and the Economic Union (UEAC). UMAC's main institution is Banque des États de l'Afrique Centrale (BEAC) that issues the common currency (Franc CFA) and manages monetary policies, exchange operations and reserves in Member States. However, UEAC is less advanced. The CEMAC Secretariat, based in Bangui, Central African Republic, the main management and administrative body, was transformed into a commission in 2007. CEMAC countries, much like WAEMU, have made efforts to improve the business climate through their membership in the Organization for the Harmonization of Business Law in Africa (OHADA) by simplifying procedures, and taking initiatives to combat corruption. Areas yet to be harmonized include customs formalities, free movement of persons and goods, non-tariff barriers, the sanitary and phytosanitary measures and technical regulation regimes (with exception of the passport and international transhumance certificate for cattle). In border tax regimes, national suspensions of import taxes and of VAT undermine the harmonized regime. The Community introduced the CEMAC passport in 2000, although it is not yet in circulation.
Economic community of Central African States (ECCAS)[59] CEMAC states: Cameroon Central African	ECCAS was created in October 1983. The Union was inactive from 1992–98 as a result of conflicts in the majority of its member states. On February 1998, a decision to reactivate ECCAS was taken in Libreville, Gabon. In 2007, a strategic plan of integration, Vision 2025, was adopted. ECCAS, as an

[59] See more from the official Secretariat website at: http://www.ceeac-eccas.org/index.php /fr/.

Annex 11.4 (*cont.*)

RTA	Description
Republic Chad Congo Gabon Angola Burundi DRC Equatorial Guinea* Rwanda Sao Tomé and Principe*	FTA, has been effective since 2004 and is geared towards a customs union. ECCAS has a preferential tariff regime, a transit regime, and its own rules of origin. All the CEMAC countries belong to the Economic Community of Central African States (ECCAS). ECCAS represents CEMAC in the African Economic Community, since as an entity it is not one of the designated eight pillars for the implementation of the AEC. A steering committee was established in 2010 to harmonize ECCAS and CEMAC.
Western African **Economic and** **Monetary Union** **(WAEMU)**[60] Benin Burkina Faso Côte d'Ivoire Guinea-Bissau Mali Niger Senegal Togo	WAEMU was created in 1994 to replace the West African Monetary Union (WAMU) and became a customs union with a common external tariff by 2000. The WAEMU Commission installed in January 1995 and based in Ouagadougou has exclusive authority over the common trade policy of its members *vis-à-vis* third-party states. It is funded by the community solidary levy of 1 per cent, applied to imports from third countries, paid in full to the WAEMU Commission. WAEMU's macroeconomic policies have been harmonized, as evidenced by the Banque Centrale des États de l'Afrique de l'Ouest (BCEAO), implementation of the West African Accounting System (SYSCOA), legislation in terms of VAT and the creation of the Regional Stock Market (BRVM) since 1998 as well as the establishment of the Institution of the National Economic Policy Committee and adoption of a Harmonized Consumer Price Index (HICP). The instruments harmonized within WAEMU include customs valuation (guiding principles); contingency measures; other import duties and taxes (statistical fee (RS), community solidarity levy (PCS)); bank

---

[60] See more from the official Secretariat website at: http://www.uemoa.int/Pages/Home .aspx.

Annex 11.4 (*cont.*)

RTA	Description
	domiciliation of trade transactions; rules of origin; competition policy; and control of veterinary medicines. Additionally, the ECOWAS rules of origin were broadly harmonized with those of WAEMU in 2003. Notably, there are ongoing efforts at convergence of national regimes on internal taxation (value added tax (VAT), excise duties, tax on petroleum products, advance payment of profits tax); prohibitions and licensing; standards, technical regulations and accreditation procedures; sanitary and phytosanitary safety; and government procurement. Areas reserved to national competence include import inspection programmes and customs duties and taxes of equivalent effect levied by Member States on their exports. WAEMU, like CEMAC, is signatory to the Treaty on the Harmonization of Business Law in Africa (OHADA). All WAEMU countries are members of ECOWAS and thus, the introduction of a CET in 2015 affected all WAEMU countries.
Economic Community of West African States (ECOWAS)[61] WAEMU states: Benin Burkina Faso Côte d'Ivoire Guinea-Bissau Mali Niger Senegal Sierra Leone Togo Non-WAEMU states:	ECOWAS was created by the Treaty of Lagos in May 1975. It was revised in 1993 in order to accelerate economic integration, eventually leading to the establishment of a common market and a single currency. The ECOWAS Secretariat based in Abuja, Nigeria, was transformed into a Commission on January 2007. Some trade policy instruments are harmonized within ECOWAS, albeit to a lesser extent, namely the ECOWAS community levy, rules of origin (similar to those of WAEMU), competition regulations (not yet operational) and the Inter State Road Transit (TRIE) regime, which is still unevenly implemented. ECOWAS has achieved the free movement of its population. It has made efforts in the area of investment through the establishment of the

---

[61] See more from the official Secretariat website at: http://www.ecowas.int/.

Annex 11.4 (*cont.*)

RTA	Description
Cabo Verde The Gambia Ghana Guinea Republic of Liberia* Nigeria *Mauritania withdrew* *from ECOWAS in* *1999*	ECOWAS Common Investment Market and the Development of Common Investment Code and Policy. Another initiative of ECOWAS is the West African Power Pool (WAPP), the purpose of which is to expand trade in electricity among the fifteen member countries. Additionally, efforts are being made to harmonize macroeconomic policies and private sector promotion. ECOWAS CET commenced in January 2015 and has a five-year window implementation for conformity. Within this period, member states are allowed to maintain certain exemptions currently in place. Other issues to be addressed within this period are the full Harmonisation Community Customs Procedure Code; exemption regimes harmonization; and free circulation. Work is ongoing on the revenue-sharing formula and is hoped to be completed within the five-year window (Andoh 2014).
Common Market for Eastern and Southern Africa (COMESA)[62] Burundi (2004) Comoros* (2006) DRC Djibouti Egypt Eritrea* Ethiopia* Kenya Libya*(2006) Mauritius Malawi Madagascar Rwanda (2004)	COMESA was formed in 1994 to replace the former Preferential Trade Area for Eastern and Southern Africa, which existed from 1981. COMESA became an FTA in October 2000 and the launch of the customs union was in 2009. The CET of COMESA launched in 2009 is said to be harmonized with that of EAC, thus moving closer towards becoming a single FTA and customs union. Overall coordination is achieved through the Secretariat, which was established in 1994, in Lusaka, Zambia. COMESA has made progress in harmonizing trade facilitation instruments. COMESA also has programmes addressing improved efficiencies in agriculture, which are in support of the Comprehensive Africa Agricultural Development Programme (CAADP). There is also the COMESA clearing house (until a common central bank is established) to settle all

---

[62] See more from the official Secretariat website at: http://www.comesa.int/.

Annex 11.4 (*cont.*)

RTA	Description
Seychelles Swaziland Sudan Uganda Zambia Zimbabwe *Tanzania left in* *2001; Namibia left in* *2004; Angola* *suspended itself in* *2007*	payments in respect of all transactions in goods and services within the common market. The Clearing House introduced the Regional Payment and Settlement System (REPSS), and started live operations on 3 October 2012. Efforts are ongoing regarding harmonization of macroeconomic policies.

Sources: TPRs and the RTA Secretariat Official Websites
Note: * Non-WTO member.

Annex 11.5 *Availability of tariffs on 43 African WTO members, as of January 2016*

	Member	Data from TPRs	Data from WTO IDB		
			Range	Missing years from range	Total no. of years available
1	**Angola**	2004, 2006	2004–2015	2006, 2007, 2008	9
2	**Benin**	1997, 2003, 2009	2003–2015	None	13
3	**Botswana**	1997, 2000, 2001, 2002, 2008, 2009, 2014	2002–2014	2003, 2004, 2006	10
4	**Burkina Faso**	1997, 2003, 2009	2003–2015	None	13
5	**Burundi**	1993, 2003, 2012	2002–2014	2004, 2005, 2006, 2007, 2008, 2009	7
6	**Cabo Verde**	2014	2006–2015	None	10
7	**Cameroon**	1995, 2000, 2007, 2013	2001–2014	None	14
8	**Central African Republic**	2007, 2013	2002–2013	None	12
9	**Chad**	2007, 2013	2002–2013	2012	11
10	**Congo**	2006, 2013	2002–2013	2012	11
11	**Côte d'Ivoire**	1994	2002–2015	None	14
12	**Democratic Republic of the Congo**	2010	2009–2010	None	2
13	**Djibouti**	2006, 2014	1998–2014	2000, 2001, 2002, 2003, 2004, 2007, 2008, 2010, 2013	8

Annex 11.5 (cont.)

	Member	Data from TPRs	Data from WTO IDB		
			Range	Missing years from range	Total no. of years available
14	**Egypt**	1991, 1999, 2004	1998–2015	None	18
15	**Gabon**	2001, 2007, 2013	2000–2013	2001, 2006	12
16	**The Gambia**	2000, 2003, 2007, 2010	2003–2013	2004, 2005, 2006, 2008,	7
17	**Ghana**	1991, 2000, 2007, 2013	2001–2015	2004, 2005, 2006, 2011, 2014	10
18	**Guinea**	1998, 2005, 2011	1998–2012	1999, 2000, 2001, 2002, 2003, 2006, 2007, 2008, 2010, 2011	5
19	**Guinea- Bissau**	-	2003–2014	None	12
20	**Kenya**	1999, 2005, 2012	1999–2014	2000, 2003	14
21	**Lesotho**	1997, 2000, 2001, 2002, 2008, 2009, 2014	2005–2014	2006	9
22	**Madagascar**	2001, 2008	1996–2014	1999	18
23	**Malawi**	1997, 1998, 2001, 2002, 2009	2000–2012	2001, 2002, 2004, 2005, 2006, 2007, 2008	6
24	**Mali**	1997, 2003, 2009	1996–2015	2000, 2001, 2002	16
25	**Mauritania**	2000, 2011	2001–2014	2002, 2003, 2004, 2005, 2012, 2013	8
26	**Mauritius**	1995, 2001, 2007, 2014	1996–2015	1997, 2003	18
27	**Morocco**	1995, 2002, 2008, 2009	1996–2015	1998, 2004	18
28	**Mozambique**	2000, 2008	2008–2014	None	7

29	Namibia	1997, 2000, 2001, 2002, 2008, 2009, 2014	2002–2014	2003, 2004, 2006	10
30	Niger	1997, 2002, 2009	2002–2015	None	14
31	Nigeria	1998, 2003, 2009	1996–2013	2004, 2007, 2012	17
32	Rwanda	2004	2000–2014	2001, 2004, 2005, 2006, 2007, 2008	9
33	Senegal	1994, 1995, 2002, 2009	2002–2015	None	14
34	Seychelles	None	None	None	1
35	Sierra Leone	2004	2004–2012	2005, 2007, 2008, 2009	5
36	South Africa	1997, 2000, 2001, 2002, 2008, 2009, 2014	1996–2015	1998, 2004, 2006	17
37	Swaziland	1997, 2000, 2001, 2002, 2008, 2009, 2014	2002–2015	2003, 2004, 2006	11
38	Tanzania	1999, 2005, 2012	2003–2014	2004	11
39	Togo	1998, 2005	1996–2015	None	20
40	Tunisia	1994, 2004, 2005	2000–2013	2001, 2006, 2007	11
41	Uganda	1995, 2001	2001–2014	2002, 2003, 2004, 2006, 2007, 2008	8
42	Zambia	1996, 2002, 2009	2001–2014	2009	13
43	Zimbabwe	2011	1997–2012	2003, 2004, 2005, 2006, 2008, 2009	10

Source: WTO Integrated Data Base and Trade Policy Reviews.
Note: This table reflects data available for HS Code 6 sub-headings.

Annex 11.6 *Evolution of tariffs in Africa per region, 1996–2015*

	1996	1997	1998	1999	2000	2001	2002	2003	2004	2005	2006	2007	2008	2009	2010	2011	2012	2013	2014	2015
AFRICA																				
All products	**18.8**	**17.6**	**19.1**	**21**	**18.6**	**16.2**	**16.4**	**16.2**	**14.3**	**13.8**	**14.4**	**12.9**	**12.6**	**12.8**	**12.1**	**12.3**	**12.1**	**12**	**11.4**	**10.5**
Agricultural products	22.4	24	25.3	29.5	29.9	23.9	25	23.5	20.8	19.5	19.6	17.7	17.9	17.1	17.1	17.5	17.3	16.8	16.1	16.9
Non-agricultural products	18.5	16.5	18.1	19.6	16.7	14.9	15.1	15	13.2	12.9	13.5	12.1	11.7	12.1	11.3	11.5	11.2	11.1	10.7	9.36
Sample size	*7*	*7*	*9*	*10*	*12*	*14*	*25*	*26*	*22*	*31*	*24*	*30*	*31*	*38*	*40*	*39*	*37*	*35*	*30*	*17*
NORTH AFRICA																				
All products	**30.5**	**33.9**	**28.1**	**30.6**	**30.6**	**30**	**28.9**	**29**	**24.3**	**24.5**	**22.3**	**20**	**20.1**	**18.8**	**16.8**	**15.9**	**15.3**	**14.1**	**14.3**	**14.5**
Agricultural products	47.9	56.4	74.1	66.7	66.7	64.2	64.8	64.7	67.7	59.1	57.5	55.4	50.3	48.3	44.4	47.1	47	38.1	45.4	14.5
Non-agricultural products	27.6	30.2	21.1	24.7	24.8	24.5	23.1	23.1	17.4	18.9	16.7	14.4	15.4	14.1	12.5	10.9	10.1	10	9.15	9.2
Sample size	*1*	*1*	*1*	*2*	*3*	*2*	*3*	*3*	*2*	*3*	*2*	*2*	*3*	*3*	*3*	*3*	*3*	*3*	*2*	*2*
SUB-SAHARAN AFRICA																				
All Products	**16.9**	**14.9**	**18**	**18.7**	**14.6**	**13.9**	**14.7**	**14.5**	**13.3**	**12.7**	**13.6**	**12.4**	**11.8**	**12.3**	**11.7**	**12**	**11.8**	**11.8**	**11.2**	**9.94**
Agricultural products	18.1	18.6	19.3	20.3	17.7	17.2	19.5	18.1	16.1	15.2	16.2	15	14.4	14.4	14.9	15	14.7	14.8	14	13.1
Non-agricultural products	16.9	14.2	17.7	18.4	14	13.3	14	13.9	12.8	12.3	13.2	12	11.3	11.9	11.2	11.5	11.3	11.3	10.8	9.38
Sample size	*6*	*6*	*8*	*8*	*9*	*12*	*22*	*23*	*20*	*28*	*22*	*28*	*28*	*35*	*37*	*36*	*34*	*32*	*28*	*15*

REGIONAL GROUPS

Group																		
SACU (5)	17.3	17.6	13	12.4	9.65	10.2	10.9	9.02	10.7	7.5	7.2	7.3	7.2	7.2	7.1	7.2	7.2	7.2
SADC (14)							14.8	12.6	12.6	10.7	9.42	8.6	8.7	9.3	9.1	9.11	8.34	8.7
EAC (5)							18	18.1	18.3	13.4	12.9	14.2	12.4	12.4	12.7	12.6	12.6	12.6
CEMAC (5)						18	18.1	18.3	18.3	18.3	17.9	17.9	17.9	17.9	17.9	18	18	18.3
WAEMU (8)		15	12.2	12.3	12	12	12	12	12	12.3	11.9	11.9	11.9	11.9	11.9	11.9	11.9	12.1
ECOWAS (14)		19.1	17.1	15.1	13.8	11.6	12	12	12.3	12	11.9	12	12	12	11.9	12	12.1	12.1
COMESA (13)	22.1	24.3	16.4	16.6	15.7	16.9	16.7	14	14.2	15.6	11.7	10.9	12.8	11.5	12.3	12.4	11.2	12.2

Source: WTO Integrated Database, based on available data (see sample sizes).

Note on composition of categories: **Africa**– 43 WTO members; **North Africa**– Egypt, Morocco, Tunisia; **SSA**– Nigeria, Sierra Leone, Cabo Verde, The Gambia, Ghana, Benin, Burkina Faso, Côte d'Ivoire, Guinea, Guinea-Bissau, Mali, Niger, Senegal, Togo, Mauritania, Cameroon, Central African Republic, Chad, Gabon, Congo, Djibouti, Kenya, Burundi, Rwanda, Uganda, Tanzania, Mozambique, Angola, Namibia, Lesotho, Botswana, South Africa, Swaziland, Mauritius, Madagascar, Democratic Republic of the Congo, Zambia, Zimbabwe, Seychelles; **SACU**– Namibia, Lesotho, Botswana, South Africa, Swaziland; **EAC**– Kenya, Burundi, Rwanda, Uganda, Tanzania; **COMESA**– Djibouti, Egypt, Kenya, Burundi, Rwanda, Uganda, Seychelles, Swaziland, Mauritius, Malawi, Madagascar, Democratic Republic of the Congo, Zambia, Zimbabwe; **SADC**– Tanzania, Mozambique, Angola, Namibia, Lesotho, Botswana, South Africa, Swaziland, Mauritius, Malawi, Madagascar, Democratic Republic of the Congo, Zambia, Zimbabwe; **WAEMU**– Benin, Burkina Faso, Côte d'Ivoire, Guinea, Guinea-Bissau, Mali, Niger, Senegal, Togo; **ECOWAS**– Nigeria, Sierra Leone, Cabo Verde, The Gambia, Ghana, Benin, Burkina Faso, Côte d'Ivoire, Guinea, Guinea-Bissau, Mali, Niger, Senegal, Togo; and **CEMAC**– Cameroon, Central African Republic, Chad, Gabon, Congo.

Annex 11.7 *List of other duties and charges identified in Trade Policy Reviews, 1995–2015*

Member	Other duties and charges
SACU	–
Botswana	– Flour levy at a rate of 15 per cent on imports of wheat flour – Additional duty of 40 per cent on imports of UHT milk – Fuel levy of P 0.12 per litre of petrol and P 0.07 per litre of diesel. The levy is collected at point of entry and finances the National Petroleum Fund (NPF) that is used to stabilize the price of oil products in the domestic market.
Lesotho	– Levy of 2.5 per cent to imported dairy products
Namibia	– Special Meat Classification Levy – General levy of 0.8 per cent of the selling price on imports of cattle, sheep, goats, pigs, meat or meat products – In order to protect its cement industry, Namibia imposed an IIP on cement in July 2012 in the form of a 60 per cent duty which is set to decrease up to 12 per cent in 2018.
South Africa	– Fuel levy and the road accident fund levy on specific goods imported for, *inter alia*, domestic consumption by diplomats . . .
Swaziland	– Fuel levy of E 0.70 per litre – Import levies on milk and dairy products at rates of 10 per cent or 12 per cent of the invoice value
EAC	–
Burundi	– Overtime fees – Fees for cautionary visits – Licence fees – Fees for services to the public
Kenya	– Import declaration fee of 2.25 per cent is payable on the c.i.f. value of all imports. – 7 per cent levy applies on the value of imported sugar – Overtime fees – Fees for cautionary visits – Licence fees – Fees for services to the public
Rwanda	– Road maintenance fees – Visa fees – Rwanda Bureau of Standards (RBS) fees – Overtime fees – Fees for cautionary visits – Licence fees – Fees for services to the public
Tanzania	– Overtime fees – Fees for cautionary visits – Licence fees – Fees for services to the public

Annex 11.7 (*cont.*)

Member	Other duties and charges
Uganda	– Second-hand cars of eight years or older are subject to 25 per cent import duty, 18 per cent VAT, 6 per cent withholding tax, and an environmental levy at 20 per cent. – Overtime fees – Fees for cautionary visits – Licence fees – Fees for services to the public
CEMAC/ ECCAS	– Community integration contribution (CCI), levied at the rate of 0.4 per cent on imports from outside ECCAS and intended to finance ECCAS and its institutions – Organization for the Harmonization of Business Law in Africa (OHADA) levy, charged at the rate of 0.05 per cent on imports from non-member countries – Communal tax of 10 per cent of the VAT – Community integration tax (taxe communautaire d'intégration (TCI)
Cameroon	– Inspection and monitoring tax is levied for services provided by the SGS – Levy on river and maritime freight by the Conseil National des Chargeurs du Cameroun (CNCC) – Temporary import surcharge of up to 30 per cent – Computer fee of 0.45 per cent on imports whose declarations are processed in computerized offices, – Phytosanitary taxes (*taxes phytosanitaires* (TPS)) or sanitary/veterinary inspection taxes – Storage fees – 'Fee on intellectual works', which has been imposed since 2011 on a number of electronic musical media, such as computer hard disks, mobile telephones, printers, USB keys, at a rate of 5 per cent of the f.o.b. import value
Central African Republic	– 0.50 per cent levy on computer equipment for finance (REIF) – 0.1 per cent COMIFAC levy – 0.5 per cent Scanner management fee
Chad	– Community preference tax (TPC): initially intended to finance the Community's Economic Commission on Livestock, Meat and Fishery Resources (CEBEVIRHA). Although the other countries have replaced this levy with the TCI, Chad still collects it on tariff lines relating to fish, meat, dairy products and other products of animal origin – Down payment of 4 per cent of the c.i.f. value of the imports, charged in the form of personal income tax – Statistical fee of 2 per cent of the c.i.f. value of imports, charged on all imports, irrespective of origin – The Rural Intervention Fund (FIR) duty, charged at rates varying from 0.3 per cent to 0.5 per cent, on 9 per cent of tariff lines

Annex 11.7 (*cont.*)

Member	Other duties and charges
	(products of plant origin, meat and fish). It is transferred to the Ministry responsible for agriculture. – For goods in transit through Cameroon, an information fee of CFAF 500 and a communications network and en route assistance fee of CFAF 2,000 is charged per journey, payable to Cameroon's Land Freight Management Bureau (BGFT)
Congo	– A 2 per cent automation fee – Inspection charges for transactions subject to inspection – Minimum 5 per cent customs duty is also in place for goods exempt under either the Customs Code, or international agreements and treaties (see 2012 Finance Law) – 15 per cent tax on imports of timber products and wood products with the exception of those intended to supply local industries – 5 per cent levy by way of an advance payment on income taxes (ADIT) – 0.2 per cent statistical tax on imports of all origins
Gabon	– The fee for use of the customs ADP system (RUSID), which is proportional to the amount of time actually spent on the system – Scanning fee (RDS) of CFAF 85,000 per TEU has been introduced for containers which are scanned
WAEMU/ ECOWAS	– WAEMU statistical fee (RS) at a rate of 1 per cent – WAEMU Community solidarity levy (PCS), at a rate of 1 per cent – ECOWAS community levy of 0.5 per cent – ECOWAS Community Integration Levy
Benin	– Port charges such as docking and handling (CFAF 1,000/t (US$ 1.5/t)) – Port commission (CFAF 1,300/t (US$ 2/t)) – Fee for placing seals (CFAF 25 per seal) – Levy of the Benin National Dockers' Council (CFAF 300/t (US$ 0.5/t) on exports and CFAF 400/t (US$ 0.7/t) on imports) – Fiscal export levy – Special re-export tax – Computer fee – Statistical tax – Temporary import tax – Vehicle tax
Burkina Faso	– 1 per cent of the f.o.b. value to the import inspection programme (PVI) – Transit levy to Chamber of Commerce and Industry of Burkina Faso (CCI-BF) – 'Deduction at source' at a rate of 20 per cent
Côte d'Ivoire	– Countervailing duty on meat – Special tax on tomato concentrates – Equalization tax on sugar

Annex 11.7 (*cont.*)

Member	Other duties and charges
	– Special textile tax
	– Tax for the development of agro-food production
	– Special import tax (TCI)
Guinea-Bissau	– Fuel, rice, and cement levies to finance national activities
	– Special import tax (TCI)
	– Goods crossing the customs cordon are subject to the payment of personal (*emolumentos pessoais*) and travel fees (*deslocações*) for customs services rendered
	– Fuel imports are subject to a levy of 4 per cent of the c.i.f. value
	– Levies on rice and cement imports at the rate of CFAF 1 per kg to finance the Chamber of Commerce
Mali	– Advance payment on several levies and taxes (ADIT), at a rate of 3 per cent of the c.i.f. value for imports
Niger	– TIPP (special internal tax on petroleum products)
Senegal	– Tax on fabrics
	– COSEC levy
	– Pastoral fund levy
	– Additional tax
	– Surcharge
	– Petroleum products tax
	– Equalization tax
	– Para-fiscal tax of 1 per cent is imposed on fabrics and is based on the c.i.f. customs value
Togo	– Infrastructure protection tax (TPI)
	– Special import tax (TCI)
ECOWAS only	– ECOWAS community levy of 0.5 per cent
	– ECOWAS Community Integration Levy
Benin	– Port charges such as docking and handling (CFAF 1,000/t (US$ 1.5/t))
	– Port commission (CFAF 1,300/t (US$ 2/t))
	– Fee for placing seals (CFAF 25 per seal)
	– Levy of the Benin National Dockers' Council (CFAF 300/t (US$ 0.5/t) on exports and CFAF 400/t (US$ 0.7/t) on imports)
	– Fiscal export levy
	– Special re-export tax
	– Computer fee
	– Statistical tax
	– Temporary import tax
	– Vehicle tax
Burkina Faso	– 1 per cent of the f.o.b. value to the import inspection programme (PVI)
	– Transit levy to Chamber of Commerce and Industry of Burkina Faso (CCI-BF)
	– 'Deduction at source' at a rate of 20 per cent

Annex 11.7 (*cont.*)

Member	Other duties and charges
Côte d'Ivoire	– Countervailing duty on meat – Special tax on tomato concentrates – Equalization tax on sugar – Special textile tax – Tax for the development of agro-food production – Special import tax (TCI)
Guinea-Bissau	– Fuel, rice, and cement levies to finance national activities – Special import tax (TCI) – Goods crossing the customs cordon are subject to the payment of personal (*emolumentos pessoais*) and travel fees (*deslocações*) for customs services rendered – Fuel imports are subject to a levy of 4 per cent of the c.i.f. value – Levies on rice and cement imports at the rate of CFAF 1 per kg to finance the Chamber of Commerce
Mali	– Advance payment on several levies and taxes (ADIT), at a rate of 3 per cent of the c.i.f. value for imports
Niger	– TIPP (special internal tax on petroleum products)
Senegal	– Tax on fabrics – COSEC levy – Pastoral fund levy – Additional tax – Surcharge – Petroleum products tax – Equalization tax – Para-fiscal tax of 1 per cent is imposed on fabrics and is based on the c.i.f. customs value
Togo	– Infrastructure protection tax (TPI) – Special import tax (TCI)
OTHERS	
Angola	– Stamp duty of 1 per cent of the c.i.f. value on imports – Statistical tax of 0.1 per cent, applies to petroleum products and goods for direct and exclusive use of extractive industries
Democratic Republic of Congo	– DGDA, for example, levies 1 per cent of the c.i.f. value of goods – OCC applies a 2 per cent tax on the c.i.f. value of imports, consisting of 0.75 per cent on behalf of BIVAC and 1.25 per cent for the OCC itself and also a flat rate of US\$ 5/tonne for tally operations – The Fund for the Promotion of Industry (FPI) imposes 2 per cent duty on the c.i.f. value of goods imported, with the exception of raw materials and imported goods exempt from customs duty – The Multimodal Freight Management Office (OGEFREM) takes a 1.8 per cent commission on freight, 0.59 per cent for transhipment and the cost of the electronic import information form

Annex 11.7 (*cont.*)

Member	Other duties and charges
	– The National Transport Office (ONATRA) collects US$ 20/tonne for handling ships at the quayside and US$ 32/ tonne for transit fees
	– All import/export operations require a licence issued by a private bank against payment of US$ 12
	– Turnover tax (ICA) on imports
	– Administrative fee
	– Fees charged for forms
	– Computer fees
	– Electronic surveillance and merchandise inspection fee (AUFS)
	– Administrative service tax (diamonds, gold, heterogenite, copper, cassiterite, coltan, wolframite and other precious materials used for artisanal purposes)
	– *Ex officio* storage tax
	– Private warehouse surveillance tax
	– Private warehouse opening tax
	– Storage charges
	– Graduated and cumulative tax
	– Container entry card
	– Ministry of Energy tax (CNE fee)
	– Fine by way of settlement for failure to obtain a licence or for not subjecting goods to pre-shipment inspection
	– Tax on the import of medicines
Djibouti	– Business licence fee of DF 8.4 is levied on each gross kg of khat imported or produced locally. This is increased by 7 per cent for the community centime tax levied on behalf of the Djibouti Chamber of Commerce.
	– Tax for the youth, sports and leisure fund applies as follows: DF 50 per kg of khat; and 10 per cent on the value of other imported goods
Egypt	–
Madagascar	– On specific products, e.g. beer: MGA 250/litre; wine: from 50 per cent to 200 per cent; other alcoholic beverages: from 50 per cent to 250 per cent for the *ad valorem* tariff and from MGA 75/litre to MGA 1,450/litre for the specific rate; cigarettes and other tobacco: 50 per cent to 325 per cent; imported second-hand motor vehicles: 10 per cent; and mobile telephone services: 7 per cent
Malawi	– Implicit surtax rate of 13 per cent
	– Stamp duties on instruments such as leases, mortgages, bonds and insurance policies
	– A fuel levy is charged at MK 7.35 per litre on petrol, MK 6.18 per litre on diesel and MK 2.99 per litre on paraffin, to fund road construction and maintenance.
Mauritania	– A UM 2,000 computer fee is charged on each declaration, whatever the customs procedure.
	– Statistical fee

Annex 11.7 (*cont.*)

Member	Other duties and charges
Mauritius	– Maurice Ile Durable (MID) levy is collected on various fuels and a levy is collected on various energy-inefficient household appliances (refrigerators, dishwashing machines, ovens, household room air conditioners, tumble dryers and electric lamps). – Processed tea is subject to a clearance fee of MUR 20 per kg or part thereof for black tea products for blending purposes, MUR 40 per kg or part thereof for green tea products in packets of 125g or above and MUR 300 per kg or part thereof for other tea products
Morocco	– 'Parafiscal' taxes (0.25 per cent of customs value) – The 'stamp' duty – The 'storage' tax (4–14 per cent of the customs value if the goods stay more than three days in customs) – The 'administrative' fees – The 'computer' tax – Tax for the control and stamping of imported handmade carpets (5 per cent)
Mozambique	– Import surtaxes on sugar; cement; and certain galvanized steel products
Tunisia	– Levies on motor vehicles, alcoholic beverages and tobacco – Inter-trade contribution to the Fund for the Development of Industrial Competitiveness (non-agricultural products) – Environmental protection tax (chemical products, cells, batteries) – Tax on fish – Animal health tax (animals, meat, hides) – Municipal slaughter tax (meat) – Trade tax for the benefit of the funds for the development of competitiveness in the agriculture, fishing and agro-food industry sectors – Advance income/company tax at 10 per cent of the c.i.f. value of certain imported products
Zambia	– Refundable 3 per cent advance tax
Zimbabwe	– COMESA surtax is levied on certain imports at either 2 per cent (1,078 HS 8-digit lines) or 1 per cent (69 HS 8-digit lines) – Imports of fuel are subject to a NOCZIM debt redemption levy and a carbon tax; their respective rates are US\$ 0.028/litre and US\$ 0.013/litre on diesel, and US\$ 0.082/litre and US\$ 0.04/litre on petrol – Trade development surcharge of 0.1 per cent is levied on the f.o.b. value of imported and exported goods for the purpose of financing any trade development organization involved in the promotion of Zimbabwe's exports

Source: TPRs.
Note: The list of ODCs in this annex is not exhaustive.

Annex 11.8 *Use of preshipment inspection, 1995–2015*

	1995	1996	1997	1998	1999	2000	2001	2002	2003	2004	2005	2006	2007	2008	2009	2010	2011	2012	2013	2014	2015
SACU																					
Botswana																					
Lesotho																					
Namibia																					
South Africa																					
Swaziland																					
EAC																					
Burundi	X	X	X	X	X	X	X	X	X	X	X	X	X	X	X	X	X	X			
Kenya	X	X	X	X	X	X	X	X	X	X	END										
Rwanda	X	X	X	X	X	X	X	X	X	END											
Tanzania					X	X	X	X	X	END											
Uganda	X	X	X	X	X	X	END														
CEMAC																					
Cameroon	X	X	X	X	X	X	X	X	X	X	X	X	X	X	X	X	X	X	X		
Central African Republic	X	X	X	X	X	X	X	X	X	X	X	X	X	X	X	X	X	X	X		
Chad	X	X	X	X	X	X	X	X	X	X	X	X	X	X	X	X	X	X	X		
Congo	X	X	X	X	X	X	X	X	X	X	X	X	X	X	X	X	X	X	X		
Gabon	X	X	X	X	X	X	X	X	X	X	X	X	X	X							
WAEMU																					
Benin	X	X	X	X	X	X	X	X	X	X	X	X	X	X	X	X					
Burkina	X	X	X	X	X	X	X	X	X	X	X	X	X	X	X	X					
Cote d'Ivoire	X	X	X	X	X	X	X	X	X	X	X	X	X	X	X	X	X	X			
Guinea Bissau																					
Mali	X	X	X	X	X	X	X	X	X	X	X	X	X	X	X	X					
Niger	X	X	X	X	X	X	X	X	X	X	X	X	X	X	X						
Senegal	X	X	X	X	X	X	X	X	X	X	X	X	X	X	X						
Togo	X	X	X	X	X	X	X	X	X	X	X	X	X	X	X	X	X	X			

Annex 11.8 (*cont.*)

	1995	1996	1997	1998	1999	2000	2001	2002	2003	2004	2005	2006	2007	2008	2009	2010	2011	2012	2013	2014	2015
ECOWAS only																					
Cabo Verde																					
Ghana	X	X	X	X	X	X	END														
Guinea		X	X	X	END																
Nigeria	X	X	X	X	X	X	X	X	X	END											
Sierra Leone	X	X	X	X	X	X	X	X	X	X	**X**										
OTHERS																					
Angola	X	X	X	X	X	X	X	X	X	X	X	X	X	X	X	X	X	X	END		
Democratic Republic of the Congo	X	X	X	X	X	X	X	X	X	X	X	X	X	X	X	**X**					
Djibouti	X	X	END																		
Egypt																					
Madagascar	X	X	X	X	X	X	X	X	X	X	END										
Malawi	X	X	X	X	X	X	X	X	X	X	X	X	X	X	X	**X**					
Mauritania	X	X	X	X	X	X	X	X	X	X	X	X	X	X	X	X	**X**				
Mauritius																					
Morocco																					
Mozambique			INTR	X	X	X	X	X	X	X	END										
Tunisia																					
Zambia	X	X	X	END																	
Zimbabwe																					

Source: TPRs.

Notes: X – Use of PSI; **X** – Latest available information in TPRs; END – End of the use of PSI.

Annex 11.9 *State trading enterprises in Africa, based on latest available information in TPRs*

	Member	State trading activity	Notification
1	**Angola**	SONANGOL (Sociedade Nacional de Combustíveis de Angola), a SOE, controls all activities relating to oil and natural gas, including exclusive import rights for oil products, except for lubricants.	NO
		Angolan Diamond Marketing Company (SODIAM), a SOE, holds the exclusive right of marketing of diamonds.	
2	**Benin**	Some enterprises that specialize in certain categories of product (for example, brand-name drugs and fertilizer) are granted exclusive import rights.	NO
		Since 1997, monopolies on the import of fertilizer (SONAPRA) and crude petroleum (SONACOP) were abolished.	
3	**Botswana**	The Botswana Meat Commission (BMC), which is 100 per cent state-owned, has a statutory monopoly on beef exports.	X*
		Debswana, the diamond mining company (50 per cent state ownership), holds a *de facto* monopoly over exports of rough diamonds.	
4	**Burkina Faso**	The Textile Fibre Company (SOFITEX) still has a monopoly of the processing of seed cotton and its marketing.	NO
		The Burkina Hydrocarbons Company (SONABHY) has an import monopoly of hydrocarbons (excluding lubricants).	
		The State holds a monopoly on the importation of tobacco products whose selling prices are fixed by the Ministry responsible for trade.	
5	**Burundi**	N.A.	NO
6	**Cabo Verde**	Sociedade Caboverdiana de Tabacos, SA, a former SOE, was granted in 1997 with the exclusive import and wholesale marketing rights for tobacco and tobacco	X

Annex 11.9 (*cont.*)

	Member	State trading activity	Notifi-cation
		derivatives for a period of 15 years (renewable).	
		EMPROFAC, created to ensure access to basic medicines for the entire population, holds exclusive rights to import and distribute pharmaceuticals.	
		Exclusive purchasing and distribution rights on fuels and lubricants, held by two private enterprises (Shell and ENACOL), were terminated in 2006.	
		Exclusive rights to import food products by two SOEs – EMPA (Empresa Pública de Abastecimento) and MOAVE (Moagem de Cabo Verde), were terminated.	
7	Cameroon	The Cameroon Oil Storage Company (SCDP) has a *de facto* monopoly on imports of oil products.	NO
8	Central African Republic	A monopoly of 90 per cent of sugar imports has been given to the private company SUCAF RCA.	NO
		The SOCASP, 51 per cent state-owned, is exclusively responsible for the storage and handling of all petroleum products and derivatives.	
9	Chad	The State-owned Chad Cotton Company (COTONTCHAD) has a monopoly on cotton marketing, including exports.	X*
10	Congo	Saris Congo is the only company producing and importing sugar.	NO
11	Côte d'Ivoire	The government holds the exclusive right to import and distribute certain animal vaccines.	X
12	Democratic Republic of the Congo	N.A.	NO
13	Djibouti	N.A.	NO

Annex 11.9 (*cont.*)

	Member	State trading activity	Notification
14	**Egypt**	No STEs within the of Article XVII:4(a) of GATT 1994.	X*
15	**Gabon**	A domestic private company holds the import monopoly for cement.	NO
		The state-owned enterprise SOGARA has the monopoly on the production and importation of petroleum products.	
		The private company SMAG has the monopoly on the production and importation of flour.	
		SIAT-Gabon, a private company, holds a monopoly on the production of edible oils, as well as the importation and marketing of edible oils of non-CEMAC origin.	
16	**The Gambia**	The Gambia National Petroleum Company (GAMPETROLEUM), established in 2004, has a monopoly on the import of petroleum products.	NO
17	**Ghana**	The Cocoa Marketing Company, a subsidiary of the Ghana Cocoa Board, has the monopoly right to export cocoa beans.	X*
		The import monopoly on crude oil by the Ghana National Petroleum Corporation was terminated in 1996.	
		The exclusive exporting rights for gold and diamonds held by the Precious Minerals Marketing Corporation and Miramex were terminated.	
18	**Guinea**	There is a *de facto* monopoly on imports of rice, sugar, flour and medicines.	X*
		The Guinean Petroleum Company (SGP), 49 per cent state owned, has an import monopoly on petroleum products.	
19	**Guinea-Bissau**	N.A.	NO
20	**Kenya**	No STEs within the of Article XVII:4(a) of GATT 1994.	X*

Annex 11.9 (*cont.*)

	Member	State trading activity	Notifi-cation
21	**Lesotho**	N.A.	NO
22	**Madagascar**	Three companies have a *de jure* monopoly: HASYMA, for the production of cotton lint; KRAOMA, for the extraction and marketing of chromium; and the Malagasy Tobacco Board (OFMATA) for the production and import of tobacco.	NO
23	**Malawi**	The marketing and export of sugar are controlled by the parastatal Sugar Corporation of Malawi.	X*
		The parastatal Petroleum Control Commission (PCC) ceased its monopoly on the importation of petroleum products in 1999.	
24	**Mali**	The Mali National Tobacco and Matches Company (SONATAM), a SOE, ceased the monopoly on imports of tobacco products and matches in 2000.	X*
25	**Mauritania**	N.A.	NO
26	**Mauritius**	The Agricultural Marketing Board (AMB) holds a monopoly over imports of whole garlic.	X
		The State Trading Corporation (STC) is the only authorized importer of petroleum products, liquefied petroleum gas (LPG) and flour, as well as the *de facto* sole importer of long grain (ration) rice.	
27	**Morocco**	The state's monopoly on the import and wholesale distribution of raw and manufactured tobacco, by the Tobacco Board, a State owned company, ended in 2010.	NO
28	**Mozambique**	No STEs within the of Article XVII:4(a) of GATT 1994	X*
29	**Namibia**	No STEs within the of Article XVII:4(a) of GATT 1994	X*
30	**Niger**	The Société nigérienne des produits pétroliers (SONIDEP) has a monopoly on the import of hydrocarbons.	No

Annex 11.9 (*cont.*)

	Member	State trading activity	Notifi-cation
		The French company Areva had a *de facto* monopoly on exports of uranium produced by the Compagnie minière d'Akouta (COMINAK); the same applied to the Société des mines de l'air (SOMAIR) until 2009 when the State decided to sell uranium directly on global markets in order to take advantage of a higher selling price than that agreed with Areva.	
31	**Nigeria**	No STEs within the of Article XVII:4(a) of GATT 1994.	X*
32	**Rwanda**	No companies in Rwanda have a monopoly on imports or exports.	NO
33	**Senegal**	The African Refining Company (SAR) imports crude oil and has a *de facto* monopoly on the production of petroleum products.	No
35	**Sierra Leone**	N.A.	NO
36	**South Africa**	No STEs within the of Article XVII:4(a) of GATT 1994.	X
37	**Swaziland**	The National Agricultural Marketing Board, National Maize Corporation, Swaziland Cotton Board and Swaziland Dairy Board have the statutory power to regulate imports and exports of several agricultural products.	NO
38	**Tanzania**	The crops marketing boards (coffee, cashew nuts, cotton, sugar, tobacco, tea, sisal and pyrethrum) and other public companies are operating under monopoly or hold exclusive rights in their respective field of activity.	NO
39	**Togo**	At the end of 2008, the State resumed the exclusive right to import petroleum products.	NO

Annex 11.9 (*cont.*)

	Member	State trading activity	Notifi-cation
40	**Tunisia**	The Tunisian Trade Board (OCT) imports sugar (de facto monopoly) and, without exclusive rights, various basic staple foods, in particular, tea (black and green), unroasted coffee and certain 'business cycle products' (mainly potatoes), and distributes them wholesale.	X
		Tunisian Petroleum Enterprise (ETAP) has a monopoly on the importation of crude oil and petroleum derivatives (LPG, diesel, jet fuel, fuel oil, paraffin, bitumen, basic oils) and natural gas.	
		Tunisian Refining Industries Corporation (STIR), with ETAP, holds a monopoly on the production of and domestic trade in petroleum products.	
		The Grain Board has a monopoly on the importation of durum wheat, soft wheat and barley.	
		The National Oils Board imports oilseed oil (soya, colza, olive) and exports olive oil, without exclusive rights.	
		The National Alcohol Agency (RNA) holds the exclusive right to import pure alcohol.	
		Medicines and pharmaceutical products are imported exclusively by the Central Pharmacy of Tunisia (PCT).	
		The Tunisian Lubricant Company (SOTULUB) has a *de facto* monopoly on the exportation of greases and lubricants.	
		The other products subject to an import monopoly include cigarettes and other tobacco goods, playing cards, matches and gunpowder.	
41	**Uganda**	No STEs within the of Article XVII:4(a) of GATT 1994.	X*

Annex 11.9 (*cont.*)

	Member	State trading activity	Notification
42	**Zambia**	No STEs within the of Article XVII:4(a) of GATT 1994.	X*
43	**Zimbabwe**	The Minerals Marketing Corporation of Zimbabwe, 100 per cent state owned, acts as the exclusive agent for the marketing and sale of all minerals.	X*

Source: TPRs and notifications to the Working Party on State Trading Enterprises.
Notes: X indicates that at least one notification has been submitted to the Working Party.
X* indicates notification(s) stating that no STEs within the meaning of Article XVII: 4(a) of GATT 1994 are maintained.
NO indicates that no notification has been submitted to the Working Party.

Annex 11.10 *Export taxes, duties and charges used by African members*

	Member	Export Taxes, Duties and Levies
1	**Angola**	– Export taxes apply to hides and skins (20 per cent), un-worked ivory (10 per cent) and minerals in the rough state (5 per cent).
		– A customs service fees (1 per cent) and a statistical tax (0.1 per cent) apply to petroleum products and goods intended for direct and exclusive use by extractive industries.
		– 400 UCF (AOA 35,200) applies for re-export or in transit per declaration and a tax of 239.90 UCF (AOA 21,111) on each transhipment order.
2	**Benin**	– Export duties were abolished in 1993, but a fiscal export levy of 3 per cent applied on cocoa beans, crude petroleum and precious metals.
		– Certain taxes (statistical, road, stamp duty, etc.) levied on an *ad valorem* basis, cumulative rates ranging from 0.85 per cent (local products) to 18.1 per cent (re-exports) on goods exported, re-exported or in transit.

Annex 11.10 (*cont.*)

	Member	Export Taxes, Duties and Levies
3	**Botswana**	– Export levy (of P30) applies to cattle of per head. – Export levies apply to hides and skins, bonemeal, bloodmeal and carcass meal in place, but not charged since 2010.
4	**Burkina Faso**	– Exports taxes were abolished in 1991, except for livestock, including bovine animals (CFAF 3,000 per animal); sheep and goats (CFAF 250 per animal); poultry (CFAF 50 per bird); and raw hides (CFAF 100 per kilo). – Export statistical tax was abolished in 1993. – Export levy (CFAF 500 per certificate) applies to artwork to support the National Cultural Promotion Fund.
5	**Burundi**	– Export taxes and charges were abolished on 1 January 2003; prior to the abolition, a 5 per cent tax was imposed on most products, and higher rates applied on fresh vegetables, flour, cereals and grains (15 per cent); tea (6 per cent); green coffee beans (31 per cent, but not collected since 1999); raw hides and skins, leather, fur skins and articles thereof (3 per cent); and mineral (1 per cent).
6	**Cabo Verde**	– No export taxes.
7	**Cameroon**	– An SGS levy of 0.95 per cent applies to all exports of shipment above CFAF500,000. – Export taxes apply to unprocessed logs (17.5 per cent), which is also subject to an export surtax (CFAF500–4,000/m^3), and sawn wood (5.65 per cent), to encourage local processing and value addition. – An export tax of 2 per cent applies to unprocessed products of animal, plant or mineral origin, except for the following cash crops: cocoa, coffee, cotton, rubber, medicinal plants, palm oil, bananas, pineapples and beans, which were removed in 1999/2000. – Export fees apply to cocoa and coffee (CFAF 25/kg) for the benefits of marketing organizations. – Veterinary and sanitary inspection tax (ISV) applies to the export of certain animals, fish and by products at different rates, sometimes *ad valorem* and sometimes specific (by head).

Annex 11.10 (*cont.*)

	Member	Export Taxes, Duties and Levies
		– Phytosanitary tax of CFAF 50/tonne.
		– A computer fee (RI, at 0.45 per cent with a ceiling of CFAF 15,000) applies to exports domiciled in a computerized customs office.
		– Single Window for Foreign Trade Operations (GUCE) fee (CFAF 15,000).
		– Electronic cargo tracking note (ECTN) fee.
		– Export duty of 2 per cent is levied on products not originating in CEMAC.
8	**Central African Republic**	– Computer equipment finance levy (REIF) of 0.5 per cent is imposed on all exports.
		– A levy applies in the form of a 3 per cent advance on the income tax (IR) or corporate tax (IS) for exports of a commercial nature, while economic operators not subject to the IS/IR pay a 3 per cent minimum flat fee (IMF), except for coffee exporters.
		– Special export duties apply to gold (1 per cent, and the mining promotion tax of 0.75 per cent of the Becdor value); diamond (4 per cent, the mining promotion tax of 1 per cent and a 3 per cent special tax on purchases of diamonds); logs (10.5 per cent); and sawn wood (4.5 per cent).
		– Export taxes apply to cattle (CFAF 1,000/head of cattle; CFAF 500/head of small livestock) and live wild animals.
9	**Chad**	– Export duties apply to animals (8 per cent), oil products (2.5 per cent), other products (2 per cent), and live animals (a rate defined by the Ministry responsible for finance).
		– Exports of livestock, skins and hides are also subject to the General Standard Rate Tax (IGL) in the range of CFAF 100–1,500/head of cattle for livestock and rate of CFAF 100/kg for skins and hides.
		– A statistical tax on exports (RSE) of 2 per cent is levied on all exports, on behalf of the CAEMC.
		– Community preferential tax (TPC) of 0.4 per cent is collected on the export of animal origin.
		– Export duty 'Rural Intervention Fund' (FIR) is collected on some types of tea (0.3 per cent), certain skins

Annex 11.10 (*cont.*)

	Member	Export Taxes, Duties and Levies
		(1 per cent) and cotton (0.5 per cent); the number of TLs subject to FIR was reduced from over 600 (2007 TPR) to 20 (2013 TPR).
		– A charge of CFAF 3 is levied on crude oil exports for issuance of the certificate of origin.
		– For fuel exports, the rate is CFAF 2.5/litre; and an additional levy of CFAF 2.5/litre is charged on fuel exports to finance the Chadian Downstream Oil Sector Regulatory Agency (ARSAT).
10	**Congo**	– All exports are subject to the 2 per cent automation fee and the 2 per cent supplementary exit duty (DAS), except for crude oil and gas.
		– Export levy of 2 per cent is levied on rough diamonds.
		– Timber export is taxed on the basis of transport costs (linked to the four logging zones), the species and processing; as well as a 1 per cent levy for the Forestry Export Products Export Controls Unit (SCPFE); a 15 per cent surcharge is imposed on rough timber exported over and above the quota of 85 per cent of the production of each forestry enterprise; and the contribution to the road fund.
11	**Cote d'Ivoire**	– 'Single exit duty' (DUS) apply to exports of cocoa and by-products in the range of 6.95–14.6 per cent; coffee (CFAF 10/kg); cashew nuts (CFAF 50/kg); and for timber (1–35 per cent of the "reference value).
		– Registration tax of 5 per cent was imposed for the export of coffee, cocoa and by-products; in 2012, it was extended to cotton, cashew, shea products and cola nuts, at 2.5 per cent.
		– Various export fees apply to coffee and cocoa, collected by the Coffee and Cocoa Subsector Management Board, culminating to up to CFAF/kg 32.81 for coffee and 2.4 per cent for cocoa.
		– Reforestation tax of 2 per cent (of the reference value) applies to wood exports, which are also subject to a felling tax (400–2,500 CFAF per m^3) and a special forest conservation and development tax (200–500 CFAF per m^3).

Annex 11.10 (*cont.*)

	Member	Export Taxes, Duties and Levies
		– Export tax of CFAF 100,000 per tonne was imposed on scrap metal and ferrous by-products, although the latter was suspended (TPR 2012).
12	**Democratic Republic of the Congo**	– Export taxes apply to green coffee (10 per cent), mineral products and concentrates thereof (10 per cent), mineral oils (5 per cent), electric power (5 per cent), logs (10 per cent), edged timber (5 per cent for a diameter less than 50 mm, otherwise 0 per cent), fresh water (5 per cent) and scrap metal.
		– Certain types of timber are subject to a charge of 2 per cent of the Ex Works (EWK) value/m^3.
		– Export levies apply to unrefined mineral ores (1 per cent), concentrates and metals (2 per cent), precious materials (4 per cent) for products covered by the Mining Code.
13	**Djibouti**	– An export tax of DF 500/tonne applies to salt.
		– A charge for a sanitary certificate is levied for the export of camels and cattle (DF 400) and of sheep and goats (DF 200).
14	**Egypt**	– No export taxes, charges or levies are applied.
15	**Gabon**	– Most of export duties and taxes were abolished, except on logs and manganese.
		– Manganese is subject to an export tax of 3.5 per cent of their reference value.
		– A felling tax of 1.5 per cent is levied on the export of processed or semi-manufactured wood.
		– Specific taxes were introduced in January 2012 on exports of wood at different levels of processing.
16	**Gambia**	– Export duties of 5 per cent apply to waste and scrap of precious metals.
		– Earlier (in TPR 2004), a 10 per cent export duty was levied on all items, except diamonds taxed at 3 per cent, while the export of fish, fish products, groundnuts and by-products, and all exports to the EU were exempted.
17	**Ghana**	– Ghana has considerably reduced its reliance on export taxes on traditional exports: in TPR 2001, a 6 per cent export tax was levied on cocoa, gold, bauxite, manganese, certain processed timber and aviation fuel; by

Annex 11.10 (*cont.*)

	Member	Export Taxes, Duties and Levies
18	**Guinea**	TPR 2014, export duties only applied to certain wood products and certain hydro-carbons. – Fiscal export duties (DFE) apply to re-exported goods of foreign origin (2 per cent), gold and diamonds exported by persons or the Central Bank (3 per cent) and gold and other precious metals and stones in the case of mining companies (5 per cent); for other mining products, the DFE is set between the state and the mining companies. – Specific export levies are imposed on coffee (US$ 13/tonne) and ferrous scrap (GF25,000/tonne). – Supplementary export tax of 0.25 per cent is imposed on agricultural products for the benefit of the National Chamber of Agriculture.
19	**Guinea-Bissau**	– Rural contribution tax (contribuição predial rústica) of 0.5–2.0 per cent is applied on the exports of rubber; groundnuts, rice, coconuts, cashew nuts, wood, palm oil; leather, skins (of crocodile, otter and other wild animals) and other natural products. – Cashew nut exports are subject to an 'extraordinary' 6 per cent tax, and the advance payment on industrial and commercial profits tax, calculated on a notional price set by the state for the purpose of levying the tax; as well as a private-sector contribution, fixed at CFAF 50/kg, and a levy (1.5 CFAF/kg) for the benefit of the Chamber of Commerce, Industry and Agriculture.
20	**Kenya**	– Export taxes apply to fish (0.5 per cent) and timber (only in TPR 2000). – Export duties and taxes on certain agricultural and mineral products were abolished in June 1994. – An export tax of 25 per cent was introduced on hides, skins and scrap metal to encourage local processing; in 2006, export taxes on hides and skins rose from 20 per cent to 40 per cent with a view to increasing value-addition in the leather sub-section, 20 per cent imposed on scrap metal to support local demand for metals.

Annex 11.10 (*cont.*)

	Member	Export Taxes, Duties and Levies
21	**Lesotho**	– An export tax of 15 per cent applies to rough, unpolished diamonds.
22	**Madagascar**	– Export duties and taxes were eliminated on vanilla and all other products by 1 May 1997, except wood products. – Export charges apply to raw logs (4 per cent) and processed wood products (1.5 per cent). – *De facto* export taxes apply to those products which are exclusively exported: gold and mining products, wood, essential oils and other forestry products, crocodile skins and other wildlife products. – A GasyNet's charges of 0.5 per cent is imposed on all exports for customs clearance.
23	**Malawi**	– Although tobacco, tea and sugar are dutiable products, the rate of export tax has been zero since April 1998. – Earlier, temporary export duties of 4 per cent to 10 per cent were applied to tobacco and sugar in 1995–97 for revenue reasons.
24	**Mali**	– Special taxes on certain products (ISCP) originally levied on all imports and exports of all products were abolished in 1991, except on gold exports; only ISCP of 3 per cent remain on gold and cotton (TPR 2010). – Export duties and taxes were abolished on most products in 1991 and on untreated skins in April 1997.
25	**Mauritania**	– Export taxes on fish (8 to 20 per cent) and shrimps and lobsters (5 per cent) were replaced by an access duty applied to bottom fishing and a territorial duty applied to small-scale fishing for almost all fisheries products. – Only export tax applies to pelagic fisheries products (2 per cent). – For cattle exports, the exporters appear to be subject to a shipment tax, ranging on average from UM 50 to UM 100 for bovine animals, from UM 8 to UM 20 for small ruminants and from UM 60 to UM 200 for camelids. – All exports are subject to a statistical fee of 1 per cent.

Annex 11.10 (*cont.*)

	Member	Export Taxes, Duties and Levies
26	**Mauritius**	– No export duties, charges or levies apply, except to sugar, which is subject to a cess of MUR 1 per tonne.
27	**Morocco**	– No export taxes, levies or charges apply. The last export taxes were abolished in 2005 (maize and plant fibre) and in 2008 (phosphate). – No inspection tax has been imposed on the export of products subject to EACCE technical control since 1991.
28	**Mozambique**	– An export duty only applies to raw cashews (18 per cent–22 per cent). – *De facto* export charges apply to those products which are exclusively exported: cotton, fishery products, forestry products and mining products.
29	**Namibia**	– Diamond export duty was abolished in April 1994, but a 10 per cent tax on unprocessed diamond exports was re-introduced in 2003. – Royalties and levies apply to mineral and fish exports. – Export levies apply to live exports of slaughter-ready cattle and small stock(specific duties). – Export levies apply to raw hides and skins (60 per cent) and pickled hides and skins (15 per cent); the 15 per cent levy on pickled hides was withdrawn in December 2013. – In April 2004, export levies apply to cattle (30 per cent), hides (30 per cent) and goat skins (15 per cent); the 30 per cent export duty on cattle was temporarily withdrawn in August 2013 and reintroduced in November 2014. – A general levy of 0.8 per cent applies to the export price of cattle, sheep, goats or pigs in November 2010. – An export levy on primary commodities and natural resources, not exceeding 2 per cent of the value of the exported goods, was scheduled to be introduced in 2015.
30	**Niger**	– A 3 per cent statistical export charge (RSE) applies to all goods except mineral substances. – A special re-export tax (TSR) of 5–15 per cent applies to the re-export of goods in transit, depending on destination.

Annex 11.10 (*cont.*)

	Member	Export Taxes, Duties and Levies
		– A special transit/re-export tax of 0.25 per cent introduced on cigarettes since 2006.
		– All export transactions for commercial purposes whose c.i.f. value is CFAF 2 million or more require presentation of the tax identity number (NIF); an advance of 7 per cent on profits tax is required for all customs and port operations by persons with no NIF; persons with a NIF but without any certificate showing exemption from payment pay an advance of 4 per cent.
31	**Nigeria**	– An export levy may be imposed on mineral or agricultural raw materials or unprocessed commodities by order of the Nigerian Export Promotion Council.
		– An administrative levy applies to exports of cocoa at US$ 5/tonne and other raw materials at US$ 3/tonne.
		– A 0.5 per cent levy applies all exports in lieu of pre-shipment inspection.
32	**Rwanda**	All export taxes, including on coffee, were abolished in 1999.
33	**Senegal**	– No export duties or taxes (2003 TPR)
		– An annual royalty of 3 per cent of the pit-head value is levied on gold exports.
34	**Sierra Leone**	– Most export taxes were eliminated in 1993, except on cocoa and coffee products taxed at 2.5 per cent.
		– A 3 per cent export tax applies to diamonds.
35	**South Africa**	– Export tax of 5 per cent (earlier at 15 per cent in 1998 TPR) on unpolished diamonds, with a view to developing local skills and promoting the domestic industry.
		– Export levies (specific duties) apply to agricultural products, including citrus, cotton, certain dairy products, deciduous fruits, dried fruits, fynbos (protea), lucerne, mango, olive, pecan nut, potato, pork, poultry, red meat, sorghum, table grape, wine and grapes, and winter cereals.
36	**Swaziland**	– Sugar export levy of 5.75 per cent on sugar to the EU was removed in 2009.
		– No export taxes are imposed.

Annex 11.10 (*cont.*)

	Member	Export Taxes, Duties and Levies
37	**Tanzania**	– All export taxes, including a 2 per cent tax on non-traditional products and minerals introduced in 1996 for revenue purposes and enhancement, were removed by 2000 TPR. – Export taxes were introduced on raw cashew nut (15 per cent or US$ 160/tonne) and raw hides and skins (increased from 20 per cent at the time of 2006 TPR to 90 per cent of the f.o.b. value or TSh 900/kg at the time of 2012 TPR) to encourage local processing and value-addition. – Export levy of 2 per cent on crop exports applied by the Commodity Boards was abolished in July 2006.
38	**Togo**	– No export duties and taxes were imposed after the abolition of the export tax on phosphates of CFAF 1,000/tonne, which was replaced by the mining royalty. – 'Export costs' are levied on the export of precious and semi-precious mineral substances at 4.5 per cent of the corresponding official value, namely diamonds (CFAF 5,000/g), gold (CFAF 1,000/g) and other mineral substances (CFAF 1,000/g). – A special re-export tax (TSR) applies to goods stored in warehouses, irrespective of final destination. – Agricultural, livestock or fisheries products for wholesale sale or export are subject to a levy of 1–5 per cent depending on the possession of the tax identification number (NIF), by way of advance payment on income tax or the flat-rate taxes payable instead.
39	**Tunisia**	– Export taxes on olive oil, fruit and vegetables, hides and skins, and cork were abolished by the 2005 TPR. – Only two export taxes remain: i) cyclical tax on exported scrap iron (90 dinars per ton), levied when scrap iron prices rise in order to discourage exports; and ii) a 'customs services fee' of 3 per cent on crude oil exports.
40	**Uganda**	– Export taxes of 1 per cent apply to coffee (collected by the Uganda Coffee Development Authority) and 2 per cent on cotton (collected by the Cotton Development Organisation) to finance promotional activities.

Annex 11.10 (*cont.*)

	Member	Export Taxes, Duties and Levies
41	**Zambia**	– An export tax of US\$ 0.8/kg (20 per cent until 2011) applies to raw hides and skins to encourage local processing and value-addition. – There were no taxes, charges or levies on exports until the 2008 introduction of an export levy of 15 per cent on copper concentrates and cotton seed (raised to 20 per cent in 2009) to encourage local value addition.
42	**Zimbabwe**	– An export tax of 15 per cent–20 per cent was imposed on chrome in 2010–11 and was replaced by an export ban in April 2011. – An *ad valorem* levy of 20 per cent applies to the export of live wildlife specimens.

Source: Various TPRs.

Note: Percentage of the f.o.b. value, unless otherwise stated.

Annex 11.11 Commitments in selected services sub-sectors

Member	Total number of commitments in all services sub-sectors	Financial services				Communication services						Transport services										Tourism and travel-related services				
		All insurance and insurance-related serces	Banking and other financial services (excl. insurance)	Other	TOTAL	Postal	Courier	Telecommunications	Audiovisual	Other	TOTAL	Maritime	Internal waterways	Air transport services	Space transport	Rail transport services	Road transport S services	Pipeline transport	Services auxiliary to all modes of transport	Other transport Services	TOTAL	Hotels and restaurants (incl. catering)	Travel agencies and tour operators services	Tourist guides services	Other	TOTAL
Angola	5		X		1						0										0	X				1
Benin	12		X		1						0	X							X		2	X				1
Botswana	19				0		X				1										0	X	X			2
Burkina Faso	2				0						0										0	X	X			2
Burundi	22				0						0										0	X	X	X		3
Cabo Verde	103	X	X		2		X	X	X		3	X					X		X		3	X	X	X		3
Cameroon	3				0						0										0	X	X			2
Central African Republic	17				0				X		1										0	X	X	X	X	4
Chad	2				0						0										0	X	X			2
Congo	4				0						0										0	X	X	X		3
Côte d'Ivoire	29	X	X		2			X			1		X				X			X	3	X	X	X		3
Democratic Republic of the Congo	12				0			X			1										0	X	X	X		3
Djibouti	13				0	X	X	X			3										0	X				1
Egypt	44	X	X	X	3			X			1	X									1	X	X	X	X	4
Gabon	15	X	X		2						0										0	X	X			2
The Gambia	110	X	X		2	X	X	X		X	4	X	X				X				4	X	X	X		3

Country	No.	1	2	3	4	5	6	7	8	9	10	11	12	13	14	15	16	17	18	19	20	21	Total
Ghana	30	X	X	X	3		X			1					X		X		2	X	X	X	2
Guinea	9	X	X		0					0		X							1	X		X	2
Guinea-Bissau	2				0					0							X		0	X			1
Kenya	40	X	X		2	X	X			2	X				X		X		2	X	X		3
Lesotho	80	X	X		2	X	X			3							X		1	X	X		3
Madagascar	2				0					0									0	X			0
Malawi	33		X		1					0									0	X	X	X	4
Mali	2				0					0									0	X			1
Mauritania	3				0					0									0	X			3
Mauritius	27	X	X		2		X			1					X				0	X	X		4
Morocco	45	X	X	X	2	X	X			1	X						X		2	X	X	X	4
Mozambique	17		X		1					0									0	X	X		0
Namibia	3				0					0									0	X	X		2
Niger	7				0					0	X				X			X	3	X	X		3
Nigeria	32	X	X		2		X			1		X							2	X	X		3
Rwanda	6	X	X		0					0									0	X			1
Senegal	29	X	X	X	2	X	X			3	X								1	X			2
Seychelles	99	X	X	X	2	X	X		X	4	X						X		2	X	X	X	2
Sierra Leone	107	X	X		2	X			X	1	X	X					X		5	X	X	X	4
South Africa	91	X	X		2	X	X			2					X				1	X	X		3
Swaziland	9				0					0									0	X			1
Tanzania	1				0					0									0	X			1
Togo	5				0					0									0	X	X		3
Tunisia	20	X	X		2		X			1									0	X	X		2
Uganda	5				0		X			1									0	X	X		2
Zambia	16		X		0					0									0	X	X	X	4
Zimbabwe	21		X		1		X			1							X		0	X	X	X	3
TOTAL		16	21	2	4	9	18	6	0	9	4	4	0	2	9	0	5	2	41	32	22	7	

Source: WTO I-TIP Services (https://i-tip.wto.org/services/)

12

Preferential Trade Agreements in Africa: Lessons from the Tripartite Free Trade Agreements and an African Continent-Wide FTA

STEPHEN N. KARINGI, OTTAVIA PESCE
AND SIMON MEVEL

Abstract

Economic transformation is an important pre-requisite for African countries to maximize the benefits of globalization. The development outcomes of the transformation process are conditioned on the one hand by the level of inclusiveness and on the other by the sustainability of the development pathways, among other factors. Building on experiences since the new millennium, in which Africa has witnessed rapid and sustained high levels of economic growth, and informed by the policy discourse that accompanied the formulation of the Common African Position on Sustainable Development Goals, African countries have charted a transformation path in which they aspire to play to their comparative advantages.

The transformation path that is also articulated in Africa's Agenda 2063 is one that rests on structural change in which industrialization plays a greater role. The comparative advantages in support of the envisaged structural transformation include an abundance of natural resources whose value can be enhanced before consumption or trade; a potentially large integrated continental market; a young, healthy and educated population; rapid urbanization complemented with falling costs of transport and communication due to increased public investments in infrastructure; and rapidly falling energy costs, especially in renewables.

Yet, in spite of the well-articulated development pathway and the existing comparative advantages, without trade, Africa is unlikely to enjoy the full benefits of its transformation process. Fortunately, the recognition of trade as a key development tool in Africa is not in doubt. Past and present

A preliminary version of this chapter was presented at the Fourth China Round Table, Nairobi, Kenya, on 13–14 December 2015.

development strategies have endeavoured to unlock latent economic potential through trade, albeit with mixed results. The regional integration process as a development imperative in Africa has consistently placed market integration at the heart of efforts to realise an integrated and prosperous African market. Indeed, contrary to widely held perceptions, Africa is on track as per the Abuja Treaty. There are also efforts to address speed bumps that could slow the process as evidenced by the Tripartite Free Trade Area (TFTA) between COMESA (the Common Market for Eastern and Southern Africa), EAC (the East African Community) and SADC (the Southern African Development Community), and the launch of the Continental Free Trade Area (CFTA) negotiations.

This chapter presents and analyses the results and empirical evidence based on the trade policy landscape in which Africa has been involved and also the prospects of the current initiatives, such as the Tripartite Free Trade Area and the CFTA. Based on the evidence, the chapter argues that it is possible for Africa to ride on trade, not only to industrialize by exploiting the continental market, but also bring about structural transformation in which services play a critical role. But for this to happen, Africa must harness regional integration to the fullest while at the same time making maximum use of the opportunities the multilateral trading system offers. In a global political economic context where there is a multiplicity of trade agreements, this chapter argues that the sequencing of actions and the scope of the agreements are important determinants of the final development outcome.

1   In Order to Achieve Sustainable Growth, Africa Needs Structural Transformation

One of the most puzzling paradoxes of the last decade is that while Africa has benefited from unprecedented growth – 4.8 per cent on average for Africa, excluding North Africa, over 2005 to 2014, with peaks in excess of 7 per cent in some countries[1] – a large part of its population has remained trapped in economic poverty, facing rampant unemployment and inequality. Africa has so far failed to achieve what economists call 'structural transformation'. Structural transformation entails a reallocation of resources from low- to high-productivity activities, typically from agriculture to industry and modern services, leading to higher economy-wide productivity and progressively raising income. In Africa, however, as shown in Figure 12.1, factors of production such as labour have not shifted from agriculture into manufacturing and industry over the past decade, but rather into services – and, some

---

[1] World Bank data

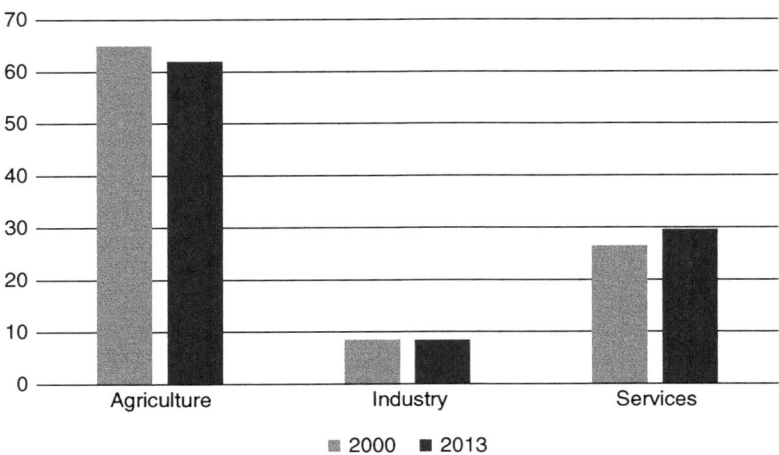

Figure 12.1   Labour force allocation among main economic sectors in Africa, 2000 versus 2013
Source: Economic Report on Africa 2015. Addis Ababa: ECA.

argue, mostly low-productivity ones (see for example Rodrik, 2013).[2] Partly for this reason, African countries remain marginal players in domestic and international markets for manufactured goods.[3]

Development history highlights the perils of high economic growth without concurrent industrial development and structural transformation. The countries that manage to reduce poverty and get richer are those that are able to diversify away from agriculture and other traditional products (Rodrik, 2013).

Africa's exports still lack diversification, both in terms of products – primary commodities, precious stones and non-monetary gold made up 80 per cent of Africa's exports in 2014[4] – and destination markets (discussed in more detail in Section 6 below).

The global economic crisis has deeply affected Africa's main trade partners (chiefly the EU28 and the US). Demand from China, which absorbed 11 per cent of exports from Africa, excluding North Africa, in 2013, is now slowing down, and reduced possibilities to sell commodities to China are affecting the continent's prospects. According to the IMF, a 1-percentage-point reduction in China's investment growth is

---

[2] For a discussion on the low level of productivity of African services see, for example, World Economic Forum (2015).
[3] UNECA (2014)   [4] ECA analysis of UNCTAD data

associated with an average 0.6-percentage-point decrease in Africa's export growth rate.[5]

The IMF reckons that growth rates in the region in 2015 will fall to their lowest since before the global financial crisis and recover only marginally in 2016.[6]

Lower commodity prices are significantly reducing revenues from African exports. Moreover, recent research summarised in the *Financial Times* found that depreciating currencies in emerging markets are failing to boost exports and are crippling imports by making them more expensive.[7] For exporters of commodities and countries with large trade deficits, both in Africa and elsewhere, this combination can prove lethal, in an economic sense. These changes threaten the sustainability of an economic model based on low value-added commodities for which prices are volatile. Without structural transformation, Africa's economic growth may run out of steam.

2 Industrialization Is a Critical Part of the Transformation Process

Industry – and manufacturing in particular – has traditionally been a source of substantial employment generation in developed countries and, more recently, in developing ones. Industry is a high value-added sector into which labour can flow and deliver higher productivity. The average manufacturing–agriculture labour productivity ratio for low-income Africa is 2.5 to 1[8] (see McMillan and Rodrik, 2011, Page, 2012 and Rodrik, 2013). Given this large difference in output per worker between agriculture and industry and the potential of manufacturing to absorb labour, industrialization presents a significant opportunity for productivity-enhancing structural change for the continent.[9]

Moreover, industrialization allows a country to tap into increasingly dispersed processes of global production via global value chains (GVCs) to produce and trade in progressively more sophisticated goods. Countries with more diversified production and export structures have higher incomes per capita (Imbs and Wacziarg, 2003; Cadot et al., 2011), and countries that produce and export more sophisticated products – those that are primarily manufactured by countries at higher income levels – tend to grow faster (Hausmann et al., 2007; UNIDO, 2009). One reason why industrial and export diversity matter for growth may be that

[5] Hruby (2015)   [6] *Financial Times* (2015)   [7] Kyinge and Wheatley (2015)
[8] This means that labour productivity in manufacture is 2.5 times larger than in agriculture.
[9] Page (2012)

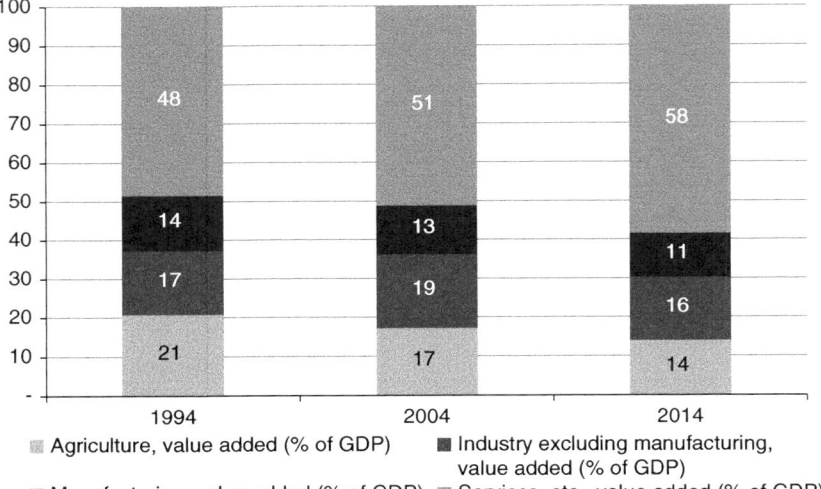

Figure 12.2   Africa excluding North Africa, value added to GDP by sector in percentage over time
Source: Authors' analysis of World Development Indicator data.

more diverse economies are better able to take advantage of opportunities in global markets as they emerge.[10]

Africa's economic progress, however, has scarcely resulted in industrialization and in the creation of value chains linked to Africa's vast agriculture potential and extractive industries.

As shown in Figure 12.2, the share of industry excluding manufacturing[11] in the GDP of Africa excluding North Africa[12] actually decreased from 17 per cent in 1994 to 16 per cent in 2014. Manufacturing – a subsector of industry that is often a source of high productivity – shrank over the same period and represented

---

[10] Page (2012)

[11] Manufacturing refers to industries belonging to ISIC divisions 15–37. Industry excluding manufacturing corresponds to ISIC divisions 10–45, minus ISIC divisions 15–37. It comprises value added in mining, construction, electricity, water and gas. Value added is the net output of a sector after adding up all outputs and subtracting intermediate inputs.

[12] Data based on the World Bank grouping for Sub-Saharan Africa. North Africa comprises, according to the World Bank classification, Egypt, Tunisia, Morocco, Algeria, Libya and Djibouti. However, some data, chiefly for Djibouti and Libya, are missing for several years within 1994–2014. Given the data limitations, the average presented is to be considered an estimate.

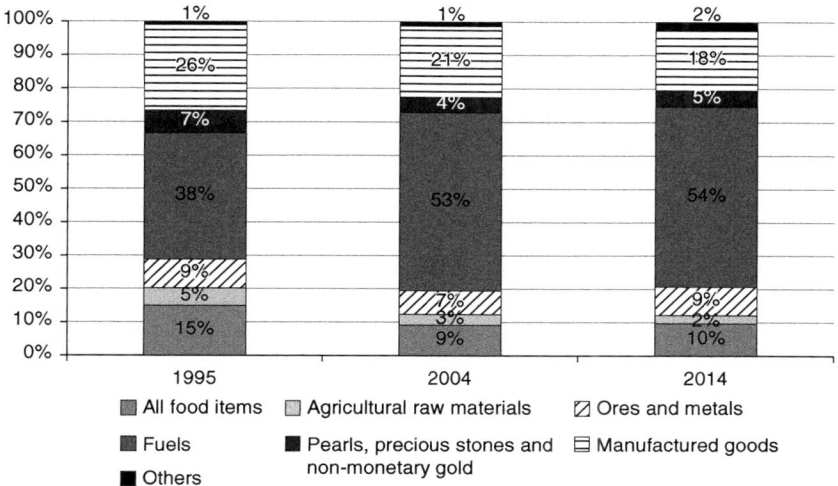

Figure 12.3   Africa's exports by main product category, 1995–2014
Source: ECA analysis of UNCTAD data.

11 per cent of GDP in 2014. Estimates for North Africa suggest that the share of manufacturing in GDP fluctuated over the period and is now approximately 16 per cent of GDP, not much above the 1994 level (14 per cent).

Figure 12.3 further shows that manufacturing as a share of Africa's exports has decreased over the past two decades, going from 26 per cent in 1995 to 21 per cent in 2004 and to 18 per cent in 2014. Fuels, by contrast, have taken up a larger share of the continent's exports (54 per cent in 2014).

Africa's manufacturing sector is dominated mostly by small and informal (and thus less productive) firms. Fewer than 10 per cent of African workers find jobs in manufacturing, and among those, only a tiny fraction – as few as one-tenth – are employed in modern, formal firms with adequate technology.[13] Additionally, few productivity increases have taken place in Africa's manufacturing sector, in comparison to benchmark middle-income countries.[14] According to Page (2012), the relative productivity of industry other than manufacturing in Africa is greater than that for selected benchmark middle-income countries, indicating that natural resources – the largest component of non-

[13] Rodrik (2013)   [14] Page (2012)

manufacturing industry – are significant even in African economies that are not classified as resource-rich.

3 Services Can Also Be an Avenue for Economic Transformation

While industry and particularly manufacturing unrelated to natural resources have stagnated across Africa, services have been thriving. In 2013, services represented the main sector contributing to GDP in the majority of African countries: thirty-five out of fifty-four. Africa's exports of services increased from US$ 55.1 billion in 2004 to US$ 79.5 billion in 2014.[15] Despite being remarkable, this growth should be seen in the context of increasing trade in services globally: Africa's share of global services exports actually decreased over 2004 and 2013. The 13 per cent share of services in Africa's total exports in 2013 looks low when compared to that of other regions: in 2013, services accounted for 37 per cent of US's exports, 31 per cent of India's, 26 per cent of Europe's, 17 per cent of China's.[16] Nonetheless, the rise of the services sector in Africa is undeniable.

From 2000 to 2010, the agriculture labour force share fell by about 10 per cent while services grew by eight per cent (McMillan and Harttgen, 2014).[17] This shift took place largely in the market service sector – most notably in retail, distribution and other trade services – employing 25 per cent of the working-age population in Africa.[18] Over the past two decades, services were the fastest growing sector in Africa: from 1995 to 2011, they accounted for 62 per cent of cumulative growth in GDP per capita on the continent, compared to 24 per cent for industry and 13 per cent for agriculture.[19]

The increased predominance of the services sector has both positive and negative implications for Africa. On one hand, services are essential inputs in the manufacturing process: transport, energy, construction, finance, insurance, legal and accounting services and business services allow local firms to be competitive. According to the OECD, as much as 30 per cent of value added of the manufacturing sector's exports is accounted for by services inputs (OECD, 2013). Beyond their support to other sectors of the economy, services make a direct contribution to GDP and job creation, attract investments into local firms, are a magnet for foreign direct investments – 40 per cent of FDIs into Africa went into services in 2012 compared to 24 per cent in 2011[20] – and are an important

[15] International Trade Centre data   [16] ECA analysis of International Trade Centre data
[17] McMillan and Harttgen (2014)   [18] WEF (2015)   [19] World Bank (2014)
[20] UNCTAD (2013)

component of global value chains participation. In Africa, growth in services value added is strongly correlated with GDP growth and growth in manufacturing value added.[21]

On the other hand, the scarcity of data on employment, output and productivity among the services sub-sectors in Africa makes it difficult to assess whether resources have shifted from agriculture into high-productivity services, or rather into low-productivity, non-tradable ones. Services exports have gone down as a percentage of Africa's GDP, excluding North Africa, between 2009 and 2012, suggesting that growth is taking place mostly in services that are not exported.[22] Moreover, most service sector jobs in Africa are informal and thus unrecorded in official statistics.[23] Though services have higher productivity than much of agriculture, they are not technologically dynamic in Africa and have been falling behind the world frontier.[24] Moreover, in many African countries, the impressive growth witnessed in services sectors such as construction, financing and insurance has often not benefited local small and medium-sized enterprises (SMEs). In Mozambique, for example, the financial sector has been growing spectacularly, but has largely positioned itself to lend to big mining projects and foreign investors, while local SMEs remain credit-constrained.[25] Some policy recommendations for governments to reinforce and direct the growth of the services sector towards high-value-added activity and support for local firms are given in the conclusions of this chapter.

4 Agriculture Remains an Essential Contributor to African Economies, and the Sector Needs to Be Linked to Regional and Global Value Chains

In 2013, agriculture accounted for 57 per cent of GDP in Africa, excluding North Africa, and accounted for 51 per cent in North Africa. Much of the sector in Africa, however, remains basic, subsistence agriculture. Africa's average yields still remain much lower than those in any other region. Although Africa's total factor productivity in agriculture is estimated to have increased in recent decades, its food production per capita remains essentially unchanged since 1960.[26]

Despite this low starting basis, the ambition for the continent is to build technologically advanced agro-processing to add value to Africa's enormous agricultural resources. More than any other sector, thanks to

---

[21] ECA analysis of World Bank data   [22] ECA analysis of WITS data   [23] Sy (2014)
[24] Rodrik (2013)   [25] UNECA (2015b)   [26] McArthur (2013)

its large employment and GDP share, agriculture has the potential to spur inclusive economic growth and poverty reduction in Africa. Growth in agriculture in the developing world has a multiplier effect on expenditures in poor households: research shows that, in Africa, a 1-percentage-point increase in GDP driven by agriculture leads to a massive 6-percentage-point increase in expenditure growth for the poorest 10 per cent.[27] For these reasons, Africa needs to be ambitious in trade negotiations for agriculture and link the sector into regional and global value chains. Africa can support the potential of its agriculture sector by pushing for strategic trade agreements that address the right barriers and unlock the potential of the sector. For example, agriculture exports to the United States have grown significantly since the African Growth and Opportunity Act (AGOA) was established, from US$ 59 million in 2001 (the first year of AGOA) to US$ 261 million in 2014, but still remain small in absolute terms.[28] US trade with Africa remains dominated by crude petroleum exports, which account for 69 per cent of US AGOA imports.[29] The US retains various trade barriers on a range of agriculture goods that, if reduced, would likely lead to increased and more varied exports for African countries.[30] This example shows how trade agreements by themselves are not necessarily conducive to export diversification for Africa. AGOA (discussed more extensively in Section 6) and other existing preferential trade arrangements (PTAs) can be improved to unlock the potential of Africa's agriculture.

5   Trade Can Drive Industrialization, through a Variety of Channels

Increased and more effective trade could greatly help Africa to drive industrialization, find lucrative markets for its products and achieve sustainable economic growth, through several channels. In classic economic theory, trade fosters economic growth by allowing countries to capitalize on their comparative advantage; through trade, Africa can exploit its large mineral and agricultural endowments and, ideally, use them as a stepping stone to progressively export higher value-added products. By providing a market for local products and access to cheaper and more varied inputs, trade can stimulate production and therefore employment.

By creating jobs and bringing revenues, trade has a direct link with poverty reduction. At the industry level, efficient trade networks allow

---

[27] Hanson and Dare (2014)   [28] Meltzer (2015)
[29] http://trade.gov/agoa/pdf/2014-us-ssa-trade.pdf   [30] Meltzer (2015)

industries to source the inputs they need for production conveniently, improving their competitiveness. Export revenues allow firms to invest and grow. Trade can be a source of learning, allowing African countries to pick up new technologies and ways of doing things, provided that adequate channels for such learning to happen are in place. Trade can be used strategically to foster industrialization, for example by reducing barriers to target export markets for mature firms and by temporary shielding infant industries from foreign competition, allowing them to build capabilities. Of course, any such shielding should be time-bound and continuously evaluated against learning and productivity improvements.

6   Preferential Trade Arrangements Do Not Seem to Have Significantly Fostered Africa's Industrialization

Preferential trade agreements (PTAs) are agreements between two or more countries giving reciprocal preferential market access to each other on either all or just some goods and services. The degree of reciprocity can be full or partial. As per WTO definitions, PTAs are synonymous with regional trade agreements (RTAs) defined as 'reciprocal trade agreements between two or more partners' and should not be confused with 'unilateral trade preferences',[31] granted by more advanced (developed and developing) economies to individual developing and/or least-developed countries on a non-reciprocal and non-contractual basis. All these trade configurations are against the principle of the most-favoured nation (MFN) non-discriminatory treatment, but have been allowed by the WTO either through Article XXIV of the General Agreement on Tariffs and Trade (GATT) or Article V of the General Agreement on Trade in Services (GATS), in the case of reciprocal preferential agreements between involving developed countries, or waivers or the Enabling Clause (i.e. the 'Decision on Differential and More Favourable Treatment, Reciprocity and Fuller Participation of Developing Countries'), in the case of reciprocal trade agreements among developing countries or non-reciprocal preferences for developing and/or least-developed countries.

This section assesses whether preferential trade arrangements are helping Africa achieve its structural transformation objectives.

Trade preferences are not exclusively granted by developed countries, but also by a growing number of emerging economies. For example,

---

[31] See https://www.wto.org/english/tratop_e/region_e/rta_pta_e.htm.

Table 12.1 *Africa and African LDCs shares of exports to five main partners, cumulative 2000–14.*

Main partners/share of total exports directed to main partners, cumulative 2000–14	African LDCs	Africa
China	28%	11%
EU28	20%	38%
US	16%	15%
India	5%	5%
Japan	3%	3%
Total share of exports going to five main partners	72%	71%

Source: ECA analysis of UNCTAD data.

India and China have set up trade preferential schemes with least-developed countries (LDCs), which came into effect in 2008 and 2010, respectively, with product coverage which has been progressively expanding since then. Trade preferences have a significant influence on Africa's exports: as shown in Table 12.1, over the period 2000–14, the top five export destinations for African countries were all preference-giving countries (EU28 topped the list). When looking only at Africa's LDCs (thirty-four out of fifty-four African countries, with forty-eight LDCs total worldwide), as much as 72 per cent of cumulative exports from 2000 to 2014 were directed towards the same countries, with a different order (China topped the list).

But have these ever-more-numerous preferential trade arrangements helped Africa achieve export growth and diversification and accelerate structural transformation? Figure 12.4 shows Africa's LDCs' exports to their five larger trading partners by main goods categories, comparing the average for 2004–06 with that for 2012–14. Between the two periods, the percentage of manufactured goods has gone down in LDCs' exports to all trading partners. Trade preferences to LDCs do not seem to have fostered greater value addition and diversification in their exports.

As we will see below, the general failure of preferential trade agreements to promote Africa's structural transformation is due to two main factors: first, Africa's own failure to upgrade its productive capacities, becoming competitive in higher value-added products, and strategically

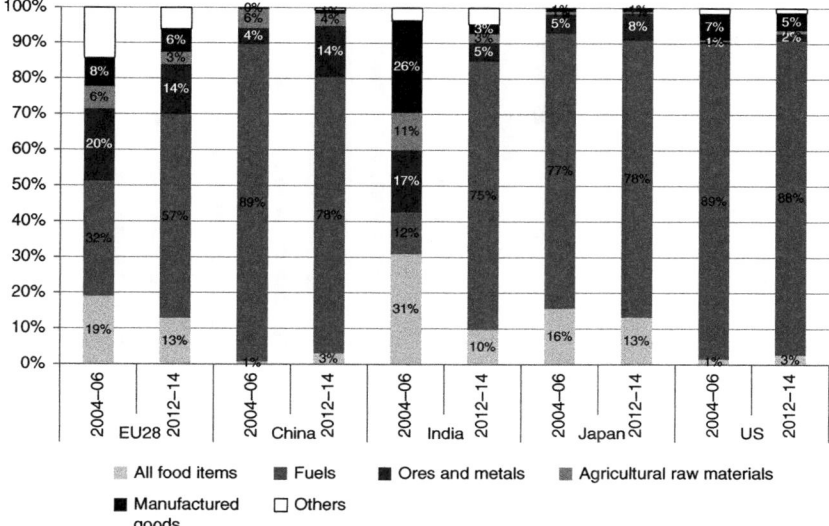

Figure 12.4 African LDCs' exports to five main partners by main category of goods, 2004–06 average versus 2012–14 average

Source: ECA analysis of UNCTAD data extracted in September 2015.

to take advantage of trade preferences; and second, poorly designed trade preference schemes.

We will look at the example of AGOA (which has just been renewed by the United States for the next ten years, to 2025) to examine the first factor. AGOA is a trade agreement which significantly enhances – beyond the preferential treatment already granted in the Generalized System of Preferences (GSP) – access to the US market (via a further reduction in tariff barriers) for selected countries[32] from most of Africa, excluding North Africa.[33] Data on exports to the United States from AGOA participants reveal a wide variation in the percentage of products exported through AGOA. This is true even when considering only countries where oil exports are not dominant.[34] While 80 per cent of

---

[32] For more details on countries' eligibility, see here: http://agoa.info/about-agoa/country-eligibility.html.

[33] As of 13 November 2015, thirty-nine African countries are currently eligible to adhere to AGOA; see http://agoa.info/about-agoa/country-eligibility.html.

[34] ECA classifies African countries as oil-rich when their oil exports are at least 20 per cent higher than their oil imports. As of 2014, this classification included Algeria, Angola, Cameroon, Chad, Côte d'Ivoire, Congo, Equatorial Guinea, Gabon, Libya and Nigeria.

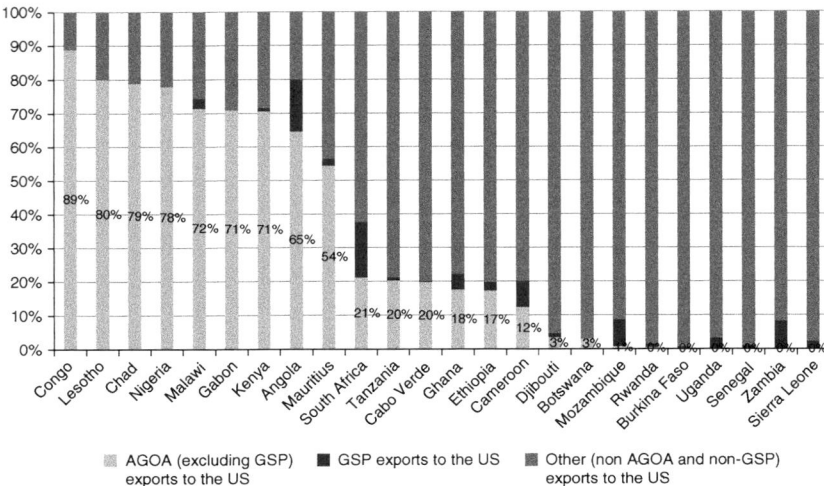

Figure 12.5   Exports of selected* AGOA-eligible African countries to the United States by preference used
* Only countries which have held AGOA continuously since at least 2004 have been included in the analysis. Some countries that met this criterion (Benin, Namibia, Sao Tomé and Principe and Seychelles) have been excluded due to lack of complete data.
Source: ECA analysis of US Department of Commerce, International Trade Administration data.

Lesotho's exports to the United States are traded through AGOA, just 17 per cent of Ethiopia's and virtually none of Sierra Leone's are (see Figure 12.5).

In many cases, a low percentage of exports to the United States through AGOA indicates that local firms are having difficulties accessing the US market. Zambia, for example, has struggled to penetrate the US market over the last fifteen years. One reason has been that Zambia's exports are concentrated on copper (more than 60 per cent of Zambia's exports in 2013). Zambia's non-traditional exports are still developing and struggle to compete internationally due to lack of adequate capacity, quality standards and investments.[35] In 2015 Zambia launched an AGOA-specific National Response Strategy to help Zambian firms export under AGOA.

In the case of Rwanda, local exporters have failed to make much use of AGOA due to, among other causes, high shipping costs linked

[35] http://agoa.info/news/article/5668-zambia-to-boost-agoa-with-strategy.html

Forecourt of the Kenyatta International Convention Centre, Nairobi, Kenya, venue for the Tenth WTO Ministerial Conference from 15 to 18 December 2015. (© WTO/Admedia Communication)

WTO Director-General Roberto Azevêdo and H. E. Mr Shouwen Wang, Vice Minister of Commerce of the People's Republic of China, open the Fourth China Round Table, which took place on 13–14 December 2015. The Government of China pledged at the Round Table to contribute a further USD 500,000 (CHF 494,636) to the China Programme for 2016. (© WTO/Admedia Communication)

H.E. Mr Wang Shouwen, Vice Minister of Commerce of the People's Republic of China, delivering one of the opening addresses during the Fourth China Round Table on 14 December 2015. (© WTO/Admedia Communication)

H.E. Mr Uhuru Kenyatta, President of Kenya, gives a keynote speech at the Opening Ceremony of the High Level Session of the Fourth China Round Table on 14 December 2015. (© WTO/Admedia Communication)

Mr Roberto Azevêdo, WTO Director-General, at the Opening Ceremony of the High Level Session of the Nairobi Fourth China Round Table on 14 December 2015. (© WTO/Admedia Communication)

H.E. Mrs Amina Mohamed, Cabinet Secretary for Foreign Affairs and International Trade of Kenya, speaking at the High Level Session of the Fourth China Round Table on 14 December 2015. (© WTO/Admedia Communication)

Mr Chiedu Osakwe, Director of the Accessions Division of the WTO, speaking at the High Level Session of the Fourth China Round Table on 14 December 2015. (© WTO/ Admedia Communication)

H.E. Ms Fatima Haram Acyl, Commissioner for Trade and Industry, African Union Commission, speaks at the Nairobi Fourth China Round Table on 14 December 2015. (© WTO/Admedia Communication)

H.E. Mr Okechukwu E. Enelamah, Minister of Industry, Trade and Investment of Nigeria, speaks at the Nairobi Fourth China Round Table on 14 December 2015. (© WTO/Admedia Communication)

H.E. Mr Rob Davies, Minister of Trade and Industry of South Africa, speaking at the High Level Session of the Fourth China Round Table on 14 December 2015. (© WTO/Admedia Communication)

H.E. Mr Joshua Setipa, Minister of Trade and Industry of Lesotho, speaking at the High Level Session of the Fourth China Round Table on 14 December 2015. (© WTO/Admedia Communication)

Ms Arancha González, Executive Director of the International Trade Centre, speaking at the High Level Session of the Fourth China Round Table on 14 December 2015. (© WTO/Admedia Communication)

Mr Joakim Reiter, Deputy Secretary-General at the United Nations Conference on Trade and Development, speaking at the High Level Session of the Fourth China Round Table on 14 December 2015. (© WTO/Admedia Communication)

Ms Anabel González, Senior Director of the Global Practice on Trade and Competitiveness of the World Bank Group, during the High Level Session of the Fourth China Round Table on 14 December 2015. (© WTO/Admedia Communication)

H.E. Mrs Ellen Johnson Sirleaf, President of Liberia, meeting with H.E. Mr Uhuru Kenyatta, President of Kenya, during the Tenth WTO Ministerial Conference in Nairobi, Kenya, on 15 December 2015. (© WTO/Admedia Communication)

H.E. Mr Uhuru Kenyatta, President of Kenya, and WTO Director-General Roberto Azevêdo, accompanied by other participants in the High Level Session of the Fourth China Round Table on 14 December 2015. (© WTO/Admedia Communication)

to unreliable freight agencies and scarce airline connections.[36] The national carrier, RwandAir, has an eight-plane fleet operating in fewer than eighteen destinations, but plans to expand considerably in the coming years.

Ethiopia's AGOA exports – principally apparel and textiles, leather products and horticulture – have increased by 150 per cent since AGOA went into effect 2001. While this might sound encouraging, Ethiopia's AGOA exports were a mere US$ 35 million in 2013. The country is keen to improve this performance and has been one of the first to implement an AGOA Strategy, a draft of which was completed in October 2013.[37] Such a strategy can be an example for other countries to help local firms make better use of AGOA and other PTAs. Ad hoc strategies can help promote the utilization of trade preferences by providing key information on the strengths and limitations of various export sectors, proposing mechanisms for overcoming barriers to trade, and listing the diverse set of actors and resources available to support exporters seeking to take advantage of AGOA.[38]

The AGOA examples illustrate how preferential trade arrangements, are not enough, alone, to stimulate exports growth and diversification. Countries benefiting from trade preferences need to adopt appropriate strategies to help local firms make use of them, put in place the infrastructure required to support exports, increase workers' skills and productivity, attract investments and diversify export into several sectors (possibly correlated to different factors of volatility).

We now look at the second reason behind preferential trade arrangements' failure to promote structural transformation. Beyond the level of development of a country's entrepreneurship and infrastructure and its strategic ability to take advantage of trade preferences, the current design of some preferential schemes also affects their capacity for fostering structural transformation in Africa. Firstly, many preferential trade arrangements include restrictive conditions: for example, an ECA and Brookings study (2013)[39] shows that trade gains for Africa could significantly increase under AGOA if products currently excluded from duty-free, quota-free market access were included by the US. Secondly, many PTAs have rules of origin (RoO) imposing minimum levels of local production that most African countries cannot achieve.

---

[36] http://www.newtimes.co.rw/section/article/2015-08-26/191902/
[37] Schneidman (2015)   [38] Kimenyi (2015)   [39] Mevel et al. (2013)

To prevent third countries from passing goods through countries that receive preferences, a minimum amount of processing of a product in the country with preference is necessary.[40] But the RoO for many products are very difficult to achieve.

For example, the EU-GSP requires a two-stage transformation process for textile and clothing products to qualify for preferential rates under rules of origin for non-LDCs.[41] More generally, available evidence suggests that, in the case of apparel, there has been a substantial supply response to preferences in a number of developing countries when rules of origin have been non-restrictive.[42] The third-country fabric (TCF) provision in AGOA – allowing eligible African countries to use foreign fabrics in the manufacture of products manufactured for the United States – can provide a meaningful illustration; many argue that it is thanks to the TCF provision under AGOA if exports of textiles and apparel from Africa to the United States continued following the 2005 WTO agreements in textile and clothing (ATC) – which suppressed quotas for exports of textiles and clothing from developing countries to developed countries, resulting in growing competition with Asian textile and apparel exporters on the US market.[43] There are direct costs associated with the completion of rules of origin of about 3 to 5 per cent which can reduce exports under preferential schemes. Rules of origin can also make it more difficult to achieve economies of scale, since input requirements may vary according to destination markets of the final products. Additionally, RoO are often an incentive to purchase intermediates in the country conceding the preference, which can result in trade diversion if there is a more efficient producer of intermediates elsewhere.[44] Finally, RoO can even be used as a means of protection for the importing country, with some studies showing that the larger the difference in tariffs, the more restrictive the associated RoO tend to be.

On the other hand, it should be highlighted that an excessive relaxation of RoO risks having perverse effects, for example in the case of Africa, by favouring import of cheaper inputs from outside the country/region instead of building the capacity to transform and add value to product locally (or regionally, thereby limiting exploitation of regional value chains in Africa).

In summary, and in order to foster development, RoO should be transparent, simple, not apt to be used as protectionist tools for

[40] UNECA (2005)   [41] UNECA (2015a)   [42] Brenton and Ozden (2013)
[43] UNECA (2015a)   [44] UNECA (2006)

importing countries, and should facilitate exports from LDCs. Some of these dysfunctional PTA clauses, such as RoO, that penalize LDCs, are the result of the scarce negotiating power of Africa's trade delegations: Africa is still not speaking with one voice in trade agreements (as the CFTA is still a work in progress, African markets remain rather small) and Africa's trade delegations often lack the resources or skills to negotiate effectively with the delegations of global superpowers. More capacity building is required to enable African governments and businesses alike to better understand rules of origin in order to take full advantage of trade preferences and become better engaged in the negotiation process. This also applies to norms and standards, which are amongst the main barriers to trade. Governments should know, and disseminate knowledge about, the main barriers affecting the country's exports. Governments can also play an active role in facilitating compliance with international norms and standards.

7   North-South PTAs: Africa's Trade Agreement with the Developed World

PTAs/RTAs have proliferated in recent years, as shown in Figure 12.6. The growth in PTAs/RTAs is partly a result of countries' disappointment with the repeated blockages, unequal negotiation power and mitigated expected gains from the multilateral trading system. In an environment where WTO trade negotiations are becoming ever more complex and demanding, countries have turned to regionalism for alternative ways to expand their trade.[45]

In 2010, African countries were involved in fifty-five PTAs/RTAs, of which forty-three were South–South and twelve were North–South. PTAs/RTAs have also increasingly become cross-regional. Of the fifty-five African PTAs/RTAs, thirty-one are cross-regional.[46] Perhaps as a consequence of increased PTAs/RTAs, the number of export partners for Africa, excluding North Africa, has decreased from 158 in 2009 to 118 in 2013.[47]

In the next section we are going to briefly describe some major North–South trade agreements in which Africa is currently involved and their potential evolution and assess whether these are helping Africa to achieve its structural transformation goals.

---

[45] UNECA (2015a)   [46] De Melo and Tsikata (2014)   [47] ECA analysis of WITS data

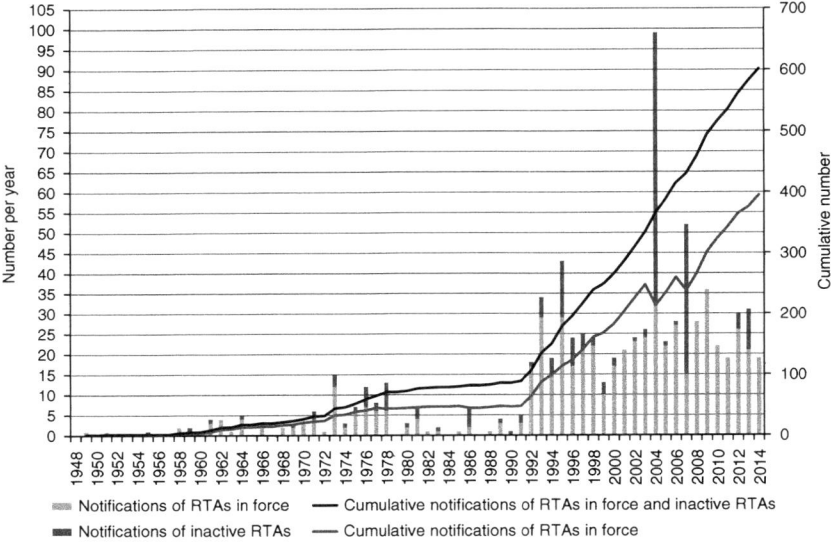

Figure 12.6   Regional trade agreements worldwide, 1949–2014
Source: WTO.

7.1   Economic Partnership Agreements between Europe and African Countries Risk Bringing Uneven Gains

Economic partnership agreements (EPAs) are reciprocal trade agreements between the European Union and seventy-nine African, Caribbean and Pacific (ACP) countries. However, they are asymmetrical in nature, as the European Union is expected to grant 100 per cent duty-free, quota-free market access to its ACP counterparts upon signing of the EPAs, whereas ACP countries must gradually open their markets duty-free and quota-free for approximately 75 to 80 per cent of their imports from the European Union. When African countries and the European Union engage in EPAs, they are starting from very different levels of protection from each other. African countries have already given large preferences on their exports to the European Union (thanks to the European Union's Everything But Arms initiative for LDCs, and EU-GSP for all African countries). Only a few agricultural sectors in the European Union are still protected for African exports. The European Union, on the other hand, has imposed significant tariff barriers on its exports to Africa in most sectors and stands to gain considerably from the opening up of Africa to its products. Therefore, gains from EPAs are likely to be unevenly distributed among African countries and the European Union. Additionally, unless trade barriers within Africa fall at an accelerated rate, the increase in Africa's exports to the European Union risks coming at the expense of intra-African trade, as intra-African trade risks becoming more expensive than EU–Africa trade after the EPAs.[48]

A study by Mevel, Valensisi and Karingi (2015)[49] examined the implications of EPAs on Africa's structural transformation, focusing on two of the five African regional groupings, the West African and the Eastern and Southern Africa (ESA) regions. The study confirms that initial asymmetric protection conditions will generate unequal trade gains for Africa and the European Union, with the European Union gaining twice as much as West Africa and ESA together in absolute terms. Moreover, after complete and effective implementation of ECOWAS's and ESA's EPAs with the European Union, intra-African trade is expected to be reduced by US\$ 3 billion in 2040, as some of the existing trade between African countries would be replaced by exports from Africa to the European Union. Finally, African governments would see notable reductions in their tariff revenues that would limit real income gains for African countries following the EPA reforms.

If EPAs do generate exports for Africa, these are expected to be essentially concentrated in a few agricultural sectors (e.g. rice, sugar, milk, meat and vegetables, fruit and nuts). It is worth noting that such gains could well be overestimated, considering African nations' current difficulty in meeting the European Union's sanitary and phytosanitary requirements, a factor that was not considered in the analysis by Mevel et al (2015). Furthermore, non-LDCs would be the main African beneficiaries, while trade gains for LDCs would be marginal. In fact, exports towards the European Union could even be reduced for some LDCs (e.g. Ethiopia, Malawi and Zambia) due to an erosion of preferences that could result from increased competition with African non-LDCs on the EU market with EPAs. As a consequence, EPAs will have a limited positive impact on Africa's industrialization, economic growth and diversification, especially for its LDCs. The reforms, however, are expected to bring larger trade gains to the European Union, especially in industrial sectors.[50]

---

[48] UNECA (2015a)
[49] https://www.gtap.agecon.purdue.edu/resources/res_display.asp?RecordID=4754
[50] UNECA (2015a)

It should be acknowledged that EPAs are not just about reducing tariff barriers, and the EU Foreign Affairs Council, aware of some of the trade-related costs implied by EPAs (especially for LDCs) is to provide financial compensation to African countries. Funds are to be disbursed between 2015 and 2020 under the EPA Development Programme (PAPED, for Programme de l'Accord de Partenariat Economique). Yet, offsetting EPA's expected negative effect on intra-African trade may well require greater financial resources.[51]

7.2   Euro-Mediterranean Agreement for North Africa

Beside the CFTA, North African Countries (NACs)[52] are involved in two other major regional integration processes: the Greater Arab Free Trade Area (GAFTA), with the countries of the Arab League, and the Euro-Mediterranean Partnership (EUROMED) process with the European Union.

Nearly all countries on the Mediterranean have concluded EUROMED agreements with the European Union, aimed at removing barriers to trade and investment, with the exceptions of Syria and Libya. Together, the countries of the region represent 8.6 per cent of total EU external trade.[53]

North Africa recorded the second-lowest manufacturing value-added growth rate of all African regions in 2008–12. Despite leading in terms of manufacturing value added per capita among African regions, North Africa's level falls far behind that of the world's most dynamic regions.[54] As shown in Figure 12.7 below, the European Union appears to have a positive trade balance with all the NACs with which it has signed EUROMED agreements – Algeria, Egypt, Morocco and Tunisia – except with Algeria, which exports large quantities of mining and fuel products to the EU.

The EU exports mainly machinery and imports mainly fuels from Egypt and Algeria (49.5 per cent of EU 2013 imports from Egypt and

---

[51] UNECA (2015a)

[52] Here defined as Algeria, Egypt, Morocco, Libya, Tunisia and Sudan. Note that Sudan does not have a EUROMED agreement with the European Union.

[53] The Euro-Mediterranean Free Trade Area, which aims at removing barriers to trade and investment between the EU and Southern Mediterranean countries and between the Southern Mediterranean countries themselves, includes Algeria, Egypt, Israel, Jordan, Lebanon, Morocco, Palestine, Turkey and Tunisia.

[54] Mevel et al. (2015)

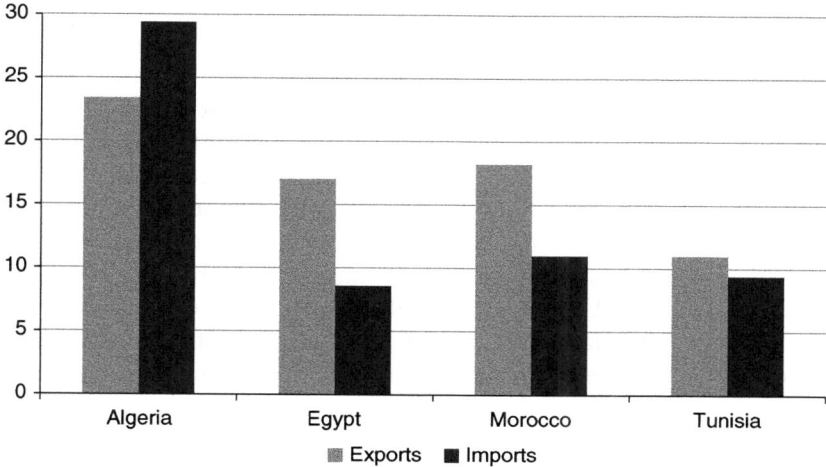

Figure 12.7 EU trade with North African countries which have signed EU-Mediterranean Association Agreements, billions of Euros, 2013
Source: Authors calculations based on Eurostat data.

97 per cent of EU imports from Algeria). On the other hand, Morocco and Tunisia have managed to export higher shares of manufactured products to the EU. In 2013, Tunisia's and Morocco's main exports to the European Union were electrical and electronic equipment, and textiles and clothing also had important shares. These data suggest that resource-poor North African countries have managed to export relatively more manufactured products to Europe than their resource-rich counterparts.

Europe is currently negotiating deeper trade agreements with some countries in the region, notably Morocco. Negotiations for a Deep and Comprehensive Free Trade Agreement (DCFTA) between the European Union and Morocco were launched on 1 March 2013. This DCFTA will extend significantly beyond the scope of the existing Association Agreement to include trade in services, government procurement, competition, intellectual property rights, investment protection and the gradual integration of the Moroccan economy into the EU single market, for example in areas like industrial standards and technical regulations or sanitary and phytosanitary measures.

EUROMED agreements have scope for improvement in their support to North Africa's trade structural transformation. Simulations from

Mevel, De Alba and Oulmane (2015)[55] show the increase in trade that would result for North Africa if the CFTA were to be put in place, together with a Pan-Arab FTA and a deepening of EUROMED agreements introducing FTA in all sectors (the current EUROMED agreements focus on manufacturing sectors). In this ambitious scenario, exports to the European Union and all other countries of the Mediterranean alliance would rise considerably. Export benefits would nearly quadruple for North Africa as a whole (in absolute terms, with the largest expansions for Morocco and Tunisia), compared to a situation where only the CFTA and the Pan-Arab FTA are in place. The greater the free trade area, the larger the export gains would be for North Africa; trade facilitation measures would further expand the benefits, with export gains in industrial products always the highest in absolute terms.[56]

7.3   Trade, Development Cooperation Agreement between South Africa and European Union

The Trade, Development and Cooperation Agreement (TDCA) establishes preferential trade arrangements between the European Union and South Africa with the progressive introduction of a free trade area. The European Union is South Africa's main trading and investment partner. The free trade area provides for the liberalization of 95 per cent of the European Union's imports from South Africa within ten years, and of 86 per cent of South Africa's imports from the European Union in twelve years. In order to protect the vulnerable sectors of both parties, certain products are excluded from the FTA and others have been only partially liberalized. For the European Union, these are mainly agricultural products, while for South Africa, they are industrial products, in particular certain motor vehicle and textile and clothing products. However, since December 2006 there have been provisions for strengthening trade liberalization in the motor vehicle sector.

The Agreement sets out detailed rules of origin in order to ensure that products benefiting from the preferential arrangements come only from South Africa or the European Union. To take account of modern international production processes, special provisions make the rules of origin more flexible.[57] South Africa's primary exports to the European Union are fuels and mining products, machinery and transport equipment, and

---

[55] Mevel et al (2015)   [56] Mevel et al (2015)
[57] http://eur-lex.europa.eu/legal-content/EN/TXT/?uri=URISERV:r12201

other semi-manufactured goods. EU exports to South Africa are dominated by machinery and transport equipment, chemicals and other semi-machinery.[58]

South Africa joined the EPAs negotiations as part of the SADC group in February 2007, but the EPA between the country and the European Union has not been signed yet.

8   Intra-African Trade Integration Is Patchy but Accelerating

In this section we analyse the current status of Africa's internal trade integration and assess the potential of recent initiatives to deepen it, such as the Tripartite Free Trade Area (TFTA) Agreement and the CFTA.

African countries are currently engaged in eight regional economic communities[59] (RECs) recognised by the African Union (AU), which have been moving at different speeds to implement the Abuja Treaty. The Abuja Treaty, which entered into force in 1994, provides a roadmap to advance regional integration in Africa, with key benchmarks such as the establishment of a CFTA by 2017, a customs union by 2019 and an African Economic Community by 2028.

Twenty-eight African countries currently belong to three or more RECs[60] and there is a simultaneous challenge in managing external trade relationships such as EPAs with the European Union, trade with the emerging powers and multilateral negotiations under the WTO Doha Round. Economic reasons are not the only motives for African countries to enter RECs: political and security considerations also matter greatly. Trade agreements increase the opportunity cost of conflict. African countries' borders and unequal resource distribution also play a role in the proliferation of RECs: small, fragmented and isolated economies with resources distributed very unequally among them make a compelling case for regional integration.[61]

Despite some progress, commitments made at regional level have often not been carried out by individual states.[62] The cost of exporting a full standard twenty-foot container from an African country to Europe

[58] http://ec.europa.eu/trade/policy/countries-and-regions/countries/south-africa/
[59] SADC, ECOWAS, ECCAS, AMU, COMESA, IGAD, EAC, and CEN-SAD
[60] http://www.moibrahimfoundation.org/downloads/publications/2014/2014-facts-&-figures-regional-integration-uniting-to-compete.pdf
[61] De Melo and Tsikata (2014)
[62] http://www.africaneconomicoutlook.org/fileadmin/uploads/aeo/2014/PDF/Chapter_PDF/03_Chapter3_AEO2014_EN.light.pdf

in 2014 was US$ 2,000, more than double the cost estimated for Asia (US$ 900).[63]

The eight African RECs are very heterogeneous building blocks to the continental regional integration process. Their sizes vary from 92 to 551 million people and their per capita GDP from US$ 98 to US$ 974.[64] Just as an example, in SADC, the average income of a person living in the Seychelles is forty-nine times higher than that of someone living in fellow SADC member the Democratic Republic of the Congo. Efforts to facilitate free movement of people within the continent are also lagging behind. Cumbersome visa requirements affect the mobility of people on the continent.[65] Aviation in Africa, while booming, is falling short of the continent's needs: flying around within the continent remains more expensive than in any other area of the world. Africa still has only a handful of intercontinental carriers in Africa, with non-African airlines accounting for 80 per cent of the intercontinental market share.

As shown in Figure 12.8, Africa's RECs have very different 'success rates' when measured in terms of percentage of internal trade: while the EAC and SADC trade, respectively, 20 per cent and 17 per cent within the REC and are not far behind similar regional agreements in other continents (and ahead of MERCOSUR in Latin America), in other African RECs, in particular ECCAS, internal trade has yet to take off.

As shown in Figure 12.9, Africa trades very little with itself. Despite the continent's well-recognised abundance of agricultural resources, in 2014 Africa imported 85 per cent of all food items and 90 per cent of agricultural materials from the rest of the world. These figures are even starker when looking at manufactured items, especially those requiring higher skills and technologies: 93 per cent of medium-skill and technology-intensive manufactures and 91 per cent of high-skill and technology-intensive manufactures were imported from outside of Africa in 2014. Overall, manufactures as a share of intra-African exports declined from 59 per cent in 1995 to 41 per cent in 2014.

The share of manufactures in Africa's internal trade, however, is substantially higher than that of manufacturing in Africa's exports to the rest of the world (41 per cent versus 18 per cent in 2014; although

---

[63] http://www.moibrahimfoundation.org/downloads/publications/2014/2014-facts-&-figures-regional-integration-uniting-to-compete.pdf

[64] http://www.moibrahimfoundation.org/downloads/publications/2014/2014-facts-&-figures-regional-integration-uniting-to-compete.pdf

[65] http://www.moibrahimfoundation.org/downloads/publications/2014/2014-facts-&-figures-regional-integration-uniting-to-compete.pdf

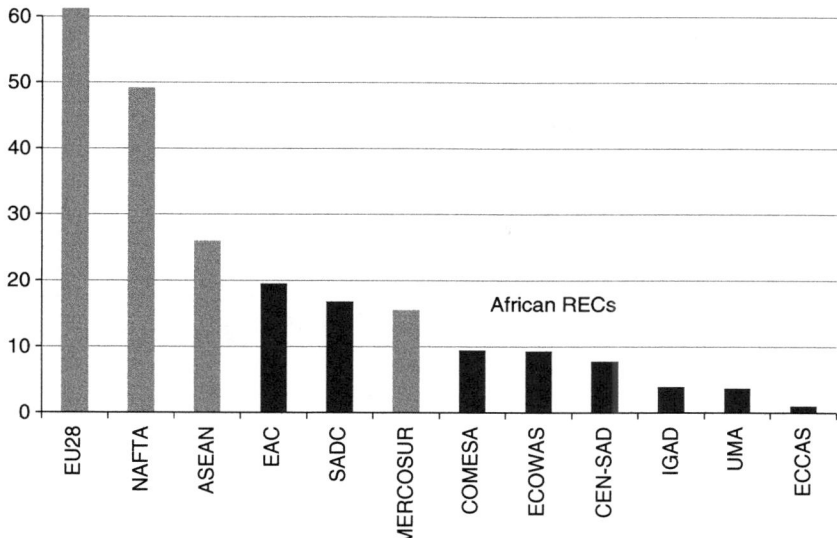

Figure 12.8 Percentage of intra-regional exports across various regional economic communities, 2014
Source: ECA analysis of UNCTAD data (accessed on 1 October 2015).

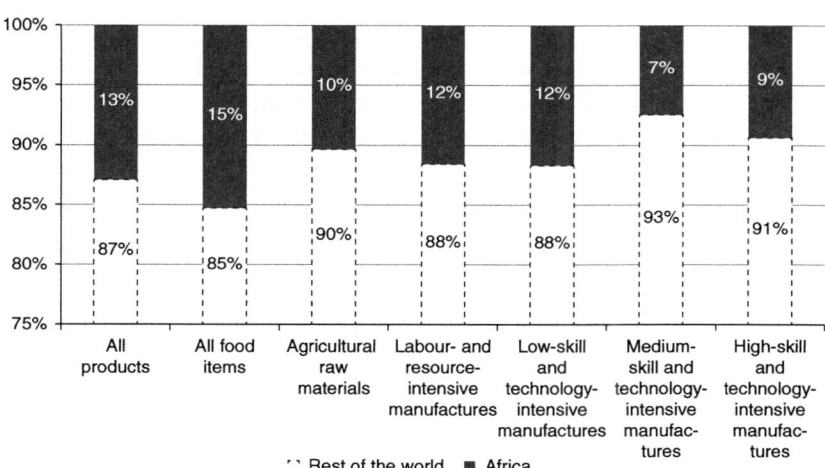

Figure 12.9 Africa's imports from Africa and from the rest of the world, 2014
Source: ECA analysis of UNCTAD data (accessed on 1 October 2015).

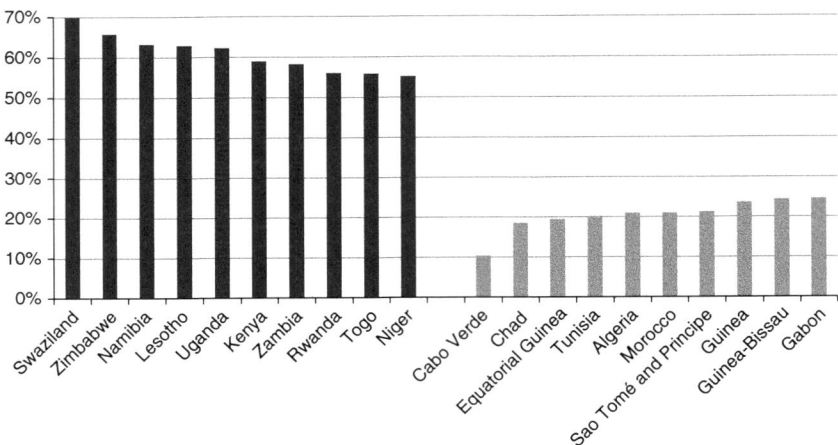

Figure 12.10   Share of trade* conducted within Africa 2012–14 average, ten highest and lowest shares
*Share of trade is defined as the average of the shares of imports and exports traded within Africa over 2012–14.
Source: ECA analysis of UNCTAD data.

manufactures as a share of intra-African exports actually declined from 59 per cent in 1995 to 41 per cent in 2014).[66] Increasing intra-African trade therefore has the potential to boost Africa's manufacturing. For example, while Kenya exports to Europe consist mostly of tea, flowers, coffee and vegetables, its exports to African countries mainly consist of processed goods such as cement, medical products and refined fuel oil.[67] This suggests that easing barriers to trade within Africa might offer a greater incentive for countries to focus on value-added products.[68]

As shown in Figure 12.10, there is wide disparity in the level of trade conducted by African countries within Africa. While Namibia, Swaziland and Zimbabwe trade significantly within the continent, Cabo Verde, Chad or Equatorial Guinea trade very little with fellow African states. It is notable that four countries (Algeria, Chad, Equatorial Guinea and Gabon) out of the ten with the lowest intra-African trade shares over 2012–14 are oil-rich.[69] This compares to zero oil-rich countries among the ten top traders

---

[66] ECA analysis of UNCTAD data   [67] Mutiga (2014)
[68] http://ti.au.int/en/sites/default/files/REVISED%20QA%20-%20Final%20_3_%20under lined.pdf
[69] Defined as countries for which oil exports exceed oil imports by at least 20 per cent. ECA 2014 classification.

with Africa. This points to the fact that oil is mostly exported crude from Africa to the rest of the world, and re-imported refined, mostly from non-African countries. Also, countries with high intra-African trade shares tend to be members of successful RECs (mostly EAC and COMESA).

9   Africa's Trade in Intermediate Inputs Is Dynamic but Has Large Scope to Grow

The scarce intra-African trade is also visible in intermediate inputs – production inputs to be transformed domestically and then possibly re-exported. African firms do not seem to find the inputs they need for industrial production within Africa. Between 2001 and 2010, Africa's imports of intermediate inputs grew almost four-fold. However, only 12 per cent of imported intermediate inputs were sourced from the continent in 2012.[70] Such a reliance on imported inputs from outside Africa points to the unavailability of suitable intermediates locally and at competitive prices, which in turn reflects the limited degree of economic diversification.

In 2011, only six countries, namely Algeria, Egypt, Morocco, Nigeria, South Africa and Tunisia, accounted for roughly three-quarters of the continent's total intermediate imports. However, the value of intermediate imports is increasing rapidly also in other African countries (such as Ethiopia, Mozambique, Rwanda, Uganda, Zambia), although from a very low base. Interestingly, those countries that appear to be more integrated in global production networks and that imported the larger shares of intermediates (Algeria, Egypt, Morocco, South Africa and Tunisia) sourced less than 5 per cent of these inputs from Africa in 2011.[71] This may indicate that countries more linked up in global production networks have access to sourcing opportunities for inputs that are more favourable than the ones they can find on the continent.

10   Intra-African Trade Is Entering a New Phase, through Transformative Agreements Such as the TFTA and the CFTA

10.1   The Current TFTA Framework More Cautious Than Ambitious

The COMESA-EAC-SADC Tripartite Free Trade Area (TFTA), which brings together twenty-six African countries or 58 per cent of the continent's GDP, was signed on 10 June 2015 and is expected to enter into

[70] UNECA (2013)   [71] UNECA (2013)

Table 12.2 *Summary of TFTA tariff liberalization schedule*

Tariff lines liberalized upon entry into force	60–85 per cent
Tariff lines to be negotiated over a period of five to eight years after entry into force	40–15 per cent

Source: Luke and Mabuza (2015).

force in January 2016. Bringing together countries which already belong to different trade regimes is not an easy task, and tripartite negotiations started back in 2008. Negotiations are conducted in two phases.

Negotiations on trade in goods for which an agreement was reached in June 2015 took place first. It should be noted, however, that not all issues have yet been resolved. For example, as shown in Table 12.2, the schedule of tariff reductions under the TFTA still needs to be finalised. At the time of the TFTA launch, not all of the TFTA countries had finalized their tariff offers. The Third Meeting of the Tripartite Council of Ministers, held in Sharm-el-Sheikh, gave countries until June 2016 to finalize their offers. Upon entry into force of the agreement, the target for trade liberalization in goods is 60 to 85 per cent, while negotiations will continue for the remainder tariff lines with the expectation that liberalization will take place over the next five to eight years (see Table 12.2), implying that it will take at least that number of years for the TFTA to match the existing levels of liberalization in some of the RECs, for example in the EAC. Luke and Mabuza (2015)[72] noted that this poses challenges for countries that have fairly liberalized trade regimes (with more than 80 per cent of their tariff lines at zero per cent MFN) *vis-à-vis* the principle of building on the *acquis*. A more coherent approach would have been to possibly set the floor for market access at the existing levels of liberalization in the RECs.[73] Sodipo (2015)[74] also underlines that from a legal perspective, the wording of the current TFTA leaves ground for ambiguity on what provisions would apply to RTAs eventually signed by TFTA members among themselves and with external partners. In particular, the current wording does not make it unequivocally clear on what basis PTAs signed by any TFTA members would extend to all TFTA members (MFN, reciprocity, non-discriminatory basis etc.). The current TFTA is still a work in progress, and governments have scope to improve it. Beyond the tariff liberalization matter, negotiations on the delicate issue of rules of origin and trade

---

[72] Luke and Mabuza (2015)   [73] Sodipo (2015)   [74] Sodipo (2015)

remedies are also yet to be completed. Rules of origin have been negotiated and agreed for only about 25 per cent of the product list so far. The Third Meeting of the Tripartite Council of Ministers undertook to finalize the tripartite rules of origin within twelve months of the TFTA launch.

Negotiations on services, intellectual property rights, competition policy and cross-border investments will take place in a second phase.

Additionally, the direct gains from the TFTA alone are likely to be unevenly distributed in absolute terms. While, in the first scenario, only South Africa enjoys significant real income gains, with moderate gains for Lesotho, Namibia and Swaziland, in the second scenario all countries would enjoy a positive aggregate welfare gain.[75] Other studies have underlined how gains from the TFTA are likely to be unevenly distributed among the participating economies under any scenario, and potentially detract from the rest of the continent.[76] Jensen and Sandrey (2011)[77] have shown that, if the TFTA is implemented together with a 2 per cent reduction in non-tariff barriers, only South Africa and Mozambique stand to gain from it. South Africa's welfare is set to increase by US$ 1,321 million, or 0.29 per cent of GDP, after the agreement, thanks to increased demand for its exports and to appreciations of the real exchange rate. Mozambique is set to gain US$ 57 million. According to their simulations, results for the rest of SACU (i.e. Lesotho, Namibia and Swaziland) are disappointing, with a welfare loss of US$ 84 million. Botswana stands to lose US$16 million. It should, however, be stated that these are tiny figures and that all African countries outside of the TFTA stand to lose from the agreement. This calls for broader integration reforms – going beyond strictly tariff barriers, and encompassing African countries outside of the TFTA. Furthermore, other studies have highlighted that, despite possible welfare losses for some countries following strict reduction of tariff barriers (Mevel and Karingi, 2012), production and exports gains could be considerable and may not just benefit big countries. Mold and Mukwaya (2014), looking at sectors which are key in the first stages of industrialisation (i.e. processed food, textile and apparel and light manufacturing), demonstrate that industrial production would be stimulated for most countries with establishment of the TFTA, and countries such as South Africa and Egypt would actually not be the main beneficiaries.

Moreover, the TFTA is not just about trade but encompasses industrialization (through an industrial pillar), infrastructure and even the movement of businesspeople. In other words, the TFTA remains

---

[75] Willenbockel (2013)   [76] Jensen and Sandrey (2011)   [77] Jensen and Sandrey (2011)

a critical starting point to building confidence and getting regional integration moving effectively on the African continent. It is expected to be an important stepping stone towards the CFTA, the goal of which is to liberalize trade among the entire continent by 2017.

10.2   CFTA Agenda and Ambition

Although economic integration has for decades been a key element of Africa's development strategy, intra-African trade remains a limited share of Africa's total trade (around 13 per cent of Africa's imports came from the continent in 2014). As shown in Figure 12.11, this compares to 55 per cent of intra-regional imports in developing Asia, 18 per cent in developing America and much higher shares in most of the developed world (with developed Asia as a striking outlier). When looking at Africa's internal imports by region, Southern Africa is the most integrated sub-region – mostly due to South Africa – with 12.2 per cent of imports coming from within the area. This compares to 2.3 per cent in Middle Africa and 3.8 per cent in Northern Africa.

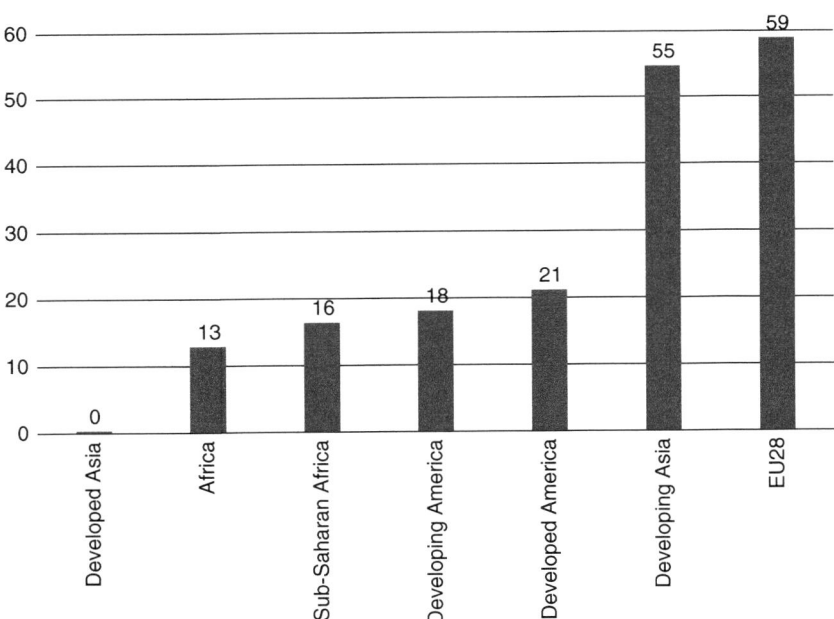

Figure 12.11   Shares of intra-regional imports by area, 2014
Source: ECA analysis of UNCTAD data.

In order to enhance Africa's market integration and increase the contribution of trade to the continent's growth, in January 2012, the African Union Summit of Heads of States and Government approved an action plan for boosting intra-African trade and the establishment of a CFTA by an indicative date of 2017. Negotiations for the CFTA were officially launched on 15 June 2015 at the last AU Summit in South Africa. The CFTA aims to eliminate tariffs and quotas on the trade of most goods and services among fifty-four African countries with a combined population of more than 1 billion people and a combined GDP of more than US\$ 2 trillion.

The CFTA would enlarge markets for goods and services, facilitate economies of scale, resolve the problem of multiple and overlapping membership of RECs, enhance customs cooperation and broader trade facilitation, promote harmonization and coordination of trade instruments and nomenclature, and ensure broader relaxation of restrictions on the movement of goods, persons and services. The collaboration and cooperation of RECs through the CFTA should further improve regional infrastructure and consolidate regional markets through improved interconnectivity in all forms of transport and communication as well as promote energy pooling to enhance the regions' competitiveness.[78] In short, the CFTA will help to ensure that trade becomes more effective in playing its transformative role by providing opportunities for value addition and industrialisation and serve as a driving force behind economic development.

Research has found that the CFTA could stimulate intra-African trade by up to US\$ 35 billion per year, or 52 per cent above the baseline in the year 2022. It could also lead to a US\$ 10 billion decrease in imports from outside the continent, while boosting agriculture and industrial exports by up to US\$ 4 billion (7 per cent) and US\$ 21 billion (5 per cent), respectively. Gains in real income and employment could be even higher if the CFTA is complemented by trade facilitation reforms, reductions of non-tariff barriers, improved infrastructure and measures to counter-balance some of the negative effects associated with liberalisation reforms, such as a loss of tariff revenue. If progress in facilitating trade (specifically, reducing costs of trading across borders)[79] is made in parallel to eliminating tariff barriers on goods

---

[78] AU and ECA (2012)
[79] Assuming that customs procedures are made twice more efficient and the time goods are spending at African ports is halved.

within Africa, the share of formal intra-African trade could almost double by 2022, reaching 22 per cent (Mevel and Karingi, 2012). At a country level, all African economies would get positive outcomes in both exports and real income. In other words, the trade opportunities brought by trade facilitation measures on top of the CFTA would more than offset the few losses to governments' budgets from declining tariff revenues.[80] For these effects to materialize and grow, Africa also needs to invest in upgrading its infrastructure and reducing the cost of doing business on the continent. Africa's infrastructure services, whether for power, water, road freights, mobile telephones or internet services, are also much more expensive than elsewhere.[81] According to the Africa Infrastructure Country Diagnostic, the continent's infrastructure spending needs stand at about US$ 93 billion per year, of which about 40 per cent is associated with power. African countries themselves fund a large share of infrastructure projects on the continent – 46.9 per cent or US$ 46.7 billion out of a total of US$ 99.6 billion in 2013[82] (of which around a third comes from donor funding).[83] Two-thirds of the public sector money is used to operate and maintain existing infrastructure and one-third is used to finance new projects. This leaves a financing gap of US$ 48 billion. A more efficient use of existing infrastructure (rehabilitation of existing infrastructure and better-targeted subsidies and budget execution, among other measures) could reduce the gap by US$ 17 billion.[84]

10.3 Sequencing: Deepening Africa's Integration before Opening up to the Rest of the World Can Maximize Africa's Benefits from Trade Reforms

Just as trade preferences towards African nations alone are unlikely to sustain Africa's industrialization, regional integration cannot be Africa's sole trade strategy. African economies need to open up to other partners outside the continent, as the regional market is still relatively small. But, in doing so, Africa needs to preserve policy space to guarantee that its priority industrialization efforts (such as regional integration) are not undermined.

This requires the adoption of strategic trade policies which actively support Africa's industrialization efforts and the use of smart sequencing of trade reforms. In what follows, we are going to highlight three key areas of intervention for smart sequencing: first, the reduction of tariffs and non-tariff barriers within the continent; second, the idea of

[80] UNECA (2015a)   [81] Sy (2013)   [82] UNECA (2015c)   [83] Sy (2013)   [84] Sy (2013)

introducing common external tariffs (CETs) from Africa to the rest of the world; and third, the accelerated implementation of the CFTA.[85]

Intra-African exports often face higher levels of protection *vis-à-vis* Africa's exports to the rest of the world, and the situation may worsen unless the CFTA is implemented before other reforms, such as the EPAs, are fully put in place.

The reduction of tariffs, removal of non-tariff barriers and integration of markets within Africa should be prioritized relative to liberalization efforts towards the rest of the world. Significant tariffs still remain among Africa's RECs. Average protection within Africa is about 8.7 per cent, while protection faced by Africa's exports toward the rest of the world is around 2.5 per cent. For strictly industrial products the difference is even starker: 9.0 per cent versus 2.3 per cent (Mevel and Karingi, 2013).[86] Therefore, mostly due to trade preferences granted to Africa by partners from the rest of the world, trade within Africa remains more limited by protectionism than trade outside of Africa. Efforts to reduce intra-African tariffs as much as possible and as quickly as possible should be redoubled.

Other limiting factors to intra-African trade, such as non-tariff barriers, remain high among RECs, weighing on the competitiveness of African producers.[87] According to a study by the International Trade Centre (ITC, 2012),[88] improving transport infrastructure within Africa and thereby reducing the cost and time required to export goods by half, would boost the GDP of Africa (excluding North Africa) by more than US$ 20 billion annually in 2025 and increase trade by up to 51 per cent beyond the forecast natural growth. This would mostly benefit intra-regional trade, where the relative cost and time lost because of Africa's poor transport network is the highest.

Putting in place strategic CETs from Africa to the rest of the world before further opening up trade between the continent and other regions would also be smart sequencing for the continent. The challenge would be to identify a CET that served the common interests of the continent, rather than one that would bid up external tariff rates in a way that would make intermediate inputs for specific Africa-led segments of global value chains become inaccessible. This would arrest the drive for competitiveness and global integration. A CET would avoid the creation of tariff distortions among regional groupings that would be hard to overcome. An ECA study (ARIA V, 2012)[89] shows that the adoption of a single CET

---

[85] UNECA (2015a) [86] UNECA (2015a) [87] Lopes (2015) [88] ITC (2012)
[89] UNECA (2012)

structure for the whole continent would not only preserve intra-African trade gains from CFTA reforms but could also expand Africa's global trade, especially if African tariffs on imported intermediates were reduced, thanks to cheaper imports of inputs for production. This would strengthen Africa's competitiveness, leading to export opportunities and gains outside the continent. CET structures should also favour imports of cheaper inputs critical in adding value to Africa's exports, with the objective of exploiting better trade opportunities and moving up the value chains.[90] Over time, increased competitiveness in African production would lessen the value of a CET, and the political will would need to be forthcoming to reduce the CET over time.

Finally, having the CFTA in place and operational sooner rather than later would help Africa avoid trade diversion from mega-regional trade agreements (MRTAs). The trend for MRTAs is on the rise around the world. The Trans-Atlantic Trade and Investment Partnership (TTIP) currently being negotiated between the European Union and the United States is the main example. The TTIP would deepen the largest economic relationship in the world. The combined trade between the European Union and the United States accounts for nearly 30 per cent of world merchandise trade, 40 per cent of global trade in services, and almost half of global GDP.[91] The expected impact of TTIP on Africa is unclear. On the one hand, there is potential for TTIP to positively impact global economic development, with some studies estimating that positive economic spillovers resulting from TTIP could increase GDP in the rest of the world by as much as US$ 109 billion. Furthermore, if preferences and standards are harmonized in a way that allows African businesses to meet them, TTIP could increase market access, facilitating increased trade with two of its largest trading partners. However, if preferences are not harmonized, or if standards are set too high, this could serve to crowd out African companies from accessing EU and US markets.

A study by ECA (2015)[92] investigates implications of key MRTAs for Africa looking at the TTIP, the Trans-Pacific Partnership (TPP) and the Regional Comprehensive Economic Partnership (RCEP). According to the study, total exports of MRTA members (i.e. TTIP, TPP and RCEP) would increase by US$ 1.0 trillion by 2020 with the agreements, and Africa's exports would be reduced by US$ 2.7 billion in that year following higher

---

[90] UNECA (2015a)
[91] Intra-EU trade is excluded and GDP is valued at current dollar prices. At purchasing power parity rates, the combined share in global GDP is about a third.
[92] AU and UNECA (2015)

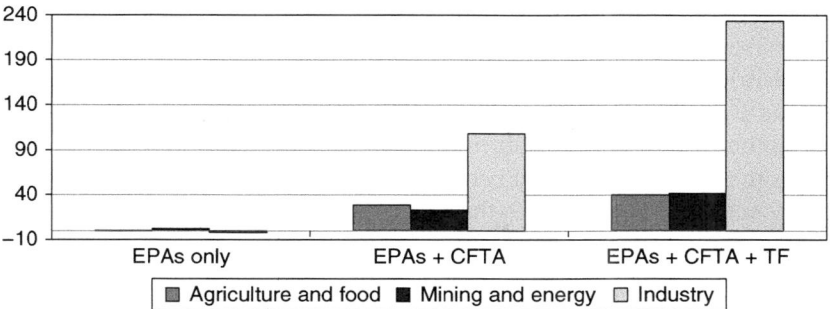

Figure 12.12 Expected change in intra-African trade by main sectors following EPAs vs. EPAs+CFTA vs. EPAs+CFTA+Trade Facilitation (TF), 2040, US$ billion
Source: ECA analysis.

competition and erosion of preferences on MRTA members' markets. Such diversion may appear relatively small, but it should be noted that Africa's exports would fall in all main sectors, especially industry. Moreover, the loss might be underestimated as the analysis only considers reductions in tariffs on goods, while the MRTAs also cover services and investments.

By deepening continental integration and consolidating African markets, the CFTA would make the continent harder to exclude from large multilateral trade negotiations and would mitigate the impact of possible trade diversion from other regions' MRTAs. According to ECA's analysis, with the CFTA, Africa's exports would increase by US$ 40 billion, of which more than two-thirds would be in industrial products.

Similarly Karingi, Mevel and Valensisi (2015) demonstrate how negative outcomes on intra-African trade from EPAs would be reversed if the CFTA were established before EPAs are fully implemented. As shown in Figure 12.12, gains for intra-African trade would be even higher if the CFTA were established together with additional trade facilitation measures.[93]

11 Conclusions and Recommendations

African governments should take actions to maximize benefits from their growing services sector. They need to ensure that services can be accessed by African firms, for example by providing growing financial institutions with incentives to lend to local SMEs. They need to direct the growth in

[93] UNECA (2015a)

the services sector towards formal, tradable and high-value added services (such as business support, finance, information technology and tourism) that can foster economic transformation, reinforce manufacturing and bring in trade revenues. At the same time, services should not be left out of liberalization efforts and trade agreements on the continent: firms in one country should benefit from the availability of good support services in other countries in the region. This will support the creation of regional value chains on the continent. Some African countries, such as Kenya and Rwanda, are already well positioned to become services hubs in their respective regions.

Africa is engaging in a multitude of PTAs, and is at the same time ambitiously pushing the agenda for trade integration within the continent. However, current trade agreements and arrangements have generally failed to promote Africa's structural transformation objectives. The continent needs to become more strategic in pursuing trade agreements that support its industrialization and exports diversification efforts. In current and future agreements with the rest of the world, Africa should preserve policy space and lobby for tariff lines, rules of origin and other requirements that can actively promote the growth of Africa's products and firms and expand Africa's exports beyond a narrow range of basic goods. At the same time, Africa needs to be more ambitious and bold on the home front, increasing the scope, streamlining the regimes and accelerating the full implementation of agreements such as the TFTA and the CFTA. Africa still has time to improve the impacts of these agreements and put them in place before further opening up with the rest of the world: what we have called 'smart sequencing'.

If Africa is able to adopt this change in vision over the coming years, trade policy will truly become an instrument of the continent's structural transformation. Trade policy, of course, cannot be the only strategy for industrialization: Africa needs to work in parallel on developing its production capacities, its human capital, its technology, its entrepreneurship, its infrastructure, its regulation and its macroeconomic and political stability.

References

African Union (AU) and the United Nation Commission for Africa (UNECA) (2012), 'Boosting Intra-African Trade. 2012'. Addis Ababa: ECA and AU. http://www.uneca.org/sites/default/files/page_attachments/issues_affecting_intra-african_trade_proposed_action_plan_for_biat_and_framework_for_the_fast_tracking_of_a_cfta_-ts6622_en_original.doc.pdf

African Union and UNECA (2015), 'Report on the Emergence of Mega-Regional Trade Agreements and their Implications for Africa's Continental Integration', prepared for AMOT meeting, May 2015. Addis Ababa: ECA-AUC.

Brenton, P. and C. Ozden (2013), *Trade Preferences for Apparel and the Role of Rules of Origin – The Case of Africa.* Washington: The World Bank. http://siteresources.worldbank.org/INTTRADERESEARCH/Resources/544824-1235150721870/ch10_Brenton_Ozden_Apparel_Preferences.pdf

Cadot, O., C. Carrère and V. Strauss-Kahn (2011), 'Export Diversification: What's behind the hump?', *Review of Economics and Statistics* 93, 590–605.

De Melo, J. and Y. Tsikata (2014), 'Regional Integration in Africa, Challenges and Prospects'. A contribution to the Handbook of Africa and Economics. FERDI Document de Travail 93. http://www.ferdi.fr/sites/www.ferdi.fr/files/publication/fichiers/wp93_de_melo_web.pdf

Financial Times (2015), 'Africa's Rise Is Stalled by Chinese Slowdown', 1 November 2015. http://www.ft.com/intl/cms/s/0/2a4f3cbc-7eff-11e5-98fb-5a6d4728f74e.html#axzz3qK96KF00

Hanson, S. and L. Dare (2014), 'Foresight Africa 2014', Brookings Institute'. http://www.brookings.edu/blogs/africa-in-focus/posts/2014/01/29-africa-agriculture-productivity-hanson.

Hausmann, R., J. Hwang and D. Rodrik (2007), 'What You Export Matters'. https://ideas.repec.org/a/kap/jecgro/v12y2007i1p1-25.html

Hruby, A. (2015), 'China's Slowdown: An Opportunity for Africa to Address Longstanding Economic Efficiencies', *Financial Times*, 26 October 2015. http://blogs.ft.com/beyond-brics/2015/10/26/chinas-slowdown-an-opportunity-for-africa-to-address-longstanding-economic-inefficiencies/

Imbs, J. and R. Wacziarg (2003), 'Stages of Diversification', *American Economic Review*, 93(1): 63–86.

International Trade Centre (2012), *Africa's Trade Potential. Export Opportunities in Growth Markets.* Geneva: ITC.

Jensen, G.H. and R. Sandrey (2011), 'The Tripartite Free Trade Agreement: A Computer Analysis of the Results'. TRALAC working paper no. N11WP06/2011. http://www.tralac.org/images/docs/4275/n11wp062011tripartitegtap20110323.pdf

Karingi, S., S. Mevel and G. Valensisi (2015), 'The EPAs and Africa's Regional Integration', *Bridges Africa* 4(6). http://www.ictsd.org/bridges-news/bridges-africa/news/the-epas-and-africa%E2%80%99s-regional-integration

Kimenyi, M.S. (2015), 'AGOA Utilisation 101', Brookings Institute. http://www.brookings.edu/blogs/africa-in-focus/posts/2015/03/23-african-growth-opportunity-act-utilization-kimenyi

Kyinge, J., and J. Wheatley (2015), 'Emerging Markets: Fixing a Broken Model', *Financial Times*, 31 August 2015. http://www.ft.com/intl/cms/s/0/945c837e-4fc7-11e5-b029-b9d50a74fd14.html?siteedition=intl#axzz3kZ7nDmNE

Lopes, C. (2015), African Trade Policies Have to Match Its Industrialisation Imperative. http://www.howwemadeitinafrica.com/african-trade-policies-have-to-match-its-industrialisation-imperative/48803/

Luke, D. and Z. Mabuza (2015), 'The Tripartite Free Trade Area Agreement: A Milestone for Africa's Regional Integration Process'. International Centre for Trade and Sustainable Development. http://www.ictsd.org/bridges-news /bridges-africa/news/the-tripartite-free-trade-area-agreement-a-milestone-for-africa%E2%80%99s.

McArthur, J., (2013), 'Good Things Grow in Sealed Packages: Africa's Agriculture Challenge in Historical Context.' Brooking Institute. http://www.brookings .edu/research/papers/2013/05/africa-agriculture-challenge-mcarthur

McMillan, M. and K. Harttgen (2014), 'What is Driving the African Group Miracle', NBER Working Paper No. 20077, April 2014. http://www.nber.org /papers/w20077

McMillan, M. and D. Rodrik (2011), 'Globalization, Structural Change and Productivity Growth', NBER Working Paper No. 17143. http://www.nber.org /papers/w17143

Meltzer, J.P. (2015), 'Reforming the African Growth and Opportunity Act to Grow Agriculture Trade', Brookings Institution http://www.brookings.edu/blogs/ africa-in-focus/posts/2015/02/23-agoa-agriculture-africa-meltzer

Mevel, S. and S. Karingi (2012), 'Deepening Regional Integration in Africa: A Computable General Equilibrium Assessment of the Establishment of a Continental Free Trade Area Followed by a Continental Customs Union', paper presented at the 7th African Economic Conference, Kigali, Rwanda, 30 October–2 November 2012. http://www.afdb.org/fileadmin/uploads/afdb/ Documents/Knowledge/Deepening%20Regional%20Integration%20in% 20Africa%20A%20Computable%20General%20Equilibrium%20Assessment% 20of%20the%20Establishment%20of%20a%20Continental%20Free%20Trade% 20Area%20followed%20by%20a%20Continental%20Customs%20Union.pdf

Mevel, S., J. Moll de Alba and N. Oulmane (2015), 'Regional Trade Integration and Trade Facilitation as a Pro-Industrialisation Tool – The Case of North African Country'. http://www.unido.org/fileadmin/user_media/Services/PSD/ WP_2015_01_RegionalTradeIntegration.pdf

Mevel, S., Z. Lewis, S. K. Mwangi, S. Karingi and A. W. Kamau (2013), 'The African Growth and Opportunity Act: An Empirical Analysis of the Possibilities Post-2015', Brookings Institution. http://www.brookings.edu/research/reports/2013/ 07/african-growth-and-opportunity-act

Mevel, S., G. Valensisi and S. Karingi (2015), 'The Economic Partnership Agreements and Africa's Integration and Transformation Agenda: The Cases of West Africa and Eastern and Southern Africa Regions', paper presented at the 18th Annual Conference on Global Economic Analysis, Melbourne, Australia,

17–19 June, 2015. https://www.gtap.agecon.purdue.edu/resources/res_display.asp?RecordID=4754

Mutiga, M. (2014), 'Africa's Path to Prosperity', *New York Times*, 24 April 2014. http://www.nytimes.com/2014/04/25/opinion/mutiga-africas-path-to-prosperity.html?_r=0

Page, J. (2012), 'Can Africa Industrialise?', *Journal of African Economies*, Vol. 21, AERC Supplement 2, pp. ii86–ii125, doi:10.1093/jae/ejr045. http://jae.oxfordjournals.org/content/21/suppl_2/ii86.full.pdf+html

Schneidman, W. (2015), 'Why AGOA Should Be Extended for 15 Years: An Ethiopian Case Study', Brookings Institution. http://www.brookings.edu/blogs/africa-in-focus/posts/2015/03/19-agoa-extension-ethiopia-schneidman

Sodipo, B. (2015), The Tripartite Free Trade Agreement: Towards Continental Integration. African Union Commission, 2015.

Sy, A. (2013), 'Financing Africa's Infrastructure Gap'. Brooking Institution. http://www.brookings.edu/blogs/up-front/posts/2013/10/09-financing-africa-infrastructure-gap-sy

Sy, A., (2014), 'Convergence or Divergence: Discussing Structural Transformation in Africa during the G-20'. Brookings Institution. http://www.brookings.edu/blogs/africa-in-focus/posts/2014/11/14-

Rodrik, D. (2013), 'Africa's Structural Transformation Challenge'. *Project Syndicate*. https://www.project-syndicate.org/commentary/dani-rodrik-shows-why-sub-saharan-africa-s-impressive-economic-performance-is-not-sustainable.

UNCTAD (2013), World Investment Report 2013. Geneva: UNCTAD.

UNECA (2005), *Economic Report on Africa 2005, Meeting the Challenges of Unemployment and Poverty in Africa*. Addis Ababa: ECA.

UNECA (2006), Expert Group Meeting on Rules of Origin. 20–22 June 2006, Rabat, Morocco.

UNECA (2012), *Assessing Regional Integration in Africa V. Towards a Continental Free Trade Area*. Addis Ababa: ECA.

UNECA (2013), *Facilitating Trade: An African Perspective*. Addis Ababa: ECA.

UNECA (2014), *Economic Report on Africa, 2014*. Addis Ababa: ECA.

UNECA (2015a), *Economic Report on Africa 2015*. Addis Ababa: ECA

UNECA (2015b), *Review of Industrial Policies and Strategies in Africa*. Addis Ababa: ECA.

UNECA (2015c), *Report on Infrastructure Development in Africa 2015*. Addis Ababa: ECA.

UNIDO (2009), *Industrial Development Report 2009*.

World Bank (2014), *Africa's Pulse*, October 2014, Washington: The World Bank.

World Economic Forum (2015), *The 2015 Africa Competitiveness Report*. http://
www3.weforum.org/docs/WEF_ACR_2015/Africa_Competitiveness_Report_
2015.pdfconvergence-divergence-structural-transformation-africa-g20-sy
Willenbockel, D. (2013), 'General Equilibrium Analysis of the COMESA-EAC-
SADC Tripartite FTA'. http://www.Trademarksa.org, http://www.trademarksa
.org/sites/default/files/publications/2013-11-06%20TFTA%20CGE%20Impact
%20Analysis%20IDS%20Final%20Report.pdf

13

African Trade Integration and International Production Networks

BERNARD M. HOEKMAN

Abstract

African trade is heavily concentrated in agricultural and natural resource-based commodities, sectors that are highly embedded in international value chains. There has been significant trade dynamism in recent years, driven by greater participation by African firms and communities in value chains, especially in products like fresh produce and flowers. Much of this trade and production is for end markets in Europe, but there is also increasing trade of this type within Africa in some manufacturing sectors as well as within services such as tourism. Intra-regional trade remains well below potential, however, and the challenge to diversify trade and increase the value-added share of African trade continues to confront most African economies. There are improving prospects for this as a result of intra-African policy changes, ranging from a greater focus on trade facilitation to the ambition of creating a continental free trade area. A steep increase in supply chain trade in Africa is possible in coming decades if efforts continue to put in place a supporting policy environment. This must centre on substantially lowering trade costs for African firms by implementing trade facilitation measures, especially for intra-regional trade flows, and improving the productivity of transport, logistics and related services that determine the feasibility of efficiently operating regional value chains.

Introduction

Global trade growth since the early 1990s has been driven in significant part by increasing specialization. International production has fragmented into value chains (VCs) that span many countries and reflect the outsourcing and investment location decisions of large multinational

A preliminary version of this chapter was presented at the Fourth China Round Table, Nairobi, Kenya, on 13–14 December 2015.

companies and retailers (so-called lead firms). While there is much discussion of global VCs, much of the associated supply chain trade (SCT) is regional in nature. Supply chain specialists expect the regional nature of supply chain trade to increase further in the coming decades (Bamber et al., 2013; Srinivasan et al., 2014) as a result of technological developments that increase the incentive of firms to re-shore or near-shore production (i.e. either to bring back production from abroad or to produce at an adjacent location) – including the availability of robotics, 3D printing (additive manufacturing – i.e. the processes used to build a three-dimensional object by layering material), etc.

Some 80 per cent of world trade is estimated to involve multinational companies (UNCTAD, 2013). All of these firms source inputs and buy services from local suppliers and subcontractors. Much SCT is 'indirect' – the value of a final good incorporates payments for many intermediate goods and services that are not exported directly. Available data indicate that about one-third of the value of all traded manufactured goods reflects the value of services that are embodied in the goods and that, overall, if account is taken of sales of services by foreign affiliates, services account for more than 50 per cent of the value-added that is traded (Francois and Hoekman, 2010). Thus, a wide range of firms and sectors, including firms providing services to firms in other sectors, can benefit from and be affected by VC-based trade and investment opportunities.

While other parts of the world have seen the share of manufactured products and services increase, African exports are heavily concentrated in fuels and other natural resources. African exports have been dynamic in recent years – the share of the African continent as a whole in world exports increased from 2.4 per cent in the early 2000s to 3.4 per cent in 2013, after falling back to 3 per cent in 2014 (WTO, 2015).[1] This compares with a steadily declining trend from the 1950s to the late 1990s (Africa accounted for 7 per cent of global trade in 1950). Much of the growth during the 2000s involved expansion along the intensive margin of trade; exports remain mostly concentrated in traditional pro-ducts/commodities.

Most Sub-Saharan African (SSA) countries have a very narrow export base, whether measured in terms of the number of products that account for most revenue earned, the number of markets exported to, or the

[1] The decline in 2014 is mostly due a reduction in the value of fuel exports – the value of exports of manufactures and agricultural products increased slightly between 2013 and 2014.

number of companies that export (Cadot et al. 2011). New products often account for just a very small share of total exports. Export growth has been driven to a significant extent by greater global demand – especially by China – and associated increases in prices (improving terms of trade) for natural resource-based products. That source of demand growth was greatly weakened in the period following the global financial crisis. This was reflected in a reduction in Africa's share in global trade and increases the importance of successful diversification of production and trade along the so-called extensive margin: selling existing products to new markets and exporting new products.

Empirical research has shown that the "survival rate" of new export relationships is very low in many African countries. While firms are just as entrepreneurial as companies in richer countries when it comes to exploring potential new markets, the problem is that they are less successful in sustaining new trade relationships. Cadot et al. (2013) find that less than 20 per cent of new export relationships established by companies in Malawi, Mali, Senegal and Tanzania survive longer than one year. Most companies that start to export in a given year no longer do so the following year. In a sample of seventeen least-developed countries (LDCs) for which there are detailed data, the export failure rate was found to average 41 per cent, with a high of 67 per cent observed in Gambia (Nicita, Shirotori and Klok, 2013). Such high failure rates are costly, as resources are incurred in entering an export market. These are lost when the exports are not sustained. Low survival rates also increase volatility in the household incomes of the workers employed in firms that fail to sustain export production.

In 2014, 50 per cent of Africa's non-fuel merchandise exports comprised manufactured products, with agricultural products accounting for another 27 per cent.[2] Both types of goods experienced double-digit growth during 2010–14: manufactured exports grew by 17 per cent per year, agricultural products by 22 per cent per year. Although the overall value of agricultural exports is dwarfed by fuels in aggregate African exports, there has been significant dynamism in other, higher value-added products. There is great potential to build on the growth to date, especially through expansion of intra-regional trade flows. In 2014, only 18 per cent of African trade was with other African countries. This compares to 25 per cent in Latin America, more than 50 per cent in Asia and North America and 68 per cent in Europe.

---

[2] The statistics in this and the following paragraph are from WTO (2015).

It has become a commonplace that the world has three regional 'factories' – Europe, East Asia and North America. These three regions produce most of the world's goods and services, in part through a complex network of intra-regional trade relationships. Countries located in these three regions account for the majority of the top forty trading nations. There were only two African economies in the list of 40 largest exporters in 2014: Nigeria and South Africa, at 39th and 40th, respectively (WTO, 2015). These two nations, along with the members of the East African Community, have the potential to become hubs of the type of value chain trade that dominates in the three 'regional factories'. As discussed below, to a limited extent South Africa is already playing such a role, but the fact that Africa accounts for only 2 per cent of global imports of intermediate products, parts and components illustrates the limited extent to which African countries participate in VCs that produce manufactured products and related services. The potential for growth in such activities is not restricted to manufactured (industrial) products – it extends to agriculture and services. Only 27 per cent of Africa's exports of agricultural produce are intra-regional. While this is higher than the average for all goods, it compares to 75 per cent, 60 per cent and 40 per cent in Europe, Asia and North America, respectively.[3]

There is great scope to increase the volume and share of value chain trade in Africa. This should not simply aim to expand production of manufactured goods. Instead, the focus of policy should centre on increasing value-added generated in Africa, whether in agriculture, manufacturing or services. Priority areas for policy reforms and action include reducing trade and operating costs for firms and increasing the productivity of services that are critical inputs into the operation of supply chains, ranging from design to distribution. Regional integration is a particularly important dimension of efforts to lower trade costs as it is a necessary condition for increasing the share of intra-regional trade in both intermediates and final goods as well as enhancing the competitiveness of African products on world markets. The experience in Asia, Europe and US makes it clear that actions to support regional integration should not aim to shelter regional firms but should be pursued with a view to expanding both intra-regional trade and trade with the rest of the world.

This chapter is organized as follows. Section 1 reviews the potential for growth in SCT in Africa. Section 2 discusses key drivers of value chain

---

[3] Finger (2016) analyses recent trade developments and performance in depth.

trade and associated investments: low trade costs and improving the productivity of services inputs, focusing on trade and transport facilitation and logistics as well as the more general importance of continuing to improve the business environment. Section 3 contains some reflections on priorities in the pursuit of regional integration.[4] Section 4 concludes.

1 Value Chains and Production Networks

An international VC involves a collection of firms (plants) located in different countries that together form a 'production line', with different parts of the production process undertaken in different countries. Depending on the location of a firm (country) in a VC or international production network, participation may either involve forward linkages, where an activity produces an output that is used in production by other firms, or backward linkages, where a downstream firm uses domestic parts and components that are inputs into production.

Participation in international supply networks offers a potentially important channel to help achieve greater diversification of exports. SCT is a mechanism that facilitates the feasibility of entry by companies into higher value activities. Pursuit of greater 'vertical specialization' (focusing on specific tasks that are part of an international supply chain) can be an effective channel for even very poor countries to start manufacturing for the international market, adding value to traditional exports or providing value-added services to foreign buyers and foreign-owned companies that invest in the country.

Although Africa accounts for only a very low share of global supply chain trade, African nations are already highly integrated into VCs. However, this involves mainly acting as suppliers of products that are processed in the rest of the world into products that are then exported to other countries. Some 50 per cent of total gross exports of African nations embody foreign value added or are used as inputs into the production of other countries' exports (AfDB et al., 2014). Sub-Saharan African (SSA) countries are already active participants in some VCs. Examples include Ethiopia, Mauritius and Lesotho in apparel and leather products. Many African countries have seen significant growth in minerals and agriculture-based VCs. ITC (2013) shows that export portfolios of many LDCs reflect significant participation in VCs, based on a measure of 'transformed exports' – the share of manufactured, semi-manufactured and

---

[4] A more extensive discussion of this subject is provided in Karingi (2016).

processed primary products in total exports. In value terms, exports of transformed products increased between three and five times in SSA economies. Five African countries – Lesotho, the Seychelles, Swaziland, Tanzania and Zimbabwe – are among the world's top thirty countries in terms of VC participation (AfDB, OECD and UNDP, 2014).

There is great potential for African firms and farmers to increase their participation in international VCs, whether as a supplier of food-stuffs to local supermarket chains in neighbouring countries, to global retailers, or as suppliers of specialized intermediate inputs that exploit specific regional comparative advantages (UNECA, 2013; UNCTAD, 2013; Pesce, Karingi and Gebretensaye, 2015). Foreign direct investment (FDI) by multinational companies is a channel for knowledge transfer and learning and creates opportunities for indirect exports through backward linkages and the supply of services and other inputs to VC players. In the case of Lesotho, for example, skills and capabilities that were generated by workers and managers in the production of apparel, motivated inward investment by international auto parts suppliers that source leather from Botswana to fabricate seat covers for automobiles used in the production of cars in South Africa and elsewhere (Banga et al., 2015).

Bhattacharya and Moazzem (2013) note that VCs in SSA differ from those observed in Asian low-income countries. While both regions participate in agricultural VCs, Asian economies tend to be more active in labour-intensive manufacturing activities such as apparel and textiles, while African countries have specialized much more in mining and natural resource-intensive chains. Another difference is that Asian countries have a much higher share of inputs in their total imports, whereas consumer products account for a higher share of total imports in African countries, reflecting the greater participation of Asian countries, including Asian LDCs, in manufacturing VCs.

Numerous recent reports – see for example AfDB et al. (2014), UNECA (2013), UNCTAD (2013) and ACET (2014) – have argued that there are significant opportunities for a step increase in SCT in Africa. There are compelling reasons to expect the pattern of intra-African trade and investment to change significantly in coming decades if a SCT-supporting policy environment is put in place. Many African countries have large pools of under-employed labour. Wages in much of Africa are competitive, making the region potentially attractive for investment in labour-intensive export production of the type that has tended to be a key feature of the development strategy undertaken by

Asian countries. As real wages in China and other Asian countries increase, African countries become more attractive for manufacturing-related investment. In parallel, as average incomes increase in African nations, the region as a whole will become a more important market, increasing incentives for intra-regional trade and investment. However, the speed and extent to which this will happen will depend importantly on actions to reduce high trade costs and to address specific obstacles to VC-related investment.

Morris and Fessehaie (2015) argue that a commodity- or resource-based industrialization strategy may offer the best opportunities for African economies, given the vigorous competition from Asia for labour-intensive and low-skill manufactured products. Economic upgrading and capturing a greater share of the value of a product can start with a focus on leveraging natural resource endowments, both non-renewable and renewable (minerals, agribusiness, tourism) and strengthening local supply capacity. Minerals, ores and other natural resource-based products offer potential for economies of scope (e.g. leveraging specialized infrastructure to increase the return on investments in the mining sector or for agricultural products).

Lead firms have incentives to source locally if they can, given high transport costs and the benefits that are associated with deepening local backward linkages and outsourcing activities that are not central to their business. These examples illustrate the point that VC participation need not involve many cross-border transactions and many countries. A key element of using VCs as part of the trade development strategy may centre on efficient import substitution: the end market for a product will be sold by a lead firm or retailer, there may be a high import content associated with production; and there may also be substantial scope for backward linkages and replacement of some of the parts and components that are imported or provided in-house by a lead firm with local supply. However, such a dynamic is conditional on inward investment by lead firms that operate international VCs.

Much has already been happening. Growth in horticulture exports has been particularly apparent in Africa over the last decade, as smallholder producers have become more integrated into horticulture VCs. Horticulture exports from African countries increased more than six-fold during the 2000s, with the African share in global exports doubling from 3 per cent to 6 per cent. Goger et al. (2014) summarize the findings of a series of country studies on three sectors – apparel, horticulture and tourism – that include three African LDCs: Lesotho, Madagascar and

Uganda. The research found large differences across sectors and countries regarding the impacts of participation in VCs in these countries. In the case of apparel African countries saw stagnation of export unit values and real wages for workers (Staritz and Mayer, 2014), while the opposite pattern is observed in the horticulture and tourism sectors. The case studies for horticulture reveal that some African LDCs – e.g. Uganda and Ethiopia – have realized very high growth in both export unit values and market shares.

Swinnen (2014) summarizes a series of empirical studies co-authored with Miet Maertens and others on the effects of SCT and investment in agribusiness activities in several African countries. This finds positive economic and social impacts of VC-driven production and trade in horticulture products (fresh fruit and vegetables). Farmers that are included in contract schemes and high-value export chains benefit significantly. In the Senegalese horticulture sector, VC-linked contract-farming led to important increases in rural households' income and significant declines in poverty. High-standards vegetable export production in Madagascar, entirely based on small-scale contract farming, including thousands of very poor farmers, was found to generate higher incomes. Moreover, because of technology spillovers on food production, income stability and the food security of participating households also improved with participation in VC export production. Other empirical study papers cited in Swinnen (2014) find that smallholders' certification to GlobalGAP results in improved quality, increased volumes, higher farm-gate prices and higher net incomes from fruit or vegetable production in Kenya and Madagascar.[5]

Local suppliers generally do not have access to the skills, know-how, technology, management, capital, inputs such as fertilizer, etc. that are required to become integrated in a VC. In many cases, assistance will be needed to overcome constraints on domestic firms with limited access to capital and technology. Such support is often provided by contractor companies and/or donors. Empirical studies of Madagascar, Senegal and other LDCs conclude that VC participation can be associated with technology transfers and that this in turn can generate significant productivity increases both for the product itself and for other production activities at the farm level, further improving the food security situation of rural households (Swinnen, 2014).

---

[5] e.g., improvements in health outcomes among farmers as a result of the use of less toxic pesticides and improved farmers' pesticide management as specified in GlobalGAP requirements.

Other research provides numerous examples of how VCs in this sector can kick-start the development of broader manufacturing (World Bank, 2013). Agri-business and related processing encourages locally based supply chain growth, with the farm sector producing the inputs that are needed in manufacturing activities such as food processing, textiles, apparel, leather and footwear. Clusters that are centred on agro-based industries can also generate agglomeration economies and other spillovers through the labour market that can support broader industrial activity. World Bank (2013) points to the maize-soy-poultry complex that supported the growth of poultry exports and processed poultry products from Thailand and the sugarcane cluster in Brazil, which supplies the ethanol industry.

To emulate such experiences in Africa, the obstacles that impede the creation and growth of the relevant supply chains and the growth of competitive domestic enterprises that are a part of the chain must be addressed. ACET (2014) discusses three specific agriculture-related areas that offer such opportunities in Africa: first, processing and adding value to traditional export crops; second, scaling-up exports of fruits and horticulture by upgrading supply chains and creating employment in processing plants and agribusiness services; and third, substituting agricultural imports by developing regional VCs. Examples include poultry meat and associated inputs such as soybean cake. In practice, imports of both the inputs and the downstream products from the rest of the world have grown significantly, but there is production capacity for both parts of this VC in different African countries, providing scope for greater intra-regional trade (regional value chain expansion). As noted, in practice, natural resource-based industrialization that leverages soft commodity VCs offers significant potential for trade-based development in many LDCs.

While VCs offer the prospect for small firms and smallholder farmers to participate in trade by connecting to an international production network, it is conditional on many factors. If local firms do not have the necessary capabilities, confront excessively high operating costs, or if there are missing factors of production or key inputs, the existence of potential VC-related opportunities will not increase investment and economic activity in a region or country. National VC-focused policies need to be embedded in a broader portfolio of policies aimed at upgrading skills, physical and regulatory infrastructure, and enhancing social cohesion (Taglioni and Winkler, 2014). The private sector can be a key partner by bolstering capabilities and skills of local suppliers. ACET

(2014) notes the example of the Samsung Group, which is addressing concerns regarding a shortage of technical and engineering skills in Africa through Samsung Electronics Engineering Academies in South Africa, Kenya and Nigeria. The aim of the initiative is to develop 10,000 electronics engineers across the continent. Another example is the Global Food Safety Partnership, which brings together companies and international development agencies in a platform that includes a multi-donor trust fund that supports training and capacity-building activities in developing countries.[6]

2   Drivers of SCT: Trade Costs and Services Productivity

There are numerous drivers of SCT (Cattaneo and Miroudot, 2013). Two critical determinants are the level of trade costs associated with getting goods and services from one country to another, and the quality and costs of intermediate services that are inputs into production and exchange— such as transport, logistics and other intermediation and distribution services. High trade costs and low productivity services are two factors that explain the limited participation of African firms in international SCT. Both are associated with a common policy implication: improving the quality of economic governance.

The time it takes to get goods from a producer to a buyer is an important determinant of trade costs (Hummels and Schaur, 2013). According to the World Bank's annual *Doing Business* report, on average it takes three times as many days, nearly twice as many documents and six times as many procedures to trade in many African countries than in high-income economies (Djankov et al., 2010). Every extra day it takes in Africa to get a consignment to its destination is equivalent to a 1.5 per cent additional tax (Freund and Rocha, 2011). Without action to reduce transport costs from remote areas, improve connectivity and facilitate the movement of goods, services and people across borders, specialization opportunities cannot be exploited fully, if at all, and the potential gains from trade will not be maximized. High trade costs are one reason many African countries have a very narrow export base, whether measured in terms of the number of products that account for most revenue earned, the number of export markets or the number of companies that export (Cadot et al. 2011; 2013). As noted previously, new products often account for just a very small share of total exports.

---

[6] See http://www.worldbank.org/en/topic/agriculture/brief/global-food-safety-partnership.

Harnessing SCT opportunities requires not just a supportive invest-ment environment but may also call for targeted action to lower trade-related operating costs, including transport, trade facilitation and logis-tics services. Slow and unpredictable land transport is a major factor keeping many SSA countries out of manufacturing value chains (Christ and Ferrantino, 2011). A country cannot significantly increase exports of new products without also importing; export competitiveness depends on the ability of firms to import intermediates that are produced by 'upstream' parts of a supply chain or that not available locally. Promoting greater participation in value chains requires reducing the 'thickness of borders' (World Bank, 2012): actions to facilitate the cross-border movement of goods, services and technical personnel and to improve the quality and variety of intermediate services.

Achieving a significant reduction in trade costs is a complex, multi-dimensional challenge, as much of the agenda revolves around adminis-trative practices and procedures. Trade costs result from a variety of factors that drive a wedge between domestic and world prices for a product. Some of these factors are difficult or impossible to change – e.g. geography. Thus, a landlocked country in Africa will always have higher trade costs than countries that have access to nearby ports or are located close to large and dynamic economic agglomerations. But a large share of observed trade costs reflect policies and factors that can be affected by policy. Examples are border clearance procedures, the quality of transport and communications infrastructure, product standards and the degree of competition that prevails on services markets. International trade costs are also increased as a result of differences in regulatory requirements and redundant provisions that repeat what other autho-rities have already done.

Econometric analyses of the effects of trade costs – and the potential or actual impacts of trade facilitation often use the World Bank's enterprise survey data and/or the *Doing Business* and *Logistics Performance* indica-tors databases (World Bank, 2014). These data sources reveal that African countries often have low ratings on measures of trade facilitation and on average have the worst performance on logistics and trading across borders. Much of the econometric research employs gravity regression models. A representative example is Djankov, Freund and Pham (2010), who use export time as measured by the World Bank's Doing Business project as an indicator of national trade facilitation performance. This measure includes document preparation, inland transit, passage through customs and other border agencies and port and terminal handling.

It therefore captures a number of important elements of trade facilitation in both the broad and narrow senses. They estimate a gravity model for ninety-eight countries in which the dependent variable is the value of bilateral trade and in addition to standard gravity model control variables, the Doing Business time-to-export measure is included as an explanatory factor. They find that this is a significant determinant of bilateral trade flows. Concretely, an extra day's delay is associated with a reduction in bilateral trade of at least 1 per cent.

Research of this type has consistently found that trade costs and trade facilitation are important as determinants of trade performance – more so than import tariffs.[7] Saslavsky and Shepherd (2014) focus on trade in machinery parts and components as a proxy for goods traded within VCs. Using the World Bank's Logistics Performance Index, they find that intra-VC trade is more sensitive to improvements in logistics performance than trade in other types of goods. Indeed, the link between logistics performance and trade in VC products is about 50 per cent stronger than for other goods. Feenstra and Ma (2014) and Zaki (2015) confirm this result, finding that trade clearance-related time costs are particularly negative for intermediate goods that are processed in value chains. Hoekman and Shepherd (2015a) find that the effect of trade facilitation both promotes exports and imports but favours the former. Hillberry and Zhang (2015) come to a similar conclusion. They use trade facilitation indicators compiled by the OECD (Moïsé and Sorescu, 2013) to estimate the potential effects of implementation of the WTO Agreement on Trade Facilitation (TFA) (WTO, 2013). They determine that this will have a significant positive effect on trade by reducing the time required to clear the border: the predicted time spent in customs is estimated to fall by an average of 1.6 days for imports and two days for exports. Using a conservative estimate of the value of time in trade, such comprehensive reforms translate into a mean tariff equivalent reduction of 0.9 percentage point for imports and 1.2 percentage points for exports.

Trade costs drive a wedge between export and import prices. As a result of this wedge, producers export less than they would in a world with lower trade costs, and consumers purchase less of each traded product, as well as a narrower range of products, than they otherwise would. Trade facilitation, which reduces the size of this wedge, tends to increase producer surplus in exporting countries and consumer surplus in importing

---

[7] See, for example, Hoekman and Nicita (2011) and Marti et al. (2014).

countries. Although more trade does not directly translate into improvements in economic welfare, reductions in trade costs do, insofar as such costs are 'wasteful' and do not generate rents. Trade facilitation to some extent involves the elimination of resource waste – e.g. duplicative procedural requirements and paperwork – in contrast to trade liberalization (e.g. lowering tariffs), which mainly reallocates resources and in the process generates efficiency gains.

In addition to boosting bilateral trade – particularly trade taking place within VCs – and increasing national income, trade facilitation can also contribute to the important development policy aim of export diversification. Moving along the extensive margin of trade is important for developing countries: selling goods in which a comparative advantage exists to additional countries, and entering into the production of new types of products. Both dimensions of diversification are part and parcel of VC participation and are likely to be facilitated through such participation. The reason is that VCs allow firms to specialize in narrow activities and tasks in which they are competitive. Trade facilitation helps in entering and exploiting such niches by lowering the fixed costs of participation in international trade. Such costs are particularly important barriers to internationalization for small companies, which are of course particularly prevalent in developing countries.

Using a sample of 118 developing countries, Dennis and Shepherd (2011) find that a 10 per cent reduction in the costs associated with the aspects of trade facilitation considered by Djankov, Freund and Pham (2010) is associated with a 3 per cent increase in the number of products exported. Beverelli, Neumueller and Teh (2014) find that the WTO TFA should have significant positive impacts on diversification along the extensive margin, with the largest impacts for African countries – in large part a reflection of the fact that Africa has the lowest performance in terms of trade facilitation indicators. They estimate that the TFA could support an increase of up to 16.7 per cent in the number of products exported by Sub-Saharan African countries and an increase of up to 14.1 per cent in the number of export destinations by product.

Although actions to lower trade costs should reduce the difference between domestic and world prices, this need not be the case. It may not occur if some agents have market power in segments of the production/value chain that prevents the passing-through of the cost reductions to consumers. Alternatively, the appropriation of trade cost reductions as rents by lead firms could prevent benefits from accruing to upstream firms.[8] The firms that drive and manage production networks will generally be much larger than their suppliers and are likely to have some market (price-setting) power *vis-à-vis* their suppliers and partners. If so, they might be able to take at least a portion of the gains from trade facilitation initiatives as rents, thus depriving consumers/suppliers of expected welfare/profit gains. Monopoly power of providers of inputs and/or monopsony power on the part of buyers (trading companies; retailers) can lower domestic farm/factory gate prices and/or may result in retail prices that are higher than they would be if the relevant markets were characterized by greater competition. The crucial question, then, is whether and how much market power firms have, and given any market power, what is done with it. The degree of market power depends importantly on the extent of competition *between* value chains within the same sector, which is in part a function of the degree to which suppliers are locked into dealing with a single lead firm, i.e. switching costs.[9]

While large retailers (supermarkets) can have buying power, the same is true for major multinational food companies that have strong brands. Insofar as retailers use their market power to bargain for better prices from suppliers that also have market power (the multinationals), the battle is over the distribution of rents. Market power at any stage of the value chain can be expected to affect the distribution of the rents that accrue to the agents that are involved in the chain. Thus, buyer power by retailers can be used to extract any rents from upstream producers, be they multinationals, wholesalers or farmers in developing countries.

In many African countries, suppliers are small firms or smallholder farmers who depend on a small number of buyers that have market power (oligopsony) and are thus able to extract some of the surplus that the export market generates. Porto et al. (2011) find that greater competition among processors in a sample of African countries and export crops would benefit farmers by increasing farm gate prices. Similarly, improvements in rural infrastructure – which is a type of trade facilitation – improves the incomes of agricultural smallholders, at the same time as reducing prices for consumers. Matters are complicated however by the fact that buyers often also provide ancillary services and working capital (e.g. seeds). Pervasive market failures such as lack of access to credit mean that in practice processors may provide inputs to

---

[8] See for example, Sexton et al. (2007) and Porto et al. (2011).
[9] Lock-in effects may arise be because of a lack of competition among lead firms or because suppliers incur significant sunk costs due to a need to invest in VC-specific facilities and processes.

farmers in return for agreement to buy their harvest at a negotiated price. Given weak capacity to enforce contracts through the legal system, the feasibility of such arrangements may depend on the buyers having some market power. Porto et al. (2011) conclude that if such constraints (market failures) are taken into account, the benefits of greater competition are reduced, but the reductions relative to a benchmark without market failures are generally small.

These considerations point to the importance of competition policy and contestable markets, and more generally a pro-competitive business environment. It is not enough to pursue trade facilitation as defined in the WTO TFA. The focus of policy needs to be broader and to span the various dimensions of policy that impact on SCT and VCs, including transport and logistics (Are these competitive? Is entry feasible?) and the structure of markets more generally (Do lead firms confront effective competition?). An effective competition policy is required to ensure that such questions can be answered. But trade policy, both as it pertains to goods and services trade, is very important as well, given that an open trade and investment regime ensures that foreign firms are not excluded *a priori* from trying to contest markets where there are rents that can be competed away.

Services Productivity, Trade Policy and Downstream Industry Performance

The role of services in the economy is today more important than in the past as a result of technological changes in information and communication and other industries. This is the case no matter the level of economic development of a country. Services are critical for the efficient operation of VCs. Recent data initiatives such as the OECD-WTO Trade in Value Added (TiVA) database have shown that services account for at least 40 per cent of global trade on a value-added basis. This high share reflects the fact that a large variety of services are inputs into traded products. Indeed, many firms in manufacturing increasingly engage in so-called servicification: a shift into or increasing the production and sale of services. This is often an element of a strategy to increase productivity and move 'up the value chain' in response to competition from imports and decisions to offshore tasks that can be done cheaply elsewhere.[10] Upgrading along a value chain often implies (requires) servicification in the sense that activities that generate a higher share of the total value of a product tend to be services,

---

[10] This has been the focus of much recent analysis. See, for example, Breinlich, Soderbery, and Wright (2014) and Lodefalk (2014).

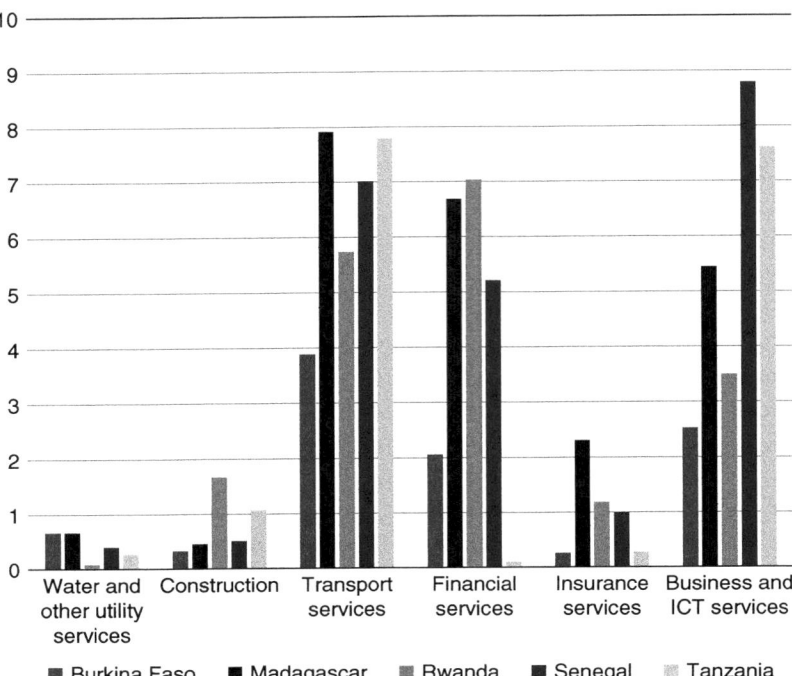

Figure 13.1   Services input intensity, selected African LDCs
Source: World Bank Export Value Added Database. Data are for 2011.

ranging from research and development and design to retail distribution and brand management.

When a service enters as an input into the production of a good that is produced nationally and then exported abroad, that service is exported indirectly, embodied in the good. Datasets such as the Export Value Added indicators of the World Bank[11] and the OECD TiVA database contain measures of services exports in value-added terms. This allows one to determine forward linkages – the value added generated by a sector, such as business services – as an intermediate input into the exports of all industries. This is a measure of services' 'input intensity' or dependence on services and an indicator of the extent to which services are indirectly exported.

Figure 13.1 plots the value of the indicator for selected LDCs in Africa.[12] Among the services sectors in the sample, financial services –

[11]   http://data.worldbank.org/data-catalog/export-value-added
[12]   The selection of countries in what follows is purely illustrative.

used as an intermediate input – account for the highest share (around 7 per cent) of total exports of value added in Rwanda and for similar shares in Madagascar and Senegal. The financial services input intensity as a share of total exported value added suggests an important role for finance as an intermediate input into export-oriented production. In Tanzania, business and ICT services appear to play a more important role, as they do in Senegal (almost 9 per cent). Transport services have the highest input intensity in Burkina Faso, Madagascar and Tanzania. As these value-added measures are also an indicator of cost, a policy implication is that in the short run, cost or efficiency improvements may be most easily obtained by focusing on services sectors that are used most intensively as inputs into export production.

Against this background, it is informative to consider scores on the World Bank's Services Trade Restrictiveness Index (STRI). The more restrictive a country is towards trade and investment in services, the more likely it is that domestic services will be less efficient than those available in the rest of the world. The STRI is a numerical summary of applied services policies believed to affect trade flows. It covers five sectors and, as appropriate, Modes 1, 3 and 4. Figure 13.2 presents overall results, in the sense of a summary number that covers all sectors and modes. A higher score indicates a more restrictive policy environment, with 100 being the highest. The SSA average STRI is 32, with policy settings varying considerably by sector as well as by mode of supply (not plotted).

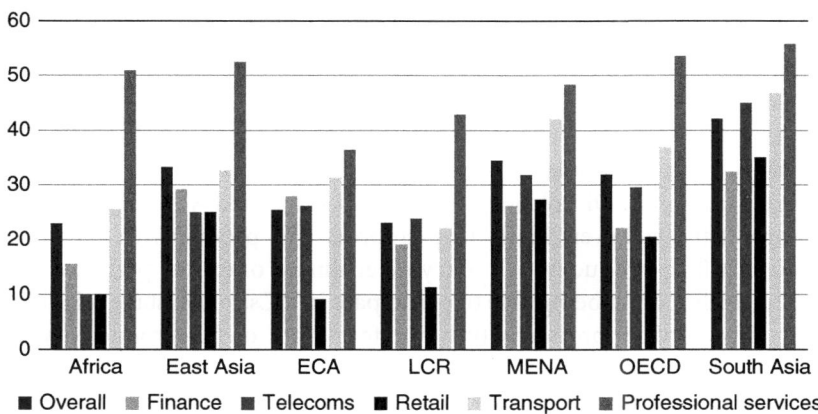

Figure 13.2   Services Trade Restrictiveness Index, 2009
Source: World Bank Services Trade Restrictiveness Database.

The general picture that emerges from the World Bank STRI database is that African countries are quite liberal when it comes to Mode 1 (cross-border supply of services), but have higher levels of trade restrictiveness in place for Mode 3 (sales through establishment by foreign affiliates, i.e. FDI). However, policy measures vary considerably by sector and country. For instance, the EAC countries typically have few restrictions on foreign investment in the retail sector, except in Uganda and to a lesser extent Tanzania. Professional services, by contrast, are more restrictive in Mode 3, as is the case in many countries around the world. Professional services are also quite restricted in relation to Mode 4 (temporary movement of natural persons supplying services), which means that policy should focus on facilitating such movement. Interestingly, the transportation sector is more restrictive in Mode 1 than in Mode 3 in all countries, and in some cases – such as Rwanda and Uganda – is relatively closed. Regulatory measures affecting transportation, such as axle load requirements for trucking, as well as cabotage restrictions, mean that there is considerable scope to reduce both the level of trade restrictions and the costs for firms that are associated with differences in regulatory regimes for this important sector – a critical determinant of the incentives to engage in SCT.

Borchert et al. (2015) note that many landlocked countries restrict trade in services that are particularly important for SCT. They show that on average air transport policies are significantly more restrictive in landlocked Sub-Saharan African countries, reducing their connectivity with the rest of the world. The result is more concentrated market structures and less access to transport services. Even moderate liberalization of air transportation services could lead to a 20 per cent increase in the number of flights.

The competitiveness of firms in the agriculture and manufacturing sectors and their ability to use VCs is in part a function of the cost and quality of services inputs they have access to. Sector-level measures of services trade and FDI policies are positively associated with manufacturing productivity: lower STRIs help improve the productivity of firms. Given that firm productivity is a key determinant of export performance and the likelihood of being able to participate in VCs, a two-stage relationship exists: services productivity is a determinant of the productivity of downstream sectors (agriculture and manufacturing), and the productivity of the latter sectors in turn determines a country's export performance.

Hoekman and Shepherd (2015b) examine both linkages using a mix of firm-level data and information on services trade and investment policies.

They show that both services- and goods-related trade policies have an impact on average productivity by affecting competition in markets. They find that local services productivity is an important determinant of manufacturing productivity at the firm level, with services productivity mattering more for those firms that use services relatively intensively in their overall input mix, and that this in turn impacts on merchandise trade performance. The strength of the productivity linkages varies substantially across African countries in their sample, reflecting differing intensities of use of services inputs in the production process.

In addition, when using a gravity model with importer-specific services trade policy information (the STRIs) and controlling for tariff protection for goods, they find that services trade policies are a significant determinant of bilateral merchandise trade. Services like retail distribution and transport are particularly important – a result that is intuitive, given that these services directly affect the ability of goods producers to get their products to market. In the case of East African countries, they conclude that if service sector trade policies were to be liberalized to the level prevailing in the leading Sub-Saharan African country (Ghana), merchandise exports of Kenya would increase by 18.6 per cent, those of Rwanda by 13.0 per cent, those of Tanzania by 19.8 per cent, and those of Uganda by 23.1 per cent. These estimated effects illustrate the potential economic gains from reform to services trade policies for increasing merchandise exports.

The effects of improved services performance that are found by Hoekman and Shepherd (2015b) differ substantially depending on whether trade data or firm-level survey data are used. The former are much larger than the latter. One reason for this may be that the former do not consider the impact of other country-level variables such as institutional development and control of corruption. In closely related research, Beverelli, Fiorini and Hoekman (2015) find that the positive economic effects of more open services trade regimes on downstream sectors are strongly conditional on the quality of economic governance and related institutions. The implication is that countries with better institutional business environments will benefit more from a more open services trade regime. Beverelli et al. argue that their finding may be due to the characteristics of services and services trade. The non-storability of many services will often require that a foreign firm invest or otherwise establish a physical presence in an importing market in order to provide a service. This in turn subjects the firm to local regulation and the prevailing business environment.

Of course, more than an open trade regime is needed to develop competitive services sector offerings domestically. Services are relatively intensive in human capital, so it is important to ensure the provision of high-quality educational services at primary, secondary, and as it becomes appropriate, tertiary levels. More generally, the development of supply side capacity in the services sector requires attention to a range of policy areas, including the investment climate and business environment. There is also an important private sector development agenda in relation to services: in some sectors, the state has historically been an important supplier, but economic reforms have meant that it has receded from that role to a notable extent. It is therefore important to develop a basis of skills and factor availability that can support the emergence of private sector service suppliers in key areas such as telecommunications, finance and transport. In the design of policy reforms and identification of priority areas from a SCT perspective, it is important to go beyond this general finding and 'unpack' how different dimensions of the business environment and economic governance institutions impact different services sectors.

3   Regional Cooperation and Integration

Regional integration of markets allows economies of scale to be realized by creating larger markets and increasing competition in markets. Regional integration can support diversification, and in the process help to achieve other objectives such as enhancing food security: for instance, allowing food to be shipped from surplus to deficit areas can reduce the negative impacts of weather-related shocks. Reducing regional trade barriers such as tariffs, rules of origin and non-tariff measures, minimizing checkpoints on inland freight corridors, reducing bureaucratic delays and transaction costs at border crossings and mutually recognizing and accepting international product standards are important parts of the policy agenda to create regional markets with sufficient scale to attract investors.

Regional integration of markets is also vital for SCT expansion – if there are high barriers to intra-regional movement of goods and service providers, it will not be cost-effective to engage in SCT and invest in VC-based production facilities. While many African countries tend to export primarily natural resource-based products to the world, the composition of intra-regional trade comprises foodstuffs, manufactured products and services. Commodity exports to the world tend to be large-scale and tend to utilize well-established infrastructure and trade relationships. Intra-regional trade in food and manufactured goods involves smaller companies and smaller-scale shipments and is much more sensitive to border delays, logistics disruptions, corruption, etc. (World Bank, 2016). This is one reason why intra-regional trade in Africa is mostly in final goods. It is too risky (i.e. too costly) to source inputs or components in one country, process them in another and sell the product in a third.

Trade facilitation has a major regional dimension. Non-tariff barriers of various kinds are substantially more restrictive for intra-regional trade flows than for goods that are exported to the rest of the world (Keane et al., 2010, World Bank, 2012). Regional integration is a politically complex process, and progress has been slow and piecemeal in Africa. In a recent paper, Afesorgbor (2015) concludes that much of the extant empirical (gravity) literature has overestimated the impact of African regional trade agreements. Using appropriate statistical techniques to control for weaknesses of the approaches that have been used to assess the effects of PTAs, Afesorgbor finds that GATT/WTO membership has had a stronger positive impact on trade than many African regional trade arrangements have had (e.g. COMESA or ECCAS). Only in the case of West Africa have regional integration agreements had a substantially greater impact in stimulating intra-regional trade than the GATT/WTO.[13]

Clearly, much more needs to be done to reduce trade costs between African countries, especially with 'hub' nations that are large enough to generate agglomeration spillovers and that have the scale and capacity to manage VC-based regional production networks. To date, this role has only been played by South Africa. The countries in Southern Africa account for 40 per cent of Africa's total participation in international value chains. South Africa provides more than 10 per cent of intermediate goods in Botswana, Namibia, Swaziland, Zambia and Zimbabwe. Overall, the South African use of intermediates from other economies in the region increased nine-fold between 1995 and 2011 (from US$ 78 million to US$ 686 million), while South African intermediates embedded in the exports of regional partners grew by a factor of five (from US$ 675 million to US$ 3.5 billion) (AfDB et al., 2014).

Regional integration goes far beyond trade and transport facilitation and reducing barriers to regional trade and movement of service suppliers. There is an important infrastructure dimension (roads, rail, ports,

---

[13] For data reasons Afesorgbor (2015) does not consider the EAC.

energy and ICT networks). Joint infrastructure investments are a key element in making regional transport corridors work. In practice, a mix of policy actions, capacity building and infrastructure development will be needed. World Bank (2013), for example, notes that constraints to the development of agribusiness in Africa can be classified into four types of factors: erratic policies in agricultural output and input markets and trade; limited access to land and respect for community land rights; poor infrastructure and high transportation costs; and difficulties for smallholders and small firms to access technologies, information, skills, and finance. In practice, a key challenge and priority will revolve around reducing non-tariff barriers to trade, which will require mechanisms for government agencies from the countries concerned to cooperate and also for agencies within a government to coordinate and work together.

From a SCT perspective, what matters most immediately is to enhance regional connectivity through trade facilitation and cooperation between customs and tax agencies so they can establish joint border posts and single windows, cooperation between countries so they can create efficient road corridors within a country, effective transit regimes that allow trucks and cargoes to move across borders and along transport routes and cooperation in the setting and enforcement of health and safety standards for products and certification/licensing of service providers such as truckers (Arvis et al., 2010). Much effort has been devoted to this agenda already. Progress is being made, but there is still very much to be done to bring down trade and transport costs for shippers to levels that are closer to those prevailing in other regions (e.g. World Bank, 2012, Freund and Rocha, 2011, Arvis et al. 2015).

4 Conclusions

The foregoing discussion and selective review of the literature illustrates that Africa is already highly integrated in global value chains, but mainly as a supplier of products that are processed outside of Africa. There has been significant dynamism in African non-fuel exports, including greater participation in horticultural value chains, but here also this has involved goods that are largely end products – e.g. flowers and fresh vegetables. Africa accounts for only 2 per cent of global trade in intermediate manufactured goods, suggesting there is great scope to substantially increase the use of and participation in SCT. A necessary condition for this is to reduce trade costs. A significant reduction in trade costs will boost incentives for firms to operate regional value chains and expand intra-regional trade. To a large extent, the associated policy agenda is one that is already being pursued by African countries, revolving around more effective trade facilitation, improving logistics and transport services and addressing non-tariff barriers to trade.

Many African countries have large agricultural sectors and export primarily agricultural products, especially if energy-related exports are disregarded. There is much more that could be done to increase the value-added embedded in exports through intra-African VCs. The share of manufactured goods in total exports is low, but has been growing slowly in recent years. A number of African countries have promoted more inward FDI in manufacturing activities. Services trade also has the potential to increase very substantially. Necessary conditions for a step increase in intra-regional gross trade flows and an increase in the share of value added in overall exports would be to make more rapid progress in achieving long-standing regional integration objectives and to focus attention on improving the productivity of – and access to – transportation, storage, logistics and related intermediary services.

References

ACET (African Center for Economic Transformation) (2014), *African Transformation Report 2014: Growth with Depth*, Accra: ACET.

Afesorgbor, S. (2015), 'Revisiting the Effectiveness of African Economic Integration: A Meta-analytic Review and Comparative Estimation Methods', at: https://www.researchgate.net/publication/279868086_Revisiting_the_Effectiveness_of_African_Economic_Integration_A_Meta-analytic_Review_and_Comparative_Estimation_Methods.

African Development Bank (2013), *At the Center of Africa's Transformation: Strategy for 2013–2022*, Tunis: AfDB.

Arvis, J. F., Y. Duval, B. Shepherd, and C. Utoktham (2015), 'Trade Costs in the Developing World: 1995–2010', *World Trade Review*, doi: http://dx.doi.org/10.1017/S147474561500052X.

Arvis, J., G. Raballand and J. Marteau (2010), *The Cost of Being Landlocked: Logistics Costs and Supply Chain Reliability*, Washington, DC: World Bank.

Bamber, P., K. Fernandez-Stark, G. Gereffi and A. Guinn (2013), 'Connecting Local Producers in Developing Countries to Regional and Global Value Chains', Paris: OECD, Trade Policy Paper 160.

Banga, R., D. Kumar and P. Cobbina (2015), 'Trade-led Regional Value Chains in Sub-Saharan Africa: Case Study on the Leather Sector', Commonwealth Trade Policy Discussion Papers 2015/02.

Beverelli, C., S. Neumueller and R. Teh (2014), 'A New Look at the Extensive Trade Margin Effects of Trade Facilitation', Geneva: WTO, Staff Working Paper ERSD-2014-16.

Beverelli, C., M. Fiorini, and B. Hoekman (2015), 'Services Trade Restrictiveness and Manufacturing Productivity: The Role of Institutions', EUI RSCAS Working Paper 2015/63.

Bhattacharya, D. and K. Moazzem (2013), 'LDCs in the Global Value Chain', Dhaka: Center for Policy Dialogue, CPD Working Paper 104.

Borchert, I., B. Gootiiz, A. Grover and A. Mattoo (2015), 'Services Trade Protection and Economic Isolation', *The World Economy*, doi: 10.1111/twec.12327.

Breinlich, H., A. Soderbery and G. Wright (2014), 'From Selling Goods to Selling Services: Firm Responses to Trade Liberalization', CEPR Discussion Paper 10116.

Cadot, O., C. Carrère and V. Strauss-Kahn (2011), 'Export Diversification: What's Behind the Hump?', *Review of Economic and Statistics*, 93(2): 590–605.

Cadot, O., L. Iacovone, M. Pierola and F. Rauch (2013), 'Success and Failure of African Exporters', *Journal of Development Economics*, 101(C): 284–96.

Christ, N. and M. Ferrantino (2011), 'Land Transport for Exports: The Effects of Cost, Time, and Uncertainty in Sub-Saharan Africa', *World Development*, 39(10): 1749–59.

Dennis, A. and B. Shepherd (2011), 'Trade Facilitation and Export Diversification', *The World Economy*, 34(1): 101–122.

Djankov, S., C. Freund and C. Pham (2010), 'Trading on Time', *The Review of Economics and Statistics*, 92(1): 166–73.

Feenstra, R. and H. Ma (2014), 'Trade Facilitation and the Extensive Margin of Exports', *Japanese Economic Review*, 65, 158–77.

Finger, M (2016), 'Rising Africa in World Trade', this volume.

Francois, J. and B. Hoekman (2010), 'Services Trade and Policy', *Journal of Economic Literature*, 48(3): 642–92.

Freund, C. and N. Rocha (2011), 'What Constrains Africa's exports?' *World Bank Economic Review*, 25(3): 361–86.

Goger, A., A. Hull, S. Barrientos, G. Gereffi and S. Godfrey (2014), 'Capturing the Gains in Africa: Making the Most of Global Value Chain Participation', Duke University, at: http://www.cggc.duke.edu/pdfs/Duke_CGGC_2014_Capturing_the_Gains_in_Africa.pdf

Hoekman, B. and A. Nicita (2011), 'Trade Policy, Trade Costs and Developing Country Trade', *World Development*, 39(12): 2069–79.

Hoekman, B. and B. Shepherd (2015a), 'Who Profits from Trade Facilitation Initiatives? Implications for African Countries', *Journal of African Trade*, 2: 51–70.

Hoekman, B. and B. Shepherd (2015b), 'Services Productivity, Trade Policy and Manufacturing Exports', *The World Economy*, doi: 10.1111/twec.12333.

Hummels, D. and G. Schaur (2013), 'Time as a Trade Barrier', *American Economic Review*, 103(7): 2935–59.

ITC (2013), *The Participation of LDCs in Value Chains: Current Trends and Future Prospects*, Geneva: International Trade Centre.

Karingi, S. (2016), 'Preferential Trade Agreements in Africa: Lessons from the Tripartite FTA and the Continental FTA', this volume.

Keane, J., M. Cali and J. Kennan (2010), 'Impediments to Intra-Regional Trade in Sub-Saharan Africa', at: http://www.odi.org/sites/odi.org.uk/files/odi-assets/publications-opinion-files/7482.pdf

Lodefalk, M. (2014), 'The Role of Services for Manufacturing Firm Exports', *Review of World Economics*, 150(1), 59–82.

Marti, L., R. Puertas, and L. Garcia (2014), 'Relevance of Trade Facilitation in Emerging Countries' Exports', *The Journal of International Trade & Economic Development*, 23L: 202–22.

Moïsé, E., and S. Sorescu (2013), 'Trade Facilitation Indicators: The Potential Impact of Trade Facilitation on Developing Countries' Trade', Paris: OECD, Trade Policy Paper 144.

Morris, M. and J. Fessehaie (2015), 'The Industrialization Challenge for Africa: Towards a Commodities Based Industrialization Path', *Journal of African Trade*, 1(1): 25–36.

Nicita, A., M. Shirotori and B. Klok (2013), 'Survival Analysis of Exports of LDCs', Geneva: UNCTAD, Policy Issues in International Trade and Commodities Study Series No. 54.

Pesce, O., S. Karingi and I. Gebretensaye (2015), 'Trade Growth Prospects: An African Perspective', in B. Hoekman (ed.), *The Global Trade Slowdown: A New Normal?*, London: CEPR.

Porto, G., N. Chauvin and M. Olarreaga (2011), *Supply Chains in Export Agriculture, Competition and Poverty in Sub-Saharan Africa*, London: World Bank and CEPR.

Saslavsky, D. and B. Shepherd (2014), 'Facilitating International Production Networks: The Role of Trade Logistics', *The Journal of International Trade & Economic Development*, 23(7): 979–99.

Sexton, R., I. Sheldon, S. McCorriston and H. Wang (2007), 'Agricultural Trade Liberalisation and Economic Development: The Role of Downstream Market Power', *Agricultural Economics* 36: 253–70.

Srinivasan, M, T. Stank, P. Dornier and K. Petersen (2014), *Global Supply Chains: Evaluating Regions on an EPIC Framework*, New York: McGraw-Hill.

Staritz, C. and F. Mayer (2014), 'Sector Case Study: Apparel', in Winkler, D. and T. Farole (eds.), *Making Foreign Direct Investment Work for Sub-Saharan Africa: Local Spillovers and Competitiveness in Global Value Chains*, Washington, DC: World Bank.

Swinnen, J. (2014), 'Global Agricultural Value Chains, Standards and Development', EUI Robert Schuman Centre for Advanced Studies Working Paper 2014/30.

Taglioni, D. and D. Winkler (2014). 'Making Global Value Chains Work for Development', in *Economic Premise* No. 143, Washington, DC: World Bank, at: https://openknowledge.worldbank.org/bitstream/handle/10986/18421/880530BRI0EP140d0VC0knowledge0notes.pdf?sequence=1

UNCTAD (2013), *Economic Development in Africa Report 2013 – Intra-African Trade: Unlocking Private Sector Dynamism*. Geneva: UNCTAD.

UNECA (2013), *Making the Most of Africa's Commodities: Industrializing for Growth, Jobs and Economic Transformation*. Addis Ababa: Economic Commission for Africa.

World Bank (2012), *De-fragmenting Africa: Deepening Regional Trade Integration in Goods and Services*, Washington, DC: World Bank.

World Bank (2013), *Growing Africa Unlocking the Potential of Agribusiness*. Washington, DC: World Bank.

World Bank (2014), *Connecting to Compete, 2014: Trade Logistics in the Global Economy*. Washington, DC: World Bank.

World Bank (2016), 'Factory Southern Africa? SACU in Global Value Chains', at: http://www-wds.worldbank.org/external/default/WDSContentServer/WDSP/IB/2016/01/21/090224b0840e51c5/1_0/Rendered/PDF/Factory0Southe0ins000summary0report.pdf.

World Trade Organization (2013), 'Agreement on Trade Facilitation', Geneva: WTO.

World Trade Organization (2015), *International Trade Statistics 2015*. Geneva: WTO.

Zaki, C. (2015), 'How Does Trade Facilitation Affect International Trade?', *European Journal of Development Research*, 27(1): 156–85.

14

Implementing Trade Facilitation Reform in Africa

MARCUS BARTLEY JOHNS, CHRISTINA BUSCH
AND GERARD MCLINDEN

Abstract

Trade facilitation is central to Africa's competitiveness in the global economy. Costs related to trade facilitation make up a significant proportion of overall trade-related costs, which in Africa are higher than in any other developing region. This acts as a barrier for the integration of African countries into global markets, as well as greater intra-African integration. Improving trade facilitation is essential for lowering costs for African agricultural producers as well as supporting the development of higher value-added activities in agribusiness, manufacturing, and services, including participation in regional and global value chains. Diagnostic tools used by the World Bank Group, such as the Logistics Performance Index, as well as country-specific diagnostics, highlight the key challenges faced. The evidence also shows that performance varies, with some countries making significant progress on reform programs to improve trade facilitation. With other developing regions having generally more advanced trade facilitation regimes, the lessons from these regions can be instructive in designing and implementing reforms in Africa, which the World Bank Group is actively supporting at the national and regional levels. A priority for the Bank Group is implementing trade facilitation programs that do more to reduce trade-related costs facing the extreme poor, given the concentration of extreme poverty in Africa.

As developing countries in Africa have come to realize the critical importance of international trade in achieving sustainable and inclusive economic growth, they have progressively lowered their tariffs, upgraded

The authors are grateful for comments received from Paul Brenton, Ankur Huria and Karuna Ramakrishnan.

trade and transport infrastructure, established regimes to encourage foreign investment, and pursued opportunities for greater regional integration. Yet in many African countries these efforts have been undermined by weak trade facilitation regimes, characterized by the persistence of outdated and inefficient border clearance procedures, excessive red tape and uncompetitive market structures. This weak trade facilitation contributes to Africa maintaining some of the highest trade and logistics costs in the world. Research clearly demonstrates that high trade costs are amongst the most important obstacles developing countries face in exploiting trade as a driver of economic development. These costs disproportionally affect small firms, farmers and the poor, and reduce the competitiveness of the region's exports (Hoekman and Nicita, 2009). They also act as a barrier to the integration of African countries into the global economy.

While some of these trade and logistics costs are attributable to factors outside the direct control of national policy-makers, such as distance from key markets, many are responsive to sound government policy choices and reform activities. Improving trade facilitation regimes has therefore become an important component of the national development plans of many African countries. Lowering trade costs through trade facilitation reform also features prominently on the agenda of all eight sub-regional bodies making up Africa's Regional Economic Communities, and continues to be an important component of multilateral initiatives, including the WTO Trade Facilitation Agreement and Aid for Trade.

This chapter surveys some of the key evidence on trade facilitation reform in Africa, including its performance relative to other regions. It then provides some context, based on the World Bank Group's experience supporting various trade facilitation reform initiatives in Africa, including implementing key measures included in the Trade Facilitation Agreement, and identifies some of the priority considerations for future work on the trade facilitation agenda in Africa. Some observations are made on the role of trade facilitation in helping address four key trade-related challenges for African policy-makers: transforming participation in global value chains, supporting economic diversification, improving agricultural competitiveness and productivity, and deepening regional integration.

Trade Facilitation Performance in Africa

In recent years, many African countries have made substantial progress in improving their trade facilitation and logistics regimes. This progress is reflected in the fact that, during the period 2009–14, nine of the top ten reformers in the World Bank's 'Doing Business, Trading across Borders' indicators came from the African continent. Likewise, seventy countries in the region are credited with implementing at least one major trade facilitation reform during the period (Huria and Brenton, 2015).[1] Major reform initiatives include creating trade information websites, the automation of customs and trade processes, the establishment of one-stop border posts, the implementation of port community or single-window systems, the introduction of cargo tracking systems, improved transit regimes and an expansion in the use of risk-based selectivity systems.

This progress does, however, mask significant differences in performance amongst African sub-regions and individual countries. Specific reform initiatives have also not always been followed by more comprehensive efforts to improve trade facilitation including reform of the market structure governing transport and logistics services. As a result, Africa's overall trade facilitation and logistics performance on average remains poor, relative to other developing regions. Data available through the World Bank's Logistics Performance Index (LPI), suggests Sub-Saharan Africa lags behind all other regions of the world, both in terms of overall trade logistics and connectivity performance, as well as the important and reform-responsive area of customs and border management performance (see Figure 14.1).

This poor performance relative to other regions results in high transaction costs for traders, discourages productive investment and lowers national competitiveness, particularly in manufacturing and agricultural value chains, where opportunities for growth exist. As a 2011 World Bank report on light manufacturing in Africa identified,[2] poor trade facilitation and logistics performance has a significant impact on exporters, particularly for those exporters that rely heavily on imported inputs. This weak performance can add up to a 10 per cent production cost penalty to countries in East Africa across the very sectors of manufacturing where growth opportunities are greatest (Dinh et al., 2012). Figure 14.2 illustrates the trade costs in manufacturing in Africa, compared with other developing regions.

These data clearly highlight the pressing need for many African countries, particularly low-income countries that tend to perform poorly in

---

[1] Nine of the top ten reformers in the Doing Business Trading across Borders indicators between 2009 and 2014 were from Sub-Saharan Africa.
[2] World Bank (2011)

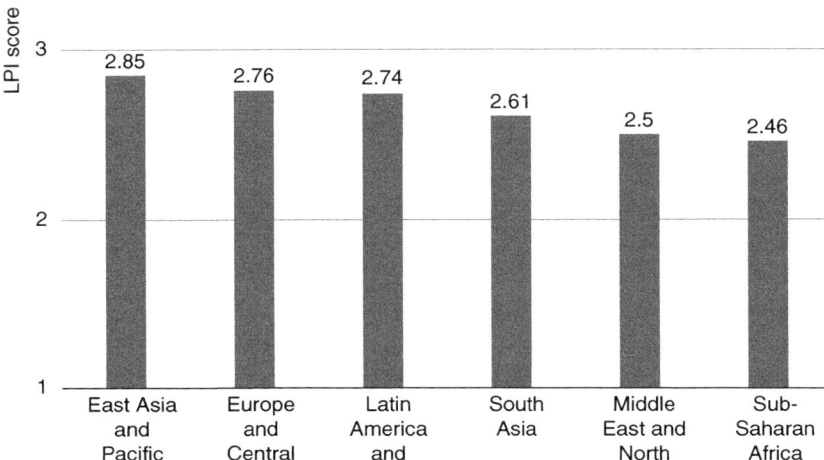

Figure 14.1   Logistics Performance Index 2014, overall score, regional comparisons
Source: Logistics Performance Index 2014, World Bank.

most aspects of trade facilitation, to accelerate and deepen their trade facilitation reform efforts, both individually and collectively. Moreover, while reform efforts are under way all over Africa, other regions of the world are not standing still and waiting for Africa to catch up. They, too, are continuing to reform and are pursuing sometimes very ambitious reform programs. As Figure 14.2 shows, trade costs have fallen in other regions in the last two decades, generally at a faster rate than in Africa. Essentially, countries and regions that are successful in improving their trade facilitation performance and lowering their trade transaction costs trade more and are better equipped to capitalize on their areas of comparative advantage, such as close proximity to raw materials or low labour costs.

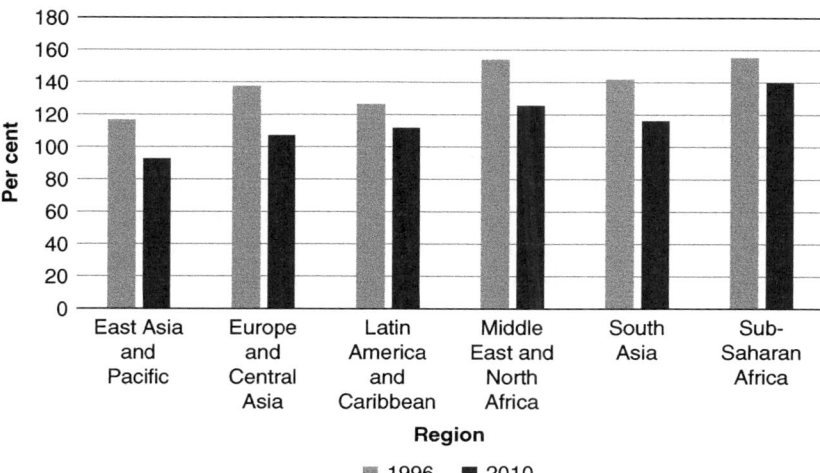

Figure 14.2 Trade costs in manufacturing by region, 1996 and 2010
Source: WB/UNESCAP Bilateral Trade Costs Database.

Implementing Trade Facilitation Reforms

How can African countries go about reducing the high trade costs that they face? Among the many factors involved, the need for investments in physical infrastructure has been identified as a priority. It is clear that significant infrastructure gaps exist in many African countries, particularly in gateway countries whose ports and road and rail networks also serve landlocked countries. These gaps will need to be addressed through long-term infrastructure development programmes requiring both significant resources and long lead times for their benefits to be fully realized.

Evidence suggests, however, that such infrastructure requirements need not deter countries and regions from also initiating major reforms in the software of trade. In many cases, procedural, regulatory and institutional reform can deliver a strong return on investment and need not be postponed while longer-term infrastructure needs are addressed. Ideally, investments in both software and hardware need to be considered and planned together. The case of one-stop border posts in Africa is illustrative of the need to carefully sequence reforms in order to ensure that re-engineered procedures and workflow requirements are developed in advance of infrastructure design and development, not following them, as has sometimes been the case.

Moreover, software improvements associated with simplifying and automating trade procedures that reduce dwell time in ports or waiting times at border stations can often reduce the need for much more costly long-term investments in trade and transport infrastructure. For example, research undertaken by the World Bank demonstrates that reducing dwell time in the port of Durban from one week to four days would more than double the capacity of the container terminal without any investments in infrastructure, and concludes that making investments in larger port storage areas can be a sub-optimal measure when efficiency gains can be obtained instead by speeding up clearance operations (Raballand et al., 2012). Evidence also suggests that reforms to improve transit systems and competition in logistics and transport services, particularly in countries along key transit corridors, can often do more to lower trade costs and increase competitiveness than investments in hard infrastructure (Arvis, 2011).

The message here is clear – in order to achieve significant reductions in trade-facilitation-related costs, countries in Africa need to go beyond an infrastructure-focused reform agenda to adopt a much broader and more comprehensive approach focused on both the hardware of trade (transport infrastructure including roads, railways, ports, border-crossing posts and cargo-handling facilities) and the software of trade (automation of procedures, re-engineering of systems, harmonizing of regulations, reduction of unnecessary red tape, institutional development of trade-related agencies, strengthened partnerships between the public and private sectors and increasing the competitiveness and professionalism of logistics service providers). Both are important, and both need to be considered in parallel as part of a coordinated and carefully planned strategy.

The conclusion that the software of trade is as important as hardware has not been lost on the many African trade negotiators who devoted a significant amount of their time to negotiating the final content and capacity-building provisions of the WTO's Trade Facilitation Agreement (TFA). The Agreement, which overhauls the now fifty-year-old trade facilitation provisions of the General Agreement on Tariffs and Trade (GATT), provides an internationally agreed set of measures to improve transparency, facilitate the movement, release and clearance of goods (including goods in transit) and promote effective cooperation between customs and other appropriate authorities on trade facilitation and compliance issues. It also contains provisions to support enhanced dialogue between the public and private sector, information exchange between countries, and the delivery of technical assistance and capacity building to developing and least-developed countries.

Estimates of the gains from full and effective implementation of the TFA vary greatly, but even the most conservative estimates suggest that its potential impact on world trade are likely to be very significant.[3] According to a recent study by the WTO, implementation of the TFA has the potential to increase global merchandise exports by up to US\$ 1 trillion per year. Likewise, based on full and effective implementation of all key TFA measures, the OECD estimates a reduction in trade costs of 14.1 per cent for low-income countries, 15.1 per cent for lower-middle-income countries and 12.9 per cent for upper-middle-income countries.[4]

More important than these global estimates, however, is the conclusion that the economic gains from implementation are likely to fall disproportionally to developing countries, as their traders typically face much higher trade transaction costs that impact negatively on their capacity to compete in regional and international markets.

Recent research undertaken by the World Economic Forum suggests that improving just two key components of trade facilitation – border administration and transport and communications infrastructure – would lead to an increase of some US\$ 2.6 trillion (4.7 per cent) in global GDP and US\$ 1.6 trillion (14.5 per cent) in global trade. Conversely, a complete worldwide elimination of tariffs would only add a further US\$ 400 billion (0.7 per cent) to global GDP. The research suggests that while gains would occur in all regions of the globe, the most significant gains would be in regions such as Sub-Saharan Africa that currently incur the highest trade transactions costs and therefore have the greatest scope for improvement.[5] It is for this reason that achieving practical trade facilitation reform based on simplifying and harmonizing trade procedures around transparent and sensible internationally standard rules has become an important development issue both for governments and the development community.

As noted above, there have been some significant success stories in improving trade facilitation performance, including in ways that contribute to effective implementation of the TFA. For example, Rwanda has focused on simplifying trade transactions and has automated key processes, together with improvements in risk management systems.

[3] Estimates of the impact of the TFA vary greatly and range from approximately US\$ 40 million to over US\$ 1 trillion. The WTO estimates that full and effective implementation of the TFA would result in a global welfare gain of US\$ 1 trillion.

[4] OECD (2014)   [5] See Arvis et al. (2014).

Likewise, Botswana, Lesotho, Malawi and Namibia have launched trade information portals that allow traders to find on one website all the rules, regulations and procedures associated with import and export activities across all government agencies. Another example is South Africa, where a comprehensive reform programme consisting of both infrastructure improvements and procedural reforms, including the implementation of a new automated system for customs, and changes to port storage charges, has led to a reduction in dwell time in the Port of Durban from seven days to four days (Huria and Brenton, 2015). Other gateway countries in Africa have also taken steps to improve trade logistics and port efficiency, including Côte D'Ivoire, Djibouti, Ghana, Kenya, the Republic of Liberia and Tanzania (Raballand et al., 2012).

Identifying priority reform initiatives and investments will depend on the key connectivity constraints and bottlenecks that impact most negatively on the performance of the entire supply chain in terms of cost, time, and above all, reliability and predictability. Like any chain, the trade supply chain is only as strong as its weakest link, so it is vitally important to correctly identify where weaknesses exist and prioritize reform efforts where they are likely to have the greatest impact. In some cases, achieving trade facilitation gains will also require leaders and policy-makers to challenge powerful local interests that may derive benefits from maintenance of the status quo.

During the past few years the World Bank Group, working together with a team of key development partners – including the WTO, the World Customs Organization (WCO), the Organisation for Economic Co-operation and Development (OECD), the UN Conference on Trade and Development (UNCTAD), the International Trade Centre (ITC) and a range of major bilateral donors[6] – has invested heavily in supporting developing country efforts to implement the provisions of the TFA, including in Africa. This work initially involved the conduct of in-country assessments to identify any gaps between current systems and procedures and the specific provisions of the TFA. The results of these assessments and subsequent validation and implementation support work are quite illustrative. While there are, of course, slight national and regional differences, the findings were surprisingly consistent and include:

---

[6] Including donors to two World Bank Group initiatives, the ongoing Trade Facilitation Support Program (Australia, Canada, European Commission, Norway, Switzerland, United Kingdom and United States) and the recently completed Trade Facilitation Facility (Canada, Netherlands, Sweden, United Kingdom).

- No country is starting from scratch, all economies have some form of trade facilitation reform and modernization plan in place, and progress has been made, although the scale and scope of programmes vary greatly.
- Implementation costs for most of the measures included in the TFA are relatively modest, with the exception of national single-window systems that are likely to incur quite heavy initial establishment costs and ongoing support and maintenance costs.
- Implementation support from the World Bank Group and others has been forthcoming and does not appear to be a binding constraint to implementation of trade facilitation reforms if countries have the necessary political and administrative will and commitment to proceed.
- High-level officials in trade agencies and private sector representatives generally support the measures contained in the TFA and believe they follow accepted good practice principles for trade facilitation.
- Coordination of activities between different government agencies involved in trade facilitation is often poor, and even when mechanisms for coordination have been established, they are difficult to maintain over the longer term.
- Dialogue and partnership between border management agencies and private sector stakeholders is often poor and characterized by high levels of distrust.
- Perhaps most importantly, customs administrations are generally far ahead of other trade-related agencies in both understanding the trade facilitation agenda and in implementing its key principles.

This last finding will not come as a surprise to many development professionals and members of the trading community. LPI respondents consistently rate their level of satisfaction with customs higher than their ratings for other border management agencies. While the latest data suggest the performance gap between customs and other border agencies is narrowing for quality and standards inspection agencies, this is not the case for health and sanitary and phytosanitary agencies.[7] In almost all African countries, as elsewhere in the world, customs have already implemented an information technology (IT)-based declaration processing system;[8] use some form of risk management to at least ensure not all cargo has to go through the same time-consuming physical inspection

---

[7] World Bank LPI 2014. p. 23   [8] Frequently UNCTAD's ASYCUDA system

procedures; have established a form of public/private dialogue; and have established cross-border consultative arrangements with neighbouring countries; and customs officials, while often focused on revenue collection as a primary objective, generally understand the need to balance control responsibilities with national trade facilitation objectives.

Customs agencies have also benefited from internationally agreed standards developed in the WCO, many of which have now been codified in the TFA. They have also benefited from a significant amount of technical assistance and capacity-building support provided over many years by the development community. Although the standard and consistency of implementation within customs administrations varies greatly, and customs reform is far from a finished agenda, it is clear that additional attention now needs to be paid by policy-makers and the development community to the reform and modernization of other border management agencies that, to date at least, have tended to lag behind customs in their level of automation, their use of modern, risk-based compliance management approaches, and their understanding of the need to balance control with facilitation.

In many African countries it is not uncommon for twenty to thirty different government agencies to play some role in the regulation of imports and exports, including agriculture, customs, health, immigration, police, quarantine and standards. Unless these agencies work effectively together to coordinate their activities and ensure that their requirements are managed in the most efficient and least time-consuming and trade-restrictive manner, their collective impact on trade costs can be very high. For example, it matters little for the trading community whether customs declarations can be submitted, risk-assessed and processed electronically, if traders still have to submit a raft of paper documents to other government agencies, which in turn need to be examined and approved and the relevant inspection fees paid, and then be taken by hand to customs before goods can be released and any duties due are paid (McLinden et al., 2011).

Add to this the sometimes-extensive permit and licensing requirements that need to be completed prior to goods arrival, and a picture of excessive administrative complexity and regulation soon emerges. UNCTAD has estimated that the average international trade transaction involves twenty to thirty different parties, forty separate documents, numerous permits, licenses and approvals, and over 200 data elements, thirty of which are repeated numerous times. The fact that each of the parties involved has different objectives, competencies and constituencies to which they answer complicates the situation further. The potential for efficiencies through re-engineering and automation of procedures and workflow is therefore enormous.

A key lesson from successful reform initiatives in Africa and other regions is that governments need to address trade facilitation challenges in a comprehensive and structured way. Likewise, government officials charged with important trade facilitation responsibilities need to think outside their own narrow organizational responsibilities and mandates to take full account of wider national development ambitions and objectives and better understand the cumulative impact of all the regulatory requirements they impose on the trading community. Non-tariff measures are legitimate vehicles for community protection, but the way they are designed and administered can easily turn them into non-tariff barriers.

Global Value Chains

A key consideration for many policy-makers in implementing trade facilitation reform is the potential benefits of African participation in global value chains (GVCs). In recent years, a growing share of international trade has been associated with GVCs. The revolution in information and communication technology, coupled with the development of ever more complex products, has allowed firms to establish production and distribution chains that are geographically dispersed across the globe. By locating various stages of production in countries where raw materials are available or costs are lower, firms decrease the marginal cost of production but increase other costs by increasing uncertainty associated with organizing activities across several locations. Changes in this trade-off between lower costs and increased complexity can be heavily influenced by national policy choices. As such, products moving across borders as part of GVCs essentially become as time- and reliability-sensitive as perishable agricultural products.

In spite of the emergence of GVCs as a dominant characteristic of modern trade, and the many economic development opportunities that participation in GVCs provides for developing countries, Africa's trade and economic policies are frequently still based on the old assumption that goods and services are produced in one country, rather than in many. Policy choices need to be informed by this new reality and should focus on facilitating the adoption of a trade facilitation and business investment environment that not only makes an economy an attractive investment location, but also promotes the creation of economic and social development flowing from GVC participation.

As in all areas of trade facilitation, it is critically important that government officials balance legitimate control and compliance measures with the need to facilitate trade. Experience suggests that conducting regulatory impact assessments before implementing new regulations can be particularly helpful in striking an appropriate balance between facilitation and control objectives. As in other areas of trade facilitation reform, it is also very helpful to engage with key stakeholders likely to be affected by new regulations to determine if legitimate objectives can be met in ways that are less costly, less time-consuming and less trade-restrictive.

Lead firms within GVCs care about efficiently connecting local factories with international production networks. As such, trade facilitation is a key factor in determining economies' levels of participation in GVC-related trade. In particular, the predictability, reliability, and time sensitivity of trade flows are important factors behind firms' decisions on where to locate and invest. In many cases, developing countries in Africa simply cannot participate in GVCs because of an inability to guarantee timely production and delivery. This is especially the case for small firms and small and medium-sized enterprises (SMEs) seeking to participate in GVCs, with small firms making up the majority of firms in many African countries.[9] These small firms have less capacity than large firms to manage the high transaction costs associated with overcoming poor trade facilitation regimes.

African countries do participate in GVCs but their participation tends to be as upstream exporters of raw materials, which are then transformed through value-added production processes in other countries. While African countries are participating in GVCs, in general this participation is not in the area of higher value-added tasks where countries in other developing regions have been able to enter GVCs. In contrast to East Asia, where GVCs have been a powerful driver of growth, Sub-Saharan Africa is yet to benefit significantly from the emergence of GVCs. Only 10 per cent of intermediate inputs imported by African countries come from within Africa, and in general there is little diversification in terms of the number of intermediate products exported, and the markets served. Analysis of the various policy factors affecting Africa's low integration into GVC trade identifies trade facilitation (measured by the border

---

[9] WB/OECD Inclusive GVCs 2015

management scores in the Logistics Performance Index) as one of the main determinants of this low GVC participation (Kowalski et al., 2015).

Diversifying the Economic Base

Along with the impact on global value chains, another priority consideration for policy-makers in the region is how trade facilitation can contribute to diversifying the economic base of African countries. Similarly, poor trade facilitation performance contributes to poor levels of export diversification in Africa. At the present time, fuels, ores and metals account for more than 60 per cent of Sub-Saharan Africa's export revenue.[10] The slowdown in commodity price growth and the apparent end of the global commodity super-cycle has already had a marked impact on African growth, which slowed from 4.6 per cent in 2014 to 3.4 per cent in 2015. This recent reduction in the rate of growth highlights the fact that dependence on a narrow range of commodity exports makes countries vulnerable to volatility in export revenues, and is associated with lower growth rates over the long run, contributing to countries being 'trapped' at lower income levels.

More effective trade facilitation regimes will be critical in lowering trade costs in ways that benefit producers in all sectors of the economy, not just those associated with extractive industries and other bulk commodity exporters. Because most trade facilitation reforms do not discriminate and contribute to lowering trade costs for all traders, not just the large and well-resourced ones, they can have a particularly strong impact on the export capacity of SMEs. Trade facilitation reforms lower the costs that such firms face in order to enter new markets, or access lower-cost imported inputs that they need to access in order to become more competitive. There is now strong empirical evidence that countries that are able to lower the costs of trade achieve greater export diversification (Dennis and Shepherd, 2011). Recent research indicates that if Sub-Saharan African countries were able to increase trade facilitation performance[11] to the regional median, they could experience a 12.8 per cent increase in the number of products exported by destination and a 29.9 per cent increase in the number of export destinations served by their products (Beverelli, Neumueller and Teh, 2015). Trade facilitation will therefore necessarily be an important element of any economic diversification programme pursued by African countries

---

[10] World Bank (2016)   [11] Measured by the OECD Trade Facilitation Indicators.

wishing to reduce their dependence on the export of a narrow range of commodities.

Strengthening Agricultural Competitiveness and Productivity

Trade facilitation reforms can also have an impact on agricultural productivity, competitiveness and food security. As population, climate and food demand patterns change in Africa, the importance of being able to import food at a low cost from either neighbouring countries or international markets grows. Trade facilitation reform is central to this agenda, as it can do much to lower the cost of intra-regional food trade and the cost of imported inputs that are necessary to boost agricultural productivity, such as access to seeds and fertilizers. Various trade barriers, including poor trade facilitation regimes and long border-crossing delays, have resulted in only 5 per cent of African food staple imports coming from other African countries, with the rest being imported from the rest of the world. With most regional trade in food staples being carried by road, and with most food staple crops having a low value-to-weight ratio, transportation costs (and border delays) have a disproportionate effect on this type of regional trade.[12]

In addition, trade facilitation reform can make a contribution to reducing the cost of imported technology like improved seeds and fertilizers that are not available domestically in African markets. As described above, poorly designed and administered regulations impose high costs on traders, and in some cases effectively eliminate the opportunity to import the technologies necessary to boost agricultural productivity. The impact of these regulations can be significant, with farmers in many African countries facing fertilizer costs that are up to ten times higher than in non-African developing country agricultural producers like India, Pakistan or Ukraine, and trade-related barriers an important driver of these high costs.[13] Reforms designed to improve the transparency of trade regulations and improve inter-agency coordination in line with the provisions of the WTO TFA are likely to pay large dividends in terms of increased food security.

Agricultural products are often perishable and therefore particularly time-sensitive in shipment. This means they are heavily affected by delays and costs associated with poorly conceived and badly implemented border management and regulatory compliance regimes. Agricultural products are typically subject to a wide range of sanitary and

[12] World Bank (2012)   [13] World Bank (2012)

phytosanitary requirements and associated technical standards imposed by various government agencies as well as frequent preshipment certification and testing requirements, often with little effective harmonization of standards across borders. While many of these regulatory requirements (non-tariff measures) are implemented for legitimate health, safety and environmental purposes, they are often left in place long after a threat has passed and are frequently administered in ways that have disproportionate and unintended trade impacts that were not fully considered by officials prior to their introduction.

Such problems are often compounded by the lack of adequate institutional and regulatory frameworks to manage food safety and agricultural health risks. This is an important area for agricultural exporting countries, where reform efforts should focus on balancing control and policing functions on imported products with quality assurance and proactive action on export products, including the promotion of good agricultural and manufacturing practices and hazard analysis and control processes. Attention should also be directed towards regional harmonization and mutual recognition of standards and towards supporting increased collaboration with neighbouring countries, by sharing capabilities and infrastructure and by specializing in certain functions, including standard setting, accreditation, certification and testing.

Trade Facilitation and Regional Integration

Over the past two decades, African leaders and policy-makers have devoted much time and political capital to the pursuit of regional economic integration. The motives for regional integration are well known and include securing better access to larger export markets and opportunities for economies of scale as well as a range of important security and political imperatives. Harmonization and regulatory coordination have been central elements of most regional integration initiatives and feature high on the stated objectives of all of Africa's Regional Economic Communities. With some exceptions, progress on streamlining and harmonizing cross-border trade procedures has, however, lagged behind ambitions, as reflected in Africa's poor trade facilitation and logistics performance relative to other developing regions of the world. To date at least, trade transaction costs remain excessively high and many firms with the potential to export remain at a competitive disadvantage relative to firms operating elsewhere in the world (Brenton and Isik, 2012).

To achieve the kind of reform necessary to change this situation, policy-makers will need to balance often-competing interests from multiple stakeholders within government (agriculture, customs, health, quarantine, standards and transport, among others) as well as private sector interests (customs brokers, freight forwarders, traders, transport companies and others). Implementing these reforms at the regional level increases their complexity (Brenton and Hoffman, 2015). However, lessons from other regions, as well as from specific corridors in Africa where progress has been good, demonstrate the high impact that can be achieved when these competing interests can be reconciled and reform can be implemented successfully. In East Asia, regional cooperation through the Association of Southeast Asian Nations (ASEAN) has been an effective driver of trade facilitation reform, with a steady reduction of trade costs contributing to the development of more integrated regional markets (Ahsan et al., 2013).

Corridor approaches, in which countries focus on improving the hard and soft infrastructure of trade facilitation along high-density routes, have been a growing priority. For example, the African Development Bank Group's Programme for Infrastructure Development in Africa (PIDA) has identified forty-two corridors that are critical for more effective regional integration, as well as links to global markets. Approaches that focus on improving performance along corridors can also facilitate more effective monitoring of results, for example through 'corridor observatories', providing a further impetus for reform (Hartmann, 2014). Experience from more successful corridor initiatives indicates that several factors are important in improving performance, including strong institutional frameworks for coordination among countries along corridors and among agencies; a focus on monitoring and improving operational logistics performance; public-private collaboration in infrastructure investments; and proven economic potential (Sequeira, Hartmann and Kunaka, 2014).

An effective approach to supporting regional integration also requires that policy-makers tackle trade facilitation constraints at borders that are not on major corridors or on key international gateways. Much trade in Africa occurs on a small scale, by individual traders carrying goods from markets on one side of a border to the other. Facilitating this trade is important for regional integration, but can also support food security (much of this small-scale trade is in food products), as well as generating a strong poverty reduction impact, including by boosting the income of women, who account for the majority of traders at many borders (World Bank Group and World Trade Organization, 2015).

Conclusion

In summary, the case for an enhanced focus on improving the trade facilitation and logistics environment in Africa is strong. While progress on reform is being made, it needs to be accelerated and deepened. Achieving significant reductions in trade transaction costs is likely to have a positive impact on the overarching goals of both inclusive economic development and poverty reduction. Immediate action needs to be taken to support:

- Enhanced economic diversification into sectors in which people are employed, and the creation of new, higher-paying jobs in agribusiness, manufacturing and services.
- Improving connectivity to global value chains through trade facilitation to provide new pathways for economic upgrading. Such efforts can lead to higher-paying and better jobs for those participating in GVCs, and can facilitate access to cutting-edge technology and knowledge, and progressively increase productivity.
- Improving food security is an essential element of addressing extreme poverty in Africa. Better-integrated regional agricultural markets present new export opportunities for African farmers, and also improve access to better inputs to boost agricultural productivity.
- Regional economic integration efforts to reduce the trade barriers that impact heavily on the many small firms that dominate the African economy and to assist small-scale traders who dominate cross-border trade in agricultural products so that they can more easily access new markets and meet product quality standards.

The poverty-reducing impact of trade facilitation reform can be maximized when it is combined with a comprehensive effort to identify the key trade-related costs that prevent people living in extreme poverty from connecting to trade opportunities.[14] For example, particular attention should be paid to undertaking trade facilitation reforms that have a positive impact for farmers in rural areas and small-scale traders, many of whom, in Africa, are women. Likewise, addressing major trade facilitation constraints at key international gateways can help reduce trade costs, not only for the country hosting the gateway, but for landlocked developing countries that depend heavily on cost-effective gateway access. The impact of these reforms would of course be enhanced if they were complemented by policies to address high domestic transport

---

[14] World Bank and World Trade Organization (2015)

costs brought about by anti-competitive transport regulations, weak domestic infrastructure connectivity and other domestic business and investment climate reforms.

While decisions to commit scarce resources and political capital to the pursuit of trade facilitation reforms must often be balanced against other competing development priorities, the return on investment in the area of trade facilitation is clearly very high. Moving ahead with the implementation of the WTO TFA and complementary upgrades to the soft and hard infrastructure of trade facilitation should be a central trade policy priority for African countries in the years ahead.

References

Ahsan, A., J.-C. Maur, A. Rillo, P. Sirivunnabood, L.Y. Ing (2013), *Association of Southeast Asian Nations (ASEAN) Integration monitoring report: a joint report by the ASEAN Secretariat and the World Bank*. Washington, DC: World Bank Group.

Arvis, J. (2011), "Transit Regimes" in McLinden, G., Fanta, E., Widdowson, D. and Doyle, T., *Border Management Modernization*, World Bank, Washington D.C.

Arvis, J. F., D. Saslavsky, L. Ojala, B. Shepherd, C. Busch and A. Raj (2014), *Connecting to Compete: Trade Logistics in the Global Economy*, Washington, DC: World Bank.

Beverelli, C., S. Neumueller and R. Teh (2015), "Export Diversification Effects of the WTO Trade Facilitation Agreement", *World Development*, vol. 76, pp. 293–310.

Brenton, P. and B. Hoffman, (2015), *Political Economy of Regional Integration in Sub-Saharan Africa*, Washington, DC: World Bank.

Brenton, P. and G. Isik, (eds). (2012), *De-fragmenting Africa*. Washington, DC: World Bank.

Dennis, A. and B. Shepherd (2011), "Trade Facilitation and Export Diversification", *The World Economy*, vol. 34, no. 1, pp. 101–122.

Dinh, H.T., V. Palmade, V. Chandra and F. Cossar (2012), *Light Manufacturing in Africa: Targeted Policies to Enhance Private Investment and Create Jobs*. Africa Development Forum. World Bank.

Hartmann, O. (2014), *Corridor transport observatory guidelines*, Sub-Saharan Africa Transport Policy Program (SSATP) working paper; no. 98. Washington, DC: World Bank Group.

Hoekman, B. and A. Nicita (2009), "Trade Policy, Trade Cost and Developing Country Trade". *Policy Research Working Paper*, 4797, Washington, DC: World Bank.

Kowalski, P., J. L. Gonzalez, A. Ragoussis, and C. Ugarte (2015), "Participation of Developing Countries in Global Value Chains: Implications for Trade and

Trade-Related Policies", *OECD Trade Policy Papers*, No. 179, OECD Publishing, Paris.

Raballand, G., S. Refas, M. Beuran and G. Isik (2012), *Why Does Cargo Spend Weeks in Sub-Saharan Ports*, Washington, DC: World Bank.

Sequeira, S., O. Hartmann and C. Kunaka, (2014), *Reviving Trade Routes: Evidence from the Maputo Corridor*. Sub-Saharan Africa Transport Policy Program (SSATP) discussion paper; no. 14. Washington, DC: World Bank Group.

OECD (2014), 'The WTO Trade Facilitation Agreement – Potential Impact on Trade Costs', OECD report, February 2014.

World Bank (2011), *Light Manufacturing in Africa – Targeted Policies to Enhance Private Investment and Create Jobs*. Washington, DC: World Bank.

World Bank (2012) *Africa Can Help Feed Africa: Removing Barriers to Regional Trade in Food Staples*, Washington, DC: World Bank.

World Bank (2015), *Africa's Pulse (October 2015)*. Washington, DC: World Bank.

World Bank (2016), *Global Economic Prospects 2016*. Washington, DC: World Bank.

World Bank Group and World Trade Organization (2015), *The Role of Trade in Ending Poverty*. Geneva: World Trade Organization.

PART III

Selected Development Experiences
and Perspectives

15

Trade Rules, Industrial Policy and Competitiveness: Implications for Africa's Development

CHIEDU OSAKWE

Abstract

Industrialization is one of the cardinal priorities for economies in dynamic transformation from a commodity base to a diversified value-added development stage. In major African economies, as in other economies worldwide, industrial policy is resurgent and back at the centre of economic policy. The sectors in focus revolve around manufacturing, textiles and clothing, footwear, automobiles, infrastructure, information technology products, petrochemicals, aluminium smelting, agro- and cut flower industries. African economies actively applying industrial policy include Algeria, Egypt, Ethiopia, Kenya, Madagascar, Mozambique, Nigeria, Rwanda and South Africa.

Although in the developed industrial economies, the re-attachment to trade activism and industrial policy are due in large measure to the rationale of spillover and network effects, in Africa the emphatic return of industrial policies is in part a response to the acute re-emergence of old challenges, such as the end of the current spin of the commodity super-cycle, a de-industrialization angst, and accumulating economic problems in a fragile and uncertain global economy. The current spur to industrialization is a reaction to the challenges emerging from the externally transmitted shocks from the 2008 Great Recession, the slowdown in Emerging Markets (EM), excessive turbulence and volatility in global markets, balance-of-payment pressures, domestic pressures for faster growth rates to respond to demographic transition of youthful populations, rising unemployment and associated social problems. The argument for resurgent industrial policy is predicated on the imperatives for domestic reforms to improve

A preliminary version of this chapter was presented at the Fourth China Round Table, Nairobi, Kenya, on 13–14 December 2015. The author is grateful for comments provided by Anna Varyanik, Dimitar Bratanov, Mustapha Sekkate, Maika Oshikawa and Vicky Chemutai.

competitiveness, reverse de-industrialization, diversify and modernize domestic economies to accelerate growth, avoid laggard status and seek convergence through integration to regional and global value chains.

The problem is three-fold. First, at its origin, industrial policy was controversial, dividing even like-minded economists because of the assumption that rapid growth and development occur behind protectionist walls. Second, African policy-makers are concerned with industrial reversal and that industrial policy is foreclosed by WTO trade rules. Third, the navigational challenges between rules-based constraints vis-à-vis sound policy fundamentals are compounded by a political economy factor that must be managed to secure policy buy-in and stability for governance. Three questions are addressed: Do WTO trade rules impede industrial policies?; What scope exists for the modern application of industrial policies and in what policy combinations to maximize their utility?; and Are there parameters for industrial policy and 'activist trade policy' for WTO consistency?

The WTO legal and policy framework and associated jurisprudence neither foreclose nor impede industrial development policies ex ante. Scope exists in multilateral trade rules for the use of industrial development policy for faster poverty-reducing growth, job creation, promotion of public goods, efficiency in resource allocation, sustainable development and intervention to reverse market failures and achieve positive externalities. There is scope for smart industrial policy in a rules-based market economy to the extent that industrial policy applications must learn from past experience and correctly interpret market and technology trends. Rational application should integrate state-of-the-art technology and apply sound market economy fundamentals. These are critical in designing twenty-first-century industrial policies, so as to avoid a repeat of the costly failures of the 1950s, 1960s import substitution and 'statist-type' policies that foundered on the grounds of discrimination, protectionism and the absence of performance criteria. Industrial policy and application must be modern, integrationist, in forward motion and lock-step with the infrastructure of the latest stage(s) of the industrial revolution and the digital economy.

1   Introduction

Let me begin by acknowledging upfront that this is an area where otherwise like-minded economists often disagree. Many economists raise the concern that any focus on manufacturing is distortionary industrial policy or misguided because they believe that manufacturing is in an inevitable and irreversible decline due to decades-long productivity and technology gains that will mean a continual loss of jobs. I want to take on those arguments because we believe that they miss important economic realities . . . and the very real benefits that manufacturing brings to our economy and that we ought to preserve. (Sperling, 2012)

1.1   Economic and Trade Policy Perspectives on Industrial Policy Development and Competitiveness

Sustained robust growth and development are fundamental priorities for governments. Most governments seek to achieve these objectives through trade expansion, attraction of investments, intellectual and other property rights, and establishing a solid industrial foundation. After generations of trial and error and experience with different growth models, policies that have been associated with prosperity are fundamentally open and market-based, geared to competition and structured for integration into wider markets through regional and global value chains. Governments that fail in delivering prosperity and welfare to their populations rapidly lose legitimacy and concede the right to govern. In this context, the question that arises is, what is the best mix of policies associated with rapid growth? Policies are never stand-alone and work in the logic of policy combinations. In whatever the policy mix, what scope exists for industrial policy interventions in a rules-based market economy?

Complex debates are involved. There are no formulae or standard recipes to apply, although there are useful lessons from economic history in the period from 1950 to 2015. There is an abundance of exhaustive diagnostic analyses that point to fundamentals from a range of development experiences. These experiences suggest what works and what does not. Yet interpreting past and current evidence for future application is neither straightforward nor always obvious. The lessons from economic history can be ambiguous and are open to varied interpretation. Regardless, there are fundamental lessons that emerge from post-war development experience to the present. These lessons clearly indicate that sustained and robust growth requires the primary foundation of sound and stable macroeconomic policies, accompanied by core GATT/WTO values of integration into the global market economy, pro-competitive domestic regulations, good governance and the rule of law. Consolidation and sustained progress will depend on the long-term building of human capital, a well-regulated financial system and a price structure where domestic prices reflect global market prices. Institutionally, a government economic management team and a separate non-governmental *competition agency* are essential in driving and sustaining an economy to rapid growth and ensuring its adaptation to uncertain changes in a fast-transforming global economy. No policy works perfectly and/or effectively in perpetuity. Domestic economic policy, legal, institutional and structural reforms must be constants in any growth model and approach to development. Experimentation, trial and error are integral to development.

In this context, this chapter focuses on industrial policy as a path for rapid growth. The various angles and questions pertaining to industrial policy are examined. As a starting point, some have argued that 'In one sense, industrial policies are unavoidable: all countries have industrial policies whether they know it or not' (Noman and Stiglitz, 2015). But how has industrial policy been defined? What is the state-of-analysis? What are the applications, and what does the record show? In what ways have results from past and current evidence been interpreted? What are the opportunities and weaknesses in industrial policy, as a development strategy for government?

Industrial policy has been defined in different ways, broadly and specifically. Narrower definitions include the notion of governments seeking to select champions regardless of market forces, channelling resources to shape specific industry sectoral allocations and hence system-wide economy directions so as to promote particular industries. On the latter lines, it has been specifically defined as 'attempts to achieve more rapid productivity growth by altering the industrial structure'. (World Bank, 1993). In the same vein, it has also been defined as 'non-neutral governmental intervention aimed at altering market signals in order to steer investment in desired directions' (Fortin, 2012). A typology with the prevailing approaches over the past 60 years has also been suggested (Low and Tijaja, 2014[1]).

Recent definitions are pitched broader from the analytic base that industrial policy goes beyond industry to encompass policies in other sectors, notably modern services like finance, information technology and sectors like agriculture. In this broad ambit, industrial policy is defined as policy that '... refers to any action that aims to alter the allocation of resources (or the choice of technology) from what the market, left to itself, would bring about' (Noman and Stiglitz, 2015).

Across many examples, a range of industrial policy objectives have emerged, notably promotion or protection of strategic domestic industries, employment creation, rapid productivity growth, reduction of inequality, national pride and prestige to promote or protect specific industries. Although the approach to promoting specific industries has

---

[1] Import-substituting industrialization; export-oriented industrialization; resource-based industrialization; export processing zones; and industrialization through innovation.

been broadly unsuccessful, the rationale is that finite resources compel prioritization, and so decisions regarding investments in infrastructure are made with a view to achieving development, strategic or other priorities.

1.2   Thinking on Industrial Policy: Revisiting the Literature

The literature on industrial policy is vast, expansive and resurgent (Wade, 2012; Luce, 2012;[2] Fackler, 2012; Rowden, 2015). In fact, several have argued that it never went out of fashion and that the real question was not whether it should be practiced, but how to practice it (Rodrik, 2010) and to focus on the 'principles' to which it must conform in design and execution in order to be 'useful' and 'succeed' (Dadush, 2016). In all, on industrial policy, several consider the challenge of implementation to be its Achilles heel. As argued, the determinant of success does not turn on the wisdom of selecting winners, 'but the capacity to let the losers go – . . .' (Rodrik, 2010).

Yet there is no denying that industrial policy has always had a controversial reception and review by economists, trade policy analysts and advisors to governments. Analysis and opinions have been divided on the pros and cons. Industrial policy has pitted its champions against classical economic orthodoxy. The theory and practice of the policy have swung between acceptance and rejection, respectability and anathema. At the core of the debate are posed some of the oldest questions in economics and trade policy regarding the role of government, on the one hand, and the relationship between governments and markets, on the other. What is the role of governments, not only at those moments when markets either fail or do not work as they were designed to, *vis-à-vis* their strategic trade and economic priorities?

Those in favour of industrial policy base their rationale on the logic of intervention by governments to provide (global and national) public goods such as reversing market failures by addressing negative externalities not priced by the market, provision of equal opportunity by law, environmental protection, accelerated growth rates for poverty reduction, economic transformation from low-skilled to high skilled jobs. Yet in all illustrated instances, the questions and arguments are complex. If, for example, as is argued and as supported by the evidence, markets

---

[2] 'Could industrial policy be creeping back into fashion? The correct answer is that it never went out of favour, even if the term itself became taboo'.

fail, it is also true that governments fail, and demonstrably with more catastrophic consequences. Hence, the question: is it better to reform and re-invent the market economy to curb its excesses or to reform governments and the institutions of governance, or both? An assumption is made that governments are pathologically lethargic to change and that even when they appear to change in partisan democratic transitions, they are inevitably recidivist in bad economic management.

The examination of the relationship between industrial policy and trade policy has been illuminated by 'New Thinking about Trade Policy' (Krugman, 1986). As argued, while it remains true that the underlying features of economies shape the patterns of international trade, a large and growing proportion of global trade consists of exchanges that are not so easily attributable to the underlying advantages of exporting countries. 'Instead, trade seems to reflect arbitrary or temporary advantages resulting from economies of scale or shifting leads in close technological races' (Krugman, 1986). The factors of large-scale production (static advantage), technology, innovation, knowledge, research and development and sheer experience have created conditions of massive trade in products in which an economy may have no underlying comparative advantage. The advocates of 'New Thinking about Trade Policy' argue that conventional economic analysis of trade policy is based on trade theory that excludes such motivations for international specialization. Technological innovation tends to generate important economic spillovers and its growing importance strengthens the need for a re-thinking of the analytical basis for trade policy (Krugman, 1986).

Conventional and traditional economic analysis is based on the 'working assumption' that markets are virtually 'perfectly competitive' (according to which there are many producers and whose 'size' makes it almost possible to influence prices or affect the future action of their competitors. This assumption has become unworkable because of the changing pattern of trade based on large-scale production, advantages of cumulative experience and transitory advantages resulting from innovation. In some industries, there is a different type of competition model in play, where it is not 'atomistic', as between small firms as in the so-called perfect competition setting, but where the firms involved face identifiable rivals and undertake 'strategic moves' to affect their rivals, as in 'imperfectly competitive markets'. The conduct of trade policy has been affected in several ways by the re-thinking of the analytical basis for trade policy (based on real change in the environment and intellectual progress in economics) and the changing character that takes account of a more complex set of factors (and departs from the simplicity of comparative advantage). The new patterns of trade, economies of scale, learning curves (experience) and dynamic innovation, lend themselves to a more activist trade policy that has the potential to yield larger 'rents' (higher profit rates or higher wages) and greater 'external economies' (high tech sectors that generate large technological spillovers to the rest of the economy). Krugman (1986) suggests that there are 'strategic' sectors in trade, a function of scale economies, advantages of experience and innovation, where capital or labour will earn significantly higher returns than they would if invested in other sectors. Although markets work well, they can be improved upon. As stated by Krugman (1986):

> . . .the idealized theoretical model on which the classical case for free trade is based will not serve us anymore. The world is more complex than that, and there is no question that the complexities do open, in principle, the possibility of successful activist trade or industrial policy.
> But this does not mean that anything goes.

Different from classical trade policy and without prejudice to the promotion or protection of sectors, some sectors are more valuable than other sectors in an economy. These are sectors with substantial 'rent' (exceptionally high returns to labour or capital) and with scope for 'external economies' (spillovers from a firms's R&D or experience). However, in seeking to identify strategic industries in selected sectors, there is the risk of backing the wrong industries, with the risk of wrongly predicting – guessing – effects in complex strategic settings. The effects of trade and economic policy on industrial behaviour are never straightforward and can be ambiguous and produce unintended effects. A degree of uncertainty will always apply to the effects of trade and economic policy on actual behaviour.

The debates attendant on the question of industrial policy and the analysis and review of relevant development experiences have also deepened our understanding on the question of the relationships between trade and industrial policies and the associated debates. Two classic World Bank Reports stand out and are of constant relevance: the 1991 World Development Report on 'The Challenge of Development' (World Bank, 1991) and the World Bank 1993 Policy Research Report on 'The East Asian Miracle: Economic Growth and Public Policy' (World Bank, 1993). The question of industrial policy, in these reports, is examined in the relationship between the roles of markets and the state. The perspectives are different, but complementary. They significantly enhance knowledge of the state/market relationship and shed light on the principal subject of scope for an activist trade policy.

World Bank (1991) describes the 'market-friendly view'. It reviews sixty-eight economies and is a synthesis of more than 40 years of development experience. It accepts that processes and drivers of economic development are not fully understood, but says that much can be learned from experience. It acknowledges that the huge amount of quantitative evidence reviewed is only suggestive and no more, and that there is 'no magic cure for economic backwardness'. It stresses that there are more ways than one to succeed. However, contemporary ideas stress price signals, trade and competition, which are the connectors to technological progress with effective government intervention only where it is most needed (World Bank, 1991). A quarter century after the publication of the 1991 Report, the experiences of these countries, several of which African, remain of continuing relevance to the questions of industrial and companion policies and the associated big-picture question of development at the centre of Africa's priorities. Even with the passage of time, the central questions remain: the role of the state, market forces, institutions, education, best practices, coping with the accelerated changes in technology and quality of governance.

Policies and institutions are critical. The key lesson drawn is that the successful promotion of economic growth and poverty reduction is at its highest when the market economy is complemented by governments. Strategies on the basis of which governments support rather than supplant competitive markets are best for development. 'Dramatic failures result when they conflict'. Markets and governments have to work together to generate the best possible results. The Report argues that the fabricated dichotomy of government intervention versus *laissez-faire* is false. The starting point is that:

> Competitive markets are the best way yet found for efficiently organizing the production and distribution of goods and services. . . . But markets cannot operate in a vacuum – they require a legal and regulatory framework that only governments can provide. . . . It is not a question of state or market: each has a large and irreplaceable role. (World Bank, 1991)

In the relationship between governments and markets, four areas are critical:

- education: building human capital
- the business environment: establishment of an entrepreneurial setting that is competition-driven, with efficient and adequate infrastructure and robust institutions, and a setting that propagates technological diffusion

- the global market: integration with the global economy (An integrated global economy has been deepened on the basis of trade, investment and factor flows, technological diffusion and information flow. In the four decades from 1950s to the 1990s, global trade expanded at approximately 6 per cent annually, more than 50 per cent faster than output growth.)[3]
- the macroeconomy: stable macroeconomic policies.

World Bank (1991) offers several observations on the 'paths to development'. It acknowledges the complexity and frequent shifts in development thinking across the 40-year period of its research. Progress has not been linear but largely experimental, with knowledge acquired through successes and failures. As stated, 'progress has not moved along a straight line from darkness to light. Instead there have been successes and failures, and a gradual accumulation of knowledge and insight. On some matters, a fairly clear understanding has emerged, but many questions still remain contentious and unanswered' (World Bank, 1991).

Theories posited to account for development which have not stood the test of time (and failed) are reviewed. These range from 'climate, culture and natural resources', to 'rapid industrialization', 'import substitution', to foster infant industries. These perspectives and the theories that underpin them failed. Governments should not attempt to micro-manage development. Trade barriers are costly. Competition should be promoted and not impeded. Interference with prices is counter-productive and costly, and undermines dynamic economic transformations.

While productivity growth is considered as the engine of development, the question asked is, 'What drives productivity?' The Report concludes that productivity is driven by technological progress, the latter influenced by history, culture, education, institutions, and policies for openness. There is a strong relationship between productivity, human capital investments and an (undistorted) market environment. The review of various country experiences in the Report suggests that improvements in economic performance follow reductions in market interventions. Yet there was the self-evident question revolving around the exceptional

---

[3] This long-term trend has changed in what is currently characterized as the 'Great Trade Slowdown', as manifested in studies that indicate sluggish trade performance in relation to world GDP. Compared to the historical trend where trade grew at rates 6 to 8 per cent faster than GDP growth, as recently as 2013 global GDP growth was 3.2 per cent, equalling 3.2 per cent trade growth (Constantinescu et al., 2015).

achievements of the East Asian economies: why did they succeed and not fail in spite of their strong state interventions in the market with infant industry protection and use of subsidies? The Report explains that the East Asian Governments in question disciplined their interventions to conform to international and domestic competition; they ensured that their interventions did not distort relative prices unduly. For instance, they neutralized export bias. Interventions were 'moderated'so that they refuted 'thoroughgoing *dirigisme*' with almost equal refutation of *laissez-faire.*

The conclusion is that the state and the market complement in specific ways. Interventions in the market are useful, if they are market friendly. Market-friendly interventions entail 'reluctant intervention' only if markets fail or if it is demonstrably better to intervene, such as in the provision of public goods. Apply checks and balances. Withdraw from a failing policy. Intervene transparently, as reflected in the preferred option of applying tariffs rather than quantitative restrictions, and subject interventions to *rules* rather than the *individual discretion* of a government official.

Weakening competition impedes the diffusion of technology and hence reduces productivity. Productivity is increased with the reinforcement of competition, the elimination of barriers to entry and exit of firms, appropriate legal codes for bankruptcy, protection of property rights and elimination of price controls. Incumbent firms should not be favoured over new industrial investments. National markets should not be sheltered from competition. High levels of domestic industry protection impede development.

Government intervention should be minimalist in those areas where markets work best. Conversely, governments should intervene where markets cannot be relied upon by themselves. Privatization of state-owned enterprises is recommended. Market-based competition should drive economic activities. Interventions on education, health, nutrition, family planning, poverty alleviation, regulations and legal infrastructure as well as resource mobilization for public expenditures ensure a stable macro-economy, in the absence of which progress is not possible (World Bank, 1991).

Political systems and economic policies interact. The factor of political economy considerations impacts and influences the state/market relationship in complex and uncertain ways. However, there are effects for buy-in, effectiveness of policy and, in instances, with effects for the stability of governments. The exact nature of the effects varies and is neither predictable nor pre-determined. They depend on the specifics of particular national economies. Economic policy choices are rarely made in a vacuum.[4]

Regardless, while sensitive to the factor of the political economy, there is no substitute for sound and rational economic policies that are effectively and consistently implemented. The 1991 Report, drawing from accumulated experience, correctly underscores the experience that:

> Many countries have suffered a vicious circle of harmful interventions that entrench special interests and lead to rent-seeking and the 'capture' of the state. Governments sometimes intervene in the market to address political instability and other political constraints. But the result is that all too often, the combination of pervasive distortions and predatory states leads to development disasters. ... Reform must look to institutions. The establishment of a well-functioning legal system and judiciary, and of secure property rights, is an essential complement to economic reforms. (World Bank, 1991)

One of the several questions addressed in the Report was entrenched orthodoxy founded on the bias against exports, according to which the role of trade in development was minimal and trade carried a risk of undermining development. Along these lines was the obsolete thesis that trade was unreliable as a source of growth. Hence, import-substitution was wrongly preferred as a basis to grow domestic industries, conserve the limited supply of hard currency (foreign capital) and encourage 'self-sufficiency' and development. As reasoned by the proponents[5] of this defunct approach, domestic enterprises could not be exposed to international markets because they would fail due to inability to compete. 'Protection' would guarantee domestic markets for growth until these domestic industries would be ready and strong enough for growth. In reality, what resulted were considerable damaging costs from infant industry protection due to misallocated resources.

In its review of how best to account for the exceptional performance of the East Asian economies, World Bank (1991) asks what should the roles

---

[4] The 1955 classic by Richard Hofstadter: *The Age of Reform*, heavily influenced this author's thinking on the theme of the interactivity between political systems and economic policies. The New Deal as economic policy was a consequence of the Great Depression, in contrast to Hofstadter's description of 'Populism' and 'Progressivism', which were functions of more prosperous eras.

[5] e.g. the economist Raúl Prebisch

of the state and market be.[6] Why did interventionist policies by the
state succeed in the East Asian economies, whereas they often failed
elsewhere? It reviews several explanations, but concludes on three propositions, namely that government intervention was subjected to international competition, market disciplines and checks and balances.
Failing instruments of protection were instantly set aside. Outward-
orientation was pursued. Intervention was 'more moderate' in the East
Asian economies than in other developing countries that experimented
with state intervention (World Bank, 1991).

The conclusion from the quantitative evidence surveyed is that
a strong market orientation, assisted by a focused and efficient public
sector, is an assured path to faster productivity growth, increased
incomes and sustained economic development. Yet there is
a political economy in any agenda for reform. Reformers are politically constrained. There are potential or actual political costs, including instability. These constraints and costs explain why it is easy or
difficult, as the case may be, for governments to change course when
policies are failing or are unworkable. In the final analysis, caution
should be exercised in intervention by governments. Government
interventions tend to create vested interests which become an impediment to flexibility for changes in policy that are failing and have to
be reversed. Once granted, protection is difficult to reverse. It creates
'rents' for labour, capital, etc. Protection also creates industrial interests which then pose huge obstacles to liberalization. It breeds corruption. There are ample remedies: for instance, open and democratic
governments, robust institutions, reform of the public sector, privatization of state-owned enterprises, involvement of civil society and
greater equity (World Bank, 1991).

A huge challenge in trade policy is the imitation of bad behaviour. Due
in part to the inertia of mercantilist behaviour, WTO members tend to
mimic economically harmful protectionist behaviour that leaves every-
one worse off, such as in the use of trade remedies that do not necessarily
countervail unfair trade practices, but instead check and curtail trade
liberalization. The evidence from trade negotiations suggests the capitu-
lation of several developing countries to the temptation of harmful trade
and economic policy behaviour.

---

[6] The East Asian economies in question comprise 'all the low- and middle-income economies of East and Southeast Asia and the Pacific, east of and including China' (World Bank,
1991).

In addressing areas of priority action for development, the 1991 Report conclusively argues that regardless of whether industrial countries play their part, and even if they fail, developing countries can advance rapidly on the basis of their own actions. In its advice to developing countries, it states that:

> It would be a tragic mistake for them to use the weaknesses of economic policy in the industrial countries as a reason to delay essential economic reforms. The right strategy for developing countries, whether external conditions are supportive or not, is to
> - Invest in people, including education, health and family planning
> - Help domestic markets to work well by fostering competition and investing in infrastructure
> - Liberalize trade and foreign investment
> - Avoid excessive fiscal deficits and high inflation.[7]

In sum, policy efforts to channel the allocation of resources via non-market mechanisms, in general, fail to improve economic performance.

The World Bank Policy Research Report 'The East Asian Miracle: Economic Growth and Public Policy' (1993) addresses the same broad question of the appropriate role of public policy in development and the relationship between government, the private sector and the market. Specifically, it examines in depth the factors underpinning the success of the East Asian Miracle of high and sustained economic growth between 1965 and 1990. How come the East Asian economies were more successful in the use of activist interventionist policy instruments in contrast to the failure by other developing countries in the use of the same instruments?

The Report notes that the eight economies[8] studied reflected a diversity of experiences in their usage of different policy combinations, from hands-off to highly interventionist instruments. It underscores the point that economic policy advice must always be country-specific; it cannot be pulled off the shelf. There are no formulae to apply.

The Report identifies the common threads that linked the High-Performing East Asian Economies (HPAEs). They conclude that rapid growth in each economy was essentially accounted for by the application

---

[7] World Bank (1991)

[8] Japan and the Four Tigers (Hong Kong, China; Republic of Korea; Singapore; and Chinese Taipei) and the three Newly Industrialized Economies of South East Asia (Indonesia, Malaysia and Thailand), together, were described as the HPAEs: High-Performing East Asian Economies.

of a set of common, market-friendly economic policies that led to higher accumulation and better resource allocation. These economies got the policy fundamentals right through: achieving macroeconomic stability and investing in education to build human capital. But, as World Bank (1993) notes, correctness and striking it right on the fundamentals did not tell the whole story. In all these eight economies, government systematically intervened in one form or another to:

- target and subsidize credit to selected industries
- maintain low deposit rates and maintain ceilings on borrowing rates to increase profits and retained earnings
- protect domestic import substitutes
- subsidize declining non-competitive industries
- establish and financially support government banks
- undertake public investments in applied research
- establish firm- and industry-specific export targets
- establish export market institutions
- share information freely between the public and private sectors
- promote specific industries over and above others.

The interesting policy-relevant puzzle that is addressed in this Research Report is, why did other economies that sought to apply and did apply, even more pervasively, the forms of intervention as were used by the East Asian economies, either fall short or fail to succeed? A distinction is made between growth-enhancing interventions, on the one hand, and growth-neutral and growth-harmful interventions, on the other.

The study suggests three prerequisites that were keys to the success of interventionist policies and instruments:

- Performance criteria were established for selective interventions for monitoring and assessing performance in a disciplined policy framework.
- Cost of intervention: if fiscal costs posed a risk to macroeconomic stability, governments retrenched those interventions.
- Price distortions were less extreme.

The core question that was addressed is the role of public policy to assist these HPAEs to rapidly accumulate human and physical capital and allocate resources to high-yielding investments. A range of explanatory factors are examined, although the focus is on two broad explanations represented by adherents to: (1) the 'neoclassical view'; and (2) the 'revisionist school'.

- 'Neoclassical View': This school argues that the HPAEs were more successful at establishing macroeconomic stability and a reliable legal framework for domestic and international competition. Orientation to international trade was positive and there was an export bias. Price controls were absent and other distortionary policies resulted in low relative price distortions. Premium was accorded to investment in education and building human capital as well as development of health systems.
- 'Revisionist View': The East Asian Economies did not wholly conform to the neoclassical model. The 'policy mix' was flexible and diverse. East Asian governments 'led the market'. As argued, markets do not consistently lead investments to industries that generate the highest systemic growth for the economy. In East Asia, governments altered the incentive structure to propel industries that, on their own, would not have prospered (Amsden, 1989). Revisionists have shown the scope of government intervention to promote industrial development in Japan, the Republic of Korea, Singapore and Chinese Taipei.

Yet the analyses showed that neither the neoclassical nor the revisionist school solely accounted for East Asia's growth 'miracle'. The 'miracle' (sustained high growth rates from 1960–90, rapid export growth, high investment rates of more than 20 per cent of GDP, etc.) reflects the use of a range of policy instruments. As the 1993 Report indicates, these included extensive government intervention in markets to channel and direct private-sector resource allocation (Japan, Republic of Korea and Chinese Taipei) and the relatively less interventionist path taken by Hong Kong (China), Malaysia, Indonesia and Thailand.

World Bank (1993) interprets and assesses the East Asian interventionist policies as responses to coordination problems within the operative framework of market economies. These interventionist policies emphasised 'cooperative behaviour' among private firms on the basis of performance criteria. The Report argues that economies in East Asia with interventionist policies not only acted on market-based competition but took it further by 'creating contests that combine competition with the benefits of cooperation among firms and between government and the private sector. Such contests range from very simple non-market allocation rules, such as access to rationed credit for exporters, to very complex coordination of private investment in the government-business deliberation councils[9] of Japan and Korea' (World Bank, 1993). What was critical in the success of these interventions was the discipline of competition, the operative context of the market economy and performance criteria monitored by the government and competing firms. In other words, success was defined by 'markets' and/or 'contests', firewalled from political interference.

World Bank (1993) assesses the promotion of sector-specific industrial policies on which most of the East Asian governments embarked.[10] Although there was government intervention and activism, it was circumscribed and targeted at investment in education, establishing a competitive, level playing field for private investors (both foreign and domestic), openness to international trade and sound and stable macro-economic policies. It is noted that all the HPAEs implemented import-substitution policies with the exception of Hong Kong, China. However, the application of these policies tended to expire much earlier than in other economies because of the need for foreign exchange in the East Asian economies. In the latter, the objective was not to 'preserve foreign exchange with stricter controls', but to 'earn additional foreign exchange'. Even in the context of industrial policy, exchange rates were liberal and there was frequent recourse to devaluation as a means to support growth. Market mechanisms were the vectors for dynamic resource allocation.

In this analysis, World Bank (1993) notes that the sector-specific promotion of industries in East Asia in the 1950s shows little evidence that such industrial policies affected either the industrial structure or the rate of change of productivity growth. The conclusion reached is that:

---

[9] 'Deliberation Councils' were also used in Singapore. In these councils, private sector groups work with the government to shape and implement policies of government that are relevant to their interests. This was seen as relatively superior to the murky politics of lobby by vested interests, seeking individual advantage over one another. They were designed to be transparent and facilitate information exchange. World Bank (1993) superbly demonstrates that manufactured export bias and growth was a strong mechanism for 'technological upgrading'. In this context of state-of-the-art technology, there are beneficial spillovers to enterprises and the wider economy, as a critical source of rapid productivity growth, addressing 'information-related externalities' not accounted for in market transactions.

[10] The use of import protection and subsidies for capital by Japan in the 1950s to promote heavy industry and similar industrial policies were imitated by Republic of Korea in the same period. More moderate industrial policy incentives were used to promote advanced industries by Malaysia, Singapore, Chinese Taipei and Hong Kong, China.

It is not altogether surprising that industrial policy in Japan, Korea, and Taiwan, China, produced mainly market-conforming results. While these governments selectively promoted capital- and knowledge-intensive industries, they also took steps to ensure that they were fostering profitable, internationally competitive firms. Moreover, their industrial policies incorporated a large amount of market information and used performance, usually export performance, as a yardstick. Efforts elsewhere to promote specific industries without better information exchange and the discipline of international markets have not succeeded (World Bank, 1993).

On the basis of this analysis and conclusion, several of the industrial policy programmes in other developing countries[11] were assessed as 'disappointing', whereas in the East Asian economies, the manner of implementation of these policies exposed their industrial sectors to international competition with the effect that domestic relative prices approximated international prices. In other words, there was a somewhat mutual co-existence of exports with domestic market protection, with sectoral policies designed for export performance, the opposite of other developing countries whose economic orientation was directed inwards. Exports were the economic performance criteria.

The purpose of industrial policy is growth and development. In all of the eight HPAEs, several lessons were distilled. A strong institutional basis was required. This was achieved with the establishment of specific mechanisms and an explicit commitment to growth. A defining characteristic of the East Asian Miracle was the combination of rapid growth and reduced inequality. Wealth-sharing programmes were designed to seek equity with growth. An economic technocracy was emplaced, separated from partisanship and politics. Institutions were established for 'domestic contests', coordination, information-sharing and transparency.

Yet the experience of the High-Performing East Asian Economies demonstrated that there was no one-size-fits-all. The instruments they applied and their experiences varied in their singular objective of achieving rapid, high growth with equity. However, the sum of their experiences is around three key factors:

- getting the market-based policy fundamentals right
- establishing a solid institutional basis for growth with equity
- policy intervention.

---

[11] Brazil, India, Indonesia and Malaysia (World Bank, 1991).

The *market-based policy fundamentals* are roundly and universally considered to have set and secured the foundation for the success of the East Asian economies. Several elements were key. They ranged from sound macroeconomic policies to developing human capital, effective financial systems, minimizing price distortions, absorption of new technology and limiting the bias against agriculture.

The micro- and macroeconomic importance of human capital development is a fundamental line of policy in any and all strategies for economic growth. The indispensable importance of human capital, to raise the literacy rate, develop the skills required by firms and enterprises and accelerate the absorption of foreign technology diffusion, is now evidenced well beyond the East Asian Miracle.[12] It was one of the foundational policies for the growth miracle of East Asia. All of the eight economies of East Asia were avid consumers of foreign technology through a range of means: reverse engineering, imported machinery, licensing and foreign investments that typically were a mix of new ideas, state-of-the-art managerial acumen, labour force and technical skills. The openness of these East Asian economies in the acceptance of modern technology contrasted in some examples in non-HPAE economies where the approach was to apply the archetypal industrial policy of import substitution of domestic standard machine tool industry with state-of-the-art foreign technology. In most if not all cases, the former fell short because of prohibitive costs and was well short of international standards.

World Bank (1993) concludes that 'Some economies – notably Japan, Korea and Taiwan, China – went beyond fundamentals and intervened in markets with industrial, trade, and financial sector policies. On balance, some of these interventions contributed to their extraordinary growth, but this was only possible because of highly unusual historical and institutional circumstances'. They succeeded in very unique circumstances because they offered incentives and government-controlled favours that were linked to economic performance criteria. And the policies were effectively implemented by a competent and honest technocracy.

In sum, in 1993 as in 1991, the conclusion is that attempting to select champions and promote specific industries tends to fail and there are many specific cases of failure. Huge economic deadweight costs are imposed on an economy from large, untargeted subsidies, negative interest

---

[12] Gary S. Becker and human capital development: http://www.nobelprize.org/nobel_prizes/economic-sciences/laureates/1992/press.html

rates that distort allocation and irrational interventions that deviate an economy away from growth. A combination of strong fundamentals and rational interventions is consistently, virtually always successful.

From being on the defensive in the economic and trade policy community, industrial policy is back *à la mode* as a growth model. In the wake of the 2008 global financial and economic crisis (the Great Recession), researchers and policy-makers have had to re-address the ever-present reality that market forces *per se* do not result in Pareto-efficient outcomes because market prices do not always account for critical national goals such as environmental protection, financial stability and inclusion, equality of opportunity and (negative) externalities.

Although there have been existentialist questions about industrial policy, eminent scholars and practitioners have reaffirmed it in theory and its viability in practice.

> All governments really do have an industrial policy. The only difference is between those who construct their industrial policy consciously and those who let it be shaped by others, typically by special interests, who vie with each other for hidden and open subsidies, for rules and regulations that favor them, usually at the expense of others. (Stiglitz et al., 2013)

1.3   Approaches to Industrial Policy

Approaches to industrial policy have differed. These approaches have been linked to questions regarding whether there are circumstances that increase the likelihood that the application of industrial policies would work. Overall, conceptually, approaches to industrial policy have revolved around several angles:

- Industrial policy and value chains
- Industrial policy and the 'facilitating' or 'developmental state'
- Industrial policy and economic transformation
- Industrial policy and manufacturing
- Industrial policy, WTO trade rules, industrial policy and permissibility questions
- Trade rules, industrial policy and trade negotiations.

Industrial Policy and Value Chains

An analytic perspective on industrial policies has been formulated from the angle of global value chains. This perspective divides along several dimensions. There is a trade policy/industrial policy-industrialization nexus. Trade policy can lead to industrialization or de-industrialization. In promoting industrialization, trade policy and agreements should seek integration to regional and global value chains and specialization in trade in tasks, including services (Economic Commission for Africa, 2015).

Industrial policy is argued to be one of several external factors that influence the decision by lead firms on the venue where they decide to locate their production activities in a global economy organized around fragmented international production structures (and multi-country processing). Such locational decisions by lead firms influence the development and diversification outcomes of a country (Low and Tijaja, 2014). The ability of a firm to participate in different parts of a value chain is in part dependent on firm competitiveness and capacity, but also in part on the operational environment, where for the latter, the role of government is central. As argued, from an industrial policy perspective, governments may aspire for higher shares of value-added on existing chains with 'upgrading' or by engaging to participate in new 'production sharing activities' (Humphrey and Schmitz, 2000, Low and Tijaja, 2014). What emerges is that in an economic environment where the objectives and motivations of firms and governments may differ, maximization of objectives and motivations is constrained. As a consequence, the challenge is for mutually accommodating outcomes between markets and the state. One conclusion reached is that, 'In the final analysis, however, it is the responsibility of governments to do whatever is required to maximize social welfare. The conception and design of industrial policy is fundamental to the successful pursuit of this objective, where governments seek to maximize alignments with firms as value chain actors' (Low and Tijaja, 2014).

The 'Facilitating' or 'Developmental State' and Industrial Policy

There has been a review of the industrial policy approach that is gaining ground in several developing countries constructed on the rationale for a 'facilitating' or 'developmental state'. As formulated, the role of government is to coordinate the clustered entry of firms into industry to achieve critical mass for competitiveness, consistent with a country's long-term or dynamic comparative advantage and to reduce or avoid a long and costly process of trial and error. This school proposes that in developing countries, governments should identify and select (new) industries consistent with comparative advantage and on the basis of priorities, allocate limited resources for infrastructure improvements for a few carefully selected industries, provide incentives and coordinate private firms in the selected industries for the rapid and successful formation of clusters. The successful performance of these roles is a determinant of long-term economic success. The rationale is elaborated to suggest that development reflects a long-run process of industrial upgrading, diffusion of technology, dissemination of knowledge[13] and the constant promotion of learning. Economic development is defined, at its essence, in terms of the diffusion of knowledge. In this framework, the constructive role of government is to promote a combination of activities and industries that assist the emergence of 'positive externalities' and facilitate learning and research. A conclusion with regard to Africa is that, 'For a region facing such opportunities and challenges, industrial policy is not a speculative intellectual exercise for academic debates but rather a necessary economic tool to address the pervasive discrepancies between private gains and social returns, and to correct major sectoral or other misallocations' (Stiglitz et al., 2013).

Industrial Policy and Economic Transformation

Relatedly, as argued, the inability for Africa to experience sustained *economic transformation*, beyond growth fuelled by commodity cycles, has been linked to the absence of industrial policy. Africa has made minimal progress in economic transformation with regard to reversing Africa's de-industrialization. Evidence from manufacturing is presented to illustrate that the share of manufacturing in GDP in 2012 was lower than it was in 1965 and barely approximated the mid-1970s level. Meaningful jobs are not being substantially created. To remedy this situation and to promote economic transformation, the vital role of industrial policies is emphasised (Noman and Stiglitz, 2015, African Centre for Economic Transformation, 2014). This school argues that industrial policy is not confined to industry *per se*, but refers to the promotion of specific types of activities encompassing learning, industrial and technology (LIT) policies (a term used interchangeably with 'industrial policy'). Societal transformation depends on learning such

---

[13] Knowledge is defined as a public good. Public goods are defined as non-excludable and non-rivalrous goods, where consumption or use by X does not reduce its availability for Y (Samuelson, 1955; Kaul, Grunberg and Stern, 1999). I argue that an efficient growth-oriented domestic economy requires the supply and existence of public goods, chief of which should be a pro-competitive regulatory framework with protection and security of intellectual and property rights.

that a right balance is struck between static efficiency and learning, which are central to successfully achieving growth and development. The economic experience of Africa is illustrative of the price and consequence of ignoring LIT policies for growth. The objective is not about selecting winners. While LIT (industrial) policies carry rewards, they also (not unusually for any policy) carry risks, and the approach should be to learn from the failures of industrial policies as from the failures of the 2008 crisis. It is important, nonetheless, in the analysis, that these studies acknowledge the risk of government failures and argue, in balance, that 'naïve faith in state interventions' should not replace 'naïve belief in unfettered markets that neglects market failures by ignoring the limitations of markets ... ' (Noman and Stiglitz, 2015).

What sets these scholars apart from the market-friendly school is on the tilt of the government/market relationship with the application of 'good and proper governance' for 'good economic performance'. The Noman and Stiglitz school, for instance, considers that the 'good governance agenda' ought to be used to develop state capacities that have marked the 'development state', rather than, in their words, the 'too-narrow focus' pushed by international institutions to 'restraining the role of government and limiting its role to enabling the private sector ... ' (Noman and Stiglitz, 2015). It is necessary to underscore that the literature makes it evident that like-minded economists are divided on what the balance should be, but that the preponderant weight of evidence is tilted heavily in favour of enabling the private sector and for clear choices to use market solutions to solve market problems, while not ignoring the role of the state.

Industrial Policy and Manufacturing

Recent literature underscores a particular manufacturing angle to industrial policy and knock-on systemic effects for the overall health of a national economy. Questions and assertions about the return of industrial policy strategy have been linked to the case made on a manufacturing strategy for the United States by Gene Sperling, Director of the White House National Economic Council (Sperling, 2013). He suggests three paradigm shifts that provide better insights through which to view the impact of manufacturing and the role of policy. First, he argues that there is a need to shift away from thinking about the promise of advanced manufacturing from the 'industrial policy' perspective, which is generally conceived as picking winners and losers, to an 'innovation spillover' model. Second, the need to shift away from the 'large factory' paradigm with a few manufacturing jobs to a 'supply chain' paradigm which acknowledges manufacturing and services jobs across integrated supply chains. Finally, to shift away from a 'static snap-shot' approach (which draws on contemporary and historical data to assess manufacturing) to an approach of 'dynamic analysis' that reviews the economic trends.

There are location spillover benefits where the manufacturing occurs. There is a relationship between the 'proximity of the manufacturing activity', on the one hand, and the 'design of the activity', on the other – the proximity of production and design relationship. The concept of the 'industrial commons'[14] is applied to describe a complex network of sup-pliers, *savoir-faire*, talents and high skills that develop around a manufacturing (production) activity. These develop over the long term and are of vital importance for the overall health of the manufacturing sector and its future growth. Manufacturing capabilities generate 'indus-trial commons', a complex and self-reinforcing network of knowledge, process skills, engineering software and research spin-off and multipliers that provide and secure the foundations for growth and innovation across industries (Pisano and Shih, 2009, 2012). This proposition is taken further with the argument that allowing the erosion of the manufacturing base would lead to the loss of 'industrial commons' and the 'dense capabilities'. Such loss would put at risk the manufacturing sector, its future growth and dependent or ancillary services (Sperling, 2013).

In sum, manufacturing is about network effects, the industrial com-mons, innovation spillovers and the systemic health of the economy, exceeding the simple calculation of its share in GDP. Competitiveness is vital. Outcomes are not pre-determined and require long-term capital investments by firms and governments. The vital importance of policy choices is underscored. A precise conclusion is reached: '. . . we believe that our first mission as policy-makers is to have our thumb on the scale in favour of encouraging US location. The President's strategy was designed to balance the need to support cost reduction with the need to invest in capabilities, to recognize the complex nature of vicious and virtuous cycles, and to appreciate the role that local economies play in promoting national outcomes' (Sperling, 2013).

Industrial Policy, WTO Trade Rules and Permissibility Questions

The relationship between WTO rules and industrial policy has been approached, in the main, from different and not always complementary

---

[14] Pisano and Shih (2009)

analytic angles. While some have emphasized the constraints, others have pointed to the opportunities in trade rules and negotiations. Those emphasizing the constraining effects of trade rules on the ability of governments to intervene draw attention to trade rules on subsidies, local content incentives, export restrictions and intellectual property rights.

At the same time, the balancing position is that the effect of WTO rules and disciplines is *not* to exclude the role of government and associated government interventions, but to transfer the emphasis to the supply side and infrastructure, building human capital, technological diffusion, capacity-building and competition policy, all in the context of sound policy fundamentals. Accordingly, these will pass the test of WTO rules because they are horizontal and generic and do not try to pick winners or promote specific industries. The evidence adduced corroborates earlier studies that industrial policy that has sought to select and promote specific industries or sectors has resulted in more losers than winners (Bora, Lloyd and Pangestu, 2000). Some have avoided the argumentation associated with the legal permissibility of trade policies required for the pursuit of different genres of industrial policy because they consider that many have been addressed, if not fully resolved, in WTO dispute settlement. However, they also consider that uncertainty remains on some industrial policies regardless of whether legal claims may not have been brought, and that this uncertainty carries a cost. Minimize ambiguity and eliminate the scope for discretion. As they argue and elaborate, 'policy and regulatory uncertainties are of greater concern than policy and regulatory density' (Low and Tijaja, 2014).

Trade Rules, Industrial Policy and Trade Negotiations

In the divided views on the relationship between trade rules and industrial policy and the balance of constraint versus the degree of freedom, analytic focus has turned on dispute settlement rulings and trade negotiations.

Six years into the Doha Development Agenda negotiations, the position was taken by the then Director-General Pascal Lamy that there was scope in current trade rules and opportunities in the Round for sustainable industrial development strategies for developing countries (Lamy, 2007).[15] As broadly stated, 'industrial development' was recognized as central to the economic objectives of developing countries in the

---

[15] Lamy (2007)

multilateral trading system well before the WTO came into force in 1995. In the WTO, since 1995, trade rules such as Special and Differential Treatment (S&D) provisions in the General Agreement on Trade in Services (GATS) and in the Agreements on Trade-Related Investment Measures (TRIMs), Trade-Related Intellectual Property Rights (TRIPS) and the Agreement on Subsidies and Countervailing Measures (SCM) provide for 'industrial development in developing countries'. As has been argued, the test of the Doha Round regarding whether it delivered on development would hinge on whether the final results of the negotiations were supportive of the industrial aspirations of developing countries. These latter would turn on enhanced market access not only for (primary stage) commodities, but elimination of tariff peaks and escalation, in instances where value has been added to those commodities, and more comprehensive commitments in the services sector. Specific to least-developed countries (LDCs), most of which are in Africa, the horizontal understanding by WTO members is that LDCs, across the board, would not undertake any reduction (liberalization) commitments in the negotiations for both agriculture and merchandise sectors so as to provide them with 'policy space' for their industrial development strategies. There is particular stress on policy reforms in the trade in services sector, which have enabled greater openness, enhanced competitiveness and provided a basis for better prudential regulations, hence industrial growth. Examples identified have ranged across government policies and liberalization commitments that have promoted investments in telecommunications, information technology, tourism, environmental services and business services. These are considered as consistent with any industrial development strategy (Lamy, 2007).

At the Tenth WTO Ministerial Conference in Nairobi, significant decisions were taken, for instance, on the elimination of export subsidies on agriculture, with immediate effect for developed countries and a short transitional period for developing countries. The Decisions on Least-Developed Countries on rules of origin, cotton and the waiver services served to support the industrial development priorities on these economies to an extent. With prejudice to the status of the Doha Round before the Membership in 2016, the outcomes from the Ninth WTO Ministerial Conference in Bali and the Tenth WTO Ministerial Conference in Nairobi support the position that trade negotiations can seriously and concretely contribute to industrial policy objectives in the rules-based Multilateral Trading System.

A final observation from the literature review is that, although the debate on industrial policy was heavily tinctured, ideologically, at its original entrance into the economic and trade policy literature, and meant different things to different scholars, the concept has evolved significantly from its origins. Although analysis is currently more practical, realistic and economy-specific, it still reflects divided views and controversy even amongst like-minded champions of trade openness and integration.

1.3   Industrial Policy Instruments

Industrial policy instruments take a multitude of forms. These various forms are neither analysed nor discussed here but are illustratively listed to provide an indication of their scope and coverage. They are trade policy instruments that have been used, in the main, for protection and associated costs. They delay necessary reforms, and a range of justifications have been invoked for their use under specific economic circumstances. They include, *inter alia,*

- subsidies: subsidized credits, directed lending, tax policies: tax breaks, firm bailouts, tax write-offs, revenue foregone, etc.
- tariffs
- quantitative restrictions
- export credits
- duty-offset / duty-drawback
- Export Processing Zones (EPZs)
- local content requirements
- buy/procure national policies
- research and development
- State Trading Enterprises (STEs)
- foreign exchange exclusions for imported products.

2   Good and Bad Examples of Industrial Policies – The Cost of Failure

There is an abundance of empirical evidence on the application of industrial policies, in developed and developing countries, to achieve varying objectives. The successful examples range from the East Asian Miracle (World Bank, 1993), the 'China Miracle' (Lin, Cai and Li, 2003) and 'The Cerrado Miracle' (Economist, 2010) to less miraculous but successful examples elsewhere. There have been successes elsewhere and in other regions, including Africa, that have been analysed (Noman and Stiglitz, 2015; Hosono, 2015).

There have also been many examples of failures entailing considerable costs. Some examples are illustrative of failed activist interventions. They include the aircraft manufacturing industry (Indonesia); iron and steel industry (Nigeria); automobile industry (Nigeria);[16] petrochemicals (Brazil); textile and clothing industry (Sweden); and the shipbuilding industry (Sweden).

Nigeria

The history of the flawed intervention by the Nigerian government in the iron and steel industry carried huge costs for the economy. It is illustrative of how the state should not attempt to micromanage the real economy. The original plan to establish an iron and steel industry was initiated in 1958 (before Nigeria's independence in 1960). The plan was taken forward as part of the First National Development Plan (1962–68), the Second Development Plan (1970–74) and the Third National Development Plan (1970–74).[17] Start-up was delayed over political disagreements regarding location. Thereafter, implementation and follow-up were affected by bureaucratic incompetence, choice of inappropriate technology, corruption and misappropriated resources. Privatization was bungled, resulting in contestation of ownership. So far, the Nigerian iron and steel industry is a failed endeavour by government at industrial policy. The costs of failure and inability to cut costs and rapidly retrench a failed policy compounded the losses. Professional sectoral assessment of the intervention and the scale of failure in the iron steel industry considered it a 'dark page' in the professional and economic history of Nigeria (Obikwelu and Nebo, 2012).[18]

There is a somewhat comparable story in the chequered history and evolution of the Nigerian Automotive Industry, which provides illustrative lessons in failure and then learning through correction. The Nigerian automotive industry started with huge promise and potential in the early 1960s with the establishment of automobile assembly plants by private companies, notably the United Africa Company (UAC), Leventis, SCOA

---

[16] The earlier failure in this industry is being reversed with the New Automotive Industry Development Policy (NAIDP).

[17] For a useful background see Ajayi, Adegbite and Iyanda (2014) and Egwuatu (2013)

[18] Obikwelu and Nebo (2012)

Nigeria PLC, BEWAC and R.T. Briscoe.[19] Government intervened wrongly in the industry from 1970 to 1980. This resulted in an uncompetitive industry, accumulation of costs and failure. Partisanship, political instability, poor infrastructure, corruption, and similar problems that affected the iron and steel industry, manifested. Car unit outputs were 'procured' for use by government departments and officials without payment. Behind-the-curve technology was in use. Corruption was systemic. Bureaucracy was incompetent. Failure and collapse logically followed from increased cost and non-competitiveness. However, learning from failures took hold in 2007, when the car and truck/light commercial vehicle plants were privatized. Learning and correction with the application of international best practices are demonstrating how industrial policy applications can be successfully turned around.

In collaboration with the Government of South Africa,[20] the Nigerian automobile industry has been re-structured. The Nigerian government, working with the National Automotive Design and Development Council (NADDC)[21], has made policy choices to establish an appropriate, market-based regulatory environment. The regulatory environment is codified in the Nigerian Automotive Industry Development Programme (NAIDP), which is a central part of the Nigerian Industrial Revolution Plan (NIRP).[22] The Government, working with the NADDC, adopted the NAIDP to encourage foreign investment in the country's motor vehicle industry and create jobs. According to external industry-sector reports, the programme has started well with concrete results and success is being registered. However, weakness in the global economy, a 'devalued' Nigerian Naira under pressure and minimal local suppliers of inputs still present challenges. But progress is being registered and jobs are being created (Economist Intelligence Unit, Industry Report, 2015).[23] The government has intervened appropriately, within the parameters of the role that governments should play in making the right policy choices,

---

[19] See http://www.nac.org.ng/industries_genesis.php

[20] The new NAIDP was initiated by Mr. Segun Aganga, former Nigerian Minister for Industry, Trade and Investment in collaboration with the Government of South Africa. The South Africa/Nigeria economic relationship, now being sectorally defined, will be a critical engine in creating regional value chains for accelerated growth for development and enhancing welfare in the Africa region as a whole. There is scope for such value chains beyond the automobile sector.

[21] National Automotive Design and Development Council (NADDC): http://www.nac.org .ng/index.php

[22] See 'Information on the Nigerian Automotive Industry Development Plan', June 2014.

[23] Also see EIU (2015).

and has stayed out of the market play, which is best left to the private sector.

In the first year, twelve manufacturers have been granted licences to assemble vehicles locally. Seven approved operations will be assembling Chinese brands (cars and lorries, including those made by Sinotruk, FAW and SAIC; BYD, the latest Chinese entrant in the market, will be producing electric vehicles).

Operating in the market and with licences to operate since the new 2014 policy are Nissan, Hyundai vehicles (with Stallion motors, their local venture partner), Kia Motors, another Korean operation, and a subsidiary of Hyundai (with Dana Motors). Nissan's Japanese competitors, Toyota and Honda, also have licences to construct local plants.

Oil and Gas Sector

Intervention by government in the oil and gas sector is another classic example of the failure of a badly conceived industrial policy with huge costs. Three facts stand out. First, policy by government to micro-manage the downstream sector, including the building of refineries, yielded inefficiencies. Second, intervention was flawed and undermined by implementation failures and political inability to retrench a plan that was not working. Third, the scale of corruption in the oil and gas industry broke the mould. It exceeded measure, in respect of subsidies to oil marketers (importers of refined downstream petroleum products in Nigeria), even in the period of the commodity down cycle with record-low oil prices that provided opportunities for subsidy elimination (Adeniyi and Alike, 2015). No policy, including industrial policy, can work under such conditions of systemic corruption. The new Government in Nigeria under President Buhari has attached the highest priority to tackling systemic corruption and insecurity and achieving greater equity through reduction of inequality. The Buhari government is registering early successes on the governance questions that are indispensable for effective implementation of government policies, and there is global acknowledgement of concrete steps in the Nigerian government's fight against corruption.[24] This includes prosecution and indictment of corrupt politicians in the previous government and the voluntary return of stolen money to the public treasury. The most obvious example is the misappropriation of US$ 2.4 billion budgeted for the military and the fight against Boko Haram.

[24] Kerry (2016)

Over the three-year period (2013–15), reports indicate that Nigerian petroleum subsidy payments and claims amounted to N1.380 trillion (approx. US$ 693 billion).[25] Sustaining this rate of subsidies, which benefit the rich and not the poor, could be viewed as a wasted opportunity, misallocation of resources that could have been better invested in infrastructure, and as a consequence, development foregone. This is an example of how the state should not intervene.

Sweden

The failures of interventionist policies with high levels of government subsidies to the Swedish shipbuilding industry in the 1970s, for the purpose of maintaining employment levels and not adjusting to changes in the world's production structure, is an example in point (Hamilton, 1983[26]). Also, there have been useful studies evaluating the risks and failures of industrial policy in the textile and clothing sector – which is of interest for many countries, developed and developing. Swedish intervention in this sector, responding to declining output and employment, was mainly defensive in nature through: direct financial support, labour subsidies and conventional trade restrictions. However, what resulted was that these policies had little or no effect on firm behaviour. Instead, inefficiencies arose due to misallocation of resources (Alänge and Jacobsson, 1994).

Brazil

In Brazil, two cases of industrial policy intervention juxtapose a successful world-class example in agriculture ('The miracle of the Cerrado'[27]) and a costly disaster in the petro-chemical sector (*Comperj in Itaborai*).[28]

The Miracle of the Cerrado

The transformation of Brazilian agriculture, in its savannah land, has been described as a 'miracle'. In less than 30 years, Brazil converted itself from a net food importer into a global agricultural producer and exporter. It achieved convergence in agriculture with the major 'big five' grain exporters: United States, Canada, Australia, Argentina and the European Union.

---

[25] Currency conversion by the author, December 2015   [26] Hamilton (1983).
[27] *The Economist* (2010)   [28] *The Economist* (2015a)

The transformation in Brazilian agriculture still astonishes. In the 10-year period between 1996 and 2006, the total value of Brazil's crops increased by 365 per cent, from US$ 23 billion to US$ 108 billion. Its beef exports increased ten-fold and it gained on and overtook Australia as the world's largest exporter. Brazil is the world's largest exporter of poultry, sugar cane and ethanol. On soyabean, Brazil accounts for approximately a third of world soyabean exports.

Because the transformation of Brazilian agriculture was standard-setting and unprecedented, it became an object of study (Hosono, 2015). The question asked was how the transformation was achieved because, as argued, 'The answer to those matters not only to Brazil but also to the rest of the world'. Specific linkages have been made to Africa. The observation has been made that '. . . the biggest single agricultural failure in the world during past decades has been tropical Africa, and anything that might help Africans grow more food would be especially valuable'. The question has been asked: '. . . can the miracle of the *cerrado* be exported, especially to Africa, where the good intentions of outsiders have so often shrivelled and died? There are several reasons to think it can' (*The Economist*, 2010).

Studies indicate that the dramatic transformation of Brazilian agriculture that established a global standard was due less to the natural endowments of arable land and renewable water than to the establishment in 1973 of the public company 'Embrapa' (*Empresa Brasileira de Pesquisa Agropecuária*; the Brazilian Agricultural Research Corporation). Embrapa pioneered new operational farm techniques, imported grass varieties from Africa (*brachiaria*) and then cross-bred it to produce an improved variety with increased yield (*braquiarinha*) for forage, treated the acidic soil in the *cerrado* with industrial quantities of lime to reduce levels of acidity, converted soyabeans into a tropical product from its temperate-climate native origins in north-east Asia and is now a global leader in GM agriculture.

Intervention by the government of Brazil succeeded for a range of reasons. There was a purposeful choice with clear objectives. State-of-the-art technology was introduced with constant innovation. Learning from past errors in Brazilian agriculture was admitted by the government and this, *inter alia*, was at the core of the dramatic world-class transformations. Government subsidies were very low, well below the OECD average for developed country agriculture subsidies. The investments by Brazil were in learning, science and technology, infrastructure and innovation.

As concluded from the East Asian Miracle, it is necessary to re-iterate the caveat that even great examples, such as the *cerrado*, are not formulae to be scientifically applied. Successful examples still have to be adapted if they are to be attempted in other countries. As noted, 'Brazil's agricultural miracle did not happen through a simple technological fix. No magic bullet accounts for it. Rather, Embrapa's was a "system approach", as its scientists call it: all the interventions worked together' (*The Economist*, 2010).

Comperj in Itaborai

There are differences and similarities in economic histories across both developed and developing countries. In many ways, Brazil's development experience across the board is broadly relevant for many African and developing countries and there are valuable lessons to be learnt. One of the lessons is from the failed intervention by the government in *Comperj in Itaborai*. The failure, at this point, has carried huge costs. In 2006, the establishment of Comperj, the Rio de Janeiro petrochemical complex, was announced. The plan included two oil refineries and petro-chemical plants. 220,000 new jobs were forecast to be created. Private firms were expected to enter into investment partnerships with Petrobas, the state-invested and controlled oil company.

As of 2015, the plan is yet to be implemented or take off. Global market and governance factors intervened. The shale gas boom in the United States reduced costs and energy demand. They contributed, *inter alia*, to the collapse of commodity prices and the drastic fall in global prices for petroleum. Weaknesses in the global economy and slow growth accompanied by weaker demand in China all contributed to reducing the demand for energy. Domestically in Brazil, Petrobras faced a continuing corruption scandal. Costs are considerable and are escalating. For instance, about 4,000 offices are estimated to be unoccupied (revenue foregone with tied-down investments).[29]

A reinforced lesson from economic history is that microeconomic intervention by the state has been unsuccessful and has led to failures with huge economic costs.

3   Africa and Industrial Policy

No country has made economic progress without positive stimulus from intel-ligent government, ... On the other hand, there are so many examples of the

---

[29] *The Economist* (2015a)

mischief done to economic life by government that it is easy to fill one's pages with warnings against government participation in economic life.[30] (Lewis, 1963)

I am clear about the role of government. It is not government who creates the scientific innovation, or translates it into growth. But we can back those who do. (Osborne, 2012)

Africa ... needs more than marginal growth. The continent requires a great leap in economic performance that will be sustainable, inclusive and transformative. Structural transformation of the African economies through industrialization is imperative. (UNECA, 2015)

Since the 1950–60s independence period, Africa has been a laboratory of different ideas on approaches to development policy. African economic policy-makers currently consider that trade and industrial policies are critical and central to their development policy. The 1995 coming into force of the WTO and the institutional participation of African countries in the rules-based system and acceptance of WTO core values yielded the benefits of integration to the global economy. Although there is unquestioned acceptance of the superior function of the market in allocative efficiency, trade liberalization and openness for growth, development experiences in East Asia, China and Brazil have made evident the vital importance of an appropriate but key role for the state. These other development experiences have pointed to lessons to be drawn with regard to stimulating industrial clustering, 'network effects', technology, infrastructure, research, learning from experience, and their effects for productivity and growth. The role of the state is also considered indispensable for addressing market failures and buffering externally transmitted shocks.

However, although Africa registered reasonably rapid growth in the past decade, with six of the world's fastest-growing economies emerging from Sub-Saharan Africa, there are key concerns with de-industrialization, the low level of manufacturing, absence of structural transformation, a small middle class, poverty and inequality. For instance, The *Economist* has suggested that, 'Unlike Asia, Africa has failed to develop industries that generate lots of employment and pay good wages. Only a few countries manufacture very much, largely because national markets are small and barriers to trading within Africa are huge'.[31] Manufacturing is essential for structural transformation and sustained economic growth, *inter alia*, for

---

[30] See quotation in Lin, Cai and Li (2003).   [31] *The Economist* (2015b)

the spillover effects that are generated, network efforts and employment opportunities created. The constellation of advice is to focus on facilitation, creation and expansion of a modern and open manufacturing base (Velde, 2016), although there are cautionary notes 'not to be obsessed with manufacturing' because its relative importance as a source of value-added and employment is declining (Dadush, 2015a) and because manufactured exports are a much smaller contributor to foreign currency earnings (Dadush, 2016).

Recent data has been presented by United Nations Economic Commission for Africa on de-industrialization, as evidenced by the decline of manufacturing as a share of GDP growth. In its 2015 Economic Report on Africa (ERA), the United Nations Economic Commission for Africa figures suggest a decline in manufactures from 4.4 per cent (1961–79) to 3.1 per cent (2000–12). Similarly, the share of industry dropped from 6.1 per cent (1961–79) to 5.2 per cent (2000–12). The point is made that industrialization is key to structural transformation, diversification and job creation.[32]

Greater economy-specific focus on individual African countries reveals an interesting picture (see Table 15.1).[33]

Morocco and Egypt have the highest levels of manufacturing as a share of GDP, followed by South Africa (the second-biggest economy on the continent) and Nigeria (the number one economy on the continent), although the figures show that manufacturing value-added in Nigeria, as a share of GDP, is growing faster than that in other economies on the continent, even if its 9.8 per cent share of GDP is below that for Sub-Saharan Africa, at 11.2 per cent.

In the context of an appropriate role for government, there is a strong economic policy push by African governments for structural transformation. This policy push is supported by operational push from the private sector. It is argued that the economic transformation of Africa will not materialize and the imagery of *Africa Rising*[34] will be aborted, if it is not industrialization-based with the application of industrial policy. Many African policy-makers and policy academics have concluded that a deliberate industrial policy framework to promote economic growth and development in Africa is imperative. Manufacturing, technology and integration are considered to be the growth drivers that would enable

---

[32] UNECA (2015).   [33] The selection by of African countries is the choice of the author.
[34] *The Economist* (2011)

Table 15.1 *Manufacturing, value-added (% of GDP)*

Countries	2006	2007	2008	2009	2010	2011	2012	2013	2014
Morocco	15.9	17.0	16.8	17.5	17.4	16.8	16.5	17.0	18.2
Egypt	17.0	16.1	16.3	16.6	16.9	16.5	15.8	15.6	16.4
South Africa	16.4	16.1	16.0	15.0	14.4	13.3	13.1	13.2	13.3
Kenya	14.3	14.5	13.6	13.4	12.6	13.1	12.3	11.9	11.1
Nigeria	2.6	2.5	2.4	2.5	6.6	7.2	7.8	9.0	9.8
Ethiopia	5.0	4.9	4.4	4.1	4.3	4.0	3.7	4.0	4.3
Sub-Saharan Africa	12.1	11.8	11.6	11.2	11.4	11.0	11.0	11.2	11.2
Germany	23.1	23.4	22.5	19.9	22.2	22.9	22.8	22.6	22.6
United States	13.5	13.3	12.7	12.3	12.5	12.6	12.7	12.4	
World	17.7	17.4	16.9	15.9	16.4	16.5	16.4	16.2	
OECD members	16.2	16.0	15.4	14.4	15.0	15.1	15.1	14.9	
Least-developed countries	11.6	11.9	11.8	11.7	11.2	11.4	11.5	11.5	11.6
East Asia and Pacific	25.4	25.3	25.0	23.4	24.5	23.9	23.6	23.3	

Source: World Bank's World Development Indicators

African countries to 'jump start development' (Sanusi, 2010 and Kuwono, 2015).

There are rhetorical policy references to the 20 November 1989 proclamation by the United Nations General Assembly (UNGA) of an 'Africa Industrialization Day' to mobilize 'the commitment of the international community to the industrialisation of Africa'. Several consider the two decades from 1980 to 2000, dedicated by the UNGA to promoting industrialization in Africa to have been a waste. There are references by academics to the 'lost quarter-century' for the African region (Noman and Stiglitz, 2015).

In most African economies, diagnostics of the problems are thorough and comprehensive. Many of these have been technically assisted by multilateral institutions, contributions from Africans in diaspora and foreign advisors. There is a systemic angst associated with industrialization failures.

The current policy pre-occupation is to identify what would be considered as the right policy alchemy to manufacture, industrialize, integrate into regional and global markets and grow. There is policy acceptance on the fundamentals of macroeconomic policy, market stability, containing inflation at single digits and good governance. There is pragmatic acceptance of reducing, if not cutting, reliance on external sources and improved mobilization of domestic resources for development. Lessons from other development experiences have made evident the need to increase the national savings rate, expand the revenue base, improve tax collection efficiency and eliminate corruption. Policy-makers understand the deficiencies in infrastructure and technology that require bridging in relation to other parts of the world. On specific sectors, there are proposals for Agricultural Value Chains (AVCs), for instance, to minimize post-harvest losses by processing agricultural produce into refined manufactured products, essential for Africa's industrialization.

A notable development is increasingly robust activism in monetary policy, no longer solely focused on price stability but on targeted intervention, with incentives and support for the development of the real sector and directed at boosting manufacturing and employment generation. The 2015 example from Nigeria is illustrative. The Central Bank of Nigeria (CBN) issued a Circular on 23 June 2015 excluding 41 items of goods and services from accessing foreign exchange at the Nigerian foreign exchange markets for their imports. The reasons given were to (i) ensure the efficient utilization of foreign exchange, (ii) encourage the local production of those 41 items, (iii) facilitate the resuscitation of domestic industries and (iv) improve employment generation. As stated in CBN (2015),

> In the continuing effort to sustain the stability of the foreign exchange market, and ensure the efficient utilization of foreign exchange and the derivation of optimum benefits from goods and services imported into the country, it has become imperative to exclude importers of some goods and services from accessing foreign exchange at the Nigerian foreign exchange markets in order to encourage the local production of these items. The implementation of the policy will help conserve foreign reserves as well as facilitate the resuscitation of domestic industries and improve employment generation.

The rationale underpinning the policy of foreign exchange exclusion for the listed items was reiterated by the Governor of the Central Bank at a press conference. In addition to the factors in CBN (2015), the Governor argued, *inter alia*, that the policy changes were forced on policy-makers from exogenous shocks and that effective policy-making required nimbleness and responsiveness to the situation forced upon the economy. The Governor stated that

> Central Banks in Developing Countries like ours cannot sit idly by and concentrate only on price and monetary stability. I argued that additional measures would be required towards identifying productive sectors of the economy and channelling credit towards these sectors, while imposing proper monitoring and performance measures in order to ensure that the goals of increased employment and poverty reduction are attained" (Emefiele, 2015).

The situation is one where monetary policy is verging on and being directed to fiscal and industrial policy objectives. What the evidence clearly points to is a policy galvanization in major African economies to industrialize, manufacture and undergo economic structural transformation for growth and development.

Studies indicate that while there have been failures in industrial policies in Africa, there have also been success stories of industrial policy application on the continent. As several have argued, failures in industrial policies are an insufficient argument for abandoning such policies, as failures in macro, monetary and financial policies, prior to the 2008 financial crisis, would not be a basis to argue for abandonment of these policies (Noman and Stiglitz, 2015). The question that remains is under what conditions such activist trade and industrial policies can be applied to ensure that they stand a chance of success and pass a litmus test of non-discrimination in a the inter-dependent, rules-based, global economy.

Several of the case studies to which reference is made of the successful application of sectoral-type industrial policies by African economies include:

- Ethiopia (leather and floriculture)
- Kenya (horticulture)
- Mauritius (textiles)
- Lesotho (apparels and clothing)
- Mali (mangoes)
- Rwanda (information and communications technology and gorilla tourism)
- South Africa (automobiles)
- Nigeria (automobiles).

Several studies consider Ethiopia to be one of the evident examples of the success of industrial policy in Africa, with broader lessons for the region. The analysis suggests that Ethiopia has used industrial policy to exploit and create dynamic comparative advantages in the sectors identified as priorities in its industrial strategy. Through a combination of incentives and targeted interventions in the leather and floriculture sectors, investments have been promoted and entrepreneurship has been nurtured (Abebe and Schaefer, 2015).

Regardless of aggregated data that indicates that manufacturing is in relative decline as a share of GDP, it is a fact that economic planners across the world still attach to it a systemic importance that exceeds the simplicity of its share of GDP. In Germany, manufacturing accounts for approximately 22 per cent of its GDP, according to 2014 figures. In 2011, to underscore the vital importance of manufacturing, the UK Chancellor of the Exchequer announced a government/'makers' pact to carry and sustain the British economy (Osborne, 2012). A comparable set of remarks by Gene Sperling mirrored the same logic of the systemic economic importance of manufacturing in terms of its spillover efforts for domestic supplier networks, research, knowledge, experience, the notion of the 'industrial commons', *savoir faire*, etc., exceeding the simple indicator of share of GDP (Sperling, 2013). In these industrial market economies, there are priorities and targets. These are linked to the competition in the league table of the global economy for market share, for influence and for leadership. As aptly characterized, '. . .countries like

ours are in a global race. . . . we face a choice: Sink or swim. Do or decline'
(Osborne, 2012).

3.1 United Nations Economic Commission for Africa, UNECA (2015), Economic Report on Africa: Industrializing through Trade

The 2015 Economic Report on Africa by the Economic Commission for Africa (UNECA, 2015) examines the trade/industrialization nexus, describing it as a 'symbiotic relationship', and two sides of the same coin. It focuses on how trade can serve as an instrument of accelerated industrialization and structural transformation in Africa. The report observes the paradox that although there is a strong growth performance in Africa (on the basis of improved management of the macro-economy, diversified trade and investment linkages with emerging economies), this growth performance has co-existed with high unemployment and poverty. It states that industrialization would resolve this paradox.

It acknowledges that trade has a major role to play in the growth performance of African economies. It underscores the critical sensitivity of trade policy, negotiations and agreements. It advises caution so that trade negotiations and agreements do not (any longer) compromise the industrialization goals of Africa.

UNECA (2015) argues that trade, under certain conditions, can promote either industrialization or de-industrialization; the virtuous link in the trade/industrialization relationship is not automatic. Appropriately applying trade policy to achieve industrialization would require adding value domestically and abandoning attempts at commodity-based industrialization, integrating and upgrading along value chains and trade in tasks for goods and services. It argues that regional integration and regional value chains (RVCs) should be a platform for learning, reinforcing a key lesson from previous industrialization and development experiences. The Report provides fundamentally sound advice that '. . .an enduring strategy is for African countries to develop capacity (to negotiate, implement, comply with obligations and defend rights) to articulate smart choices within the various trade agreements they have signed'. A case is made to sequence the conclusion of the Continental Free Trade Area (CFTA) before other trade agreements are fully implemented by Africa with others.

UNECA (2015) notes that the newly industrialized countries converged with developed countries through highly selective trade policies and argues that Africa can surpass the East Asian Miracle if it carefully designs trade and industrial approaches that draws from past lessons and current and future developments in the global environment. Correctly, the Report does not consider trade policy as a silver bullet for Africa's industrial development. Lessons and results from earlier development analyses are reinforced, that no policy works as a stand-alone policy. Companion policies are indispensable and required. While there is an important role for governments, policy-makers must understand global trade dynamics and use regional and international trade negotiations to pursue their industrialisation agenda.

There have been several reactions. For instance, several consider that, although success is being registered with regard to growth rates in Africa, there is scepticism on the long-term perspectives. Some consider it 'a long road ahead for Africa to emulate East Asia', specifically on industrialization. Africa is bearing the brunt of de-industrialization for a range of reasons, namely infrastructure deficits; perversely, the abundance of natural resources; and the absence of a 'lead goose'.[35,36] The paradox is that while the trend tends to be that economies de-industrialize as they grow richer (shifting to the services economy), in Africa de-industrialization is happening under poverty rather than under the prosperity of higher-paying factory jobs. Premature de-industrialization is happening in part because of increasing technology and also because manufacturing is less labour-intensive and more sophisticated.

The principal challenge in light of the evidence is that 'visions' and 'plans', including for industrial policy development, have been undone by systemic corruption, weak leadership and discontinuity in government and severe weaknesses in linking technology to business and strategic goals by governments.

The legal and policy framework of the WTO, the balance of rights and obligations of each individual member, remain the foundation for African countries in their integration into the rules-based global economy. Invocation of WTO rights, including the Dispute Settlement Mechanism, is more essential for African members than for the industrially developed members in levelling the playing field and resolving imbalances in trade rules and addressing fairness questions on the

---

[35] Terminology attributed to Ngozi Okonjo-Iweala, Nigeria's former Coordinating Minister of the Economy. The point is that East Asia's economic success took place under a 'flying geese' model, according to which a leading economy clears the path for others to follow. This author argues that several economies in Africa have the capacity to do so – in particular, Nigeria, South Africa, Morocco and Kenya.

[36] *The Economist* (2015c)

foundation of the rule of trade law. Relatedly, as recently argued, 'The spread of WTO discipline, and its enforcement through a very active and widely used dispute settlement mechanism, has been an important force behind the extraordinary expansion of world trade before the financial crisis. In turn, the increasing importance of trade means that WTO discipline is even more valuable' (Dadush, 2015b).

3.2   WTO Rules and Industrial-Policy-Related Jurisprudence

The relationship between industrial policy and WTO rules is still a source of primary discomfort for many African members, who perceive trade rules in the multilateral trading system as impeding their industrial policy objectives for development. Several African policy-makers, on advice, are concerned that industrial development policy objectives are either impeded or foreclosed by WTO multilateral trade rules. This is wrong. It is possible to be WTO-compliant and still practice legitimate and development-oriented industrial policy as strategic economic intervention, as the literature, experience and practice of developed and other developing members of the WTO illustrate. However, the WTO-consistency of industrial policy measures cannot be determined *ex ante*, and, if challenged, would be subject to rulings by the Dispute Settlement Body (DSB) of the WTO, pursuant to the Dispute Settlement Understanding (DSU). Prior to making domestic decisions on developing an industrial development policy framework, it is necessary to consult and check for WTO-consistency.

A question to be addressed is whether GATT/WTO rules tighten the obligations that inhibit the application (or use) of intervention and industrial-style policies. If so, it could be argued that rules that significantly tighten or preclude the use of intervention by governments would make it more difficult to emulate the examples of some of the East Asian economies such as Japan and Korea. Before the conclusion of the Uruguay Round and the coming into force of the WTO, the analysis in the 1993 World Bank Report suggested that expanded GATT obligations under the WTO could constrain the use of interventionist policies intended to protect domestic industries and subsidize exports in an export-push strategy (World Bank 1993). However, the rules, emerging jurisprudence and the continued evolution of the world economy together show that WTO trade rules neither foreclose nor impede intervention and industrial policy.

Under WTO rules, only the use of particular types of industrial policies may be restricted. Such WTO disciplines include the rules on tariff bindings, general elimination of quantitative restrictions, regulation of trade-related investment measures (TRIMs) and prohibition of local content requirements, disciplines on the use of state subsidies, TRIPS (technology transfer) and the legal and policy framework for non-discriminatory treatment. The trade performance of WTO Article XII members that have actually, explicitly, accepted these obligations, including in their WTO plus versions,[37] indicates that they have grown faster than the original members, exercise greater resilience to shocks and crises and have greater success in attracting investment because of, *inter alia*, a more predictable business environment.

It is *non-sequitur* that WTO rules impede, exclude or prohibit industrial policy because of, *inter alia*, the non-discriminatory rules on subsidy use. While WTO disciplines govern the specific types of trade-related industrial measures, general exceptions from the WTO rules allow for introduction of legitimately justified measures for industrial and economic development needs. Moreover, it may be argued that WTO disciplines facilitate industrial policy through foreign investment liberalization (e.g. through liberalizing services markets under the GATS). The WTO disciplines on S&D treatment include flexibilities granted to developing countries to temporarily increase protection of their markets, delays in implementation of WTO agreements and other preferential disciplines.

As confirmed by the WTO Dispute Settlement Body (DSB) in *China – Rare Earths,*

> [WTO] Members are perfectly entitled to pursue their own industrial policies. But they must do so in a way that is either consistent with the WTO obligations or justified by one of the relevant [WTO] provisions that explicitly provides exceptions for measures pursuing industrial policies. Both the GATT 1994 and other WTO covered agreements generally allow Members to adopt measures in pursuit of their industrial policy needs, and even recognize that, in certain circumstances, Members' industrial policy needs, and especially the imperative to protect vulnerable domestic industries, can override GATT obligations.[38]

---

[37] See Osakwe (2011).

[38] WTO Panel Report on *China – Measures Related to the Exportation of Rare Earths, Tungsten, and Molybdenum* (official WTO documents WT/DS431/R, WT/DS431/R/Add.1, WT/DS432/R, WT/DS432/R/Add.1, WT/DS433/R, WT/DS433/R/Add.1, adopted on 2 September 2014), paragraphs 7.452, 7.453.

This position has recently been endorsed by the WTO Appellate Body in *Argentina – Measures Affecting the Importation of Goods*,

> nothing [. . .] calls into question the ability of WTO Members to pursue their development policies, [. . .] in a manner consistent with the overall objectives stated in the preamble of the WTO Agreement and their commitments under the WTO agreements.[39]

Therefore, the WTO-consistency of any trade-related measure, distinguished from general statements of policy, is dependent on the substance of a legal challenge brought before the DSB, pursuant to the WTO Dispute Settlement Understanding, by a member who makes a claim that its WTO benefits have either been nullified or impaired. For any individual member, WTO membership is a legal contract, based on a specific balance of rights and obligations. Government measures are presumed to be WTO-consistent unless the DSB rules differently, whereas the mere assertion of a claim does not amount to proof. Comparable to the domestic law principle of presumption of innocence, the legal principle of WTO-consistency is made, with the burden of demonstrating WTO-inconsistency falling on the complainant with the Panel/Appellate Body as the referee.

4 Conclusions

There are several conclusions to be reached on WTO trade rules, industrial development policy and competitiveness and its implications for African development. First, industrial policy was saddled with heavy ideological baggage of negativism from its deeply flawed import-substituting, protectionist and discriminatory origins. But it has since evolved. The positive evolution of the concept of industrial policy, examples of successes and lessons being learned from its failed applications indicate that it is a policy with potential utility, given certain conditions, for accelerating productivity growth and development.

Second, the evolution in the literature reviewed indicates multiple perspectives that have improved understanding of the positive morphing of the concept and application of industrial policy. Analysis and elaboration are now less theoretical, better grounded in substantive focus and more policy-relevant, in the light of the challenges confronted by individual economies,

---

[39] WTO Appellate Body Report on *Argentina – Measures Affecting the Importation of Goods* (official WTO documents WT/DS438/AB/R, WT/DS444/AB/R, WT/DS445/AB/R, adopted on 26 January 2015), paragraph 5.150.

both developed and developing and having regard to the dynamic transformations in a rapidly changing and uncertain global economy.

Third, fundamentally, industrial policy is a strategic approach practised by governments, pursuing clear economic policy choices with associated instruments. All governments have an activist trade and industrial policy. Choices are based on specific objectives, which have differed depending on economic policy priorities, challenges facing an economy and strategic directions. They range across a multitude of objectives, spanning industrialization writ large; manufacturing, domestic reforms, market access, accelerated growth for poverty reduction and development; 'national vision plans'; achieving or maintaining sectoral leadership; sustenance of strategic power and leadership; equity, etc. Industrial policy can connote geo-political objectives.

Fourth, there are questions about whether industrial policy is a stand-alone policy, such as trade and finance are. In reality, it is a strategic point of policy intersection and coordination for other policies because of its objectives, *inter alia*, to alter structure, change direction, achieve efficiency and address externalities. Separated from its flawed origin, industrial policy is legitimate and credible like any other branch of public policy. Synonymous with the role of the state and state intervention, there is no one unitary industrial policy model. After approximately 65 years of application, industrial policy approaches, like any other branch of economic policy, have exhibited successes and failures. Notably, in its updated version, a learning coefficient has been introduced. Industrial policy presents opportunities and risks for competitiveness, accelerated growth and development.

Fifth, the substantive evolution of industrial policy was positively impacted by the conclusion of the Uruguay Round and the coming into force of the WTO in 1995, on two key dimensions:

- Although WTO trade rules constrain the economic and trade policy behaviour of its members to negotiated and contractually agreed WTO-consistent behaviour, they levelled the playing field for the conditions of competition without foreclosing or impeding industrial development policy. This was recently underscored in WTO jurisprudence by the WTO Dispute Settlement Body (DSB) in China – Rare Earths, that confirmed that '[WTO] Members are perfectly entitled to pursue their own industrial policies . . . '.
- WTO Accessions *acquis*, resulting from twenty years of WTO accession negotiations (1995 to 2015), have provided 36 governments with an instrument for WTO-consistent domestic reforms. This *acquis*

(a combination of the original rules in 1995 and WTO plus commitments from accession protocols) has consolidated *WTO core values*[40] of commitment to an integrated global market economy, trade openness, transparency, good governance and the rule of law. WTO studies have shown that the economies that have committed to these core values have grown faster than others, exhibited greater resilience to shocks and have had more success in the attraction of investments.[41] Their trade performance have not indicated erosion of the ability to use legitimate trade policy instruments for industrial policy objectives.

Sixth, neither development nor industrial policy is formulaic. Convention and orthodoxy can become inhibitors to progress. Hence, there is a degree of pragmatism and experimentalism. Because priorities and constraints vary widely across economies, policies will differ in application. However, successful policy application should be rooted on fundamentals and learning and adapting the lessons from the past to the reality of the moment. There is a multi-dimensional, complex set of interactions at the national, regional and global economy levels. It involves orientations to competition, private initiatives and market structure; civic attitudes to work linked to productivity levels at the domestic level; efficient functioning of infrastructure and public services; the size of the domestic market; conscious insertion to regional value chains; and the constraints and opportunities in global trade rules.

Although there are neither formulae nor recipes to apply for accelerated growth and development, failures and successes underscore vital lessons. Both provide pathways for development and productivity experiences that are worthy of emulation, on the one hand, and on the other hand, dead-ends. The major milestones include the 'East Asian Miracle'; the 1991 collapse and failure of centrally planned economies; and the ascendant and dominant prosperity of market economies, coupled to improved understanding of the indispensable role of the state on the foundation of a high quality of governance.

Seventh, the best policies will fail with corrupt governance and an incompetent public service, lacking talent, training and leadership. Successful implementation of industrial policy interventions depends on

---

[40] For this concept and its application, see Dadush and Osakwe (2015).
[41] WTO Director-General's Annual Reports on Accessions: official WTO documents WT/ACC/14; WT/ACC/15; WT/ACC/19; WT/ACC/21; WT/ACC/23; and, WT/ACC/25. These documents are available via https://www.wto.org/english/thewto_e/acc_e/acc_e.htm.

its application by competent, high-quality domestic governance within the parameters of a private sector, firm-driven market economy. Intervention on industrial policy in a rules-based global economy, as with any other area of policy, must be pro-competitive, open and non-discriminatory, reformist, integrationist and acceptant of state-of-the-art technology and global best practices. Enhancing and sustaining high-quality governance will establish the capacity to effectively implement policy such as industrial policy, or for that matter any other policy. Furthermore, the sustainability of high quality governance will turn largely on robust institutions that neutralize individual discretionary and arbitrary behaviour and are fire-walled from partisan politics. A range of reforms to these ends will encompass public expenditure rationalization, reform and privatization of STEs, efficiency in the delivery of public goods, civil service reforms, etc.

Many African economies are embarking on domestic reforms. Sustaining these reforms should take account of the lessons drawn. Africa is the current and future growth frontier. Maximizing the opportunities will neither happen on its own nor would it be self-fulfilling. It will eventuate in the light of the substance of growth and development experience and lessons from the past, rotating on determined, focused and clean governments that are in lock-step with contemporary technological developments.

Domestic restructuring of government departments and agencies is an urgent and pressing necessity to ensure efficiency and ensure that different government departments and agencies do not work at cross-purposes. An area of synergetic urgency is the better integration of the portfolio of foreign ministries with the portfolios of government ministries responsible for trade, industry and investments. Changes are required in improving the way governments function in the areas of trade, investment and industrial policies. One way to proceed with this would be to establish an Advisory Council for Foreign Trade, Industry and Investment Policy. This is overdue in many African economies, in the interests of policy coherence.

In the end, policy and operational performance must be subject to performance criteria. What does not work must be immediately retrenched and adjusted for competitiveness and global best practice. Maximizing the opportunities of the African market will entail reducing barriers and restrictions between African countries and increasing specific cooperative engagement between key regional economic engines. Reduction of internal barriers to African trade is moving in the right direction, as recent data shows. The share of intra-African trade has improved from 14.2 per cent in 2009 to 17.7 per cent in 2014. Total merchandise trade in exports also almost doubled from US$ 55.92 billion in 2009 to US$ 98.08 billion in 2014.[42]

The real challenge for African economic policy-makers is to understand the fundamental underpinnings of the global economy: the cyclical patterns and deeper long-run structural factors, operating in the short, medium and long term. Before appointments to governance and managerial responsibilities in African governments, prospective appointees must have a clear intellectual and policy grasp of the operative logic of the competitive functioning of the global economy, the dynamic nature of the interactions between the government and markets, and how to master and ride the complex challenges in economic governance so as to lead an economy to prosperity and place it in the league of dominant economies, globally. Economic policy-makers must be free from dogma, bureaucratic rigidities, domestic partisan rhetoric and naïve, ivory-tower counsel. In the end, economic prosperity, welfare and ascendance to the top league will result from a combination of strategic understanding and planning, constructed on the foundation of science, technology and knowledge, and, thoughtfully 'calling set plays' in a competitive global market economy where all countries, naturally, seek to out-bid, out-flank and out-gun one another, without exception, albeit within a rules-based global economy. Africa has room for neither abstractions nor complacency. If it wants to ascend the ladder to the peaks of the global economy, it must be purposeful, determined and coordinated. The question is whether African economies are up for the challenge.

To conclude, growth is under way in Africa. The potential for sustained, stronger growth must be loosened if not separated from commodity cycles. Conceptually, industrial policy has been detached and modernized from its flawed 1950s and 1960s protectionist fallacies. Modern industrial policy will be central to establishing a manufacturing base. It is a key component for increasing productivity, achieving sustained growth and structural transformation. But industrial policy pursued must be in lock-step with the rapid changes in technology – 'the technological revolution that will fundamentally alter the way we live, work and relate to one another' (Schwab, 2016). Industrial policy should not be focused on past industrial stages. Developments in the real African economy indicate that many operators are operating in the new industrial stage.[43] It is the governments

---

[42] WTO Statistics Database: http://stat.wto.org/Home/WSDBHome.aspx?Language=
[43] Fick (2016)

that are challenged to catch up. There is an abundance of duties for all, and it requires time to turn an economy around and set it on a trajectory for sustained structural transformation. The principal responsibility lies with national governments, but there is a role that multilateral institutions can play in support.

References

Abebe, G. and F. Schaefer (2015), "Review of Industrial Policies in Ethiopia. A Perspective from the Leather and Cut Flower Industries", in: Noman, A. and E.J. Stiglitz (ed.) (2015), *Industrial Policy and Economic Transformation in Africa*, Columbia University Press.

Adeniyi, O. and E. Alike (2015), 'Nigeria: Subsidy Claims By Oil Marketers Rise to N1.7 Trillion in Three Years', in allAfrica, 3 December 2015: http://allafrica.com /stories/201512031055.html

African Center for Economic Transformation (ACET) (2014), *African Transformation Report: Growth with Depth*, Washington, DC: ACET.

Ajayi, J.A., M.A. Adegbite and A.R. Iyanda (2014) 'Sustainable Iron and Steel Production in Nigeria: The Techno-Economic Backbone of National Development', Paris: World Federation of Engineering Organizations (WFEO): http://www.wfeo.org/wp-content/uploads/wecsi2014/B1/B1-1.MAINPAPER-Steel_for_Sustainable_Development-AdeAjayi.pdf

Alänge, S. and S. Jacobsson (1994), 'Evaluation of Industrial Policy: The Case of the Swedish Textile and Clothing Industry', *Small Business Economics* 6(6): 465–475: http://www.jstor.org/stable/40228861

Amsden, A.H. (1989), *Asia's Next Giant: South Korea and Late Industrialization*, New York: Oxford University Press.

Bora, B., P.J. Lloyd and M. Pangestu (2000), 'Industrial Policy and the WTO' Geneva: UNCTAD, Policy Issues in International Trade and Commodities Study Series No. 6: http://unctad.org/en/Docs/itcdtab7_en.pdf

Central Bank of Nigeria (CBN) (2015), 'Inclusion of Some Imported Goods and Services on the List of Items not Valid for Foreign Exchange in the Nigerian Foreign Exchange Markets', 23 June 2015: https://www.cbn.gov.ng/documents/ tedcirculars.asp

Constantinescu, C.-I., A. Dennis, A. Mattoo and M. Ruta (2015), 'What Lies behind the Global Trade Slowdown?', in *Global Economic Prospects* (January 2015), Washington, DC: World Bank: https://www.worldbank.org /content/dam/Worldbank/GEP/GEP2015a/pdfs/GEP15a_web_full.pdf

Dadush, U. (2015a), 'Is Manufacturing Still the Key to Growth?', Rabat: OCP Policy Center, 10 February 2015: http://carnegieendowment.org/2015/02/10/is-manufacturing-still-key-to-growth

Dadush, U. (2015b), 'The Truth about Trade', *Foreign Affairs*, 18 November 2015: http://carnegieeurope.eu/2015/11/18/truth-about-trade/im43

Dadush, U. (2016), 'Industrial Policy: A Guide for the Perplexed', OCP Policy Center, 1 February 2016: http://carnegieendowment.org/2016/02/01/industrial-policy-guide-for-perplexed-pub-62660

Dadush, U. and C. Osakwe (2015), *WTO Accessions and Trade Multilateralism. Case Studies and Lessons from the WTO at Twenty*, Cambridge and Geneva: Cambridge University Press and World Trade Organization.

The Economist (2010), 'Brazilian Agriculture. The Miracle of the Cerrado', 26 August 2010: http://www.economist.com/node/16886442

The Economist (2011), 'The Hopeful Continent. Africa Rising', 3 December 2011: http://www.economist.com/node/21541015

The Economist (2013), 'The World's Fastest Growing Continent: Aspiring Africa', 2 March 2013: http://www.economist.com/news/leaders/21572773-pride-africas-achievements-should-be-coupled-determination-make-even-faster

The Economist (2015a), 'Latin America's Economies. Learning the Lessons of Stagnation', 27 June 2015: http://www.economist.com/news/americas/21656201-memories-galloping-growth-fade-it-time-tough-thinking-about-future-learning

The Economist (2015b), 'Africa's Middle Class. Few and Far Between', 24 October 2015: http://www.economist.com/news/middle-east-and-africa/21676774-africans-are-mainly-rich-or-poor-not-middle-class-should-worry

The Economist (2015c), 'Industrialisation in Africa. More a marathon than a sprint. There is a Long Road Ahead for Africa to Emulate East Asia', 7 November 2015: http://www.economist.com/news/middle-east-and-africa/21677633-there-long-road-ahead-africa-emulate-east-asia-more-marathon

Economist Intelligence Unit (EIU) (2015) 'Entering a Faltering Market', industry briefing, 1 April 2015: http://www.eiu.com/industry/article/1573021341/entering-a-faltering-market/2015-04-01

Egwuatu, C. (2013), 'The State of Nigerian Iron And Steel Industry', Orient Daily, 30 January 2013: http://www.nigerianorientnews.com/the-state-of-nigerian-iron-and-steel-industry/

Emefiele, G. (2015), Opening Remarks, Press Conference on Foreign Exchange Ban for Rice, et al., Abuja, 24 June 2015: http://www.cbn.gov.ng/OUT/SPEECHES/2015/OPENING%20REMARKS%20PRESS%20CONFERENCE%20ON%20FX%20BAN%20FOR%20RICE%20ET%20ALJUNE%202015.PDF

Fackler, M. (2012), 'Declining as a Manufacturer, Japan Weighs Reinvention', *New York Times*, 15 April 2012: http://www.nytimes.com/2012/04/16/world/asia/amid-manufacturing-decline-japan-weighs-a-reinvention.html?_r=0

Fick, M. (2016), 'Smart Africa: Nigerian Groups Target 100% Mobile-First Market', *Financial Times*, 28 January 2016: http://www.ft.com/cms/s/0/0ad2bbe4-c044-11e5-846f-79b0e3d20eaf.html#axzz4F94lGaMy

Fortin, C. (2012), 'The World Bank and Industrial Policy: Hands Off or Hands On?', Bretton Woods Update Issue 83, 6 December. The Bretton Woods Project.

Hamilton, C. (1983), 'Public Subsidies to Industry: The Case of Sweden and Its Shipbuilding Industry', Washington, DC: World Bank, Staff working paper, No. SWP 566: http://www-wds.worldbank.org/external/default/WDS ContentServer/WDSP/IB/2002/11/28/000178830_98101903415326/Rendered/ PDF/multi0page.pdf

Hoff, K. and J. E. Stiglitz (2001), 'Modern Economic Theory and Development', in G.M. Meier and J.E. Stiglitz (eds), *Frontiers of Development Economics*, New York: Oxford University Press: 389–459.

Hosono, A. (2015), 'Industrial Strategy and Economic Transformation: Lessons from Five Outstanding Cases', in Noman, A. and J. E. Stiglitz (eds), *Industrial Policy and Economic Transformation in Africa*, Columbia: Columbia University Press.

Humphrey, J. and H. Schmitz (2000), 'Governance and Upgrading: Linking Industrial Cluster and Global Value Chain Research', Brighton: Institute of Development Studies, Working Paper 120.

Kaul, I., I. Grunberg, M.A. Stern (1999), *Global Public Goods. International Cooperation in the 21st Century*, New York, Oxford, Oxford University Press.

Kerry, J. (2016), 'Remarks at the World Economic Forum', 22 January 2016: http:// www.state.gov/secretary/remarks/2016/01/251663.htm

Krugman, P. R. (ed.) (1986), 'New Thinking about Trade Policy', in *Strategic Trade Policy and the New International Economics*, Massachussetts: The MIT Press.

Kuwonu, F. (2015), 'Using Trade to Boost Africa's Industrialization' in Africa Renewal, August 2015: http://www.un.org/africarenewal/magazine/august-2015/using-trade-boost-africa%E2%80%99s-industrialization

Lamy, P. (2007), 'Tariff Talks Crucial to Industrialization Strategies of Developing Countries'; Address to the 12th Session of the UNIDO General Council, Vienna: https://www.wto.org/english/news_e/sppl_e/sppl82_e.htm

Lewis, W.A. (1963), *The Theory of Economic Growth*, London: Allen & Unwin.

Lin, J.Y., F. Cai and Z. Li (2003), *The China Miracle: Development Strategy and Economic Reform*, Columbia: Columbia University Press: http://cup.columbia .edu/book/the-china-miracle/9789622019850

List, F., G.-A. Matile, H. Richelot and S. Colwell (1856), *National System of Political Economy*, Philadelphia: J.B. Lippincott and Co.

Low, P. and J. Tijaja (2014), 'Effective Industrial Policies and Global Value Chains', in *A World Trade Organization for the 21st Century. The Asian Perspective*, Edward Elgar Publishing Limited.

Luce, E. (2012), 'America Reassembles Industrial Policy', *Financial Times*: http://www .ft.com/cms/s/0/6cbeb150-7da4-11e1-bfa5-00144feab49a.html#axzz3t3kYXUTW

Noman, A. and E.J. Stiglitz (eds) (2015), *Industrial Policy and Economic Transformation in Africa*, Columbia: Columbia University Press.

Obikwelu, D.O.N. and C.O. Nebo (2012), 'A Critical Look at the Nigerian Steel Industry – A Dark Page on the History of Nigeria and the Metallurgical Profession', presentation at the Plenary of the 28th Annual Conference and Annual General Meeting of the Nigerian Metallurgical Society, (NMS): http://www.nigerianmetsociety.org/wp-content/uploads/2015/02/Crtical-look-at-the-Nigerian-Steel-Industry-BY-D.-O.N.-Obikwelu-and-C.O.-Nebo.pdf

Okonjo-Iweala, N. (2012), *Reforming the Unreformable. Lessons from Nigeria*, Cambridge, MA: The MIT Press.

Osakwe, C. (2011) 'Developing Countries and GATT/WTO Rules: Dynamic Transformations in Trade Policy Behaviour and Performance', *Minnesota Journal of International Law* 20(2): 365–436.

Osborne, G. (2012), Speech by the Chancellor of the Exchequer, Rt. Honourable George Osborne MP, to the Royal Society, 9 November 2012: https://www.gov.uk/government/speeches/speech-by-the-chancellor-of-the-exchequer-rt-hon-george-osborne-mp-to-the-royal-society

Pisano, G. and W. Shih (2009), 'Restoring American Competitiveness', *Harvard Business Review* 87: 7–8.

Pisano, G. and W. Shih (2012), *Producing Prosperity: Why America Needs a Manufacturing Renaissance*, Cambridge: Harvard Business Review Press.

Rodrik, D. (2004), 'Industrial Policy for the Twenty-First Century', paper prepared for UNIDO: https://www.sss.ias.edu/files/pdfs/Rodrik/Research/industrial-policy-twenty-first-century.pdf

Rodrick, D. (2010), 'The Return of Industrial Policy', Project Syndicate: http://www.project-syndicate.org/commentary/the-return-of-industrial-policy?barrier=true

Rowden, R. (2015), 'Africa's Boom Is Over', *Foreign Policy*, 31 December 2015: http://foreignpolicy.com/2015/12/31/africas-boom-is-over/?utm_content=buffer49f4c&utm_medium=social&utm_source=linkedin.com&utm_campaign=buffer

Samuelson, P.A. (1955) 'Diagrammatic Exposition of a Theory of Public Expenditure', *The Review of Economics and Statistics*, 37(4): 350–356: http://www.jstor.org/stable/1925849

Sanusi, M.S.L. (2010), 'Industrial Policy in Africa: What Needs to Be Done', 1 December 2010: http://www.makingitmagazine.net/?p=2443

Schwab, K. (2016), 'The Fourth Industrial Revolution: What It Means, How to Respond', Geneva: World Economic Forum, 14 January 2016: https://www.weforum.org/agenda/2016/01/the-fourth-industrial-revolution-what-it-means-and-how-to-respond/

Shimada, G., (2015), 'The Economic Implications of a Comprehensive Approach to Learning on Industrial Policy: The Case of Ethiopia', in Noman, A. and J.E. Stiglitz (eds), *Industrial Policy and Economic Transformation in Africa*, Columbia: Columbia University Press.

Sperling, G. (2012), 'Remarks at the Conference on the Renaissance of American Manufacturing', 27 March 2012: https://www.manufacturing.gov/remarks-by-gene -sperling-before-the-conference-on-the-renaissance-of-american-manufacturing/

Sperling, G. (2013), 'The Case for a Manufacturing Renaissance', Washington, DC: The Brookings Institution, 25 July 2013: http://www.brookings.edu/~/media/ events/2013/7/25-manufacturing/the-case-for-a-manufacturing-renaissancege ne-sperling7252013finalp.pdf

Stiglitz, J.E. (1996), 'Some Lessons from the East Asian Miracle', *World Bank Research Observer*, 11(2):151–157.

Stiglitz, J.E., J. L. Yifu and E. Patel (eds) (2013), *The Industrial Policy Revolution II: Africa in the Twenty-First Century*, Basingstoke: Palgrave Macmillan, International Economic Association Series.

te Velde, D.W. (2016), 'Nigeria Needs a Modern Manufacturing Base', *Financial Times*, 2 February 2016: http://www.ft.com/cms/s/0/fc523b10-c9c8-11e5-a8ef-ea66e967dd44.html#axzz4F94lGaMy

United Nations Economic Commission for Africa (UNECA) (2015), *Economic Report on Africa: Industrializing through Trade*, Addis Ababa: UNECA.

Wade, R. (2012), 'Return of Industrial Policy', *International Review of Applied Economics*, 26(2), 223–239.

World Bank (1991), *World Development Report (1991): The Challenge of Development*, Washington, DC: The World Bank: http://elibrary.worldbank .org/doi/pdf/10.1596/978-0-1952-0868-9

World Bank (1993), *The East Asian Miracle: A World Bank Policy Research Report*, Washington, DC: The World Bank; http://www-wds.worldbank.org/external/ default/WDSContentServer/WDSP/IB/2012/10/15/000386194_20121015021309/ Rendered/PDF/123510v20PUB0r00Box371943B00PUBLIC0.pdf

16

WTO Accession Reforms and Competitiveness – Lessons for Africa

ALEXEI P. KIREYEV

Abstract

This chapter evaluates the impact on competitiveness of reforms undertaken by recently acceded countries and draws lessons for African countries pursuing the goal of becoming emerging economies. By comparing reform outcomes before and after accessions relative to control groups using the difference-in-difference evaluation method, the chapter concludes that the recently acceded members improved their international competitiveness, although the overall impact was relatively small and differed substantially across economies, economic sectors and time. African economies aspiring to become emerging economies could build on the experience of recently acceded countries by designing long-term reform agendas similar to the accession reform packages, locking them into a credible policy framework through a series of domestic and international agreements, frontloading reforms to gain credibility and persisting in their implementation, balancing short-term costs with long-term benefits and learning from Article XII peers who have gained substantial experience in managing complex reforms.

1 Policy Setting

The membership of the World Trade Organization (WTO) consists of original General Agreement on Tariffs and Trade (GATT) members and new members. The group of original members includes 128 GATT contracting parties, which upon signing in 1994 the Agreement Establishing the WTO (the 'WTO Agreement') became 'original' WTO members. Since then, thirty-four new members have joined the WTO as

A preliminary version of this chapter was presented at the Fourth China Round Table, Nairobi, Kenya, on 13–14 December 2015. The author is grateful to C. Henn and A. Mansoor for their useful comments.

a result of negotiations under Article XII of the WTO Agreement. The latter group – known as Article XII members, new or recently acceded countries – joined the WTO through negotiations with original members on terms and conditions worked out during these negotiations. Therefore, unlike the original members, Article XII members have undertaken reforms to adapt their trading systems to WTO requirements as a precondition for the WTO membership.

The results of accession have been far-reaching and generally positive. They have contributed to greater precision, clarification and strengthening in the WTO rules-based system. On market access, the results from accession negotiations, as codified in goods and services schedules, have improved commercial opportunities for all members, hence contributing to growth and job creation. To illustrate, it is significant that the rules-based multilateral trading system has expanded to cover approximately 98 per cent of world trade in 2014, from 91 per cent in 1995, because of the enlargement of the WTO (WTO, 2015a). The WTO Accession Protocols have become integral parts of the WTO Agreement and are enforceable under the WTO Dispute Settlement Understanding. This makes them an integral part of multilateral trade rule-making and vehicles for a major extension of the multilateral trade discipline at the core of the global trading system (Dadush and Osakwe, 2015).

The goal of this chapter is to assess the impact of WTO accessions through domestic reforms and competitiveness, and to draw lessons for African countries. The chapter examines the evidence of a relationship between WTO accession reforms, the macroeconomic environment and policies, and their ultimate impact on competitiveness, the measure of an economy's advantage or disadvantage in selling its products in international markets. Competitiveness is defined as factors that determine the productivity of a country relative to other countries. A range of competitiveness indicators – price-based and (survey) non-price based – are considered to evaluate empirically the impact of accession-related reforms on competitiveness of recently acceded countries and draw lessons for Africa.

In the academic literature, the impact of WTO accessions has been studied in the broader context of the cost and benefits of WTO membership.[1] There are no conclusive results on the impact of WTO membership on trade volumes. Subramanian and Wei (2007) claim that there is robust evidence that the WTO has had a powerful, positive, but

---

[1] For a review of recent academic literature on accessions, see WTO (2015b).

uneven impact on trade, and that WTO membership has been associated with a large increase in imports mainly for industrial countries and developing countries that joined the WTO after the Uruguay Round, but not for other developing countries. The impact across sectors has been asymmetric. However, the impact on growth from WTO membership has been found to be generally positive. Tang and Wei (2009), focusing on developing countries, found that accessions to the WTO tend to raise the income of acceded countries, as higher growth and investment generally last for about five years after accession. This conclusion was valid only for those acceded countries that had undertaken substantial reforms. Li and Wu (2004) found that only high-income economies experienced significantly faster growth after accession. This conclusion implies that openness by itself is not sufficient to promote growth and needs to be combined with proper economic institutions. The reasons for the positive impact on growth from WTO accessions are not entirely clear. It can be explained by the long-lasting nature of accession commitments, which are legally binding as long as the country remains a WTO member.

2   Accession Topology

From the inception of the General Agreement on Tariffs and Trade (GATT), new members have joined the institution through the processes of succession and accession. Many countries that gained independence succeeded to GATT status under special provisions of GATT Article XXVI:5(c), which allowed former colonies of GATT contracting parties to acquire GATT membership upon achieving independence. About a half of original GATT contracting parties joined GATT through succession, including countries in Africa, the Caribbean, and parts of Asia. Succession involved a much less careful scrutiny of the trade regimes of succeeding countries for their conformity with GATT rules. This is why members, including in Africa, that joined the GATT through the succession process have lighter obligations than members that acceded to the GATT/WTO, in particular on market access, as they did not have to go through the stringent reform required by the WTO accession procedure.

In the WTO, accessions are governed by Article XII of the WTO Agreement, and successions have no equivalent. The WTO Agreement states that 'any State or separate customs territory possessing full autonomy in the conduct of its external commercial relations and of the other matters provided for in this Agreement and the Multilateral Trade Agreements may accede to this Agreement, *on terms to be agreed between it and the WTO'*. The italicized condition leads to negotiations between the acceding government and incumbent members and results in a package of reforms the acceding government needs to implement as a precondition for joining the WTO.

By end-2015, thirty-four members had joined the WTO under Article XII, usually after a prolonged negotiation period. The average duration of accession negotiations for Article XII members has been ten years, and they have already spent on average eleven years as WTO members (Figure 16.1). Obviously, the relative length of accession negotiation and the membership periods differ by member, with some of them spending substantially more or less than the average either in the status of an acceding country or as WTO members.

Several shorter periods can be singled out in the accession timeline. The first covers the period before 1995. Only after 1995, the more stringent procedures of WTO accessions through negotiations under Article XII entered into force. The second period is 1995–2004, the first ten years of the WTO. During this period twenty new members joined the WTO. By now, they have accumulated substantial reform experience and can be considered the reference sample for intra-temporal performance comparisons. The third period is 2005–14, the latest ten years of the WTO with full annual data available. During this period, thirteen new members joined the WTO. Finally, the years after 2013 can be viewed as a separate period, during which three countries joined the WTO, but the duration of their member-ships is too short for and does not allow for a meaningful assessment of the impact of the Article XII reform package on their competitive-ness. Therefore, although thirty-four countries have joined the WTO under Article XII, the sample for the evaluation of the impact of WTO accession on competitiveness includes only thirty-one countries, excluding Afghanistan, Seychelles, and Yemen, Kazakhstan and Liberia where the membership period has not been sufficiently long for analysis.

Article XII members represent a heterogeneous group. Based on the United Nations (UN) classification used in the WTO, at end-2015, seven Article XII members were designated as least-developed countries (LDCs) and twenty-seven as non-LDCs (Table 16.1). Cabo Verde, Cambodia, Lao PDR, Nepal, Samoa, Vanuatu and Yemen are or were LDC members. Cabo Verde and Samoa graduated from their LDC status

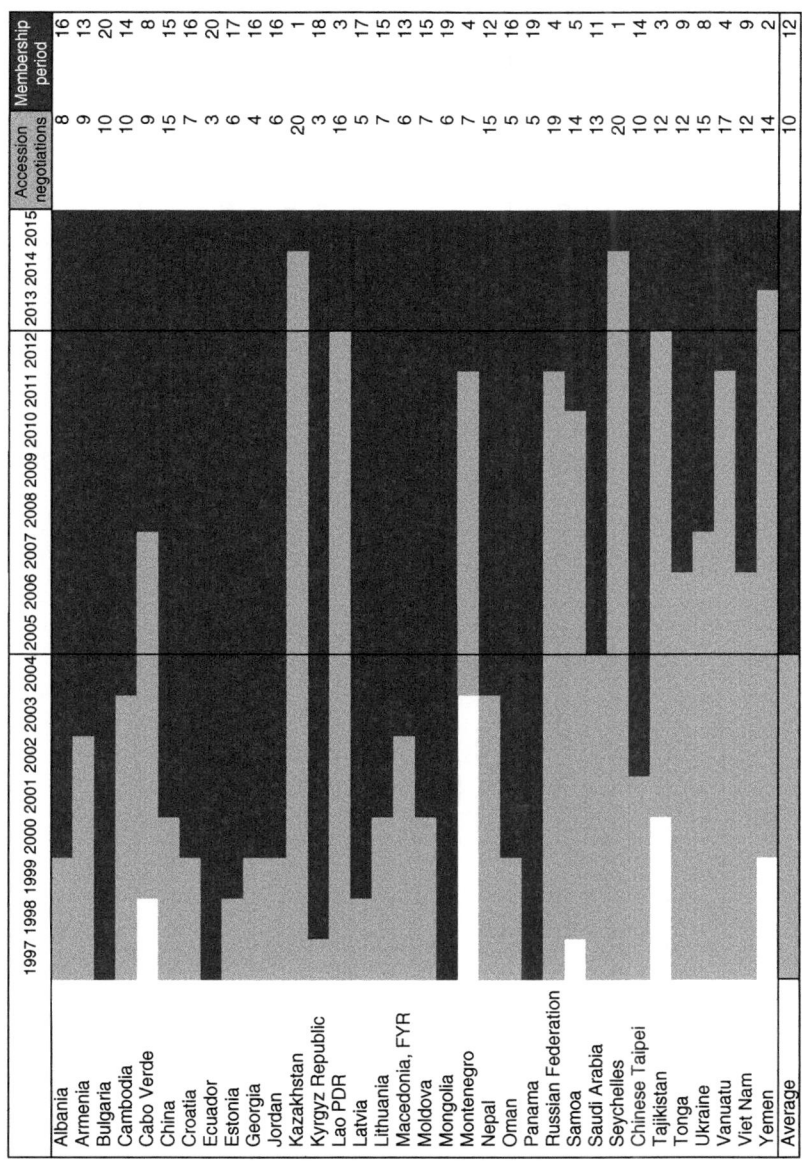

Figure 16.1 WTO Article XII members (Duration of accession negotiations and membership in years)

Source: WTO Accession Gateway, www.wto.org.

Table 16.1 *Article XII membership topology*

LDCs		Non-LDCs		
Low-income (less than US$ 1,045)	Low middle-income (US$ 1,046 – US$ 4,125)	Low middle-income (US$ 1,046 – US$ 4,125)	Upper middle-income (US$ 4,126 – $12,735)	High-income (above US$ 12,736)
Cambodia	Cabo Verde	Armenia	Albania	Croatia
Nepal	Lao PDR	Georgia	Bulgaria	Estonia
	Samoa	Kyrgyz Republic	China	Latvia
	Vanuatu	Moldova	Ecuador	Lithuania
	Yemen	Tajikistan	Jordan	Oman
		Ukraine	Kazakhstan	Russian Federation
		Viet Nam	Macedonia, FYR	Saudi Arabia
			Mongolia	Seychelles
			Montenegro	Chinese Taipei
			Panama	
			Tonga	

Source: World Development Indicators, World Bank, http://data.worldbank.org.

after their accession to the WTO but were part of the LDC group at the time of their accession and therefore are treated as LDCs for the purposes of this chapter.

By level of income, Article XII members can be divided into several groups. Based on the World Bank Atlas classification, at end-2015, three Article XII members were classified as low-income countries (LICs) with a gross domestic income (GNI) per capita of less than US$ 1,045; thirteen as lower-middle-income countries (LMCs) with a GNI per capita of US$ 1,046 – US$ 4,125; eleven as upper-middle-income countries (UMCs) with a GNI per capita of US$ 4,126 – US$ 12,735; and nine as high-income countries (HICs) with a GNI per capita of above US$ 12,736. There are overlaps between the UN designation and the World Bank classification. Article XII member LDCs include both LICs and LMCs. The lower-middle-income group includes both LDCs and non-LDCs. The upper-middle-income and high-income groups, with the exception of Angola, include no LDCs.

3   Stylized Facts

New members compare favourably to the original members on some macroeconomic indicators but less so on others. From 1995 to 2014, the average GDP growth rate of new Article XII members was about one percentage point higher than that of original members (Table 16.2).

Table 16.2 *WTO Article XII members: stylized facts (1995–2014 averages)*

	Unit	New members	Original members
Real GDP growth	Per cent	4.6	3.6
Inflation	Per cent	12.8	9.7
Growth of merchandise trade	Per cent	11.9	7.0
Growth of trade in services	Per cent	11.3	7.7
Fiscal deficit	Per cent of GDP	−2.2	−1.8
Current account	Per cent of GDP	−4.2	−2.2
Foreign direct investment	Per cent of GDP	4.9	5.0
Openness	Per cent of GDP	93.8	86.4
Export market penetration	Index	4.6	8.1
Export diversification	Index	3.3	3.3

Sources: World Economic Oulook, IMF; WTO Statistics Database.

During the same period, growth rates of merchandise trade and trade in services in new members were 11.9 per cent and 11.3 per cent, respectively, substantially higher than that of original members at 7.0 per cent and 7.7 per cent. As a consequence, the share of world trade of new members increased from 7.8 per cent in 1995 to 17.5 per cent in 2014 (WTO, 2015a). New members seem to have been slightly more open to trade than original members. In terms of foreign direct investment (FDI) attraction and export diversification, new members were broadly in line with original members, while clearly lagging behind on export market penetration and openness. The fiscal deficits and the current account balances have remained in a sustainable range for both new and original members. Somewhat higher current account and fiscal deficits of new members may be explained mainly by the more intensive use of world savings to finance structural reforms by low- and middle-income countries, which is what constitutes most Article XII members. Finally, inflation was on average higher in new members than in original members.

Price competitiveness is traditionally measured by the evolution of the real effective exchange rate (REER). The REER is a trade-weighted average of bilateral exchange rates adjusted for the difference in the aggregate price levels between the home country and its trading partners. An appreciation of the REER makes national exports more expensive relative to those of foreign competitors and imports cheaper relative to domestic production and may signal a loss of competitiveness of national producers. With the depreciation of the REER, domestic tradable products become more competitive internationally. Obviously, the evolution of the REER reflects a gamut of domestic and international factors, with the changes in a country's trade regime as a result of its accession to the WTO being only one.

On the indicators of price competitiveness, the overall performance of Article XII members has been mixed. Only a handful of members have improved their price competitiveness after their accession to the WTO (Figure 16.2). In the case of LDCs (group 1a), the improvement was not long-lived because after some depreciation, the level of the REER has broadly approached the level of the year of accession. However, several non-LDC members improved and largely preserved their price competitiveness (group 1b). In most LDC and non-LDC Article XII members, price competitiveness has not changed significantly since accession to the WTO (groups 2a and 2b). In all cases, there has been some appreciation of the REER, but it was contained below 10 per cent, suggesting that it cannot be a major source of pressure on individual countries'

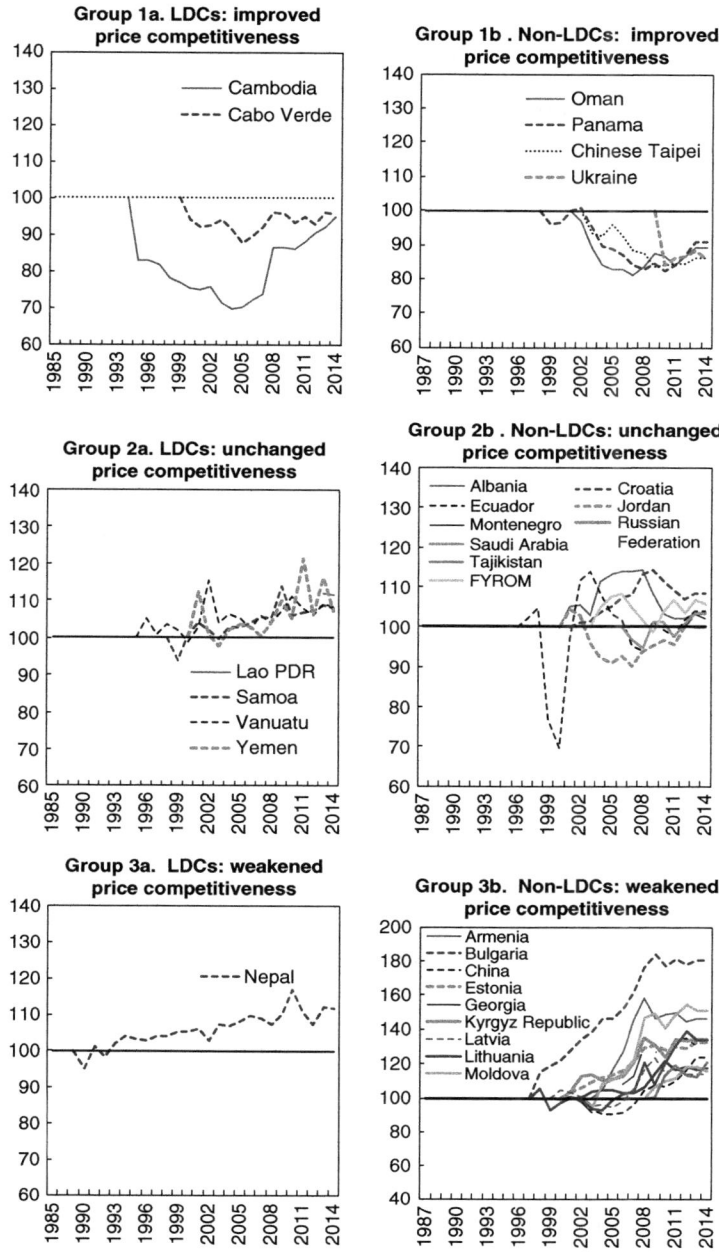

Figure 16.2   Article XII members: evolution of price competitiveness (real effective exchange rate, year of accession = 100)
Source: Information Notice System, IMF.

competitiveness. Finally, in one case of an LDC and a substantial number of cases of non-LDCs, new WTO members experienced a substantial loss in price competitiveness since their accession to the WTO (groups 3a and 3b). Most likely, this REER appreciation in most Article XII members has been driven by macroeconomic circumstances unrelated to their WTO accessions.

Non-price competitiveness reflects all factors other than relative prices that may influence the position of a country in the international market. The indicators of non-price competitiveness are usually aggregated into indices designed to capture simultaneously institutional, political, economic, and other factors that impact on the competitiveness of an economy. The Global Competitiveness Index by the World Economic Forum and the Doing Business Indicators by the World Bank are the two most comprehensive and widely used indices. The Global Competitiveness Index, for example, covers twelve areas and ranks most WTO members starting from 2006. However, for some members it is available only starting from a later date or not available at all. Also, the changes in country coverage in the calculations of non-price competitiveness indices limit the intra-year comparability of rankings.

Nevertheless, the Global Competitiveness Index portrays a broadly similar mixed picture on the evolution of non-price competitiveness of Article XII members. If the change in the ranking does not exceed five points in either direction over the past ten years or from the date of the first observation, the non-price competitiveness of a country may be considered broadly unchanged. This is largely the case on average for Article XII LDCs, for which data are available (Figure 16.3a) and for a group of non-LDCs (Figure 16.3b), although there have been some marginal improvements in some of them. At the same time, a large group of non-LDCs improved their non-price competitiveness on average by 15 points (Figure 16.3c), while the non-price competitiveness weakened in a comparably substantial group of other non-LDCs by roughly the same order of magnitude (Figure 16.3d).

4   Methodology

To estimate the impact of accessions through negotiations on competitiveness, both parametric and non-parametric methods for conducting programme evaluation are possible (Todd and Wolpin, 2006, 2008). The results obtained by applying both methods can be contrasted with their predictive content and with the conclusions drawn from

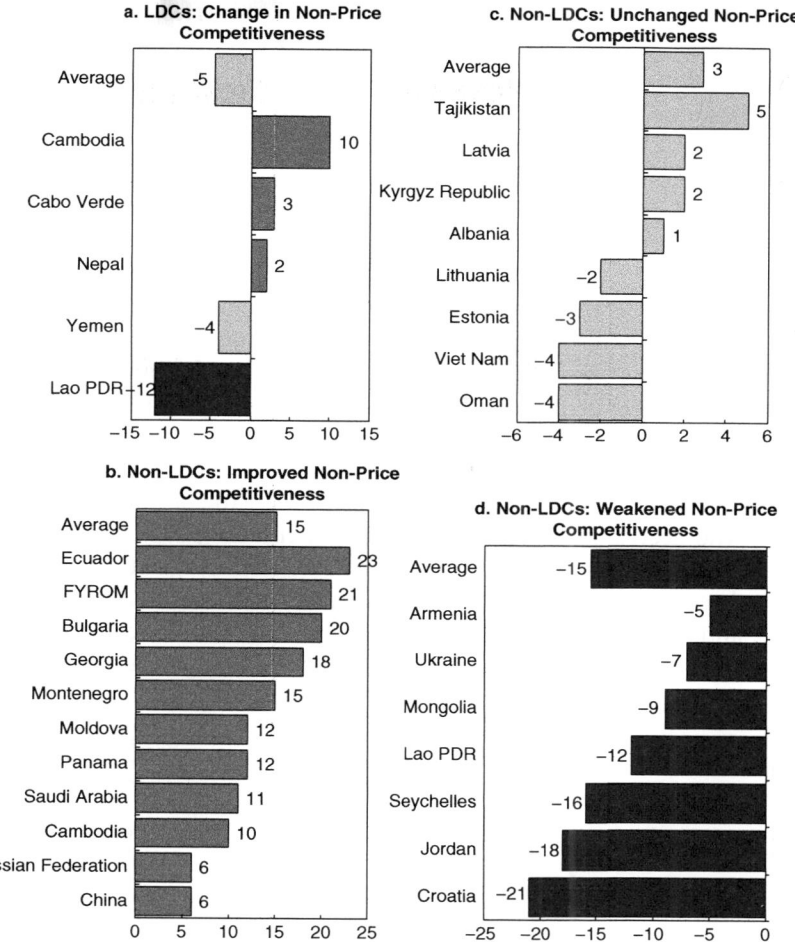

Figure 16.3 Article XII members: evolution of non-price competitiveness (change in ranking, 2006–15)

Source: Global Competitiveness Index, World Economic Forum.

counterfactual experiments (Attanasio, Meghir and Santiago, 2012). However, both approaches have limits for drawing policy conclusions (Imbens and Wooldridge, 2009). Since a social experiment is not possible in the context of the subject of this chapter, it applies the difference-in-difference (DID) method. This is a quasi-experimental approach that splits the countries into those that joined the WTO during the period under study and similar countries that have been WTO members during this period, which allows one to estimate the direction that the impact of accession-related reforms has had on their macroeconomic outcomes (Albouy, 2011). The DID is applied to estimate the effect of reforms driven by accession commitments on macroeconomic and competitiveness outcomes over time between Article XII members (treatment group) and original members (comparator group) (see Lechner (2011) for details).

Graphically, the DID method can be presented as follows. The evolution of the variable of interest Y is a function of time t. There are two groups of WTO members called here *New* (Article XII members, treatment group) and *Old* (original WTO members, comparator group) (Figure 16.4). There are also two time periods – *Before* the accession of a *New* member to the WTO and *After* its accession. Both groups are measured as an average of the variable of interest Y (point t_0) for the period immediately before the accession and for the period immediately after the accession of each Article XII member (point t_1). At t_0 the difference between *Old* and *New* represents an average constant difference because the two groups are different. At t_1 the difference between Old and New also includes the average difference between the *Before* and *After* accessions. Therefore, by subtracting the unobserved

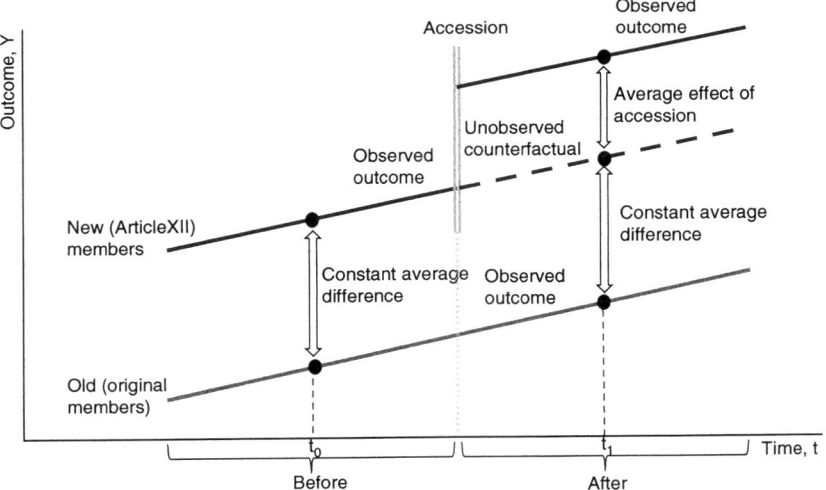

Figure 16.4 Difference-in-difference
Source: Author's presentation.

counterfactual level of the variable of interest Y for the *New* group from its observed outcome, the average impact of accession can be estimated. The counterfactual can be approximated by the DID underlying assumption that the parallel trend between the *Old* and the *New* groups exists *Before* and continues *After* accession.

More formally, the DID estimator of the impact of WTO accessions can be written in two equivalent ways. In a simple algebraic way, the DID estimator($\hat{\delta}$) can be defined as the difference in an average outcome ($\overline{Y}$) in the *New* group *After* accession ($\overline{Y}^{New}_{After}$) and *Before* accession ($\overline{Y}^{New}_{Before}$) minus the difference in the average outcome in the *Old* group *After* accession ($\overline{Y}^{Old}_{After}$) and *Before* the accession ($\overline{Y}^{Old}_{Before}$) of the member in the *New* group. Therefore,

$$\hat{\delta} = (\overline{Y}^{New}_{After} - \overline{Y}^{New}_{Before}) - (\overline{Y}^{Old}_{After} - \overline{Y}^{Old}_{Before})$$

Equally, the same estimator for each country i can be calculated from the following regression:

$$Y_i = \alpha + \beta D_i + \gamma T_i + \delta(D_i T_i) + \varepsilon_i$$

where Y_i is the outcome of interest for each country i. $D_i = 0, 1$ is a dummy variable (an artificial variable that takes the value 0 or 1 to indicate the absence or presence of an effect), which takes the value of 0 if the member is *Old* (original member) and 1 if it is *New* (Article XII member). $T_i = 0, 1$ is a common time trend dummy for the *Old* and *New* groups, which takes the value of 0 for the period *Before* accession and the value of 1 for the period *After* accession. The error term ε_i captures all determinates omitted by the model. Regressions are run for each economy separately relative to the average for the comparator group. The equations allow for estimation of four unknown parameters: α, the constant term; β, the average constant difference between the *Old* and the *New* groups; γ, the time trend common to the *Old* and *New* groups; and δ, the cross dummy variable (the dummy variable multiplied by the observed variable) that shows the impact of the *New* group in the *After* period, i.e. the effect of accession. This is the parameter of interest.

The DID method leads to unbiased results as long its underlying assumptions hold. The DID estimation requires that the Article XII member and the comparator group have parallel trends in outcome, i.e. the difference between the Article XII member and the comparator group is constant over time $cov(\varepsilon_i, D_i, T_i) = 0$. This is the most important assumption, and it has been verified by checking statistical significance of β, the average constant difference between the *Old* and the *New* groups. Also, the decision to become a WTO member should not be related to the outcome in the *Before* period in the *New* group; the composition of the *Old* and *New* groups should be stable; and there should no spillover effects between the two groups. With the exception of a few members, these assumptions seem to hold reasonably well.

The DID method can provide important insights into the outcome of accessions. It allows estimation of the causal effect using observational data if assumptions are met. Also, it allows establishment of the direction of causality from accessions. In addition, it removes biases in the *After* period comparisons between the *New* and *Old* groups that could be the result of permanent differences between them. Also, it removes the biases from comparisons over time in the *New* group that could be the result of trends. The comparison between the *New* and the *Old* groups focuses on change rather than absolute levels, and therefore these groups can initially be at different levels. Finally, the DID approach allows for an intuitive interpretation because it accounts for changes owing to factors other than accessions.

The DID approach has substantial limitations, and the conclusions should be treated with caution. The data requirements are substantial: for each variable of interest, observations for the period before the member acceded to the WTO and the period after the accession are needed. The same data for the whole comparator group are also required. The DID method cannot be used if the decision to join the WTO was driven by the outcome in the *Before* accession period. Also, if the parallel trend assumption does not hold, the estimate will be biased. The length of both *Before* accession and *After* accession periods should be substantial to allow for a meaningful evaluation of changes.

Finally, the assumption is that the implementation of accession commitments starts on the year of accession. This may or may not be the case. Some *New* members started the implementation of certain commitments before the accession as *Old* members insisted on a 'down payment' as a precondition for accession. At the same time, some other *New* members have delayed the implementation of their WTO accession commitments for a variety domestic reasons. Finally, some *New* members joined the WTO early in the year and thus have almost a whole year to implement accession reforms, whereas others joined during the later months of the year, leaving them little time for reform implementation during that year. However, because no monthly data are available for most variables used in this study, and there is no quantifiable information on the 'down payments' made by some *New* members, accession reforms are uniformly assumed to have been started on the year of accession for all Article XII members.

5   Data

Competitiveness is an outcome of the environment and policies. Therefore, the dataset of variables is designed to capture the macroeconomic conditions, policy efforts, and their impact on competitiveness (Figure 16.5). Political and macroeconomic stability represent important preconditions for successful economic reforms and increased competitiveness. The stable macroeconomic environment usually leads to high and sustainable *growth* and low and manageable *inflation.* Preserving macroeconomic stability requires good fiscal, monetary, and structural policies. The outcome of these policies manifests itself in low and sustainable *fiscal deficits* that do not lead to an excessive public debt accumulation and help maintain employment and social balance. Solid fiscal policies, in turn, help to manage the *current account balance* and strengthen the overall balance-of-payments position of the country, so that it does not give rise to disruptive exchange rate movements.

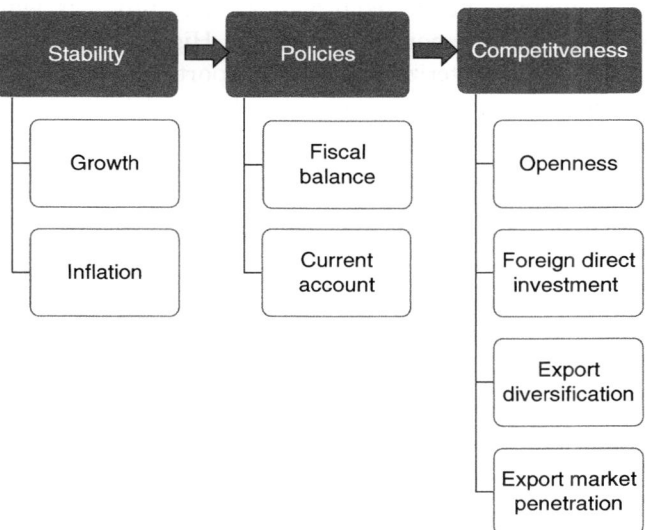

Figure 16.5   Test variables flow chart
Source: Author's presentation.

The stable macroeconomic environment and good policies are the pre-conditions for improved competitiveness. This environment is more conducive to deep structural reforms, which enhance further long-term growth and help preserve the low inflation environment.

The evolution of competitiveness in Article XII members is measured indirectly by a number of indicators. *Economic openness* – calculated here as a ratio of trade to GDP – can be considered an indicator of competitiveness, as no country has developed successfully in modern times without harnessing openness for its development. Trade openness increases the size of the market available to domestic firms, exposes them to international competition, expertise and technology, which drive up productivity and ultimately competitiveness. *FDI* – measured as an annual flow in per cent of GDP – is critical for innovations and improved competitiveness, in particular in developing countries. At the same time, competitiveness may be hindered by restrictive and discriminatory rules on FDI, which limit foreign ownership. *Export diversification* is usually found to be driven by both foreign and domestic investment and represents yet another indicator of competitiveness. Diversification is defined as a shift to a more varied production structure, involving the introduction of new products or the expansion of pre-existing products, including higher-quality products.[2] It is measured by the ratio of the total number of exported products to new products, with lower values signalling higher export diversification. Highly competitive economies are usually characterized by high export diversification. Finally, higher *export market penetration* is a desirable outcome of increased competitiveness. It is measured as the number of countries to which the given country exports a particular product, divided by the number of countries that import the product.

The data are annual for 1985–2015. Their time span covers the period from the first application for accession for countries that acceded under Article XII rules to the most recent accessions. The sources of the data and their detailed descriptions are included in Annex 16.1. The data cover all thirty-four Article XII members; Afghanistan, Kazakhstan, Seychelles, Liberia and Yemen are excluded from the analysis as their

---

[2] The dataset developed by Fund staff includes indices of diversification across products and trading partners. Product diversification indices are further disaggregated into the extensive margin and intensive margin. The main data source is an updated version of the UN–NBER dataset, which harmonizes COMTRADE bilateral trade flow data at the 4-digit SITC (Rev. 1) level (for details on calculations see IMF, 2014).

membership period in the WTO is too short and does not allow for a meaningful application of the DID methodology.

Original WTO members of a similar level of development were identified as comparators for each group of Article XII members (Annex 16.2). With the predetermined list of Article XII members (treatment group), a random selection of members for the comparator group was not possible. Therefore, all original WTO members were considered as comparators. Including all original members as comparators allows us to avoid selection biases and yields more robust estimates on the impact of accession on each variable of interest under the DID methodology. They were further divided into low-income, lower-middle-income, higher-middle-income, and high-income members, in line with the new members' classification. A group of original members considered as LDCs under the UN classification was also established.

6   Results

The overall impact of accessions has, so far, been generally positive, although marginal. About two-thirds of Article XII members have not yet felt any impact from accession-related reforms on their competitiveness, as the difference-in-difference (DID) method did not detect any statistically significant differences between the treatment and the control groups. This outcome should have been expected, as earlier empirical evidence suggested that structural reforms translate into better macroeconomic and competitiveness outcome with a substantial lag. This may be driven by the fact that accession-related reforms take substantial implementation time, as they require deep institutional changes. Also, these reforms are designed mainly to improve access for new WTO members to international markets and therefore may translate into better macroeconomic and competitiveness outcomes with time. The remaining third of Article XII members already seem to have experienced the impact of WTO accessions. In most cases, the impact was positive and statistically significant.

At a more granular level, the impact of WTO accessions can be further evaluated across three dimensions – the economic area, member group and time. In the area by member matrix, the first dimension quantifies the impact on each of eight economic areas along all Article XII members, with four of them evaluating the environment needed for competitiveness and the other four different aspects of competitiveness itself. This requires aggregation of the impact along columns of the matrix to capture the impact on the variable of interest for all Article XII members. The results indicate which sectors have benefitted the most and the least from accessions. The second dimension evaluates the impact of accession on each Article XII member across all economic sectors. The results are calculated for each member and aggregated in groups according to members' level of development. They show which members have benefitted the most and the least from accessions. Finally, the third dimension evaluates the impact of accession on Article XII members across time. For that, thirty-one Article XII members included in the sample were divided in two groups – twenty-one members that joined the WTO before the beginning of 2005 and ten members that joined thereafter. The results show whether accession-related reforms have accelerated economic performance and improved competitiveness through time.

The impact of accession-related reforms across economic areas has been uneven. Of all Article XII members experiencing any impact of accession-related reforms, the strongest positive impact was in external competiveness, as almost half of members have improved openness and one-quarter improved their export diversification (Figure 16.6a). Substantial positive results have been achieved by Article XII members relative to original WTO members in controlling inflation, attaining faster economic growth, containing the fiscal deficit and attracting FDI. At the same time, Article XII members have on average lagged behind original members on export market penetration and had higher current account deficits. While the latter should not be viewed as a point of concern, as the current accounts of most Article XII members remain in a sustainable range, the slow progress in export market penetration represents a clear challenge for them, and the underlying reasons require special investigation.

The reforms driven by WTO accession commitments affected groups of Article XII members differently. On average, the impact was substantially higher on non-LDCs than on LDC members (Figure 16.6b). For example, almost nine out of ten non-LDCs have felt positive repercussions of reforms compared to one out of ten in the case of LDCs. High-income Article XII members have managed to obtain the highest benefits of accession-related reforms where almost a third of them have felt their positive impact. The picture was mixed in the group of upper-middle-income and lower-middle-income non-LDCs, where positive and negative effects were almost equal. Among LDCs, low-income LDCs have done substantially better than lower-middle-income members. Overall, the impact by country group suggests that the faster the implementation of accession reforms, the higher the level of development of the Article XII member.

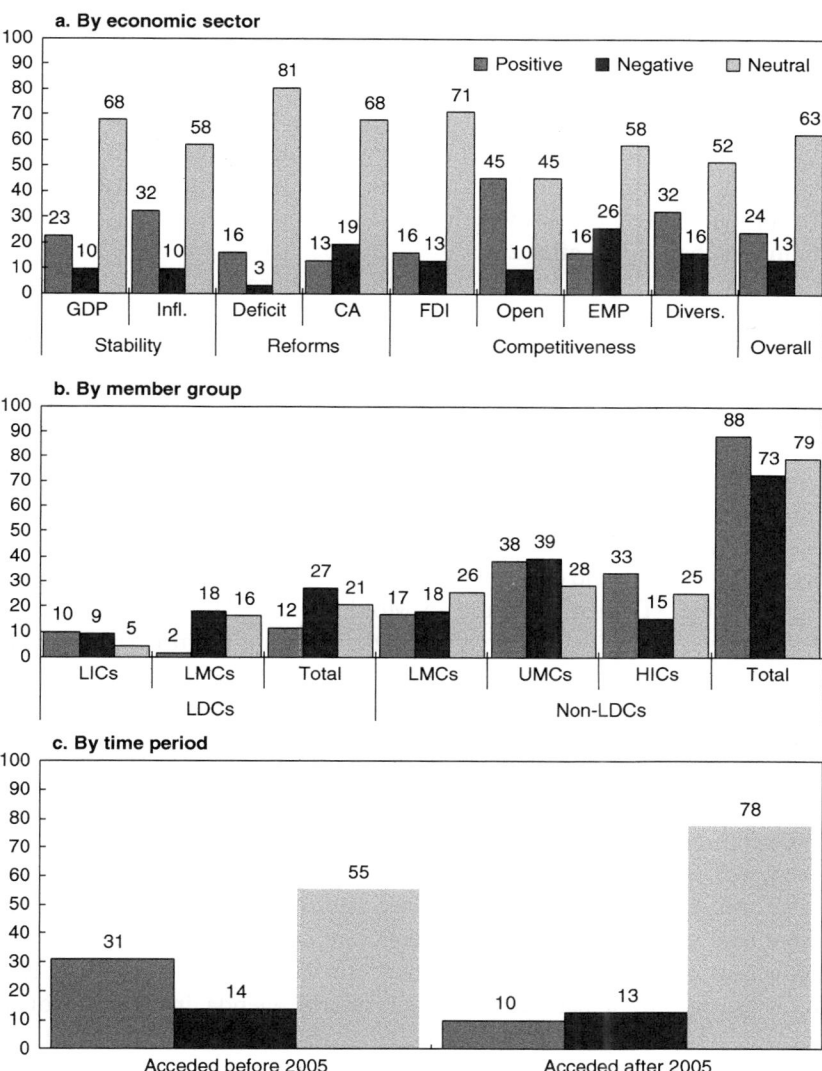

Figure 16.6 Impact of WTO accessions (percentage of Article XII members)
Source: Author's calculations.

The impact of WTO accession reforms through time has been asymmetrical. The twenty-one members that acceded to the WTO before 2005 have benefitted substantially more from reforms than the ten members that joined thereafter (Figure 16.6c). With the somewhat negative impact almost the same between the two periods, the positive impact is more than three times higher for members that joined before 2005. The percentage of members that have not experienced any impact so far is substantially higher in the later than in the earlier period. This finding may suggest that the members that joined between 1995 and 2004 have had more time for reform implementation and can already benefit from their positive results, which would transpire with some lag also for members that joined after 2005.

Finally, the DID method allows for the identification of the economies that have benefitted the most from accession. The economy-by-economy impact calculated as a simple difference between positive and negative instances of the impact of accessions suggests that roughly half of Article XII members are already enjoying strong benefits of accession-related reforms (Figure 16.7a). On average, across all eight indicators and relative to their corresponding comparator groups, five countries – the Kingdom of Saudi Arabia, Panama, Oman, Lithuania and Georgia – have extracted the largest benefits from these reforms on their macroeconomic stability and competitiveness. The impact was not yet felt in the eight Article XII members, and in Moldova and Vanuatu, transitional difficulties seem to have outweighed the benefits (Figure 16.7b). This conclusion needs to be considered as an indicator for those lagging behind of the need to catch up with the more advanced group. Also, it allows identification of possible peer-learning arrangements, whereby members that are more advanced on accession reforms could share their experience with those which are facing implementation difficulties.

Overall, accessions have had a positive, albeit small, impact on competitiveness. The impact on about half of Article XII members has been neutral so far. Most of them are very recent accessions (2012–15), and the impact cannot be evaluated yet. For the remaining Article XII economies, the impact has been positive but relatively small, as it should be, because accession is only a part of a broader reform agenda in any economy. The impact of accessions has been heterogeneous across countries, reform areas, and time, stronger for some and weaker for others. Out of all the Article XII members, low-income LDCs and lower-middle-income non-LDCs have benefitted the most from accessions. Most lower-middle-income LDCs have not yet felt the impact of accessions. The most favourable impact was felt in external competitiveness (openness, export diversification), structural reforms (current accounts, fiscal deficits) and macroeconomic performance (inflation, real growth). Export market penetration and foreign direct investment are the two areas where additional reform efforts are needed.

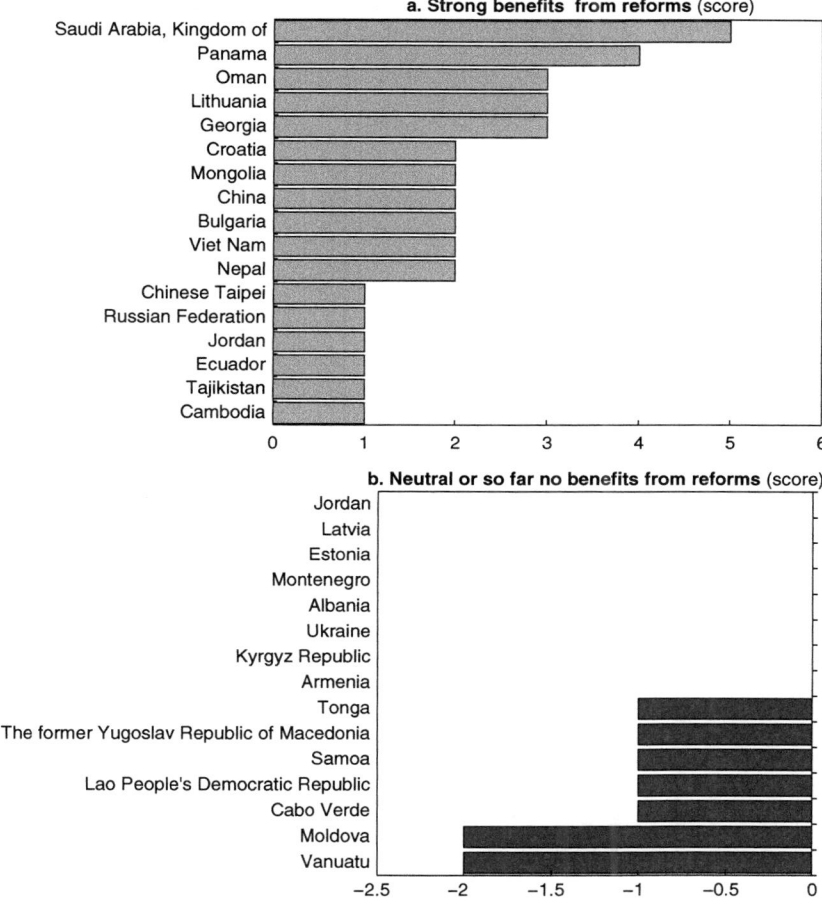

Figure 16.7   Impact of accessions by Article XII member (score)
Source: Author's calculations

7   Lessons for Africa

Africa is facing stiff competition for international markets and needs to make major improvements in its competitiveness. A broad range of indicators point to weak and deteriorating competitiveness in the region, in particular in Sub-Saharan Africa, relative to all other regions of the world (Figure 16.8). Africa is underperforming on virtually all twelve of the pillars of competitiveness included in the World Competitiveness Index, and the situation has not improved in the past decade. Moreover,

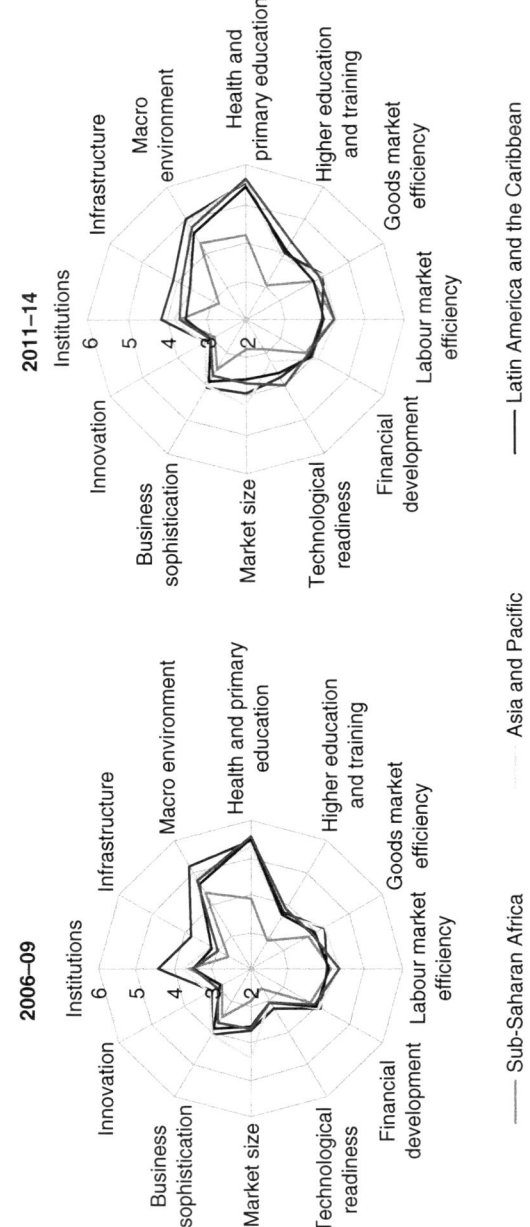

Figure 16.8 Africa's relative competitiveness

Source: IMF (2015), based on World Economic Forum, 2015.

Note: Only emerging markets and developing economies from each region are considered.

a number of price-based indicators suggest that Africa's competitiveness has been declining since the early 2000s (IMF, 2015). Although the loss of competitiveness has been fairly broad-based, the trend is particularly pronounced in commodity exporters.

Africa has a lot to learn from new WTO members undertaking accessions-related reforms. The lessons of Article XII members – both positive and negative – can be an invaluable guide not only for African economies negotiating their entry into the WTO, but also for a broader range of economies in the region aspiring to become emerging economies. Algeria, Comoros, Equatorial Guinea, Ethiopia, Libya, Sao Tomé and Principe, and Sudan are currently negotiating their accession to the WTO. For them, the experience of Article XII members is directly relevant on all levels, from the technicalities of documentation to macroeconomic implications. But for most others, in particular those already considered frontier economies, it is the fast-growing low-income economies that are attracting international investor interest. These economies, such as Kenya and Mozambique, have been deepening their financial markets, and some, such as Ghana, Nigeria, Senegal, Tanzania and Zambia, have been able to tap into international capital markets. The next natural step for them is to become full-fledged emerging economies with deep and liquid financial markets, high growth rates, low inflation, strong institutions and good governance. Reform implementation in Article XII members offers valuable lessons for these African countries. Here are some of them.

- Design a long-term reform agenda to rise to an emerging economy status. The long-term reform agenda of Article XII members may be used by African countries as a guide to emerging economy status. If replicated in African countries, this reform agenda can be viewed as one of the pillars needed to reach emerging economy status, as accession *acquis* already includes many elements critical for such transformation: a long-term vision on domestic reforms, reduction of barriers to trade, openness to competition, application of best international practices, good governance, institution-building and modernization of infrastructure. Political stability, stable macroeconomic environment and good macroeconomic policies are additional and equally important pillars.
- Lock the reform programme into a credible policy framework. The WTO accession mechanism is a package deal that locks countries into a negotiated set of policies for the length of their WTO

membership and makes them accountable to other WTO members. A similar mechanism could be used by African countries. The already existing plans for transition to an emerging status could be credibly locked into domestic and international policy frameworks. Domestically, regular accountability to national parliaments could be built in the reform programme. Significant deviations from the programme should trigger extraordinary parliamentary sessions. Internationally, key components of the reform package also could be locked in the agreements with key development partners, which usually provide policy advice, financing and technical assistance for transition.

- Start early and persist in reform implementation. Some WTO accession negotiations demand that the applicants implement important reforms before accession, in other words, provide a 'down payment', and this could be particularly useful for African countries. It is an important confidence-building measure, which could be used by African countries to gather domestic and international support for their transition to emerging status. To be trustworthy, their reform package needs an initial evidence-based confirmation of a binding commitment. In this sense, the planning of transition- to emerging-economy status should include a sufficient 'down payment' in the form of front-loaded critical measures to demonstrate the commitment to reforms and a series of milestones to measure the progress.

- Be ready to pay short-term costs to acquire long-term benefits. The experience of acceded countries confirms that any deep structural reforms take time, and there should be no expectations of overnight gains. Moreover, direct and indirect costs of accessions may be substantial. In the short term, such costs may outweigh the immediate benefits; but in the long run, better resource allocation should help re-establish the balance. African economies willing to become emerging economies could learn from Article XII members how to balance short-term costs against potential long-term benefits to position their transition plans as catalytic for a broad range of domestic policy reforms.

- Learn from Article XII peers. Reaching emerging economy status will require knowing how to navigate the political economy and technical challenges of reform implementation. The experience of Article XII members that have implemented accession reforms successfully, and possible peer learning from them, may be helpful in advancing this process. Accession experience provides valuable guidance for improvements and peer learning. Accessions and the ensuing reforms should be viewed as a dynamic process, and this heterogeneity in the impact should not be interpreted as accessions creating winners and losers; it should be seen as a guidepost for possible directions of improvements and peer learning. The experience of more advanced Article XII members could be shared through a peer-learning mechanism (e.g. periodic accession peer-learning seminars) with others whose progress has so far been lagging. Peer learning would build a shared understanding among experts, practitioners and various stakeholders about how to implement reform and would assist other low-income economies in advancing toward emerging economy status, using the experience of accessions reform implementation as a road map.

References

Albouy D. (2011), 'Program Evaluation and the Difference in Difference Estimator'. Berkeley University, *Mimeo.*

Attanasio, O., C. Meghir and A. Santiago (2012), 'Education Choices in Mexico: Using a Structural Model and a Randomized Experiment to Evaluate PROGRSA', *Review of Economic Studies* 79(1):37–66.

Dadush, U., and C. Osakwe eds. (2015), *WTO Accessions and Trade Multilateralism. Case Studies and Lessons from WTO at Twenty*, World Trade Organization, Cambridge University Press.

Farole, T., J. Reis and S. Wagle (2010), 'Analyzing Trade Competitiveness: a Diagnostics Approach', World Bank Policy Research Working Paper Series, 2010 (1).

Imbens, G., and J. Wooldridge (2009), 'Recent Developments in the Econometrics of Program Evaluation', *Journal of Economic Literature* 47(1):5–86.

International Monetary Fund (IMF) (2014), 'The Diversification Toolkit: Export Diversification and Quality Databases'. Online resource: www.imf.org/external/np/res/dfidimf/diversification.htm

International Monetary Fund (IMF) (2015), 'Dealing with the Gathering Clouds.' *Regional Economic Outlook*. IMF, Washington, DC, www.imf.org/external/pubs

Lechner, M. (2011), 'The Estimation of Causal Effects by Difference-in-Difference Methods', *Foundations and Trends in Econometrics* 4(3):165–224.

Li, D., and C. Wu (2004), 'GATT/WTO Accession and Productivity', Growth and Productivity in East Asia, *NBER-East Asia Seminar on Economics*, Vol. 13, University of Chicago Press.

Subramanian, A., and S. Wei (2007), 'The WTO promotes trade, strongly but unevenly', *Journal of International Economics* 72(1):151–75.

Tang, M., and S. Wei (2009), 'The Value of Making Commitments Externally: Evidence from WTO Accessions', *Journal of International Economics* 78:216–29.

Todd, P., and K. Wolpin (2006), 'Assessing the Impact of School Subsidy Program in Mexico: Using a Social Experiment to Validate a Dynamic Behavioural Model of Child Schooling and Fertility', *American Economic Review* 96(5):1384–417.

Todd, P., and K. Wolpin (2008), 'Ex Ante Evaluation of Social Programs', *Annales d'Economie et de Statistique* 91/92: 263–91.

World Trade Organization (WTO) (1999), *The Results of the Uruguay Round of Multilateral trade Negotiation: Legal Texts.* Cambridge University Press.

World Trade Organization (WTO) (2015a), Director General's Annual Report on WTO Accessions, WTO official document n° WT/ACC/25.

Annex 16.1 *Data sources and definitions*

Variable	Measure	Definition	Source	Link
Real GDP growth	Per cent change	Annual percentages of constant price GDP are year-on-year changes	World Economic Outlook Database, IMF	http://www.imf.org/external/pubs/ft/weo
Inflation	Per cent change	Annual percentages of average consumer prices are year-on-year changes	World Economic Outlook Database, IMF	http://www.imf.org/external/pubs/ft/weo
Fiscal balance	Per cent of GDP	Fiscal revenue minus total expenditure	World Economic Outlook Database, IMF	http://www.imf.org/external/pubs/ft/weo
Current account balance	Per cent of GDP	Current account is all balance of payments transactions other than those in financial and capital items.	World Economic Outlook Database, IMF	http://www.imf.org/external/pubs/ft/weo
Openness	Per cent of GDP	Exports of goods plus imports of goods	World Economic Outlook Database, IMF	http://www.imf.org/external/pubs/ft/weo
Foreign direct Investment	Per cent of GDP	Foreign direct investment are the net inflows of investment to acquire a lasting management interest (10 per cent or more of voting stock) in an enterprise operating in an	World Development Indicators, World Bank	http://data.worldbank.org/data-catalog/world-development-indicators

Annex 16.1 (*cont.*)

Variable	Measure	Definition	Source	Link
		economy other than that of the investor. It is the sum of equity capital, reinvestment of earnings, other long-term capital, and short-term capital as shown in the balance of payments. This series shows net inflows (new investment inflows less disinvestment) in the reporting economy from foreign investors, and is divided by GDP.		
Export market penetration	Index	The number of countries to which the reporter exports a particular product divided by the number of countries that import the product. The range of values is from 0 to 1. A value of 1 indicates that the country exports to every country that imports a particular product.	World Bank; World Integrated Trade Solution (WITS)	http://wits.worldbank.org

| Export diversification | Index | The shift to a more varied production structure, involving the introduction of new or expansion of pre-existing products, including higher quality products. Lower value of the Theil index signals higher export diversification as the index is calculated a ratio of the total number of products to new products. | IMF Export Diversification and Quality Databases | https://www.imf.org /external/np/res/dfidimf |
| Merchandise trade | Per cent | Merchandise trade covers all types of inward and outward movement of goods through a country or territory. Goods include all merchandise that either add to or reduce the stock of material resources of a country by entering (imports) or leaving | WTO Statistics Database time series on international trade. | http://stat.wto.org /StatisticalProgram |

Annex 16.1 (*cont.*)

Variable	Measure	Definition	Source	Link
		(exports) the country's economic territory (see United Nations International Trade Statistics, Concepts and Definitions, Series M, No 52, Revision 2).		
Trade in services	Per cent	Exports (credits or receipts) and imports (debits or payments) of commercial services are included in balance of payments statistics, in conformity with the classification of the sixth (2009) edition of the IMF Balance of Payments and International Investment Position Manual (BPM6) as well as the 2010 edition of the Manual on Statistics of International Trade in Services (MSITS 2010).	WTO Statistics Database time series on international trade.	http://stat.wto.org /StatisticalProgram

Annex 16.2 *Full WTO membership topology*

Low-income members		Lower middle-income members				Upper middle-income members		High-income members	
GNI per capita < US$ 1,045		GNI per capita US$ 1,046 – 4,125				GNI per capita US$ 4,126 – 12,735		GNI per capita > US$ 12,736	
Art. XII LDCs LICs	Non Art. XII LDCs LICs	Art. XII LDCs LMCs	Non Art. XII LDCs LMCs	Art. XII non-LDCs LMCs	Non Art. XII LMCs	Art. XII non-LDCs UMCs	Non Art. XII UMCs	Art. XII non-LDCs HICs	Non Art. XII HICs
Treatment group	Comparator group	Treatment group	Comparator group	Treatment group	Comparator group	Treatment group	Comparator group	Treatment group	Comparator group
2	20	5	8	7	21	11	26	9	49
Cambodia	Benin	Cabo Verde	Bangladesh	Armenia	Bangladesh	Albania	Angola	Croatai	Antigua and Barbuda
Nepal	Burkina Faso	Lao People's Democratic Republic	Djibouti	Georgia	Bolivia, Plurinational State of	Bulgaria	Belize	Estonia	Argentina
	Burundi	Samoa	Lesotho	Kyrgyz Republic	Cameroon	China	Botswana	Latvia	Australia
	Central African Republic	Vanuatu	Mauritania	Moldova	Congo	Ecuador	Brazil	Lithuania	Austria
	Chad	Yemen	Myanmar	Tajikistan	Cote d'Ivoire	Jordan	Colombia	Oman	Bahrain, Kingdom of
	Democratic Republic of the Congo		Senegal	Ukraine	Djibouti	Kazakhstan	Costa Rica	Russian Federation	Barbados
	Gambia		Solomon Islands	Viet Nam	Egypt	The former Yugoslav Republic of Macedonia	Cuba	Saudi Arabia, Kingdom of	Belgium
	Guinea		Zambia		El Salvador	Mongolia	Dominica	Seychelles	Brunei Darussalam
	Guinea-Bissau				Ghana	Montenegro	Dominican Republic	Chinese Taipei	Canada

Annex 16.2 (cont.)

Low-income members GNI per capita < US$ 1,045		Lower middle-income members GNI per capita US$ 1,046 – 4,125				Upper middle-income members GNI per capita US$ 4,126 – 12,735		High-income members GNI per capita > US$ 12,736	
Art. XII LDCs LICs Treatment group	Non Art. XII LDCs LICs Comparator group	Art. XII LDCs LMCs Treatment group	Non Art. XII LDCs LMCs Comparator group	Art. XII non-LDCs LMCs Treatment group	Non Art. XII non-LDCs LMCs Comparator group	Art. XII non-LDCs UMCs Treatment group	Non Art. XII UMCs Comparator group	Art. XII non-LDCs HICs Treatment group	Non Art. XII HICs Comparator group
Haiti					Guatemala	Panama	Fiji		Chile
Madagascar					Guyana	Tonga	Gabon		Cyprus
Malawi					Honduras		Grenada		Czech Republic
Mali					India		Jamaica		Denmark
Mozambique					Indonesia		Malaysia		Finland
Niger					Kenya		Maldives		France
Rwanda					Morocco		Mauritius		Germany
Sierra Leone					Nicaragua		Mexico		Greece
Tanzania					Nigeria		Namibia		Hong Kong, China
Togo					Pakistan		Paraguay		Hungary
Uganda					Papua New Guinea		Peru		Iceland
					Philippines		Romania		Ireland
					Sri Lanka		South Africa		Israel
					Swaziland		Saint Lucia		Italy
					Zambia		St Vincent and the Grenadines		Japan
							Suriname		Korea, Republic of
							Thailand		Kuwait, State of
							Tunisia		Liechtenstein
							Turkey		Luxembourg
									Macao, China

World Bank July 2015 classification: For analytical purposes, the World Bank divides economies by income groups according to 2014 gross national income (GNI) per capita using the World Bank Atlas method:

Low-income countries (LICs), US$ 1,045 or less;

Lower middle-income countries (LMCs), US$ 1,046–4,125;

Upper middle-income countries (UMCs), US$ 4,126–12,735; and

High-income countries (HICs), US$ 12,736 or more.

The term 'country', used interchangeably with 'economy', refers to any territory for which separate economic statistics is reported.

Source: http://data.worldbank.org/news/new-country-classifications-2015.

United Nations classification: The group of least-developed countries (LDCs) based on the UN classification used in the WTO is presented at the time of accession of each country to the WTO. 48 countries are currently designated by the United Nations as LDCs. The list of LDCs is reviewed every three years by the United Nations Economic and Social Council. Three criteria are used by the CDP to determine LDC status: per capita income (gross national income per capita); human assets (indicators of nutrition, health, school enrolment and literacy); economic vulnerability (indicators of natural and trade-related shocks, physical and economic exposure to shocks, and smallness and remoteness). Four countries have so far graduated from LDC status: Botswana in 1994, Cabo Verde in 2008, Maldives in 2011, and Samoa in 2014.

Source: http://unctad.org/en/Pages/ALDC

Malta
Netherlands
New Zealand
Norway
Poland
Portugal
Qatar
Singapore
Slovak Republic
Slovenia
Spain
Saint Kitts and Nevis
Sweden
Switzerland
Trinidad and Tobago
United Arab Emirates
United Kingdom
United States
Uruguay
Venezuela, Bolivarian Republic of

Annex 16.3 *Article XII members: stability and reform indicators*

| | Stability | | | | | | Reforms | | | | | |
| | GDP | | | Inflation | | | Fiscal deficit | | | Current account | | |
	Effect	SE	T-stat	Effect	SE	T-stat	Effect	SE	T-stat	Effect	SE	T-stat
Art. XII LDCs LICs												
Cambodia	−0.553	1.299	−0.426	−21.920	18.606	−1.178	−1.385	0.951	−1.456	−1.454	1.632	−0.891
Nepal	−2.568	0.755	−3.400***	9.814	2.725	3.601***	1.182	0.749	1.577	10.116	1.225	8.261***
Art. XII LDCs LMCs												
Cabo Verde	−5.778	1.387	−4.165***	7.490	3.592	2.085**	−0.971	2.192	−0.443	−3.630	2.292	−1.584
Lao People's Democratic Republic	0.252	2.386	0.105	−7.808	25.565	−0.305	0.813	3.179	0.256	−11.370	5.370	−2.117***
Samoa	−3.493	2.588	−1.350	7.491	7.005	1.069	−3.284	3.967	−0.828	2.196	5.070	0.433
Vanuatu	−1.837	2.541	−0.723	7.117	5.268	1.351	0.757	2.478	0.306	1.700	3.502	0.485
Art. XII non-LDCs LMCs												
Armenia	0.693	3.321	0.209	−915.215	552.106	−1.658	4.225	5.078	0.832	5.660	4.026	1.406
Georgia	11.741	5.314	2.209***	−2472.001	1367.483	−1.808	5.934	5.595	1.061	−0.441	2.497	−0.177
Kyrgyz Republic	3.988	5.446	0.732	−60.122	171.168	−0.351	3.076	5.098	0.603	−3.077	5.720	−0.538
Moldova	12.442	3.963	3.140***	−274.224	77.207	−3.552***	−3.353	−3.353	−3.353***	−0.674	2.789	−0.242
Tajikistan	7.401	3.160	2.342***	−410.076	227.896	−1.799	2.363	2.092	1.130	5.164	2.996	1.724
Ukraine	−2.459	4.297	−0.572	−452.992	457.204	−0.991	−0.093	2.592	−0.036	−5.645	2.129	−2.652***
Viet Nam	−2.189	0.777	−2.817***	8.555	121.856	0.070	−0.476	1.179	−0.404	3.256	2.309	1.410
Art. XII non-LDCs UMCs												
Albania	3.820	3.007	1.270	65.333	34.399	1.899	4.478	3.007	1.270	−4.770	1.510	−3.160***
Bulgaria	6.624	1.872	3.539***	105.085	79.593	1.320	6.735	1.872	3.539***	−0.278	2.824	−0.098
China	0.114	1.110	0.103	95.626	30.576	3.128***	0.632	1.110	0.103	2.081	1.665	1.250

Ecuador	1.022	1.358	0.752	72.589	28.648	2.534***	0.452	1.358	0.752	5.174	1.195	4.331***
Jordan	2.836	1.577	1.798	88.617	26.822	3.304***	0.115	1.577	1.798	0.227	2.799	0.081
The former Yugoslav Republic of Macedonia	2.798	1.477	1.894	12.392	36.241	0.342	-2.364	1.568	-1.508	2.460	1.472	1.671
Mongolia	6.907	2.193	3.150***	-14.776	22.338	-0.661	6.978	2.193	3.150***	5.226	4.117	1.270
Montenegro	-2.354	2.975	-0.791	-8.051	15.911	-0.506	-0.758	2.553	-0.297	8.130	8.616	0.944
Panama	3.951	1.803	2.192***	110.152	25.123	4.385***	1.297	1.803	2.192***	-5.864	2.025	-2.895***
Tonga	0.112	1.341	0.083	61.861	33.777	1.831	1.006	1.341	0.083	-4.099	1.767	-2.319***
Art. XII non-LDCs HICs												
Croatia	0.263	2.129	0.124	-228.598	154.161	-1.483	-4.844	2.129	0.124	-2.844	1.945	-1.462
Estonia	0.232	3.335	0.070	-17.336	3.913	-4.431***	-1.888	3.335	0.070	-2.058	2.744	-0.750
Latvia	3.851	3.078	1.251	-19.187	9.546	-2.010**	-2.137	1.356	-1.576	-9.030	3.544	-2.548***
Lithuania	1.258	3.158	0.399	0.302	0.039	7.677***	1.124	3.158	0.399	2.250	2.285	0.985
Oman	-0.946	1.469	-0.644	6.901	1.760	3.922***	7.488	2.288	3.273***	0.318	0.043	7.353***
Russian Federation	2.703	4.551	0.594	-151.922	235.200	-0.646	-0.870	4.068	-0.214	-5.384	3.012	-1.788
Saudi Arabia, Kingdom of	3.387	1.561	2.170***	7.619	1.804	4.224***	13.162	3.801	3.463***	21.923	3.699	5.927***
Chinese Taipei	-1.799	1.281	-1.405	3.884	1.568	2.476***	-2.089	1.281	-1.405	0.402	1.790	0.225

*** p-value < 0.01; ** p-value < 0.05.

Annex 16.4 *Article XII members: competitiveness indicators*

	Foreign direct investment			Openness			Competitiveness					
							Export market penetration			Export diversification		
	Effect	SE	T-stat	Effect	SE	T-stat	Effect	SE	T-stat	Effect	SE	T-stat
Art. XII LDCs LICs												
Cambodia	0.066	1.209	0.055	36.527	11.399	3.204***	1.406	0.397	3.545***	0.790	0.213	3.713***
Nepal	−3.318	0.477	−6.963***	−4.467	4.264	−1.048	0.624	0.115	5.418***	−0.575	0.211	−2.729***
Art. XII LDCs LMCs												
Cabo Verde	−1.642	1.899	−0.865	5.491	4.441	1.236	−0.156	0.041	−3.781***	n.a.	n.a.	n.a.
Lao People's Democratic Republic	−2.446	2.637	−0.927	32.753	20.679	1.584	n.a.	n.a.	n.a.	−0.045	0.145	−0.310
Samoa	1.834	2.116	0.867	−13.292	6.007	−2.213**	−0.135	0.069	−1.963	n.a.	n.a.	n.a.
Vanuatu	−7.905	2.357	−3.354**	−20.327	6.162	−3.299***	−0.187	0.198	−0.945	n.a.	n.a.	n.a.
Art. XII non-LDCs LMCs												
Armenia	−0.118	1.348	−0.087	−90.662	63.423	−1.429	−0.267	0.063	−4.231***	−0.583	0.290	−2.010**
Georgia	1.412	2.842	0.497	14.420	5.609	2.571***	−0.034	0.172	−0.200	−0.766	0.137	−5.591***
Kyrgyz Republic	0.996	3.031	0.329	19.095	18.991	1.005	−0.340	0.201	−1.695	n.a.	n.a.	n.a.
Moldova	1.387	1.679	0.826	−24.999	10.385	−2.407***	0.193	0.270	0.715	0.084	0.110	0.765
Tajikistan	0.213	1.666	0.128	−87.431	−87.431	−0.874	n.a.	n.a.	n.a.	−0.049	0.194	−0.251
Ukraine	−1.193	1.367	−0.872	−5.772	5.443	−1.061	1.430	0.436	3.280***	−0.310	0.188	−1.647
Viet Nam	−1.839	1.388	−1.325	56.444	15.430	3.658***	3.064	0.503	6.095***	−0.845	0.178	−4.759***
Art. XII non-LDCs UMCs												
Albania	2.716	1.144	2.374***	37.925	6.621	5.728***	−0.908	0.327	−2.772***	−0.031	0.143	−0.216

Bulgaria	6.721	3.095	2.172***	10.876	25.718	0.423	0.847	1.568	0.540	0.249	0.044	5.630***
China	−1.187	0.709	−1.675	18.332	4.719	3.885***	24.063	2.695	8.928***	0.144	0.051	2.827***
Ecuador	−2.240	0.543	−4.127***	7.942	3.003	2.645***	−1.016	0.353	−2.875***	0.053	0.095	0.556
Jordan	5.895	1.684	3.500***	3.113	6.405	0.486	−0.657	0.260	−2.523***	−0.085	0.056	−1.511
The former Yugoslav Republic of Macedonia	−0.395	1.329	−0.297	7.199	5.099	1.412	−0.395	1.329	−0.297	0.240	0.081	2.953***
Mongolia	7.369	2.703	2.726***	36.115	4.555	7.929***	−1.419	0.679	−2.090**	0.796	0.135	5.873***
Montenegro	−10.159	5.743	−1.769	−3.851	10.630	−0.362	0.006	0.146	0.044	n.a.	n.a.	n.a.
Panama	6.127	1.819	3.368***	−3.956	3.634	−1.089	−0.531	0.621	−0.856	−0.316	0.084	−3.747***
Tonga	−0.226	0.947	−0.239	3.108	3.802	0.817	−0.908	0.162	−5.609***	−0.377	0.186	−2.032**
Art. XII non-LDCs HICs												
Croatia	−0.063	0.468	−0.134	19.603	4.086	4.798***	−0.701	0.517	−1.355	−0.333	0.050	−6.596***
Estonia	−0.500	3.070	−0.163	25.520	4.545	5.615***	−0.267	0.515	−0.518	−0.280	0.142	−1.962
Latvia	−3.575	1.811	−1.974	25.381	3.783	6.709***	−0.391	0.380	−1.030	−0.757	0.138	−5.478***
Lithuania	n.a.	n.a.	n.a.	30.204	3.934	7.677***	0.329	0.454	0.723	−0.432	0.128	−3.372***
Oman	−2.952	1.153	−2.561***	31.756	4.319	7.353***	−3.811	0.469	−8.123***	−0.575	0.154	−3.739***
Russian Federation	1.861	2.153	0.865	107.118	32.679	3.278***	0.491	0.747	0.657	n.a.	n.a.	n.a.
Saudi Arabia, Kingdom of	0.023	1.178	0.020	91.396	8.472	10.789***	−0.721	0.635	−1.135	0.162	0.116	1.398
Chinese Taipei	n.a.	n.a.	n.a.	n.a.	n.a.	n.a.	n.a.	n.a.	n.a.	n.a.	n.a.	n.a.

17

Driving Economic Growth through Trade Policy Reforms and Investment Attraction in the Open World Economy: The Experience of China

YUAN YUAN

Abstract

China achieved a great leap forward in its economic development in the last thirty years, supported by profound trade policy reforms, significant infra-structure investment and utilization of foreign capital, under the overarching state policy of reform and opening-up. Shares of manufactures and services in production have kept increasing, and remarkable export performance has been scored during this period. Additions of labour and capital, as well as competitive costs have largely shaped the economy's comparative advantages up to now, and they are likely to be replaced by increasing domestic con-sumption, productivity growth and a greater reliance on services as the main factors sustaining future economic growth, albeit at a slower pace. Nonetheless, opening-up and domestic policy reforms, going hand-in-hand, will continue to play a critical role. The question that this paper addresses from China's perspective may serve as a reference for the African economies seeking to establish a strong manufacturing base, and to realise economic take-off with the help of a clear opening-up strategy and a proper trade policy toolkit.

I Starting Point of Over Thirty Years' Robust Economic Development

The story of 'win-for-all' since China joined the WTO in 2001 is now widely known. However, the process of reform and opening-up that led up to and followed China's WTO membership may not be equally familiar. Beginning well before 2001, the year of China's WTO accession,

A preliminary version of this chapter was presented at the Fourth China Round Table, Nairobi, Kenya, on 13–14 December 2015.

China's policy endeavour for domestic reform and integration into the global economy dated back to China's formal application to resume its GATT contracting party status in 1986, and to eight years earlier, when China first signalled its intention to embrace the open world economy in 1978. Comparison of major economic indicators from 2014 and those earlier dates will show how far China has gone and what progress has been made over the past thirty years.

In 1978, China's GDP stood at 364.5 billion RMB, ranking as the tenth-largest GDP in the world, and accounting for less than 1 per cent of the global economy, while by 2014, China's GDP had increased nearly 175-fold to top 63.6 trillion RMB, ranking China second globally for five consecutive years from 2010 to 2014, accounting for 13.3 per cent of the world economy in 2014. Per capita GDP grew from 381 RMB to 46,600 RMB during this period.

In 1978, China's foreign exchange reserve was only US$ 167 million, ranked as the world's 38th-largest holding of foreign exchange reserve, whereas in 2014 it totalled US$ 3.84 trillion, with China ranking first in the global economy in terms of its holdings of foreign exchange reserves, for nine years in a row.

In 1978, China's trade in goods was valued at only 35.5 billion RMB, ranking it 32nd in the world in term of the value of trade in goods, while in 2014, it reached 26.4 trillion RMB, ranking it first in the world for the second consecutive year.

In 2014, China's exports of goods registered 14.39 trillion RMB, accounting for 12.4 per cent of the world's total value of exports of goods, and China's imports of goods recorded 12.04 trillion RMB, accounting for 10.3 per cent of the global total. In the same year, China's exports of services registered at US$ 222.21 billion, and its imports of services at US$ 382.13 billion, ranking it fifth and second, respectively, in the world.

In 2014, the amount of foreign direct investment (FDI) absorbed by China totalled US$ 128.5 billion, lifting its global ranking to first, with China described as the largest developing FDI recipient, a title it has retained for eighteen years. Outbound direct investment registered US$ 107.2 billion, making China one of the world's major investors.

Since 1978, China's economic structure has improved continuously. In 2014, the added value of the tertiary industry, including the services sector, accounted for 48.1 per cent of GDP and contributed to 40.6 per cent of total employment. The urbanization rate reached 54.8 per cent, and 54 per cent of economic growth was attributed to progress in science and technology.

Significant progress has been made in poverty reduction. There were nearly 300 million rural poor in 1978, but this number fell to 70 million in 2014, according to the poverty standard of China, a decrease of 230 million in total or nearly 20 million annually. The United Nations, in its 2015 Millennium Development Goals Report (United Nations, 2015), commended the central role played by China in the global reduction of poverty and in the sharp decline of the extreme poverty rate in Eastern Asia.

Infrastructure construction has registered exponential development. By the end of 2014, China had registered advances and strong progress in operating railroads (112,000 kilometres), roads (4.464 million kilometres), highways (112,000 kilometres) and regular flight routes (4.637 million kilometres). Operating high-speed railways exceeded 16,000 kilometres, the most of any economy in the world.

On 1 December 2015, the International Monetary Fund (IMF) Executive Board decided to include RMB in their special drawing rights (SDR) basket, an international reserve asset created by the IMF to supplement its member countries' official reserves and currently based on a basket of four major currencies (IMF, 2015). This first alteration in more than fifteen years in the list of currencies included in the SDR marked an important milestone in China's global economic and financial integration, and also a recognition of China's progress in the reform of its monetary and financial systems.

China's development benefits the rest of the world. Today, China has a large number of trading partners, more than 120 countries and regions. It is the world's biggest exporting economy and its second-largest importer. Recording a growth rate of around 10 per cent for more than three decades, its economic development has been a major contributor to global economic growth for years. Since joining the WTO in 2001, China has been implementing its commitments and protecting intellectual property rights (IPR) more forcefully. It has facilitated the access of foreign goods and services into its huge market. Jobs have been created for China's trading partners. Investment opportunities and profits have been generated for their companies, accompanied by wider choices of value-for-money products and surplus provided to consumers. The World Bank once estimated that China's WTO membership would generate an extra US$ 74 billion worth of global benefits on an annual basis.

1978 was a milestone year to launch China's booming economic growth, and positive results have continued for the past thirty years.

1978 was also the year that kicked off unparalleled changes, or even a revolution, in China's outlook on the world, its choice of a path for development and corresponding national policies.

II   Vision and Determination: Background for the New Outlook

Internally, under the system of planned economy for nearly forty years and in the aftermath of the decade-long Cultural Revolution, China was one of the poorest economies in the world, on the verge of economic collapse. Its economic structure was seriously distorted, agriculture was underdeveloped, manufacturing was lagging behind, consumer goods were in short supply and the country was largely closed to the outside world. Externally, nearly all major economies were introducing reforms or policy adjustments and some were taking the lead in technological and economic development. Globalization, as a new trend of world economic development, was increasingly recognized by the international community. Against this backdrop, the thinking of reform and opening-up, and the vision to integrate and prosper in the world economy began to ferment in the minds of Chinese leaders.

Deng Xiaoping, Chairman of the Central Advisory Commission of the Communist Party of China from 1981–87, was among the first to realize that reform and opening-up were inherent needs of the economy and that these were in accord with the fundamental and long-term interests of China. His two historic overseas visits and other leaders' inspection tours abroad paved the way for the launch of the opening-up process.

During his visit to Japan in the fall of 1978, Deng said, 'The world is advancing by leaps and bounds. We are eager to bring about modernization. Toward that end, we need sound policies, and we must regard as our starting point for development the advanced technology and management know-how of the world today. We must be good at learning. We want to learn from every developed country, and we also want to draw on the good experience of our less well-off Third World friends.' These remarks reflected his thoughtful views on the urgent need for China to open up.

Following his trip to Singapore in November 1978, in a speech at home entitled 'Proposals on Economic Work', Deng said that, 'When we study financial and economic issues now, our starting point should be how to make the most of foreign capital and be good at it. It would be a great pity if we failed to use foreign funds'.

In October 1978, when meeting with a delegation of journalists from what was then West Germany, he used the term 'opening-up' in no uncertain terms for the first time, saying that, 'as to your question about whether the policy of opening-up that we are going to adopt runs counter to our tradition, my answer is that good traditions must be preserved, but we should also make new policies under new circumstances'.

At the closing of the Central Working Conference on 13 December 1978, Deng delivered his now well-known speech entitled 'Emancipating the Mind, Seeking Truth from Facts, and Looking toward the Future in Unity', which later became the central theme of the 3rd Plenary Session of the 11th CPC Central Committee, held on 18 December 1978. The Plenary Session formulated a series of new principles and policies, and most importantly, made the policy decision to shift the Party's focus of work from seclusion to openness and from rigorous dogmatism to reforms in all fields of endeavour. The guidelines for work on international economic relations were set as 'being proactive in developing economic cooperation with all countries on the basis of equality and mutual benefit, as well as self-reliance, with the goal of adopting technology and equipment at advanced world levels'.

Heralding a new era of development for China, the meeting was an historic prologue to the country's opening to the outside world. As the chief designer of China's new road of development, Deng spared no efforts in championing the vision of reform and opening-up, and successfully passed it on to successive generations of Chinese leadership.

Reform was seen as creating the institutional basis and internal conditions for opening-up. It improved China's ability to cooperate and compete globally. Opening-up promoted reform by providing a reference of experience and sources of vitality, hence serving as a starting point and constituting a component of reform. Forming an unswerving national strategy and basic policy together, these two factors have gone hand-in-hand throughout China's development, with opening-up normally staying a step ahead.

However, it is easier said than done. It cannot be overemphasized how arduous the task is to transform the world's most populous nation from a planned economy to a market-oriented one. The challenge has tested our mettle, wisdom and resolve. Courage is required for risk-taking, and perseverance for ultimate success.

In this context, Deng Xiaoping said: 'Today's world is an open one. The more we reform and the wider we open up, the stronger our ability is to stand risks. We've got to uphold the opening-up policy. This cannot be changed. If we really want to change it, all we can do is to open even wider to the outside world.' Jiang Zemin, General Secretary of the Central Committee of the Communist Party of China in 1989–2002, said, 'Opening-up to the outside world will be a basic state policy for a long time to come. We shall perfect the all-round, multi-layered and wide-ranging pattern of opening-up, develop an open economy and enhance international competitiveness'. Hu Jintao, General Secretary of the Central Committee of the Communist Party of China in 2003–12, said, 'Only by adhering to reform and opening-up can we make progress and address the thorny problems occurring in the process of our development'. Most recently, Xi Jinping, General Secretary of the Central Committee of the Communist Party of China from 2012 to the present, said, 'In the era of economic globalization, no country can develop behind closed doors. The more we develop, the more open we are. China's door of opening-up will never be closed. Reform and opening-up have no end, and they will always be on their way'.

History has proven the effect of this determination. A clear goal of integration into the global economy has been established and a series of opening-up policy measures have been taken ever since, to absorb foreign capital, break up monopolized trading and conduct reforms on enterprises, pricing, finance, taxation and foreign trade. Each minor step forward in the opening-up endeavour has triggered a giant stride forward in China's national development. Trade policy reforms and investment attraction have been in the vanguard of this process.

III   Trade Policy Reforms Contributing to Economic Development

International trade not only generates foreign exchange and improves people's livelihood; it also promotes technological progress and accelerates industrial restructuring. The rapid growth of foreign trade over the last three decades has injected vigour into China's economic development, and is largely attributable to the reform of its foreign trade policy.

The building and perfection of a foreign trade legal system enshrining international rules and market economy principles has provided stability, transparency and predictability to China's trade policies. Foreign trade is operated and administered by law.

- Between 1949 and 1978, though there were a few laws and regulations regarding foreign trade in China, they reflected the highly concentrated foreign trade operation featuring state monopoly of purchase and marketing.

• Between 1978 and 1992, as foreign trade experienced qualitative changes in both value and structure, the process of foreign trade legislation accelerated. The number of laws was increased, with ever-widened jurisdiction.

The Customs Law of the People's Republic of China and the Provisional Regulations of the People's Republic of China on the Licensing System for Imported Goods were formulated in 1987. The Foreign Economic Contract Law and the Regulations on the Management of Technology Import Contracts were enacted in 1985 (although the Regulations were abolished in 2002), and the Implementing Rules (i.e. the Detailed Rules and Regulations for the Implementation of the regulations on Administration of Technology Import Contracts of the People's Republic of China) in 1988. The Provisional Regulations of the Customs of the People's Republic of China on Origin of Imported Goods came into effect in 1986. The Measures for Re-inspection of Import and Export Commodities came into being in 1989. The Provisional Stipulations on the Foreign Trade Agent System was unveiled in 1991. China also acceded to the United Nations Convention on Contracts for the International Sale of Goods and other international economic and trade treaties.

Between 1992 and 1999, the foreign trade legal system took shape, and the administration and operation of foreign trade in China approximated international practices. With the objective of building a socialist market economy established in 1992, and rule by law identified as the basic strategy in 1997, a large amount of legislative work took place.

On 11 January 1994, the State Council of China issued the Decision on Further Deepening the Reform of Foreign Trade Regime, stating that 'the country regulates foreign trade activities mainly through legal and economic means, efforts will be made to establish a fairly sophisticated foreign trade legal system as soon as possible, and all national regulations and policies involving foreign trade shall be made public by the Ministry of Foreign Trade as authorized by the State Council'. Transparency was mentioned for the first time in the field of foreign trade.

Another milestone legislation was the Foreign Trade Law endorsed at the 7th meeting of the 8th National People's Congress (NPC) on 12 May 1994. Serving as the basic law for foreign trade administration, it quoted and used for reference relevant GATT rules and was in line with international norms, thus laying down a solid foundation for China's accession to the WTO seven years later.

A series of laws, regulations and measures were formulated, governing international buying and selling of goods, administration of import and export commodities, inspection and customs supervision, trade remedies and trade in services. One case in point was the Contract Law endorsed in 1999, which absorbed the relevant content of the Foreign Economic Contract Law enacted in 1985 and replaced it, making sure that the same legal terms apply to all contracts. Other examples included the Provisional Measures on the Administration of Export Commodities in 1992, the Interim Measures for the Administration of the Import Quota for General Goods, and the Provisional Measures on the Administration of Import of Electro-mechanical Products in 1993, the Provisional Measures on the Operation Administration of Import Commodities in 1994, the Implementing Regulations of the Law on the Inspection of Import and Export Commodities in 1992 and the Regulations on Antidumping and Countervailing promulgated by the State Council in 1997.

Since 1999, China's foreign trade legal system has matured and China has begun more intensively to reflect WTO principles and rules in its domestic laws and make them applicable.

Over 2,300 laws, regulations and departmental rules were drafted, revised and revoked at the central government level, and more than 190,000 local regulations, rules and other policy measures were adjusted and/or formulated at sub-central government levels. The scale and intensity of work was unusual among WTO members.

On foreign trade administration, a batch of laws, regulations and departmental rules were formulated or revised, including but not limited to the Customs Law, revised in 2000; the Regulations on the Administration of Import and Export Goods, the Regulations on the Administration of Import and Export of Technique, the Measures on the Designated Operation and Administration of Import Goods and the Measures on the Bidding of Export Quotas in 2001; the Law on the Inspection and Quarantine of Import and Export Commodities, revised in 2002; the Regulations of the People's Republic of China on Import and Export Duties in 2003; the Measures on the Administration of Export Licenses and the Measures on the Administration of Import Licensing in 2004; the Regulations on the Protection of Geographical Indications in 2005; and the the Regulations of the People's Republic of China on the Origin of Import and Export Goods in 2008.

A trade remedy system was fully established in 2002 with the enactment of the Anti-dumping Regulations of the People's Republic of China and the Countervailing Regulation of the People's Republic of China, which replaced the 1997 Regulations on Anti-dumping and Countervailing, as well as the implementation of Regulation of the People's Republic of China on Safeguard Measures. The three regulations were revised in 2004.

Laws and Regulations have been implemented in major service sectors, such as Telecommunications Regulations of the People's Republic of China in 2000, Law of the People's Republic of China on Commercial Banks in 2003, Securities Law in 2004 and Insurance Law in 2009.

IPR protection has tremendously improved, with the formulation or revision of laws at par with international standards, including the Trademark Law in 2001, the Patent Law revised three times since 2000, the Copyright Law in 2010 and a series of other regulations as well. The Anti-Monopoly Law came into force in 2007, making a big stride in competition legislation. China has joined the Paris Convention for the Protection of Industrial Property, the Madrid Agreement Concerning the International Registration of Marks, the Universal Copyright Convention, the Berne Convention for the Protection of Literary and Artistic Works, the Patent Cooperation Treaty, and the Rome Convention for the Protection of Performers, Producers of Phonograms and Broadcasting Organizations.

The most significant legislative progress in this period was the revision of the 1994 Foreign Trade Law, aimed at applying the basic principles and rules of the WTO. Endorsed at the 8th meeting of the 10th NPC on 6 April 2004 and implemented on 1 July, the law liberalized trading rights, bringing to an end the fifty-year-long foreign trade examination and approval system in China, and delivering the relevant WTO commitment half a year in ahead of time.

As a result of these legal drafting efforts, China's economic development, and trade growth in particular, is equipped with a legal-level institutional guarantee, and the stability, transparency and predictability of China's trade and related policies have constantly improved.

Continuous Reforms of the Foreign Trade Regime Have Released Tremendous Institutional Vitality

Before 1978, foreign trade was regarded only a means to 'supply each other's needs and regulate surpluses and shortages', and was subject to rigid planning, central finance and operation monopoly in China. Foreign trade was recognized later as way to generate foreign exchange, improve people's livelihoods and promote technological progress and industrial restructuring, especially as a way to benefit and maximize comparative advantages in the international distribution of labour. All-round reforms were conducted on China's foreign trade regime, covering trading right, trade administration and operation, and trade liberalization and facilitation, to address the various institutional constraints.

Welcoming All to Trade

Before 1978, import and export were basically subject to the uniform management of eleven specialized foreign trade corporations under the Ministry of Foreign Trade, which in 1982 was merged into the Ministry of Foreign Economic Relations and Trade, or MOFERT (renamed Ministry of Foreign Trade and Economic Cooperation or MOFTEC in 1993, and renamed Ministry of Commerce or MOFCOM in 2003).

The drawbacks of this highly centralized foreign trade system became increasingly pronounced with the development and expansion of the national economy. The purchase of export commodities by local branches before they were sold abroad by their head companies according to unified plans alienated producers from sellers and detached industries from the international market. Coordination and enthusiasm were lacking.

Starting with the National Import and Export Work Conference in November 1979, the monopolistic foreign trade system began to be transformed by delegating power and reducing controls.

The export of some commodities was entrusted to localities and relevant departments, while provinces, municipalities and autonomous regions were allowed to establish specialized trading companies to deal in local commodities. Relevant departments of the State Council were allowed to set up companies to export commodities produced by factories under their administration. The right of manufacturing enterprises to engage in foreign trade was expanded, and various pilot companies that combined manufacturing and trade were established.

With the gradual application of the foreign trade agent system since 1984, companies with trading rights, within their business scope and in their own names, began to sign import and export contracts with foreign businesses on a commission basis for the domestic entities providing or purchasing goods. Such practices yielded good results, as manufacturers were turned into mandatees and were connected with the international market, and as their interests merged with those of trading companies they became proactive in making tradable goods and expanding exports.

Companies with trading rights, as agents, were also encouraged to improve their service quality.

The process of liberalizing trade of the vast majority of commodities began 1987. In the Regulations on the Transformation of Operating Mechanisms by Industrial Enterprises Owned by the Whole People, promulgated by the State Council in 1992, it was made clear that qualified enterprises could enjoy the right to import and export according to law, upon approval.

Between 1978 and 1992, besides the 6,000 specialized foreign trade companies, over 620 large- and medium-sized enterprises and manufacturing groups were permitted to trade. A great number of foreign-invested enterprises (FIEs) with trading rights were established, as were more and more rural and township enterprise groups and research institutions. By the end of 1993, more than 1,400 manufacturing enterprises, 100 research institutions and more than 130,000 FIEs could import and export. Both the rapid increase in the number of trading companies and the ever-fierce competition sharpened the sensitivity of enterprises to cost, consumers' demand, profits and losses. Their progress in technology, organization and management was effectively and constant promoted.

Following the complete liberalization of trading rights in 2004, the filing and registration system of trading rights was established, and the vitality and initiatives of market players set free. In less than two years, the number of foreign traders in China grew by nearly 100 per cent, with the vast majority being private companies. By the end of 2007, 634,000 enterprises had been granted the right to foreign trade. In 2014, exports by private companies accounted for 43.2 per cent of China's total exports, contributing to 71.8 per cent of that year's national export increment. Also in 2014, another 351 entities were authorized as archival filing and registration agencies for trading rights.

Turning Trading Companies into Independent Market Players

The assumption of responsibility for profits and losses by the state rather than the companies resulted in poor economic outcomes under the planned economy.

In 1984, the State Council issued the Notice on Transmitting the Report of MOFERT on the Propositions of Reforming the Foreign Trade Regime (Guo Fa No. 122), advocating the separation of government administration from enterprise management as a basic reform principle.

Foreign companies were separated from their former governing bodies so as to engage in independent accounting, take responsibility for their own profits and losses, and gradually develop into professional companies, with a free hand and inspired enthusiasm. The autonomy was later extended to foreign trade companies at city and county levels, manufacturing enterprises and research institutes. Restrictions on the business scope of foreign trade companies were also lifted.

In 1987, the State Council issued the Reform Plan for the Foreign Trade Regime in 1988 (Guo Fa No. 90), proposing to 'hold trading companies accountable for their own profits and losses' and that 'subsidies under the egalitarian "big pot" system should be abandoned, trading of vast majority of commodities liberalized, distribution of labour and responsibilities between government and enterprises implemented, and macro administration of foreign trade enhanced by applying the scientific economic regulatory system through policy and legal means'.

All companies engaging in foreign trade were guided to trade in a business manner, empowered to assume sole responsibility for their own management decisions, profits and losses. The financial disciplines imposed on them were strengthened, and they could no longer depend on central finance. The sectors of light industry, arts, crafts and clothing were chosen for pilot reform measures. After the connections between foreign trade corporations and MOFERT were de-linked, conglomerates were encouraged, as an organizational form of trading companies, to improve economic benefits and competitiveness by engaging in both domestic and international trade, and allowing free entry and economies of scale. Industrialization, conglomeration and internationalization became the development direction of trading entities. By the end of 1992, financial subsidies for export were no longer made available, and all trading companies were held responsible for their own profits and losses.

Transforming the Development Mode of Foreign Trade and Optimizing Trade Structure

Processing trade was transformed and upgraded, with the quality and benefit of foreign trade lifted to a higher level.

In the early stage of China's opening-up and trade development, processing trade played a fairly important role in importing technology and equipment, introducing foreign capital, generating foreign exchange and creating jobs, together with other forms in the 'three-plus-one' trade pattern, i.e. export processing with client-supplied materials, samples or components, plus compensation trade. The trade pattern referred to the practice by which foreign businesses supplied designs, raw materials and equipment to factories in China to be processed into commodities for export to the world market. The materials supplied by foreign businesses or imported by Chinese enterprises and needed for processing were exempted from import tariffs. Chinese factories and local governments drew processing and administrative fees from the profits, and ownership of the imported equipment reverted to the Chinese side after a period of time.

This policy was first introduced in the coastal regions, especially the Pearl River Delta in 1978, and achieved success in the special economic zones (SEZs) before being spread to the hinterland. Processing trade was quick to catch on due to its prompt results in increasing output, revenue and employment effects with little investment. Most FIEs formed in Shenzhen after 1982 were transformed from export processing firms. By 1996, processing trade had become the trading mode that generated the biggest trade volume and made up half of China's total imports and exports.

However, the disadvantages of processing trade became increasingly evident as China tried to move higher up in the industrial chains. Path dependence made the elevation from labour-intensive industries to technology- and knowledge-intensive ones very difficult, and differences in such endowments as resources and labour capacity hindered balanced development of trade among various regions.

With a view to restructuring trade and raising the position of China's manufacturing in the global value chains, the strategies of 'Success through Quality', 'Market Diversification' and 'Reinvigorating Trade by Science and Technology' were carried out in 1991.

The State Council termed 1991 the Year of Quality, Variety and Benefit. By the end of 1992, China had established economic and trade relations with 221 countries and regions, and foreign trade markets were diversified. 1996 saw the formulation of Outline for Quality Revitalization (1996–2010). Efforts were made to improve the quality and reputation of goods, optimize the export structure and create brand products by intensifying legislation and law enforcement on quality control, increasing the technology content and added value of products, introducing quality management systems in line with international standards, and strengthening total quality management. In March 2011, a campaign entitled the Year for Advancing the Quality of Foreign Traded Goods was launched.

After China's accession to the WTO in 2001, transformation and upgrading processing trade became a new orientation for development.

The export of highly polluting, energy-consuming and resource-intensive products was discouraged. The shift from the expansion of the scale of trade to the improvement of its quality and benefits was encouraged, as was the shift from the utilization of low-cost advantages in resources, energy and labour force to sharpening comprehensive competitive edges. In November 2011, MOFCOM joined forces with other departments to issue the Guiding Opinions on Promoting the Transformation and Upgrading of Processing Trade, calling for the structural upgrade of industries and products, optimization of regional layout and a move to the high end of industrial value chains.

Administration policy for processing trade was perfected by revising regulations in regard to bonded goods for sale in the domestic market, supervision of goods in processing trade and processing trade involving different regions.

In October 2012, the State Council issued the Guiding Opinions on Promoting the Scientific Development of Customs Special Surveillance Zones. Such zones, taking various forms such as export processing zones, duty-declaring logistics parks, cross-border industrial zones, bonded ports and qualified bonded areas, will gradually be integrated as comprehensive bonded areas, with more sophisticated and diversified functions of bonded processing, bonded logistics and bonded services, thus attracting processing trade to relocate there. In 2014, innovation was introduced in the modality of processing trade, and the Catalogue for Prohibited Categories of Processing Trade was adjusted.

Policy measures were explored to facilitate new business types in foreign trade, like cross-border electronic commerce, market purchase and comprehensive foreign trade services platforms, as well as trade in services and service outsourcing.

In May 2012, five cities – Shanghai, Chongqing, Hangzhou, Ningbo and Zhengzhou – were chosen for pilot services for cross-border e-commerce. In August 2013, the State Council transmitted the Opinions on Implementing the Supportive Policies for Retail Export by Cross-Border E-Commerce jointly formulated by MOFCOM and other departments, identifying support measures to be implemented in the regions with proper conditions on customs supervision, export inspection, foreign exchange settlement, cross-border payment services, taxation and credit system construction. The outline of the Development Plan for China's International Service Outsourcing Industry (2011–15) came out in 2012.

So far, positive headway has been made in the mode transformation and structural adjustment of trade. The quality of exported commodities has been constantly enhanced and the competitive pressure from opening-up has promoted product improvement by domestic enterprises. In the first eleven months of 2015, export through general trade accounted for 53.9 per cent of China's aggregate export.

In Terms of Trade Flow, Efforts Were Made to Realize Coordinated and Balanced Import and Export

A special endeavour for balancing the growth of import and export has been undertaken since 2010. Trade surplus has not been deliberately pursued, though the major source of trade surplus was FIEs and processing trade.

Provisional import duties lower than the most-favoured nation (MFN) tariff rates (i.e. treating trading partners equally and without discrimination) were applied to goods under more than 600 eight-digit tariff headings in 2010 and 2011, respectively. The number of tariff headings subject to provisional tariff was increased to 730 in 2012, with an average tariff rate of 4.4 per cent, more than 50 per cent lower than the applied MFN rate, and to more than 780 in 2013, with an average rate of 4.4 per cent and a preferential margin of 56 per cent. Though that number was slightly reduced (to 730) in 2014, the average tariff preferential margin went up to 60 per cent.

Moreover, starting from 1 July 2009, key parts, components and raw materials for major technological equipment have been exempted from import tariff and import value-added tax (VAT), with a view to expanding imports.

Import administration procedures have also been further streamlined. MOFCOM eliminated automatic import licensing administration on more than 27 and 130 goods in July 2012 and September 2013, respectively, under the 10-digit HS code. In 2014, the number of items subject to the Catalogue of Automatic Import Licensing Administration was substantially reduced.

From the perspective of trade promotion, at its 100th session in 2006, the world-renowned Canton Fair changed its full name from Chinese Export Commodities Fair to Chinese Import and Export Commodities Fair. The China Import Promotion Website went online at the end of 2013. In 2014, MOFCOM issued the Several Opinions on Strengthening Import.

Providing More Market Access Opportunities through Trade Liberalization and Facilitation

Market access is at the core of trade development, and can only be realized through continuous liberalization efforts and facilitation arrangements. The opening-up process of China was accompanied by its reduction of tariffs and non-tariff barriers at unilateral, bilateral and multilateral levels.

At the end of 1992, China initiated tariff-cutting with the widest goods coverage and largest margin of duty reduction, involving 3,371 dutiable items of imported commodities, or 53.6 per cent of the total in the Customs Tariff of Import and Export Commodities, including oil and crude oil. That was another new contribution made unilaterally by China to the GATT Uruguay Round, following its reduction of tariffs on more than 225 dutiable items and elimination of import regulatory tax earlier that year.

On 1 January 1993, Provisional Measures on the Administration of Export Commodities formulated by MOFERT were implemented. With a view to enhancing macro regulation of export and accelerating the development of foreign trade, the document referred to the international trade practices and represented a major reform of China's foreign trade regime. Since then, the varieties of commodities subject to export licensing administration were cut by half, the right of distributing quotas and licenses was further delegated to lower levels of government, and the number of export goods under quota and licensing administration gradually declined. For the sake of transparency, the annual results of allocation and implementation of quotas have been made public, except for those involving trade secrets.

At the end of 1993, 283 kinds of commodities were removed from the list of import administration. In 1994, another 195 types of commodities were no longer subject to import licensing and quotas. This was another new move in the reform of China's import administration regime and its process of resuming the GATT contracting party status, aiming at establishing an import management system in keeping with international norms, using tariff regulation as the primary means.

Liberalization efforts continued after China became the 143rd member of the WTO in 2001.

By 1 January 2005, the tariffs for all information technology (IT) products were abolished according to the ITA. As of 1 January 2008, China's overall tariff level was lowered from 15.3 per cent at the time of

accession to 9.8 per cent, with that for industrial goods cut from 14.8 to
8.9 per cent and that for agricultural products from 23.2 to 15.2 per cent.
100 per cent were bound tariffs. Non-tariff measures (NTMs) were
removed and state trading of silk was eliminated, as committed to in
Annex 3 to China's Accession Protocol. The tariff rate quota (TRQ)
administration system improved, with the amount of TRQ increased,
as committed, year by year, and TRQ administration of ten tariff headings, including plant oil (which covered soybean oil, palm oil and rape-
seed oil), was removed on 1 January 2006.

By 1 January 2010, China had fully honoured its WTO commitments,
reduced the tariffs for agricultural products and industrial products by 8
and almost 6 percentage points, respectively, both at bound rates, eliminated NTMs for products under 424 tariff headings, and opened 102 out
of the 160 service sectors categorized by the WTO.

A series of trade facilitation measures have been taken, such as improving trade finance, simplifying customs clearance procedures, introducing
paperless customs declaration, establishing electronic ports and adjusting
the catalogue of commodities subject to entry-exit inspection and
quarantine.

It is fair to say that the miracle of China's foreign trade growth over the
last thirty years was mainly attributable to its unswerving reform efforts,
and that its achievements in foreign trade have made significant contributions to the national economy.

IV   Investment Attraction Contributing to Economic Development

Bringing in foreign capital was the biggest and boldest step in China's
opening-up, a breakthrough in the old development philosophy of complete independence and self-reliance (from before 1978). More importantly, the practices and processes of FDI utilization present a miniature
of China's overall opening-up, epitomized in the idiom of 'fording the
river by groping for stones', and running experimental zones before
nationwide policy application.

Recognizing the benefits of foreign investment, including tax revenue
for the country, income for the workers and promotion of the service
industry, Deng Xiaoping made it clear in 1978 that funds and technology
from abroad could be used in China's construction, and joint ventures
were acceptable in the bid to absorb foreign investment. Guided by this
strategic decision, China's FDI utilization was started from scratch and
its achievements were recognized worldwide.

1   Pilot Zones of Various Kinds Were Run as Testing Fields for New Policy Measures and Institutional Arrangements

The Bao'an Industrial Zone Was Constructed in July 1979

Responding to the request of Hong Kong, China businesses to open factories in Guangzhou, and considering local conditions, Guangdong Province made up its mind to move first in the reform and the opening-up. In January 1979, together with the Ministry of Transport and Communications, a higher-level entity of the Hong Kong, China-based Merchants Group, it reported to the central government the idea of establishing an industrial zone in Shekou People's Commune of Bao'an County (later renamed Shenzhen City). By fully utilizing the inexpensive local land and labour resources to bring in overseas funds, technology and raw materials, it was intended to use foreign capital in the zone to boost industries, especially export-oriented ones. The Chinese leadership gave the green light to the proposal, and relevant central departments provided the zone with special policies, for example a taxation rate similar to that of Hong Kong, China, preferential import and export duties, the authority to endorse industrial projects of up to US$ 5 million in investment, and permission to borrow from foreign banks.

Breaking ground on 20 July 1979, the Shekou Industrial Zone thrived and scored a number of 'firsts', including FDI attraction, borrowing from overseas, autonomy in project approval, and assumption of sole responsibility by enterprises for their operation and profits and losses. High speed, high efficiency and high returns were the direct deliverables of the zone. In only two years, more than 100 enterprises had been established there.

Special Export Zones Were Run on a Trial Basis

Encouraged by the guiding principles of the central government, the provinces of Guangdong and Fujian requested more autonomy to intro-duce overseas funds and technology, operate compensation trade for export and develop ports. Initiatives for "export bases" and "export processing zones" were initiated and implemented.

At the Central Working Conference to discuss economic issues held in April 1979, Deng Xiaoping responded positively to the proposal and mentioned the term 'special zones' for the first time, meaning to identify a few places and apply to them certain special policies and flexible measures for foreign economic activities, and to explore approaches to speed up socialist economic development. It was decided at the meeting that special export zones would be run on a trial basis in the four cities of Shenzhen, Zhuhai, Shantou and Xiamen. These places would be given more decision-making authority, with a new management system coming into effect in planning, foreign trade, finance, monetary affairs, materials, commerce, wages and prices. Joint ventures and wholly foreign-owned enterprises (WFOEs) could be established to reflect the attractiveness of these zones. These trial special export zones made remarkable achievements. And the curtain was lifted on the trailblazing phase of opening-up in China.

Special Economic Zones (SEZs) Proved Great Success

It did not take long before striking results were achieved in the special export zones. At the same time, the two provinces of Guangdong and Fujian came to realize that these zones could not play a role as trailblazers for the opening-up initiative if they were limited to export processing and production bases. They should serve as 'windows' for China to observe the world's development and changes, and as 'testing grounds' to shift advanced foreign technology, management expertise and useful experience to the rest of the country. The term 'special export zone' did not do justice to these zones' broad functions.

It was suggested at a working meeting of special export zones in Guangdong in October 1979 that the zones be renamed 'special economic zones' (SEZs). The idea was endorsed by the central government in May 1980. In document Zhong Fa No. 41 of 1980, it was made clear that certain areas would be identified in the four designated cities to run SEZs on an experimental basis, and to be constructed mainly by incorporating foreign investment, with their economies regulated by market forces.

On 26 August 1980, the Regulations of Guangdong Province on SEZs were endorsed by the 15th meeting of the 5th NPC Standing Committee, and came into effect immediately, stipulating the following:

- As for their foundations and nature, SEZs represent a special approach to encouraging and using foreign capital and speeding up economic development in selected areas by adopting different systems and a more open policy than the hinterland. They are engaged in a comprehensive economic undertaking, broader in scope than ordinary export processing zones.
- As for the fundamental principles of organization and management, state sovereignty must be safeguarded. Foreigners shall be screened

and granted permission to invest in the SEZs, and shall obey the administration of the Chinese government.

- As for preferential policies, foreign investors would be allowed to run WFOEs after passing approval formalities; foreign banks and insurance companies would be allowed to set up affiliated institutions; import and export goods would be exempted from customs duties; tax rates on enterprises in the zones would be lower than in the hinterland and slightly lower than in Hong Kong, China and Macao, China; entry-exit procedures would be streamlined for the convenience of departures and arrivals; foreign exchange control would be properly relaxed; and foreign businesses, foreign workers and staff members would be permitted to transmit their lawful profits and wage incomes out of China through banks in the SEZs, provided that the relevant taxes were paid. Foreign businesses would be accorded more preferential treatment than their counterparts outside the zones regarding fees and term for using production sites.

The special measures for opening-up and economic development in the SEZs have yielded marked effects. Taking Shenzhen SEZ as an example, in a little more than two years from the birth of the city in January 1979 to March 1981, it accomplished a quantum leap from a tiny desolate border country of Bao'an with 250,000 residents subsisting on farming and fishing, to a municipality under a mayor with a vice governor's portfolio, and later, a metropolis inhabited by millions of people. Toward the end of June 1981, Shenzhen Municipality had signed more than 720 economic contracts with foreign parties, including seventeen WFOE projects, seven equity joint ventures and seventy-three contractual joint ventures. In the breakdown, 623 were projects for processing, assembly and compensation trade, totalling HK$ 2.458 billion in investment and bringing in 6,000 sets of machinery and equipment. In 1980, Shenzhen reported a total industrial and agricultural output value of 186 million RMB, up 20 per cent from 1979, and 720 million RMB in 1983, increasing by more than 10 times over that before the birth of the SEZ.

After nearly seven years, in a report to the 9th meeting of the 6th NPC Standing Committee on 7 January 1985, four special features of the SEZs were summarized as follows: 1) they live mainly on foreign capital, 2) their economic activities are regulated in the main by the market, 3) they offer investors policy preferences and entry-exit convenience and 4) their decision-making power on economic activities is greater than that delegated to certain provinces.

During his tour to the SEZs in early 1984, Deng Xiaoping fully affirmed their achievements, and wrote that 'the development and experience of Shenzhen has proven that our policy to establish SEZs is correct'.

As Deng rightly commented, SEZs, as both windows and bellwethers for China's reform and opening-up for more than thirty years, have played an important role in leading the efforts toward opening-up, institutional innovation and industrial upgrading, and in spreading them to the entire country.

Economic and Technological Development Zones Opened the New Chapter of Opening-Up

On 24 February 1984, Deng said to a few colleagues that, 'apart from the SEZs we have now, we may consider opening up some port cities, such as Dalian and Qingdao. These places will not be called SEZs, but can apply some of the policies as in the SEZs'.

Before and at a seminar held on 26 March 1984, in which some coastal cities participated, another twelve cities – Shanghai, Tianjin, Yantai, Ningbo, Wenzhou, Beihai, Nantong, Lianyungang, Guangzhou, Zhanjiang, Fuzhou and Qinhuangdao – were added to the above list of cities, and all were named 'economic and technological development zones'.

In the minutes of the meeting transmitted by the central government in document Zhong Fa No. 13 on 4 May 1984, 'accelerating the pace in utilizing foreign investment and importing cutting-edge technology' was mentioned, and the note endorsing the minutes pointed out that the coastal port cities must make the first step with a view to their fine locations, economic foundation, managerial experience, technology and markets. As a priority, these cities should strive to transform old enterprises and launch a number of medium and small projects that call for less investment, have quick capital turnover and yield fine returns. Instead of giving them money, the central government mainly provided them with incentives, i.e. preferential treatment and lower taxes to foreigners making investments or offering advanced technologies. More autonomy in foreign economic activities was given to coastal port cities. Some of these cities designated certain areas for establishing economic and technological development zones with well-defined boundaries. No efforts were spared in these zones to bring in the badly needed advanced technologies and run clusters of equity and contractual joint ventures, WFOEs and Sino-foreign cooperative research institutions. Some zones were also developed into international transit trade centres. All these zones had roughly the same decision-making power to endorse foreign-invested projects as SEZs.

One case in point was Tianjin Economic and Technological Development Zone. Established on 6 December 1984, the Zone has a planning area of 33 square kilometres. In early 1986, its builders' intention was to make things convenient for investors and help them make money, and by the middle of the year, their intention was to simulate an ideal international investment environment. With a government loan of only 370 million RMB, it focused its development plan on one piece of land at a time. Once profit was made in one area, there was movement to the next. Foreign investors were invited when construction was still going on, to ensure that development was sustained. The zone had signed thirty-five contracts with investors from eleven countries and regions and twenty factories started production in less than two years. The inscription from Deng Xiaoping on his tour to the Zone in August 1986 stated that 'The development zones hold great promise'.

The opening of the fourteen coastal cities and the construction of the first batch of economic and technological development zones marked the beginning of the nation's all-round openness to the world. In the 1990s, other provinces in China were opened in succession. By 1997, foreign investment could be found in nearly all Chinese cities, and by 2007, WFOEs were allowed in the vast majority of industries.

Marking the 30th anniversary of the establishment of the first batch of national economic and technological development zones, a national working meeting was convened in 2014. Policy measures were unveiled to promote the transformation and upgrading, innovation and development of these zones. The construction of international cooperative ecological parks or zones will be promoted.

The Shanghai (Pilot) Free Trade Zone Was Set up, Opening up Further, Not with Policy Preferences, but through Institutional Innovation

When China entered the stage of "New Normal" in recent years, new challenges emerged during the transformation from high- to moderate-speed economic growth, from scale and pace to quality and benefit of economic development, and from an investment-driven to an innovation-driven economy. China's traditional comparative advantages like low-cost labour, land, energy and resources needed to be replaced by new competitive edges. Another round of higher-level and more proactive opening-up was launched as a response.

The 3rd Plenary Session of the 18th CPC Central Committee held in November 2013, in its resolution entitled 'Decision on Several Major Issues of Comprehensively Deepening Reforms', set the goal of building a new system for the open economy and called for the market's decisive role in resource allocation. More innovative moves on China's own initiatives have been taken and the concept of zones came up again, but with a brand new connotation this time.

The Shanghai Pilot Free Trade Zone (FTZ) was launched in September 2013, twenty-three years after the establishment of the Shanghai Wai Gao Qiao Bonded Area. An FTZ indicates a single sovereign country or region, for the purpose of reducing costs and to promote the development of international investment and trade, and the application of special regulatory measures regarding foreign investment, customs bond, and exemption of tariffs. As a unilateral opening step to promote development and reform, it focuses on institutional innovation, serves as a testing field for establishing new administrative mechanism, especially for foreign investment, and expands market access to foreign services, aiming at leading in the building of a cross-border investment system in line with the requirements of internationalization and legalization, and cultivating a legalized, internationalized and market-oriented business environment.

The 'Special Administrative Measures on the Access of Foreign Investment to the China (Shanghai) Pilot Free Trade Zone (Negative List)' was released in 2013. According to the authorization of the 4th meeting of the 12th NPC and the decision of the State Council, eleven items subject to administrative examination and approval were involved in the three foreign investment-related laws in China, and thirty-two such items stipulated in fifteen administrative regulations and three administrative normative documents were provisionally adjusted. Reform was conducted on the existing administration of foreign investment, featuring case-by-case examination and approval, and exploration was made on the management modality of implementing pre-establishment national treatment plus a negative list. For sectors outside the negative list, projects with foreign investment were no longer subject to the ratification system, but to the filing system instead.

By the end of March 2014, foreign investment issues regarding the establishment and changes outside the negative list accounted for 93 per cent of the total application items by foreign investors. An administration system dominated by filing management had been built. A commitment had been made to issue certificates such as business licenses and company codes four days after receipt of companies' applications. In the field of trade facilitation, thirty-two measures were taken by the customs, inspection and quarantine authorities. The reform of the registration system of shipping insurance products was launched, and the pilot classified supervision of goods was expanded to all logistics enterprises in the bonded area. The initial version of the 'Single Window' for international trade went online, involving seventeen port and trade regulatory agencies, and more than 700 companies served online. Based on its one and a half years' experiment, twenty-eight reform measures of the FTZ had been spread across China and six copied to special customs surveillance zones.

On the market access front, auto parts manufacturing, grease processing and the six service sectors (financial, shipping, commercial, professional, cultural and social services) were further opened to the outside world. By the end of November 2014, the number of companies in the zone amounted to 22,300, of which 14,000 were newly established ones, including 2,114 foreign-invested enterprises. 280,000 jobs were created in the zone.

At the end of 2014, three new FTZs had been approved to be established in Guangdong, Tianjin and Fujian, reflecting the replicable experience of the Shanghai FTZ and its success as a pilot. Together with the Shanghai zone, all these FTZs apply the measures outlined in the 'Special Administrative Measures on the Access of Foreign Investment to the Pilot Free Trade Zone (Negative List)', which was printed and distributed by the State Council General Office in April 2015 (Guo Ban Fa No. 23) and includes 122 measures, down from 190 in the 2013 version. In the breakdown, eighty-five were restrictive measures, and thirty-seven were prohibited ones.

The construction and refined improvement of a foreign investment legal system enshrining international rules and the principles of market economy has provided stability, transparency and predictability to the investment policies and environment. FIEs are operated and administered by law.

In October 1978, during the visit of Thomas Murphy to China for technical consultations on China's import of heavy-truck technology, the CEO of General Motors, the world's largest automaker, extended an official offer to China for long-term partnership in the form of joint ventures, as the first leader of a major transnational corporation ever to do so. He said that to run a joint venture means that both sides would pool money and efforts and share profits and losses, like 'a family bound together by marriage'. Agreeing that 'joint ventures were workable', Deng Xiaoping also pointed out that rule of law should be guaranteed, especially where the use of foreign capital and import of technology were concerned, and no time should be lost in enacting economic statutes.

The Law of the People's Republic of China on Chinese-Foreign Equity Joint Ventures was endorsed at the 2nd meeting of the 5th NPC on 1 July 1979. As the first law governing foreign capital, it furnished the legal backing for the efforts of FDI attraction and was instrumental in the rapid and sound growth of joint ventures in China.

This law not only provided for the principal legal matters on joint ventures, but also introduced for the first time concepts like boards of directors, limited liability companies and company structure into the modern corporate system.

A series of administrative regulations, departmental rules and other normative documents were formulated thereafter. The Implementing Regulations of the Law on Chinese-Foreign Equity Joint Ventures promulgated by the State Council on 20 September 1983 addressed the practical operational issues in a comprehensive and specific way.

On 4 April 1990, the 3rd meeting of the 7th NPC endorsed the Amendment to the Law on Chinese-Foreign Equity Joint Ventures. Implementation started on the same day. Equal protection for foreign investment was reflected and enhanced, stipulations regarding nationalization and expropriation were added and taxation preference was reduced. Most importantly, the provisions regarding Chairman's qualification were revised. Unlike previously, the position of Chairman could be held by the representative from both Chinese and foreign partners of the joint venture, instead of by the Chinese side only.

The Law on Foreign Capital Enterprises was endorsed at the 4th meeting of the 6th NPC on 12 April 1986. The permit to WFOEs signalled the improvement of China's opening-up and the level of FDI utilization. The implementation rules of this law were promulgated by MOFERT (Decree No. 1) on 12 December 1990. Interpretation of Several Provisions in the above Implementation Rules was issued by MOFERT on 6 December 1991.

The Law on Chinese-Foreign Contractual Joint Ventures was endorsed at the 1st meeting of the 7th NPC on 13 April 1988, providing a more flexible form for foreign investment. Instead of dividing equity shares between them, two parties of a contract joint venture would agree on the way and proportion for profit distribution in their contract, based on equality and mutual benefit. The Chinese party normally provided land, site, existing plants, facilities, labour resources and labour services, while foreign investors offered funds, technology, equipment and fine brands as direct investment. Foreign investors could withdraw their investment earlier if certain conditions were met.

On 4 September 1994, the Ministry of Foreign Trade and Economic Cooperation (MOFTEC) promulgated Implementation Rules of the law (Decree No. 6), and on 22 October 1996, issued the Notice on the Introduction to Several Provisions in the Implementation Rules of the Law on Chinese-Foreign Contractual Joint Ventures (Wai Jing Mao Fa No. 658).

Foreign investment-related laws were systematically revised around China's accession to the WTO, removing the non-compliant elements. On 31 October 2000, the 18th meeting of the 9th NPC Standing Committee adopted the amendment to the Law on Foreign Capital Enterprises, and decided to revise the Law on Chinese-Foreign Contractual Joint Ventures. On 15 March 2001, the 4th meeting of the 9th NPC endorsed the second amendment to the Law on Chinese-Foreign Equity Joint Ventures.

Requirements for the balance of foreign exchange, local content and export performance, the provision of filing production plans by FIEs, and the stipulation that FIEs must use advanced technology and equipment were deleted, bringing the 3 laws in full compliance with WTO rules.

A series of new laws have been formulated since China's WTO accession, leading to a more level playing field for domestic and foreign companies. The new Foreign Investment Law being drafted will represent historic progress in the administration of foreign investment.

Regulations on the Administration of Foreign-funded Financial Institutions came into effect in 2002. Stipulations on the Establishment of Investment Companies by Foreign Investors were promulgated in 2004, allowing investment-type FIEs to be set up and to provide services to other companies with their investment. Interim Stipulations on the Takeover of Domestic Enterprises by Foreign Investors were implemented in 2006.

On 1 January 2008, the new Law on Enterprise Income Tax took force, unifying the 25 per cent income tax and other relevant preferential policies for domestic and foreign-funded companies. On 25 November 2009, Measures for Administration of the Establishment of Partnership Enterprises within the Territory of China by Foreign Enterprises or Individuals were released by the State Council (Decree No. 567), adding one more form of commercial presence of foreign investors besides WFOE, equity joint venture and contractual joint venture.

On 28 December 2013, the decision to amend the Company Law was made at the 6th meeting of the 12th NPC, for reforms of companies' registered capital and other items subject to registration. The Notice on Printing and Distributing the Reform Plan of Registered Capital and Registration System was released by the State Council on 7 February 2014, which provided for the shift from paid-in to subscribed registered capital, and the conditions for registration of companies were relaxed considerably.

As required by the 3rd Plenary Session of the 18th CPC Central Committee to unify laws and regulations applicable to domestic and foreign funds, the drafting of a Foreign Investment Law kicked off in 2014. After inviting opinions from 54 central government agencies and 16 local commerce authorities, the draft of the law was made public on the MOFCOM website for public comment on 19 January 2015. Aiming at cultivating a more stable, transparent and predictable legal environment for foreign investors, the legislation focuses on providing more market access, protecting the legitimate rights and interests of foreign investment, and strengthening administration in process and afterwards, instead of prior approval. The new administration model to be adopted, which combines pre-establishment national treatment and negative list, fully reflects China's determination to open up wider and its courage to push reform further.

2   Investment Liberalization and Facilitation Have Generated More Investment for China and More Business Opportunities for the Rest of the World

Foreign investment in the early days of opening-up featured small scale, little amounts, a low number of companies, and a high proportion of funds from Hong Kong, China. Since the initiation of FDI attraction until the end of 1979, only six joint ventures were established in China. By the end of June 1981, the ninety-two joint ventures approved had brought in

US$ 197 million. By the end of 1982, only forty-eight joint ventures were in place.

Along with China's application process for GATT contracting party status and its participation in the Uruguay Round of talks on trade in services since the 1990s, China adjusted its policies to permit foreign investment into such areas as finance, insurance, real estate, commercial retailing, consultancy, accounting firms and information services on a conditional basis. The investment climate has continued to improve, leading to fast development of FDI in China, both in terms of scale and performance.

In 1991, export of FIEs accounted for 16.7 per cent of the country's total. In 1992, import and export of FIEs took up over one-quarter of the national aggregate, and that proportion increased further to one-third and 37 per cent in 1993 and 1994, respectively.

1992 was the first year in which FDI surpassed US$ 10 billion. 1993 witnessed the approval of 83,265 FIEs, equalling the total number in the first fourteen years of reform and opening-up. 1994 saw more than US$ 30 billion worth of FDI, and 1995 saw US$ 37.8 billion. By the end of July 2004, 490,000 FIEs were established in China, which actually brought in US$ 540 billion. One hundred and ninety countries and regions, and 400 of the Fortune 500 companies had investments in China. Thirty regional head offices and more than 600 research and development (R&D) centres were set up.

In the Several Opinions of Doing a Better Job of Utilizing Foreign Investment released by the State Council in April 2000, more areas were required to open to foreign investment, for example high-end manufacturing, high-tech, modern services, new energy, energy-saving and environment protection, and foreign investors were welcomed to participate in the reorganization, transformation and mergers and acquisitions (M&A) of domestic enterprises.

The Industrial Catalogue for Foreign Investment was revised in 1997, 2002, 2004, 2007, 2011 and 2015, after its first release in 1995. The latest version has cut the number of prohibited entries to thirty-six and reduced the restricted entries to thirty-eight. The limit on foreign equity ratio was lifted and new opening-up measures were introduced in certain areas. Foreign access to medical treatment, care for the aged, commerce and logistics, as well as e-commerce, was further liberalized.

The Several Opinions on Building a New System for the Open Economy, released by the CPC Central Committee and the State Council on 5 May 2015, are the new FDI regulatory approach. They feature pre-establishment national treatment and were test run in the four FTZs. One of the goals of the Several Opinions is to innovate the foreign investment administration system. Other objectives included improving the investment environment, expanding market access to services, further opening up the manufacturing industry, stabilizing the scale and speed of FDI attraction and enhancing its quality. Another objective is to reform the foreign investment administration mode of examination and approval, as well as industrial guidance, and to promote institutional innovation and the transformation and upgrading of development zones.

V   Experience of China and Outlook for Cooperation with Africa

Looking back on the past thirty years, China's economic development has been, to a large extent, driven by its trade policy reforms and investment attraction, and fundamentally by its steadfast determination and unremitting efforts for integration into the open world economy. China has contributed to that open world economy and benefited from it. China's experience has testified to the inexorable law that a nation declines whenever it shuts itself behind closed doors, and thrives whenever it embraces the world. The answer to the great development achievements made by China boils down to its opening-up efforts, a long-term process of exploring, learning and maturing.

Five milestone years are worth remembering. First, 1978, the year China adopted the opening-up policy and began doing business with the outside world and running SEZs on a trial basis. Second, 1986, the year China applied to resume its GATT contracting party status and began to learn more about international trade rules in its ever-intensified external economic relations. Third, 1992, the year China set the goal of establishing a socialist market economy and the opening-up endeavour gained full momentum. Fourth, 2001, the year China ushered in a new stage of opening-up with its WTO membership and a maturing world-oriented home economy. Fifth, 2013, the year China set the goal of constructing a new system for its open economy, ran FTZs on a pilot basis and launched a new round of higher-level and more proactive opening-up.

And six key points of experience are worth mentioning. First, the importance of seizing opportunities, making decisions and taking action without hesitation when chances come about. Second, moving forward step-by-step. Radical policy changes incur heavy costs. Taking the easiest task first, adopting a dual track initially and running pilots on an experimental basis to help with a smooth start, with the least possible resistance, accumulating experiences and avoiding huge losses. Third, adapting to the changing situation. Specific policy measures cannot stand still after their formulation, because circumstances do not. Adjustments to local conditions and modulations on proper occasions in a practical and flexible manner can help respond better to reality. Fourth, working with perseverance. Never give up easily or be afraid of making mistakes. Unremitting efforts, including trial and error, will eventually pay off. Fifth, exercising the rule of law. The building and refined improvements of legal systems for trade and investment provide stability, transparency and predictability for the policies and business environment. Sixth, playing by the rules. Economies get the most out of a fair, reasonable and transparent system of international commerce and trade rules, when they all comply. And that is why the WTO is so important and significant for all its members.

Africa now faces a golden opportunity in its economic take-off. As the resource advantages, market potential and demographic dividend gradually improve, it has become one of the top investment destinations, and one of the potentially huge consumer markets. Africa is poised to become a new pole in the global economy.

As its largest trading partner for six consecutive years and an important source of FDI, China enjoys a traditional friendship as well as fruitful economic and trade cooperation with the African continent. In 2014, bilateral trade registered US$ 222 billion, twenty-one times that of 2000; China's investment stock in Africa exceeded US$ 30 billion, more than sixty times that in 2000. China provided duty-free treatment to 97 per cent of exported products to China from 33 African least-developed countries (LDCs). Chinese companies set up twenty economic and trade cooperation zones in Africa and trained a wide array of experts, totalling 83,000 individuals.

China welcomes an open and a more prosperous Africa. At the UN Sustainable Development Summit held on 26 September 2015, President Xi Jinping announced the establishment of an assistance fund for South–South cooperation and to increase investment in the LDCs. At the FOCAC Summit held on 4–5 December 2015, President Xi announced new measures including ten Cooperation Programs to enhance practical collaboration between the two sides for the next three years, from which Africa would benefit. The complementarity of development between China and Africa also provides vast space for collaboration in such fields as industrialization, regional connectivity and trade in services in general, and manufacturing, finance, tourism, telecom, aerospace and television and broadcasting, *inter alia*. China stands ready to help LDCs to the best of its capacity, and join hands with Africa in further boosting two-way trade and investment, along with their comprehensive strategic partnership.

References

Cheng, S.W. (2001), *Studies on Economic Reforms and Development in China*, Oxford University Press.

Editorial Group (2002), *Complementary Reader of the Report of the 16th CPC Central Committee*, Beijing: People's Press.

Editorial Group (2015), *Complementary Reader of Proposals of the CPC Central Committee on the Formulation of the 13th Five-year Plan for National Economic and Social Development*, Beijing: People's Press.

International Monetary Fund (IMF) (2015), 'IMF Survey: Chinese Renminbi to be Included in IMF's Special Drawing Right Basket', Washington, DC: IMF. http://www.imf.org/external/pubs/ft/survey/so/2015/new120115a.htm

Li, L.Q. (2008), *Breaking Through: The Birth of China's Opening-Up Policy*, Beijing: Central Party Literature Press.

Li, Z.J. (2013), *New Thoughts on China's Reform*, Beijing: Publishing House of Electronics Industry.

MOFTEC Department of Laws and Treaties (2002), *Legal Education Materials for Foreign Trade Departments Across China*, Beijing: Law Press China.

United Nations (2015), The Millennium Development Goals Report 2015, New York: United Nations. www.un.org/millenniumgoals/reports.shtml

World Trade Organization (WTO) (2006), *Trade Policy Review – Report by China*, Geneva: WTO, official WTO document number WT/TPR/G/161.

WTO (2008), *Trade Policy Review – Report by China*, Geneva: WTO, official WTO document number WT/TPR/G/199.

WTO (2010), *Trade Policy Review – Report by China*, Geneva: WTO, official WTO document No. WT/TPR/G/230.

WTO (2012), *Trade Policy Review – Report by China*, Geneva: WTO, official WTO document number WT/TPR/G/264.

WTO (2014), *Trade Policy Review – Report by China*, Geneva: WTO, official WTO document No. WT/TPR/G/300.

Yuan, Y. (2015) 'Looking Back 14 Years after Accession: Case of China', Speech at the Dushanbe Third China Round Table on WTO Accessions. https://www.wto .org/english/thewto_e/acc_e/Session2YuanYuanPostAccessionLookingback14 yearafter.pdf

Zhang, Y.J. (2009), *Insights: Observation of Commerce in China for 20 Years*, Beijing: Jiu Zhou Press.

Zhou, X.C., et al. (1996), *Changes in the Way of Thinking towards an Open Economy*, Shanghai: Shanghai Yuandong Press.

18

Conclusions

PATRICK LOW, CHIEDU OSAKWE AND MAIKA OSHIKAWA

To summarize as wide-ranging a book as this in a way that does justice to all its contributions is not an easy task. These brief paragraphs seek to capture the main messages.

Africa is on the brink of an economic transformation, and the depth, quality and speed of that transformation will largely depend on policies, the way they are implemented and the quality of the governance implementing them. While the market economy and sound policy fundamentals form the foundations for implementation, governance and a lock-step relationship with global best practices and technology are critical pillars in economic transformation and development.

In recent years, Africa has grown faster than the world economy and increased its shares of both global GDP and trade. The challenge, however, is to sustain this trend. As commodities still dominate the composition of the continent's export base, greater diversification would reduce vulnerability, establishing a platform for Africa's structural transformation.

The bulk of Africa's trade is geographically concentrated in three markets, i.e. China, the European Union and the United States, and a major opportunity exists for expanding intra-continental trade, which still makes up little more than one-tenth of its countries' total exports. The mutual benefits accruing to African economies from closer cooperation are enormous. It is very largely in the hands of African governments to make this happen through a broad range of market-opening, regional integration and facilitation measures.

Product and geographical concentrations will lessen as domestic economies pick up the pace of diversification from primary commodity production towards manufacturing and services.

Africa's economic transformation will depend crucially on access to knowledge and technology, and amongst its other attributes, trade is a valuable transmission mechanism. Increased participation in global and regional value chains allows countries to specialize, add more domestic value and upgrade product sophistication in ways that were previously not possible.

Good policy design and efficient implementation are essential if governments are to shape progress, helping rather than hindering growth and development.

Markets support growth, development and job creation, but policy can contribute as an enabler, and can shape outcomes to meet certain social and economic ends not provided by the market. Virtually all governments seek to shape their economies with what are sometimes referred to as industrial policies, but success depends very heavily on the quality of interventions and government capabilities.

African economies, like many others, could do much to create a more conducive macro-environment with better infrastructure and less cost-ridden policy conditions, which would foster trade, development and growth, not least through strengthened intra-African links.

China's experience of dramatic growth and transformation over three decades has showcased what is possible, at a relatively early stage of economic diversification, with a judicious mix of incentives, facilitated trade, learning and entrepreneurship.

Commitment to WTO core values is critical for the structural transformation of Africa. WTO accession packages can be a blueprint for long-term policy reform. The WTO can also serve as an anchor for coherent domestic policy and a guarantor of consistent and non-discriminatory policies on the part of trading partners.

Following the WTO's Tenth Ministerial Conference in Nairobi in December 2015, the WTO is exploring a new agenda for rule-making and trade regulation. The exploratory focus is directed, *inter alia*, on the policy underpinnings for a new agenda and linked business priorities for the WTO. Areas of trade policy frequently featuring in the exchanges amongst members are revolving around trade in cross-border data flows, investment and competition policy, e-commerce and the digital economy, small and medium-sized enterprises (SMEs) and food security.

Operationally, in the real economy of Africa, the trends point to increased economic activity in SMEs and smart technology. The business world in the twenty-first century is increasingly typified by SMEs in the private sector employing smart technologies and utilizing e-commerce. For most African businesses, success is measured by their usage of up-to-date technology, particularly mobile technology. In Sub-Saharan Africa alone, mobile penetration has almost doubled since 2010. With the increasing accessibility and affordability of mobile phones, mobile technology has become a *sine qua non* for business start-ups as it aids operations, particularly in terms of deepening market penetration. Also, the possibilities for broader consumer reach have attracted foreign companies that are willing to invest heavily in these businesses, an indication of the crucial role of technology in spurring global growth. SMEs consist of myriad multi-sectoral setups, and as they are strongly linked to private sector employment, women's economic empowerment, income distribution and poverty reduction, it is particularly crucial for Africa that the associated trade issues such as accessibility to international markets and newer technologies be addressed on a multilateral platform.

Providentially, the recent expansion of the WTO's Information Technology Agreement at the Nairobi Ministerial Conference will see an elimination of tariffs on 10 per cent of global merchandise trade, increasing trade in information technology products. However, there is need for a collaborative engagement between the African private sector and the WTO, with a goal of ensuring that the impediments to the participation of SMEs in global trade are not overlooked. Trade facilitation remains fundamental to economic progress, as it not only enhances stability and predictability, but may also result in a surge of foreign investment and job creation throughout this burgeoning continent.

ANNEX: CONTRIBUTOR BIOGRAPHIES

Editors

PATRICK LOW, from Spain/Kenya, is a fellow at the Asian Global Institute of the University of Hong Kong where he undertakes research into global supply chains, international trade and global governance. He was the Chief Economist at the World Trade Organization from 1997 to 2013, having previously worked at the GATT Secretariat from 1980 to 1987. After joining the WTO, he worked on trade in services for two years before his appointment as Chief Economist in 1997. From 1999 to 2000, he served as WTO Director-General Mike Moore's Chief of Staff, after which he returned to his previous post as Chief Economist. Between leaving the GATT and joining the WTO, Dr Low taught economics at El Colegio de México in Mexico City, from 1987 to 1990, and during this time worked as a consultant for a range of governments and inter-governmental institutions. From 1990 to 1994, he worked as a senior economist in the World Bank's research complex (International Trade Division). His main areas of research at the Bank were trade policy, trade and the environment, fiscal policy and customs reform. Dr Low was also an Adjunct Professor of International Economics at the Graduate Institute of International and Development Studies (Switzerland) from 2008 to 2013. He taught courses there on trade theory and the theory of trade policy, and the economics and politics of the environment, trade and climate change. He holds a BA in Economics from the University of Kent (United Kingdom) and a PhD in Economics from Sussex University (United Kingdom), and has written widely on a range of trade policy issues.

CHIEDU OSAKWE, from Nigeria, is currently Advisor to the Minister of Industry, Trade and Investment of the Federal Republic of Nigeria while he is on special leave from the WTO. The most recent position he held was the Director of the Accessions Division (2009–2016). He is also an

Adjunct Professor at the International University in Geneva (IUG) in International Trade, Diplomacy and Negotiations. Previous WTO positions he held include Special Coordinator for LDCs (i.e. least-developed countries) and Head of the Secretariat Working Group on the Integrated Framework for LDCs, Office of the Director-General (1999–2001). In this position he was Chairman of the Inter-Agency Working Group (IAWG) for the Integrated Framework. He has also held the positions of Director, Technical Cooperation Division (2001–02); Director, Textiles Division (2003–05); and Director, Doha Development Agenda – DDA Special Duties Division, Office of the Director-General (2005–08). Prior to joining the WTO Secretariat, Dr Osakwe was a Nigerian Foreign Service Officer (1979–98). During this period, he served at the Permanent Mission of Nigeria to the United Nations in New York (1983–86) and to the GATT/WTO (1993–98). As Nigerian delegate to the WTO, he was Chairman of the Committee on Rules of Origin (1995–96) and Chairman of the Committee on Preshipment Inspection (1997–98). He coordinated the WTO African Group in 1995. In recognition of his contributions to the Foreign Service, Nigerian President Goodluck Jonathan appointed him Ambassador *in situ* in 2010. Dr Osakwe was educated at the Universities of Ibadan (Nigeria) and Oxford (United Kingdom) and at New York University (United States), where he obtained his PhD. He has published in several areas, including trade policy, the rule of law and national security. Dr Osakwe has been decorated and honoured by several governments.

MAIKA OSHIKAWA, from Japan, is Officer in Charge of the Accessions Division of the WTO. Prior to joining the Accessions Division, she was Head of the Asia and Pacific Regional Desk at the Institute for Training and Technical Cooperation (ITTC) of the WTO. At the ITTC, she was responsible for managing training and technical assistance activities for thirty WTO members and observers in the Asia and Pacific region, as well as of partnership arrangements with organizations and institutions based in the region. Before joining the ITTC in 2010, she worked in several divisions at the WTO Secretariat, including the Development Division (2003–10), the Technical Cooperation Division (2001–02), the Office of the Director-General (2000–01) and the Trade Policy Reviews Division (1998–2000). Ms Oshikawa obtained a MS in Development Studies from the London School of Economics, a DES in International Economics from the Graduate Institute of International Studies

(Switzerland) and a BS in Foreign Services from Georgetown University (United States).

Contributors

FATIMA HARAM ACYL, from Chad, is the Commissioner for Trade and Industry at the African Union Commission since her election in 2012. As Commissioner, Mrs Acyl has championed key elements of Agenda 2063, including preparing for the launch of the African Continental Free Trade Area (CFTA) and establishing the African Minerals Development Centre (AMDC) as an AUC institution. She is steadfastly committed to Africa's structural transformation and has worked to advance trade, industry and responsible mineral resource development as fundamental drivers of that transformation. Prior to joining the Commission, she gained a wide range of dynamic public and private sector experience. She has served as Deputy Director General of the Agricultural Bank of Chad, Director of Finance and Administration at the United Nations Office for Project Services (UNOPS), Audit Manager at Crowe Chizek and Company LLC and Manager at PricewaterhouseCoopers USA, where she rose from an associate to a managerial position. Commissioner Acyl has an MBA in Finance, with Honours, from Xavier University, (United States), and a BS in Business Administration (Operational Research) from the University of Moncton (Canada).

MOULAY HAFID ELALAMY, from Morocco, has been Minister of Industry, Trade, Investment and the Digital Economy of the Royal Kingdom of Morocco since 10 October 2013. With a degree in information systems from the University of Sherbrooke (Canada), where he was also Governor of the Faculty of Administration, Mr Elalamy began his professional career in Canada as a senior advisor to the Ministry of Finance of Quebec prior to becoming Director of Information within a Canadian insurance company. In 1995, he created his own company, operating in finance, insurance, assistance and consumer credit. This company acquired two of the most important insurance companies in Morocco, as well as a pan-African insurance group. Mr Elalamy has launched two programmes dedicated to entrepreneurship: the Sherpa Club, which actively participates in the emergence of sustainable, competitive and job-creating structures in Morocco, and the 'MHE Young Entrepreneurs competition', which offers financial support and guidance to young promoters for the creation of their companies. Mr Elalamy was President of the General Confederation of Businesses of Morocco from 2006 to 2009. He is also Vice-President of the Moroccan Federation of Insurance and Reinsurance Companies and a member of the Investment Committee of the *Caisse Interprofessionnelle Marocaine de Retraite*. A member of the Mohammed V Foundation for Solidarity, Mr Elalamy is also Treasurer of the Lalla Salma Association for the prevention and treatment of cancer.

UKAMAKA ANAEDU, from Nigeria, is a research assistant in the Accessions Division of the WTO. She previously worked as a treasury officer with Liman Bravo Mortgage Finance. She also worked with 'Rediscover Nigeria' project and Ruyi Communications, both in the advertising and publishing industry in Nigeria. Ms. Anaedu is a graduate of the University of Nigeria and holds a Master of Arts in International Law and Diplomacy from the University of Lagos (Nigeria).

ROBERTO CARVALHO DE AZEVÊDO, from Brazil, is the Director-General of the WTO. Ambassador Azevêdo holds degrees in electrical engineering from the University of Brasilia (Brazil) and in international relations from the 'Instituto Rio Branco', the graduate school of international relations and diplomacy run by the Brazilian Ministry of Foreign Relations. He joined the Brazilian Foreign Service in 1984. His first diplomatic posting was to Washington, DC, in 1988. He subsequently served in the Brazilian embassy in Montevideo before being assigned to the Permanent Mission of Brazil in Geneva in 1997. In 2001 he was named head of the Brazilian Foreign Ministry's Dispute Settlement Unit where he remained until 2005. During his tenure he acted as chief litigator in many disputes at the WTO and served on WTO dispute settlement panels. From 2006 to 2008 he was Vice-Minister for Economic and Technological Affairs at the Foreign Ministry in Brasilia. In that capacity he was Brazil's chief trade negotiator for the Doha Round and represented Brazil in MERCOSUR negotiations. In 2008 he was appointed Permanent Representative of Brazil to the WTO and other International Economic Organizations in Geneva. Ambassador Azevêdo has been a frequent lecturer on topics related to international economics and has published numerous articles on these issues.

CHRISTINA BUSCH, from Germany and the United States, works in the Trade and Competitiveness Global Practice of the World Bank Group. She joined the Bank's Trade Facilitation and Logistics team in 2013. She co-authored the World Bank's 2014 Logistics Performance Index (LPI) and the forthcoming 2016 LPI edition. Before joining the World Bank Group, Christina served as Director of Programs at the Friedrich Naumann Foundation's Transatlantic Dialogue Program in Washington, DC. She also worked in the Economic Policy Programme of the Bertelsmann Foundation in Germany. Christina holds an MSc Degree in Economics (Diplom-Volkswirtin) from Humboldt-Universitaet zu Berlin (Germany) and a Master of Public Administration degree from Columbia University (United States). She is currently pursuing a PhD in Economics at Technische Universitaet Berlin (Germany).

VICKY CHEMUTAI, from Uganda, is an Economic Affairs Officer in the Accessions Division of the WTO. She has assumed the role of Secretary and Co-Secretary on the Working Parties of various accession dossiers. Prior to working at the WTO, Ms Chemutai worked in the National Social Security Fund in Uganda as a Data Integrity Officer. She holds a BSc in Quantitative Economics from Makerere University (Uganda) and a Postgraduate Diploma in International Trade Policy, Trade Law and Development, and she is currently pursuing an MSc in International Trade Policy and Trade Development from Lund University (Sweden) in association with the Trade Policy Training Centre in Africa (TRAPCA) (Tanzania).

ROB DAVIES, from South Africa, is the Minister of Trade and Industry of South Africa. He has previously served as Deputy Minister of Trade and Industry. Davies was Chairman of the Parliamentary Portfolio Committee on Finance. He has overseen the development and implementation of annual three-year rolling Industrial Policy Action Plans as well as steering South Africa's participation in important trade relations, including the COMESA-EAC-SADC TFTA, BRICS, Economic Partnership Agreement with European Union, the US African Growth and Opportunity Act and World Trade Organization's Bali Package. An Anti-Apartheid activist for many years, before entering Parliament,

Rob Davies was Professor and Co-Director of the Centre of Southern African Studies at the University of the Western Cape (South Africa) and before that Professor Auxiliar at the Centro de Estudos Africanos at Eduardo Mondlane University (Mozambique). Academically he holds an Honours Degree in Economics from Rhodes University (United States), a Masters in International Relations from the University of Southampton (United Kingdom) and a Doctorate in Political Studies from the University of Sussex (United Kingdom).

OKECHUKWU ENELAMAH, from Nigeria, is the Minister of Industry, Trade and Investment of Nigeria. Prior to taking office on 11 November 2015, he worked as the Chief Executive Officer (CEO) of Africa Capital Alliance (ACA), an investment and financial advisory firm which he co-founded in 1998. Previously, he was employed at Arthur Andersen and Goldman Sachs, before moving on to Zephyr Management LP in New York as an investment manager. He was one of the original principals of Zephyr Capital and South Africa Capital Growth Fund, Ltd. He served as a Director of Emerging Markets Private Equity Association. He is a Member of the Advisory Boards Africa Leadership Initiative West Africa and a Fellow of the Aspen Institute. He is a qualified medical doctor, a Chartered Financial Analyst and a qualified Chartered Accountant in Nigeria. He holds an MBA degree with high distinction from the Harvard Business School (United States), where he was a Baker Scholar.

MICHAEL FINGER, from Germany, worked as an international economist in the GATT/WTO Research Division for more than three decades. During his time in GATT/WTO, he regularly contributed to the organization's flagship publications, in particular by providing the sections reviewing the current international trade developments. Among the articles he authored are: 'Ten years of the WTO Information Technology Agreement' and 'The Evolving Wave of Competition in International Markets: Challenges for Africa through the Rise of China and India'. He has lectured on WTO and global trade issues worldwide. Since leaving the WTO, he has continued to work on international trade issues. For the ICC Research Foundation, he prepared the ICC Open Market Index.

ANABEL GONZÁLEZ, from Costa Rica, is Senior Director of the World Bank Group Global Practice on Trade and Competitiveness (since July 2014). In this capacity, she leads a team of 500 people to design and implement the World Bank Group's global and country agenda in the areas of trade, investment climate, competitiveness, innovation and entrepreneurship. Previously, she served as Costa Rica's Minister of Foreign Trade (2010–14). During her tenure, she led Costa Rica's efforts to join the OECD, negotiated, approved, and implemented six major free trade agreements, and implemented investment climate enhancement policies that contributed to attracting over 140 new investment projects. She also had a lead role in Costa Rica's Competitiveness and Innovation Council. During her more than fifteen years of service with the Ministry of Foreign Trade, she held various positions including Director General for International Trade Negotiations (1990–97), Vice-Minister of Foreign Trade (1998–2001) and Ambassador-Chief Negotiator (2003–04). She also served as Director of Costa Rica's Investment Promotion Agency (2001–02), Director to the Agriculture and Commodities Division of the World Trade Organization (2006–09) and Senior International Consultant on Trade and Investment at the Inter-American Development Bank (2009–10). She is the current Chair of the World Economic Forum Global Agenda Council on Competitiveness (2014–16), after serving as Chair of the Council on Trade and Foreign Direct Investment (2012–14). She has lectured in over forty countries and written on many trade and competitiveness issues. She holds an LLM from Georgetown University (United States) and a law degree from the University of Costa Rica.

ARANCHA GONZÁLEZ, from Spain, has been Executive Director of the International Trade Centre (ITC) since September 2013. Before joining the ITC, Ms. González served as Chief of Staff to former Director-General of the WTO, Pascal Lamy, from 2005 to 2013. During her tenure at the WTO, she played an active role in launching the WTO's Aid for Trade initiative and served as Mr Lamy's representative at the G20. Prior to working at the WTO, Ms González held several positions at the European Commission, conducting negotiations of trade agreements and assisting developing countries in trade-development efforts. Between 2002 and 2004, she was the European Union spokeswoman for trade and adviser to the European Union Trade Commissioner. She began her career in the private sector advising companies on trade, competition and state-aid matters. She served as an associate at Bruckhaus Westrick Stegemann, a major German law firm, in Brussels. Ms. González holds a degree in law from the University of Navarra

(Spain) and a postgraduate degree in European Law from the University of Carlos III (Spain).

BERNARD M. HOEKMAN, from the Netherlands, is the Director of the research strand 'Global Economics: Multilateral Cooperation and Policy Spillovers' at the European University Institute. He has held various senior positions at the World Bank, including Director of the International Trade Department and Research Manager in the Development Research Group. He has also worked as an economist in the GATT Secretariat and held visiting appointments at Sciences Po (France). Other positions include Chairperson, Global Agenda Council on Logistics and Supply Chain Systems at the World Economic Forum. Mr Hoekman is a graduate of the Erasmus University Rotterdam (Netherlands) and holds a PhD in economics from the University of Michigan (United States). He is a Research Fellow of the Centre for Economic Policy Research (CEPR) (United Kingdom) and a Senior Associate of the Cairo-based Economic Research Forum for the Arab Countries, Turkey and Iran (Egypt). He has published widely on trade policy and development, the global trading system and trade in services. His most recent co-authored book is *The Political Economy of the World Trading System* (Oxford University Press, 2009).

MARCUS BARTLEY JOHNS, from Australia, is a Trade Specialist in the World Bank Group's Geneva Office. He is the focal point for the Bank Group's engagement in the WTO and other Geneva trade and economic institutions. This includes serving as Geneva-based coordinator for Bank Group activities in support of effective implementation of the WTO Trade Facilitation Agreement. He also jointly leads engagement in the G20 trade agenda. He was one of the lead authors of the World Bank Group-WTO 2015 flagship report *The Role of Trade in Ending Poverty*, and has written and presented on a range of issues related to trade and economic affairs. Before joining the World Bank Group, Marcus worked for the Australian Department of Foreign Affairs and Trade and Australian Agency for International Development. He was posted to Australia's Permanent Mission to the World Trade Organization from 2011 until 2014. Prior to that, he held assignments in Bangkok with the Australian Agency for International Development (2009–11) and with the Department of Foreign Affairs and Trade (2008–09), and worked in headquarters in 2007–08. Before joining the Australian government, he worked on foreign policy, trade and development issues for a Member of

Australia's national parliament. He has an MSc in Finance (Economic Policy) from the School of Oriental and African Studies, Honours in International Relations from the Australian National University and a BA from the University of Sydney (Australia).

STEPHEN N. KARINGI, from Kenya, is currently the Director of the Regional Integration, Infrastructure and Trade Division of the United Nations Economic Commission for Africa. He joined the United Nations in April 2004. Before joining the United Nations, Mr. Karingi was a Senior Analyst and the Head of Macroeconomics Division in the Kenya Institute for Public Policy Research and Analysis in Nairobi. He received his BSc degree in Agricultural Economics at Egerton University (Kenya), and received a Master of Economics degree and a PhD from the Faculty of Economics, Business and Law of the University of New England (Australia) after winning a John Crawford Merit Scholarship. Prior to joining KIPPRA, he was a Lecturer of Economics at Egerton University (Kenya) and was also a researcher with the University of New England (Australia) and Griffiths University (Australia). He has been involved in consultancy and capacity building assignments with international and regional organizations such as the World Bank, World Food Programme, United Nations Development Programme, Common Market for Eastern and Southern Africa, Macroeconomic and Financial Management Institute, the African Economic Research Consortium and the Southern African Tax Institute. Previously, he has been awarded several research grants from institutions such as the International Food Policy Research Institute and Rockefeller Foundation. He has affiliation with Harvard University (United States) after being appointed the Zolt-Gilburne Visiting Fellow of the International Tax Programme at the Harvard Law School. Within the United Nations, he has been able to mobilize significant funding in support of trade capacity building for African countries.

UHURU KENYATTA, from Kenya, is the President of Kenya.

ALEXEI KIREYEV, from Russia, is a Senior Economist at the International Monetary Fund and the former IMF representative to the WTO (2000–03). He has led advanced IMF missions to member countries, provided advice on macroeconomic policies to countries with IMF-supported programmes, and reviewed IMF policy advice, financing and technical assistance. Prior to joining the IMF, he was an economic advisor to President Gorbachev, an economist at the World Bank and a professor of international economics at universities in Russia and the United States. His degrees include an MA in Economics from George Washington University (United States) and a PhD in Economics from Moscow State Institute of International Relations (Russia). Dr Kireyev has researched and published extensively on international economics and trade, applied macroeconomics, principles of economics and economic problems of low-income countries. His most recent publication includes a two-volume book on *International Microeconomics and International Macroeconomics* (2013).

GERARD MCLINDEN, from Australia, joined the World Bank in 2004 and is currently a Lead Trade Facilitation Specialist in the Bank Group's Trade and Competitiveness Global Practice, based in Singapore. He is responsible for the design and implementation of a wide range of customs, trade facilitation and border management projects and knowledge activities, and since moving from Washington, DC, in late 2015, he now focuses on the World Bank Group's trade activities in the East Asia, Pacific and South Asia regions. He has been heavily involved in coordinating the World Bank Group's trade facilitation programme and related partnerships with key international organizations, including the WCO, UNCTAD, IMF and the OECD. He has written and presented widely on trade facilitation issues and the implications of the WTO agenda for developing countries. He was the lead editor of the World Bank's *Border Management Modernization* handbook, released in 2011. Prior to joining the World Bank Group, Gerard worked in a variety of senior positions for the Australian Customs Administration and served a five-year term at the WCO. He also served as Senior Australian Customs Representative for the Asian region, and worked for three years as Project Director for a series of Australian government-financed customs development projects in the Asia/Pacific region. He holds a Bachelor's Degree in Political Science and Economics and a Master's Degree in Management, and he has worked on trade facilitation related issues in all of the World Bank's regions.

SIMON MEVEL is an Economic Affairs Officer at the United Nations Economic Commission for Africa (ECA). Prior to joining the United Nations in 2011, he worked as a research analyst at the World Bank in

Washington, DC, the International Food Policy Research Institute (IFPRI) in Washington, DC, and the *Centre d'Etudes Prospectives et d'Information Internationales* (CEPII) in Paris. He holds a Master's Degree in International Economics from the University of Pau (France). Often assessing policies through economic modelling, he has worked and published articles primarily on international trade but also on genetically modified organisms, energy and climate change, each time with a strong focus on economic development.

AMINA MOHAMED, from Kenya, is Cabinet Secretary for Foreign Affairs and International Trade of Kenya. Before being appointed to this post by President Kenyatta in May 2013, Ambassador Mohamed was the Assistant Secretary-General and Deputy Executive Director of the United Nations Environment Programme (UNEP). From 2010 to 2011, she served as the President of the United Nations Conference and Transnational Crime in Vienna. From 2008 to 2011, she was the Permanent Secretary in the Ministry of Justice, National Cohesion and Constitutional Affairs of Kenya. From 2006 to 2007, Ambassador Mohamed was the Director of Europe and Commonwealth Countries and Director for Diaspora Matters at the Ministry of Foreign Affairs. From 2000 to 2006, she was Ambassador and Permanent Representative of the Kenyan Mission to the United Nations and other International Organizations in Geneva. Ambassador Mohamed holds a postgraduate diploma in International Relations from the University of Oxford (United Kingdom) and an LLM at the University of Kiev (Ukraine) and the Kenya School of Law.

JOSHUA SETIPA, from Lesotho, is the Minister of Trade and Industry of Lesotho. Honourable Setipa is the former CEO of the Lesotho National Development Corporation. Prior to this post, he served as a Counsellor to former WTO Director General Pascal Lamy, where he reinforced WTO relationships with global institutions including the World Bank, IMF, UN Specialised Agencies and regional institutions like the African Union, African Development Bank and Regional Economic Communities. He is well skilled in regional economic development issues in Southern Africa, with emphasis on the economic sector reform and export diversification matters. Mr Setipa holds a BA in Political Science from NUL (Lesotho), a graduate diploma in International Trade and International Affairs from ANU Canberra (Australia) and an MBA from the University of Bradford (United Kingdom).

OTTAVIA PESCE, from Italy, is an Economist at the United Nations Economic Commission for Africa, where she conducts research and provides technical assistance to African countries on issues related to trade and industrial policies. Her recent research includes a review of industrial policies across six African countries, an analysis of trade in services in Africa and an assessment of the impact of lower oil prices on the continent's prospects. Before joining the UN, Ottavia worked for the OECD, in their Central Asian Competitiveness Programme, where she focused on helping the region of Atyrau (Kazakhstan) diversify beyond oil extraction and improve vocational education training. Before the OECD, Ottavia was an economist at Frontier Economics, a leading economic consulting firm based in London, UK, where she worked on sectors ranging from energy to health policy and air transport, advising government bodies and global companies. Ottavia holds a double degree Masters in Public Affairs from the London School of Economics and Sciences-Po Paris and a BA in Economics and Management from Bocconi University in Milan, Italy.

JOAKIM REITER, from Sweden, is Deputy Secretary-General at UNCTAD and former Chairman of the Working Party on the Accession of Liberia. Previously, he was the Ambassador and Permanent Representative of Sweden to the WTO, during which period he served as Chairman of the Council for Trade in Services in WTO. Ambassador Reiter was Head of the Trade Policy Unit and Minister Counsellor at the Swedish Representation to the European Union (2008 and 2011), representing Sweden in the Trade Policy Committee of the Council, which he chaired during the Swedish Presidency in 2009. Prior to that, Ambassador Reiter was posted to the European Commission's Directorate-General for Trade (2004–08). In this capacity, he served as EU negotiator in various trade negotiations and was in charge of tariffs and trade in goods in the EU-Korea free trade agreement, as well as non-agricultural market access and rules for regional trade agreements within the Doha Development Agenda of the WTO.

YUAN YUAN, from China, is Director of the Division of Trade Policy Review and Notification, Department of WTO Affairs of the Ministry of Commerce (MOFCOM) of China. Previous MOFCOM positions she held include Director for Trade Negotiation Coordination of the Secretariat for China International Trade Representative, Director for New Media Communication of the General Office, Deputy Head of

China (Xiamen) International Investment Promotion Center, Assistant Spokesperson of the Ministry and Deputy Director for Press Affairs of the General Office, Deputy Director in the Department of Foreign Affairs and Lead Interpreter for China's major economic and trade talks like Sino-EU Textile Talks, Trade/Economic Ministers' Meeting of APEC and ASEM, Sino-US JCCT, and the first three sessions of Sino-US SED. As a participant in the multilateral and bilateral negotiations on China's WTO accession since 1998, she witnessed the historic moment of WTO endorsing China's membership in Doha in 2001, and was one of translators of the *Compilation of the Legal Instruments on China's Accession to the World Trade Organization* (China Law Press, 2002). She was conferred with two national awards for youth work and outstanding division director, and awarded a MOFCOM Third-Class Merit, Exemplary Public Servant and other honours for distinguished service. She received her Bachelor's Degree in Economics from the University of International Business and Economics (China), her Master's Degree in Public Administration (MPA) from Peking University (China) and an MPhil Degree in International Relations from the University of Cambridge (United Kingdom) as a Chevening Scholar. She was a visiting scholar to Stanford University (United States) in 2013.

INDEX

Note: Italic locators indicate figures, tables or boxes.